Intergenerational Caregiving

Also of interest from the Urban Institute Press:

Meeting the Needs of Children with Disabilities, by Laudan Y. Aron and Pamela J. Loprest

Medicare: A Policy Primer, by Marilyn Moon

Health Policy and the Uninsured, edited by Catherine McLaughlin

Kinship Care: Making the Most of a Valuable Resource, edited by Rob Geen

Edited by
Alan Booth, Ann C. Crouter, Suzanne M. Bianchi,
and Judith A. Seltzer

Intergenerational Caregiving

THE URBAN INSTITUTE PRESS
Washington, D.C.

THE URBAN INSTITUTE PRESS
2100 M Street, N.W.
Washington, D.C. 20037

Library of Congress Cataloging-in-Publication Data

Intergenerational caregiving / edited by Alan Booth ... [et al.].
       p. cm.
    Includes bibliographical references and index.
    ISBN 978-0-87766-747-6 (alk. paper)
    1.   Intergenerational relations. 2.   Caregivers. 3.   Family. I. Booth,
Alan, 1935-
    HM726.I46 2008
    306.87--dc22

                                                                2008032361

Printed in the United States of America

10 09 08   1 2 3 4 5

THE URBAN INSTITUTE is a nonprofit, nonpartisan policy research and educational organization established in Washington, D.C., in 1968. Its staff investigates the social, economic, and governance problems confronting the nation and evaluates the public and private means to alleviate them. The Institute disseminates its research findings through publications, its web site, the media, seminars, and forums.

Through work that ranges from broad conceptual studies to administrative and technical assistance, Institute researchers contribute to the stock of knowledge available to guide decisionmaking in the public interest.

Conclusions or opinions expressed in Institute publications are those of the authors and do not necessarily reflect the views of officers or trustees of the Institute, advisory groups, or any organizations that provide financial support to the Institute.

In memory of Steven Nock—
family scholar, teacher, and friend—
who will be missed

Contents

vii

Preface

Dramatic changes in American families over the past half century have transformed the nature of intergenerational relationships. Nuclear families have become smaller as fertility has declined, but extended families have become larger with gains in life expectancy leading to more generations within families. Divorce and nonmarital child-bearing, remarriage, and cohabitation, all more common now than a half century ago, add further complexity to intergenerational relationships. They weaken ties to biological fathers while at the same time reinforcing some grandparent–grandchild ties. Step-children and step-grandchildren increase the number of family members on whom an elderly person can potentially rely for help, but the strength of these familial ties may be insufficient to generate the desired care. These changing family ties also increase the importance of understanding how adult siblings, including step-siblings, negotiate intergenerational caregiving roles. Finally, women's greater employment also alters the "caregiving reserve" that families have and drives up the costs to women who forgo employment to care for family members. In dual-earner families, the demands of two jobs create their own tensions, with men and women often having to negotiate, and renegotiate, how to divide housework, paid work, and dependent care. In this book, scholars from different disciplines consider factors that account for variation and changes in relationships within and among generations, the strengths and weaknesses of current information that can be used to understand change in inter- and intragenerational relationships, as well as implications for social policies.

The contributions to this book are based on papers presented at the 14th Annual Penn State Symposium on Family Issues, "Caring and Exchange within and across Generations." The two-day interdisciplinary symposium is held in October on the University Park campus of Penn State. This edited volume is the culmination of those two days of stimulating and provocative presentations and discussions.

Intergenerational Caregiving is organized into four sections, each of which addresses a distinct goal. Each section includes a chapter by lead authors, followed by shorter chapters by discussants. Care has been taken to bring together perspectives from diverse disciplines. The book concludes with an integrative commentary.

In the first section, an interdisciplinary team of economists and sociologists sets the stage by laying out contemporary trends and contexts of care and exchange across generations. The team is composed of Kathleen McGarry, Suzanne Bianchi, V. Joseph Hotz, and Judith A. Seltzer, all of whom are members of a group funded by the National Institute of Child Health and Human Development (NICHD) that has been charged with developing new models for explaining family change and variation. Discussants' chapters weave in additional insights, including international perspectives. Rebeca Wong, a demographer, includes examples from Mexico in her chapter. Francesco Billari and Aart Liefbroer, demographers from Italy and the Netherlands respectively, draw on international data to make the point that caregiving varies considerably across nations. Melissa Hardy, a sociologist with expertise on adulthood and aging, emphasizes the kind of data and research designs needed for this field of study to move forward.

Economist Donald Cox leads off the second section with a chapter on the theoretical models that various disciplines have used to explain patterns of caregiving and exchange within and across generations, including ideas drawn from economics, sociology, and bioevolutionary theory. The three discussants—Merril Silverstein, a gerontological sociologist; Jeremy Freese, a sociologist; and Steven Zarit, a scholar whose training fuses life-span human development with clinical psychology insights about aging and family caregiving, provide thoughtful reactions. At times, the discussants question how feasible it is to test hypotheses drawn from evolutionary theory.

In the third section, authors take a look *inside* families. Older adults who need care often have several children to whom they could possibly turn, and those adult children may have spouses and children who, in turn, are additional sources of possible help. The lead chapter by sociologists Karl Pillemer and Jill Suitor examines unusual data on aging families and multiple siblings. The discussants bring a rich set of expertise from different disciplines and periods of the life course. The first discussant chapter, coauthored by Marsha Mailick Seltzer and Jan S. Greenberg, both professors of social work; Julie Lounds Taylor and Gael I. Orsmond, both developmental psychologists; and Matthew J. Smith, a social work researcher, adds insights from research on families raising children with disabilities. Susan M. McHale and Ann C. Crouter, scholars in human development and family studies, describe patterns of sibling relations and parental differential treatment of siblings in middle childhood and adolescence that may underlie subsequent patterns of care later in life. The final chapter in this section, by Robert Pollak, Barbara Schone, and Liliana E. Pezzin, brings an economic perspective.

The book culminates in an intriguing comparison of different family caregivers, addressing the question, "Who feels an obligation for whom?" Sociologists Steven Nock, Paul Kingston, and Laura M. Holian summarize survey data collected with an experimental design. Respondents were asked to rate how much responsibility a variety of hypothetical family caregivers should take in different situations, varying the situation in terms of "degrees of removal" as defined by biological ties, step-ties, and in-law ties. Psychologists James Jackson, Toni C. Antonucci, Besangie Sellars, Edna E. Brown, and Svein Olav Daatland; Adam Davey, whose work focuses on the psychology of aging; and economist Robert Willis offer complementary perspectives.

The final chapter is an integrative commentary by Cassandra Dorius and Laura Wray-Lake, graduate students at Penn State in Sociology and Human Development and Family Studies, respectively. This interdisciplinary team deftly summarizes the themes woven throughout the volume and suggests next steps for research.

Acknowledgments

The editors are grateful to the many organizations at Penn State that sponsored the 2006 Symposium on Family Issues and this resulting book, including the Population Research Institute; the Children, Youth, and Families Consortium; the Prevention Research Center; the Center for Work and Family Research; the Center for Health Policy Research; the Center on Population Health and Aging; the Gerontology Center; and the departments of human development and family studies, labor and industrial relations, economics, psychology, sociology, and the women's studies program. The editors also gratefully acknowledge essential core financial support in the form of a five-year grant from NICHD, as well as ongoing, substantive guidance and advice from Christine Bachrach of NICHD and Lynne Casper, formerly of NICHD and now at the University of Southern California. The ongoing support of all of these partners has enabled us to attract excellent scholars from a range of backgrounds and disciplines—the sort of group on whom the quality and integrity of the series depends.

A lively interdisciplinary team of scholars from across the Penn State community meets with us annually to generate symposia topics and plans and is available throughout the year for brainstorming and problem solving. We appreciate their enthusiasm, intellectual support, and creative ideas. This book represents collaboration between Penn State and the Generations Group within the NICHD-funded Explaining Family Change and Variation Project. The Generations Group not only provided coeditors Suzanne Bianchi and Judith Seltzer but also wise counsel from V. Jeffrey Evans, V. Joseph Hotz, and Kathleen McGarry, as well as from S. Philip Morgan, the project's principle investigator. We also sincerely thank Nancy Landale, David Eggebeen, Valarie King, and Rukmalie Jayakody for presiding over symposium sessions.

The many details that go into planning a symposium and producing a book cannot be overestimated. In this regard, we are especially grateful for the assistance of our administrative staff, including Tara Murray, Barbara King, Kim Zimmerman, and Sherry Yocum. Finally, we could not have accomplished this work without the incredible organizational skills, hard work, and commitment of Carolyn Scott. Her attention to the many details that go into organizing a good conference and edited book made it possible for us to focus on the ideas.

Alan Booth
Ann C. Crouter

PART I
Intergenerational Ties: Contemporary Trends and Contexts

1

Intergenerational Ties
Theories, Trends, and Challenges

Suzanne M. Bianchi, V. Joseph Hotz, Kathleen McGarry,
and Judith A. Seltzer

Relationships between parents and children are the province of diverse academic disciplines, including the social sciences, humanities, and biological sciences. One need only compare the plot in Shakespeare's *King Lear* with the exchange model offered by economists to see the breadth of interest in intergenerational transfers. However, despite this widespread interest, discipline-specific language and methodologies have hampered the sharing of ideas and principles about caring and exchange in families. These structures, which affect the questions asked and the frameworks used to study intergenerational relationships, make viewing the similarities and differences across disciplines difficult. It is similarly difficult to compare what has been learned by the various approaches and to draw broad conclusions that span disciplines.

This chapter discusses theories of altruism (or caring) and exchange (or reciprocity) commonly found in the economics literature on intergenerational relationships and also found in sociological discussions of family ties. We discuss theoretical perspectives in language accessible to those outside our disciplines of economics and sociology. We also include a brief review of the evolutionary perspective receiving increased attention in economics. By laying out the framework that economists and, to a lesser extent, sociologists and demographers use to understand family relationships, we seek to enrich the theory development needed to guide empirical study of intergenerational relationships.

The chapter also includes a discussion of the "facts"—what we think we know descriptively about intergenerational caring and exchange and the changing contexts that affect generational ties. We focus on relationships between parents and adult children, although we recognize that these relationships cannot be understood without considering what happens earlier in life. However, in couching our discussion in terms of caring and exchange between adult kin, we provide insights into how intergenerational relationships play out when both parties are (at least potentially) independent and participating in the decision process.

The chapter is not meant to provide a comprehensive assessment of theoretical insights from the many disciplines that inform us about intergenerational relationships. Rather, it provides a starting point for cross-disciplinary development of theories of intergenerational family relationships. Future theoretical development should ideally incorporate insights from additional perspectives (e.g., developmental perspectives on attachment, feminist perspectives on the role of gender, life course perspectives on early-life influences on later-life behaviors, biological perspectives on hormones, and cognitive functioning and other factors that influence caregiving and exchange). Theoretical insights from these perspectives, however, are largely beyond the scope of this chapter.

Understanding intergenerational relationships is becoming increasingly important as the demographic, social, and economic environments facing families are transformed. Already we have seen sweeping changes in factors affecting family behaviors: More women than ever before are employed in the labor force; they are having fewer children and are having them at later ages. Cohabitation and childbearing outside marriage have increased. Divorce rates are high, and the prevalence of stepfamilies formed by marriage or cohabitation means that families can include a wide array of biological and social relationships. At the same time, increases in life expectancy have contributed to a rise in the number of three- and four-generation families. On the policy front, changes in Social Security, Medicare, and Medicaid programs are likely in the near future, and these changes will necessarily affect the distribution of resources across generations.

These demographic changes raise new questions about the definition of family and familial obligations. Just who is part of the modern family and who should help family members in need? Childbearing outside marriage and divorce weaken ties between nonresident parents and children, but cohabitation, remarriage, and the increase in multigeneration families introduce new kin and quasi kin (e.g., cohabiting partners of older parents and adult children of cohabiting partners) into the family picture. Similarly, household members may not be members of the same legal family, as in the case of some cohabiting couples, and family members need not live in the same household to share significant emotional and material bonds. These issues make it difficult to define family and determine how broadly familial obligations are spread.

The demographic changes also have different implications for women's and men's family experiences. For example, because of the high rates of divorce and out-of-wedlock births, men are increasingly likely to live apart from their young children and may therefore have weaker ties than women to their offspring later in life. In contrast, women are now more likely to be single mothers, often relying on their extended kin, especially their own mothers, to fulfill their parenting obligations. Despite the importance of these demographic changes, the literature lacks even basic descriptive information about many of these new intergenerational relationships and how families function in light of the changes.

How and Why Are Generations Connected? Theoretical Perspectives

Various disciplines have put forth a number of perspectives, explanations, and models of intergenerational behavior. Although these ideas differ in numerous respects, there are clear camps into which many of them can be placed. The first is the idea that intergenerational relationships are based on self-interested behavior with transfers made with the expectation of some form of reciprocity or exchange. The second posits that behavior is based on caring or altruistic preferences on the part of the individual making the transfer. Economists refer to these competing ideas as exchange and altruism, although terms like reciprocity and caring appear frequently in other disciplines. Within these broad categories are several related models that we briefly note. None of these ideas is likely to explain all behaviors, but rather, we expect that they all play a role in comprising the complicated relationships observed among family members.

The catalogue of ways of thinking about what motivates and influences intergenerational relationships, outlined below, is intended as a brief overview of the literature and a starting point for further theoretical development and integration across disciplines. We encourage researchers interested in these issues to pursue this goal.

Perspectives on Family Behaviors

Historically, the dominant model of family decisionmaking in economics assumes that one member—the head—makes all decisions and does so in the best interest of the family members (Becker 1974, 1991). Although this *unitary* model has provided a useful theoretical foundation for understanding family dynamics, it is predicated on assumptions that are difficult to reconcile with social behavior. Any decision that involves negotiation between two individuals with divergent preferences or goals (e.g., the decision to divorce or leave the nest) can be difficult to place into the framework of a unitary family or household. Moreover, the empirical predictions of the unitary model have been rejected in a wide array of settings. Recent theoretical literature on the family instead has turned to highlighting the individuality of each family member. In these latter *collective* models of the family (Chiappori 1988; McElroy and Horney 1981; Alderman et al. 1995), family members—spouses, parents, offspring (siblings), and kin in general—are viewed as having their own preferences and their own sources of "power" relative to others in the family. This power guides their bargaining, or interactions, with other family members with respect to the allocation of resources and consumption decisions. This framework also has been increasingly used to characterize the interactions between generations and includes both cooperative and noncooperative behavior (Bergstrom 1997).

Related literature in sociology notes that cooperation or conflict can guide family relationships. In cooperative models, families are characterized as exhibiting solidarity along several dimensions—affection, emotional support, their willingness to provide material resources and care for each other—and this solidarity helps them function as cohesive units to fulfill members' needs (Bengtson 2000). In contrast to this idea of solidarity and cooperation, scholars have recognized that parents and children, husbands and wives, adult children and elderly parents sometimes hold different interests, that individual family members vary in their ability to achieve their goals in part because power differentials exist among actors in the family, and that social networks within and outside the family can affect the "winner" in these contests.

Conflict perspectives on family behavior often align with "quid-pro-quo" models of exchange. Solidarity models of the family share more affinity with altruistic motivations for family behavior. But the congruence is not perfect: altruistic actors, such as the parents of a young adult child or the adult children of a frail elderly mother, may encounter resistance when they do what they believe is in the best interest of those for whom they care. Conversely, when all parties understand and accept the rules for exchange and all parties benefit from the exchange, self-interested behavior may occur under conditions of minimal conflict.

Understanding intergenerational ties requires theory about individuals' motivations for behavior as well as an appreciation of the larger context that surrounds generational interactions. We provide perspective on the larger demographic and policy context later in this chapter.

Exchange and Reciprocity

The exchange model views the interactions among family members as being very much like the interactions between any two parties: each member has his own objectives (preferences) and resources (sources of power) and each member can potentially improve his situation by trading different goods and services to maximize individual well-being. From this perspective, elderly parents can "buy" the care and attention of their offspring with promises to provide the latter with bequests or other transfers (Bernheim et al. 1985). Transfers need not be reciprocated at the time they are made but can be paid back at a later date and in different currencies. Care for elderly parents, for example, could be given in response to resources received long ago, perhaps in return for parental investment in schooling, help with a down payment on a home, care for a young grandchild, or in response to expected future compensation, as with a bequest.

In its simplest form, the parties involved in the transaction exchange goods and services, subject to the "comparative advantage" of each family member in producing, or supplying, these items. In this context, the "price" of services provided to parents will depend on the opportunity cost of their children's time, with services purchased from high-income children being more costly on a per-hour basis than those purchased from children with lower time costs. Thus, in the context of interactions between elderly parents and their adult children, one would expect the child with the lowest opportunity cost of time to be most likely to provide services to the parent. However, because the total value of the time transferred from a child to a parent depends on both the price per hour and the number of hours provided, the total value of the time transferred from a high-income child (price × quantity) could be greater than that from a low-income child, despite the provision of fewer hours of care by the high-income child.

In sociology, the idea of reciprocal, or quid-pro-quo, behavior is nearly identical to that found in economics: individuals engage in actions that maximize their personal rewards and minimize their costs (Cook and Rice 2003). They do this either by a "backward-looking" strategy, where they base future exchanges on the reinforcement and information they have obtained from prior exchanges (Homans 1961), or via a "forward-looking" strategy, where decisions are based on expected future benefits from engaging in a particular exchange (Blau 1964). In repeated interactions, such as occur in families, actors can use the considerable information from the outcomes of prior exchanges to predict likely outcomes from future exchanges. Actors also develop perceptions about the "fairness" of ongoing exchanges and overlay exchange relationships with an emotional response (Lawler and Yoon 1998; Molm, Takahashi, and Peterson 2000). Hence, repeated exchanges in families may have both rational and emotional aspects that need to be incorporated into theoretical predictions about intergenerational exchanges.

A motive for interactions between generations that is closely related to maximizing (future) well-being is the provision of insurance against unforeseen events, such as accidents or job loss, and the related provision of credit. While markets exist for most types of insurance and credit, families may play a crucial role in providing these services because the problems of adverse selection and moral hazard can plague such markets.[1] Kotlikoff and Spivak (1981) examine the family's role in providing members with substitutes for market annuities, that is, insurance against outliving one's resources. The private annuity market is known to be inefficient due to the presence of adverse selection, and Kotlikoff and Spivak show that even small families may significantly improve their members' well-being by sharing the longevity risk. In Kotlikoff and Spivak's example, children promise to provide for their parent if the parent lives longer than expected and exhausts her savings. Conversely, if the parent dies sooner than anticipated, the children reap the benefit of the parent's unspent resources through a bequest. With respect to credit, a parent may be better able to judge the creditworthiness of a child just starting out on his own than would a formal lending institution (or be better able to enforce repayment) and, thus, be able to make a mutually advantageous loan (Cox 1990). These behaviors are a type of exchange in which both parties benefit. The parent receives a higher return on the loan than she might through other investments, and the child receives a lower interest rate than he would from a bank.

A key issue in these simple characterizations of exchange-based interactions between parents and children (or any other family members) is the extent to which kinship plays a role in the exchange. Certainly reciprocal behavior occurs in many relationships. Why, then, should parents rely on their children to provide care when these services may be obtained from other providers, such as nursing homes or hired help? Market transactions for such services may be fraught with problems of adverse selection and moral hazard, as in the annuity market, and finding such services or assessing the quality of service providers outside the family may be difficult. This latter issue may be especially important with respect to such services as caring for a cognitively impaired parent or for an infant. In this context, parents may engage in transactions (exchanges) with family members they feel they can "trust." In addition, children, knowing their parents' preferences and needs, may provide such services more efficiently than outsiders. As in the case of the parental loan discussed above, families may be better able to enforce reciprocity than would the private sector.

In this vein, the exchange processes may be viewed as rooted in normative principles that obligate repayment of a debt, financial or otherwise (Silverstein 2005). Terms like "enforceable trust" and the idea that intergenerational relationships carry a social obligation that is "owed," suggest that families have power to ensure reciprocal transfers beyond what the market might produce.

A related idea in social psychology is the concept of a "support bank" (Antonucci 1990)—a reserve of gifts or goodwill produced and consumed over an individual's lifetime. Parents invest early by transferring resources to their children and withdraw these resources later after they have built up a reserve. In effect, children owe their parents and "good children," who have internalized the notion of filial responsibility, provide a return to these investments.

Altruism or Caring Behavior

Despite the likely importance of this self-interested behavior, ties between family members would be expected to differ from those between unrelated individuals for reasons other than market efficiency. As Becker (1974, 1991) emphasizes, family members have unique motivations and bonds that guide their interactions, namely they care about one another and one another's well-being. Such altruistic feelings can motivate a parent to finance a child's education and thereby improve the child's future well-being—even if there is no "repayment" from the child—or motivate a child to care for his frail mother despite no possibility of a bequest.

This model is often couched in terms of parents being the donors and children being the recipients, perhaps because the majority of transfers in the United States appear to flow "downstream." It can, however, be two-sided if each party cares about the other, or can operate in the opposite direction with the child as the donor or caregiver. In following the common terminology, we will tend to speak of transfers from parents to children.

In the formal specification posited by economists, the utility function, or well-being, of the parent (donor) U_p depends upon the well-being of the child (recipient) U_k such that

$$U_p = U\left(C_p, U_k\left(C_k\right)\right),$$

where C_k is the consumption of the child and C_p the consumption of the parent. This structure does not require that the parent put equal weight on her own consumption and that of her child, but rather allows for there to be a "weight" or scaling factor attached to the child's well-being. An altruistic parent chooses the amount to transfer to her child—and, thus, the parent consumes what income remains—so as to maximize U_p. As a result, the parent will allocate her resources to equalize the marginal utility of her consumption with the (weighted) marginal utility of her daughter's consumption.

There are several predictions and implications that follow from this model of family decisionmaking. First, children who are poorer—that is, who have fewer of their own resources—will receive larger transfers from their parents than children who are, themselves, better off. This compensatory action by parents accords with an intuitive notion of the consequences of having altruism guide intergenerational interactions. But, there also are additional, less intuitive, predictions from the simple altruism model of family decisionmaking:

- The altruism model implies that the family, through the parent, will choose the consumption levels of its members as a function of the family's *total income;* that is, the distribution of incomes across family members will not affect consumption outcomes. This is sometimes referred to as the *income-pooling* restriction of the altruism model.

- The desire of the altruistic parent (donor) to equalize the marginal utilities of consumption across family members implies that, all else equal, an exogenous increase in the income of children (recipient) will reduce the amount of the transfer the parent (donor) provides. We refer to this as the *transfer-recipient income* prediction.

- An increase of $1 in the income of the parent (donor), accompanied by a decrease of $1 in the income of the child (recipient) will result in a $1 increase in the amount of the transfer. This prediction is referred to as the *transfer-income derivative* restriction.

A number of studies have attempted to test these implications of altruism with alternative data sets and in alternative settings.

As with models of reciprocity, this simple altruism model is applicable to a wide variety of transfers. Because well-being depends on many factors, a parent can increase a child's happiness by transferring cash, providing time assistance, and providing in-kind transfers, such as shared housing or food. Even less-easily quantified commodities, such as attention or good parenting behavior, can be provided to benefit the child. The choice of the specific transfer currency (or currencies) will depend on the preferences or tastes of the donor and recipient—that is, how much different types of assistance are valued or how much disutility or unhappiness their provision implies—and the relevant prices. An adult child wishing to provide assistance to a frail elderly parent can do so herself or can hire a professional caregiver. A child with a high cost of her time, that is, a high wage, would likely find it more cost-effective to purchase professional care for a needy parent, while a low-wage child might be better off reducing hours of paid work and providing the care herself. In addition, the parent may have preferences for care coming from different sources and, thus, would receive different benefits from each type of care.[2]

Because the value of additional units of any commodity—dollars, time, or goods and services—is assumed to decline with the amount of the item the individual has (decreasing marginal utility), this model predicts that more resources will be directed to individuals who are less well off, those who value the transfer the most. This prediction follows from the formal model and agrees with intuition: an altruistic or caring parent would provide more help to the child who needs it more, implying a negative relationship between the resources of the child and the magnitude of the transfer.[3]

Altruism, Exchange, and Related Models

It is certainly plausible to assume that both altruism and exchange may guide the interactions of family members. In a carefully developed model, Cox (1987) presents an exchange model in which the parent is altruistic toward her child but also values the service or good the child can provide. If provision of the service lowers the utility of the child—say, the child dislikes providing care or caregiving takes time away from paid work and is therefore costly—the parent will want to compensate the child in some way, offsetting the negative effect of caregiving.

Similarly, one can imagine alternatives to these basic models. Related to the idea of exchange is the "demonstration effect" model Cox and Stark (2005) developed. In this model, an adult child, who only cares about her own well-being, may choose to care for an elderly parent in the hope of instilling in her own child the belief that one ought to care for one's parents, thus increasing the probability that she herself will be looked after in her old age. In effect, she cares for her parent with the expectation of receiving care in return, albeit from her child rather than the parent. Although intriguing and possibly important in certain contexts, the model is fairly new and has been subject to little formal testing. Some difficulties are readily apparent. For example, the model cannot explain why adult children with no children of their own would provide care for a parent. Yet the literature suggests that unmarried children (who are likely to be childless) are more likely to provide care than their married siblings (Logan and Spitze 1996).

This demonstration effect in economics is similar to social learning theories that have been prominent in developmental psychology (Bandura 1977) and role modeling in sociology. The supposition is that by modeling certain types of behavior, parents increase the likelihood that children will imitate these behaviors and eventually internalize the idea that they "should" behave in this manner. In sociology, there has been increased attention to children's agency in socialization processes. An interesting empirical question is under what circumstances demonstration effects are an effective strategy for establishing an obligation and under what conditions they are resisted or rejected.

Other alternatives also exist. An altruistically minded parent, rather than caring about the child's overall happiness, might care about what the child consumes. Here, a parent might provide resources to finance a college education but not to buy a new car, or might be willing to give the child a down payment on a home but not fund a trip around the world. This model is referred to as a paternalistic model (Pollak 1984).

A second alternative model has been termed the "warm glow model." Here the parent enjoys giving, not because of the improved well-being of her child, but simply because the act of giving makes her happy (Andreoni 1989). The warm glow from giving could be internal or could be due to the praise or adulation the parent receives from others. The idea that a warm glow could come from social "applause" begins to connect economic theories to more sociological theories of norms and identities. That is, if others' opinions motivate an individual, the social network in which the individual is embedded becomes relevant along with shared notions of appropriate behavior within that social network. It then becomes a relatively short step to considering the role of culturally approved and sanctioned norms of behavior, which individuals internalize, and the role these norms might play in setting the context for understanding intergenerational obligations.

Norms, Obligations, and Social Identities

When discussing such motivations as altruism and its related warm glow model, the theories are silent as to the origin of the altruism. Why do family members care for one another or feel an obligation to assist one another? To address these issues, sociologists have moved outside these formal theories to investigate the roles of norms and social identities.

Norms are a core concept in theories about the family in general and intergenerational relationships in particular (Mason 1983, 1991; Rossi and Rossi 1990; Smith 1989). Although difficult to define, norms are perhaps best thought of as social understandings about how individuals ought to behave, in this case, how family members ought to behave toward each other. Norms obligate certain actions, set binding constraints on individuals, and prescribe widely recognized and accepted rules for behavior (Rossi and Rossi 1990, 158).

Such norms help explain why family relationships are special (Finch 1989) and the ways in which family relationships differ from relationships with nonkin. For instance, as Nock, Kingston, and Holian indicate in chapter 13, norms may explain why individuals are willing to give more money to family members than to strangers in need. Norms also may explain why parents treat all of their children equally with respect to bequests but not with respect to inter vivos transfers or support and emotional closeness (McGarry 1999; Pillemer and Suitor, this volume; Wilhelm 1996). Norms also may account for why individuals in the United States report feeling greater obligations to parents and children than they do to aunts and uncles or cousins (Rossi and Rossi 1990; Nock et al., this volume). The specific attributes of these obligations may vary across cultural contexts (e.g., in a matrilineal kinship system, the mother's brother has father-like responsibilities for his sister's children) or historical periods (e.g., when children owe more to parents than parents owe to children, as in Caldwell's [2005] theory of wealth flows).

Despite the centrality of norms for intergenerational relationships, they are often inadequately conceptualized and measured. Measurement is difficult because norms arise from social interactions (Mason 1991; Pollak and Watkins 1993) and, thus, the social group to which the individual belongs is obviously paramount. However, individuals typically belong to several social groups (e.g., family of origin, family of procreation, workplace, clubs) and may face conflicting rules about how to behave. Furthermore, as individuals age, they may move through several different social groups, resulting in exposure to changing sets of norms over time. Thus, not only do individuals' current reference groups matter, but the varied experiences they have throughout life affect their understanding of intergenerational obligations.

To study the potential importance of social norms, it can be useful to examine situations where there is a disruption from what is viewed as normal—situations where the "routinized" or normal experience has been dislodged. Rossi and Rossi (1990) give the example of coresidence with one's 10-year-old child. In the United States, it is normal to expect such coresidence, and, indeed, there could be legal sanctions against a parent who did not provide adequate shelter for a 10-year-old child. However, among some immigrant groups, it might be considered perfectly acceptable—indeed, normative—for parents to leave a 10-year-old child in the home country in the care of another relative. Even in the United States, the norms of coresidence with children become less clear once children reach age 18. Many parents offer coresidence to young-adult children, but the norms are less universal and the obligation certainly not legally binding.

Stepfamilies formed after divorce and nonmarital cohabitation are examples of kin or quasi-kin relationships in which the commonly accepted rules about responsibilities to relatives are still evolving. The lack of consensus about how to behave in these family relationships indicates that these are incomplete institutions (Cherlin 1978; Nock 1995). Examining how individuals adapt to these situations and how these quasi-kin relationships develop may help us understand how norms are formed and how they affect individuals' behaviors. While making studies of intergenerational ties more difficult, these expanded definitions of family also provide an opportunity to address fundamental concepts.

Another example in which norms come into play is the coresidence of adult children and elderly parents. Since World War II, there has been a large increase in the United States in independent living among the elderly (Costa 1999; Kobrin 1976; McGarry and Schoeni 2000; Michael, Fuchs, and Scott 1980). Yet, when an elderly widowed mother has a serious health crisis and can no longer live alone, it is often her adult children who must choose a course of care. They must decide, with or without the mother's involvement, whether she will live with one of her children and which one, or move to an institution. Models based on either altruism or exchange consider the economic opportunity costs of the possible caregivers and the potential for a child to be reimbursed for the care. Omitted from these analyses are the norms under which decisions are made, such factors as what is expected of children in a particular society or whether more distant kin will play an important role. Our predictions about the frequency and variation in the likelihood of coresidence would thus be improved by knowing whether the social setting is one in which being a "good adult child" requires taking one's parent into the household and whether the setting has strong, gender-differentiated norms about daughters' and sons' responsibilities. Variation in patterns of coresidence by racial groups, for example, is not sufficiently explained by differences in the economic resources of adult children and parents (Coward, Albrecht, and Shapiro 1996; Hernandez 1989; Hofferth 1984; Laditka and Laditka 2001) but likely also depends on variation in norms and internalized meanings of filial obligation.

Finally, these norms, and their attendant meanings for individuals, imply an element of social control. Individuals who violate these norms likely face a cost or penalty for doing so. In the example of coresidence with a parent, a child may allow her elderly mother to live with her not only because she feels obligated to do so as part of being a good daughter but because the cost of violating this expectation outweighs other potential costs, such as the loss of privacy or tension in the child's marriage that may arise from coresidence.

The Evolutionary Biology Perspective on Intergenerational Exchange

Although norms likely play a key role in driving intergenerational relationships, an alternative explanation that has its roots in biology has recently begun to receive attention. As Cox (chapter 5) argues, a desire to ensure the survival of one's genes may motivate much human behavior. With respect to intergenerational transfers, this evolutionary perspective hypothesizes that the older generation invests in the younger generation to further their genetic line rather than out of concern for the happiness or well-being of their offspring. In particular, parents care for their children to ensure that they are healthy and survive to reproductive age and, in more modern times, invest in their schooling so that they will be successful and have children. This investment by parents in their genes' survival need not stop with the next generation, but ought to carry on to later generations as well. For example, Cox and Stark (2005) posit that parents can use cash transfers to "purchase" grandchildren. If adult children are delaying childbearing until they can afford a home, for example, a parent might hasten the process by providing funds for the home's purchase.

Interestingly, and perhaps most controversially, the evolutionary perspective also predicts differences in the ties between mothers and fathers and their children. Because ties are based on the desire to pass along genetic material, the strength of the tie depends on the strength or certainty of a genetic link. A mother is always certain that the child to whom she gave birth is her own child, and thus half of the child's genes are hers. A father, however, may be less certain of his paternity. In this model, then, a mother has greater incentive to invest in her child and the ties between mother and child will be stronger than those between a father and his purported child. Similarly, ties to a grandchild born of a daughter will be stronger than ties to the child of a son. In principle, these predictions are testable and provide a way of validating the evolutionary model.

A major weakness of the evolutionary model is its failure to predict transfers that flow upstream to elderly individuals. Once an individual's capacity for reproduction has been exhausted, the species no longer needs the individual to survive. One could argue that the older generation assists in the survival of the younger generation and thus, there is an incentive to prolong the life of the grandparent (Lee 1997). However, younger family members regularly assist elderly individuals who are far too infirm or cognitively impaired to provide any assistance to the young.

Concluding Observations on Alternative Models of Intergenerational Ties

The perspectives described above provide some interesting predictions concerning interactions of all types between generations, as well as a framework with which to examine familial behavior. Common sense and introspection tell us that no one model applies to all individuals or situations. As individuals move through life, for example, different needs may dominate, affecting the salience of various behaviors. Privacy, greatly valued by elderly individuals in the United States, may be less important for younger individuals who seek companionship and have not yet grown accustomed to having their own home. In economic terms, this change in preferences affects the price or value an individual is willing to place on independent living. Individuals who do not have children are unlikely to be inspired to certain behaviors by the desire to demonstrate for their progeny by example, whereas those with children may find that the possibility of a demonstration or role modeling effect provides strong motivation. Similarly, past experience, happenstance, culture, and social norms likely also play a role in determining the relative importance of alternative motives and behaviors.

The majority of empirical studies—some of which are discussed below—have failed to find convincing evidence in support of a single model of behavior. We argue that focusing on one model paints too narrow a picture and we encourage the reader to consider that the different models outlined in this section (and in the other chapters) may be more or less important in different types of families, in different contexts or cultures, and at different points in individuals' lives. Yet despite the multiplicity of motives, identifying when and why a particular model is operating is important for understanding intergenerational behavior, and more specifically, the impact and appropriateness of various public policy measures.

What We Know about Intergenerational Ties

The bulk of demographic research on intergenerational relationships has concentrated on three types of ties: coresidence, transfers of time or care-giving, and financial support.[4] Here we outline the patterns observed for coresidence, the provision of time assistance (primarily home health care), and financial assistance. These behaviors are related, although the nature of the relationship is not always clear. Assistance provided through one form of support may be either a substitute or complement for some other type. For example, financial assistance from a child to a parent may pay for a caregiver, indicating that cash and time help are substitutes. Conversely, an elderly parent who is very infirm might live with a child so that the child can provide help with personal care needs more efficiently. In this case, the transfer of shared living arrangements and caregiving are complements. Similarly, families that are close emotionally may exhibit several of these behaviors and support may flow in multiple directions.

Unfortunately, only a few studies examine transfers in more than a single currency (Boaz, Hu, and Ye 1999; Freedman et al. 1991; Hogan and Eggebeen 1995; Schoeni 1997) and, thus, we know relatively little about the interaction of the various types of transfers. In contemplating the areas in which future research efforts might be most productively employed, we encourage scholars to consider the joint determination of multiple forms of transfers as well as transfers flowing in each direction.

Coresidence

Coresidence can facilitate intergenerational support in numerous dimensions. The arrangement may be an alternative to financial support, as in the case of a parent providing room and board for an adult child struggling to make ends meet. It may improve the efficiency of the provision of care, as, for example, in the case of an adult child caring for an elderly parent or of a grandparent caring for a grandchild. Coresidence also likely increases the emotional support the parties can provide for each other and may thus strengthen family ties, or conversely, lead to additional stresses in a relationship resulting from loss of privacy or autonomy.

Much of the literature has been limited primarily to documenting the extent of coresidence and describing which family characteristics are correlated with a propensity to coreside. Many studies have focused on the living arrangements of the elderly. We provide a brief summary of what we know from this literature.

- There was a dramatic decline in elderly individuals and couples who coresided with their children over the 20th century in the United States (Costa 1997; McGarry and Schoeni 2000; Ruggles 2005). Economists have explained this by focusing on the role of increases in income, citing the sharp rise in Social Security benefits and general economic conditions throughout the 20th century that have made independent living more feasible—and concluding that independence is preferred to coresidence.

- Coresidence of elderly parents with children—and support for coresidence—is higher among blacks and Hispanics (Burr and Mutchler 1999; Coward et al. 1996; Freedman et al. 1991; Hernandez 1989; and Hofferth 1984) and immigrants (Cohen and Casper 2002) than among native-born whites.

- Elderly parents who are married are less likely to reside with one or more of their children (Boaz et al. 1999), suggesting that coresidence of an elderly parent with adult children does not occur until one parent dies.

- Health problems of the elderly parent can precipitate coresidence with children, just as the deteriorating health of a parent can trigger the transition out of coresidence and into an institutional arrangement (Choi 2003).

- Identifying who is helping whom can be difficult, and coresidence may indeed benefit both parties. For example, until parents are quite old, multigenerational families often reside in the home of the parent rather than the adult child. Similarly, parents are more likely to share their home with adult children who are single parents than with those who are married (Cohen and Casper 2002), with unmarried sons than daughters, and with unemployed than employed children. These patterns all suggest that support flows from parents to children (Choi 2003).

- In the past decade, interest in arrangements in which grandparents and grandchildren coreside, either with or without the middle generation, has increased. Much of this research stems from recent welfare reform legislation with new requirements that teenage mothers live with a parent or guardian. There also has been an increase in grandparents raising grandchildren, most often in situations where the parents are experiencing problems (Casper and Bryson 1998; Pebley and Rudkin 1999). One study in this area hints at the potential importance of the "demonstration effect" discussed earlier;

Goldscheider and Lawton (1998) find that the experience of having lived with grandparents is later correlated with an individual's commitment and support for providing residential support for aging parents.

- Coresidence is more common among low-income families, suggesting that finances play a crucial role. However, to disentangle the effect of income from other factors that may be correlated with the decision to coreside is difficult. Although such endogeneity is probable with respect to many explanatory variables, it is perhaps most problematic with respect to income because income and living arrangements are so likely to be jointly determined. A number of studies of the living arrangements of the elderly have attempted to surmount this "endogeneity problem" by analyzing how living arrangements change in response to exogenous changes in government benefits (Costa 1997, 1999; McGarry and Schoeni 2000). These studies conclude that privacy is a normal good; individuals with more resources choose to live alone. Other factors that may be potential determinants of independent living among the elderly, such as changes in fertility and social norms, appear to play a much smaller role.[5]

Living with family members can reduce costs in two important ways. The first is through the returns to scale embedded in a shared-living arrangement—the old saying that "two can live as cheaply as one," while not quite true, is close to the mark. The second is through the more direct route of income pooling or sharing. Economists have been particularly interested in how much income is pooled or shared among household members. Although little attention has been paid to income pooling in intergenerational households, a good deal of work has examined pooling within nuclear families. Even in these cases, where the decision-makers are husbands and wives, researchers have shown significant differences in household expenditure patterns that depend on which spouse controls the resources. These patterns suggest that income is not completely shared and different individuals prefer to spend money on different goods.[6] Based on these conclusions, one might imagine that income pooling within extended families is even less likely.[7] Unfortunately, little data exist to measure consumption and income pooling within the household, although this remains an important avenue for future work.

Time Assistance

The provision of time assistance is obviously tied to the decision to live together, as a shared residence vastly improves the efficiency of providing care. Yet despite the efficiency gain, studies have shown substantial time transfers are made even among non-coresident family members. In fact, families provide more in-home care of the elderly than paid caregivers or caregiving organizations provide.[8] This section examines home health care provided to elderly parents, as well as some limited data on help with chores. We also investigate briefly the provision of child care by family members other than the child's parents. Certainly assistance is provided over a wide spectrum of other tasks as well, but few large-scale studies examine help outside these dimensions. Studies also vary in how time assistance is measured, the types of help considered, and the time period in which help is observed, for instance, in the past month or past year. Yet existing literature provides the following broad-brush picture of the provision of time assistance among family members:

- For elderly individuals needing assistance with activities of daily living (ADLs) or instrumental activities of daily living (IADLs),[9] the most likely caregiver is the spouse: among the frail elderly over age 70, spouses made up 27 percent of all primary caregivers and 67 percent of primary caregivers for married individuals (McGarry 1998). Wives are more likely to be caregivers than are husbands, largely because women tend to marry older men and outlive their husbands.
- Children were the next most common assistant: 20.5 percent of caregivers for the elderly were non-coresident children and another 11.3 percent were coresident children. The unbalanced sex ratio holds among children as well; 70 percent of non-coresident children who are providing care are female (McGarry 1998). Spitze and Logan (1990) find the key to receiving help is to have at least one daughter.
- Adult children with more education and higher wages are less likely to provide assistance to elderly parents with ADLs and IADLs than are children with less education or lower wage rates (Coward and Dwyer 1990; Henretta et al. 1997; Laditka and Laditka 2001). Gender and socioeconomic differences in adult children's caregiving propensities may be intertwined. If the opportunity cost of a daughter's time is less than that of a son's, economic theory predicts that the daughter will provide the care. Because women's wage

rates have historically been lower than men's, they would traditionally have had a lower cost of time. Similarly, women who have
left the labor market to raise children face a lower opportunity cost
of their time. The recent rise in women's labor force participation
and the increase in the ratio of female to male wages, therefore,
would be expected to decrease the fraction of female caregivers.

- As with coresidence, transfers of time may go in both directions:
  conditioning on the existence of a living child, 23 percent of elderly
  parents give help to children and 38 percent receive help with
  household chores from children (Freedman et al. 1991). Here, too,
  there are gender differences, with divorced or never-married
  daughters with children especially likely to have contact with and
  receive help from parents (Spitze et al. 1994). Grandparents, usually
  grandmothers, often provide child care for grandchildren. For example, grandparents are the primary child care providers for preschoolers with working mothers for 14 percent of married mothers and a
  quarter of unmarried mothers (Casper and Bianchi 2002).

Financial Assistance

Much of the research examining financial assistance has focused on
transfers from parents to children and vice versa.[10] As any parent may
attest, even after children are grown and living on their own, a substantial amount of money flows downstream. Estimates about how commonly transfers occur and the amount of money transferred depend, in
part, on how survey questions are posed (for instance, whether the question asks about all transfers or only transfers above a certain amount).
The following highlights major findings on the provision of financial
assistance within families:

- Gale and Scholz (1994) estimate annual flows of inter vivos cash
  transfers between family members of $63 billion (in 1986 dollars). Of
  this amount, $41.2 billion was transferred directly with 80 percent
  flowing to children and 12 percent to grandchildren.[11] An additional
  $105 billion was transferred through bequests.[12]
- McGarry and Schoeni (1995) found nearly 30 percent of parents in
  their fifties made a cash transfer of $500 or more to at least one of
  their children, while 9 percent made a transfer to one or more of
  their parents. Conditional on giving, the average amounts of these

transfers were large: $3,500 for each child who received a transfer and $2,100 for each parent. Even among parents age 70 and older, transfers to children were common, with 25 percent transferring $500 or more to at least one child.

- Among elderly parents age 65 and over, 18.7 percent report giving money to a child, while only 11.9 percent of elderly parents receive money from a child (Freedman et al. 1991).

- Among children age 19 and over, 15 percent receive regular financial assistance from an older parent, while 8.8 percent give older parents financial assistance (Freedman et al. 1991).

- Financial factors are important. Children's economic status affects the type and amount of assistance provided. For example, an increase in children's wage rate—that is, an increase in the opportunity cost of time—increases financial transfers and decreases time transfers (Couch, Daly, and Wolf 1999; Zissimopoulos 2001;).

- Transfers are negatively related to the incomes of the recipients, although the responsiveness of transfers to income is smaller than the altruism model would predict (Altonji, Hayashi, and Kotlikoff 1997; McGarry and Schoeni 1995, 1997).

- In contrast to the compensatory nature of inter vivos transfers, bequests are nearly always divided equally among children (Wilhelm 1996; McGarry 1999), a result that is difficult to reconcile with either the altruism or the exchange model.

Summary of Empirical Patterns of Intergenerational Transfers

The empirical trends and evidence presented above look at assistance at a point in time or at broad trends based on examination of repeated cross sections. Studies suggest there are numerous ties between generations with assistance provided in many ways. However, almost nothing is known about the persistence of assistance to or from particular family members (for an exception, see Szinovacz and Davey [2006]). In the case of home health care, it is important to know for how long, on average, a parent receives care, and what fraction of care each child contributes. Does care progress from informal familial support to paid home care to institutionalization? Or is it more common for a family to rely on a particular form of care? In transfers made in the other direction, we do not know how the provision of child care affects the labor supply of older women or their daughters, whether this care represents a hardship, or whether they receive utility from spending time with a grandchild. In terms of cash assistance, we do not know whether transfers are made repeatedly to the same children.

Even when examining behavior at a point in time, our understanding falls far short of the ideal. Some empirical patterns, however, are clear. Transfers between family members appear to be compensatory—more cash and coresidence is provided to members with lower income. More cash assistance flows from parents to children than vice versa, and caregiving is predominantly provided by women. In no case, however, is the motivation for transfers clear. Understanding the motivation will help us understand what we can expect from families when the political, demographic, and economic environments change.

Distinguishing between Altruism and Exchange: Empirical Strategies and Challenges

Empirical studies have attempted to distinguish between the two most prevalent theoretical motives for intergenerational transfers, altruism (or caring) and exchange (or reciprocity). This section discusses the strategies used, their limitations, and two studies that use direct measures of parents' motives to distinguish between these alternative theories.

Recall that the altruism model makes strong predictions about how resources are shared within families and the responsiveness of transfers to changes in donors' and recipients' incomes. These predictions provide straightforward means of testing the model's validity. Such tests, when implemented, appear to discredit the altruism model. For example, Altonji, Hayashi, and Kotlikoff (1992) use consumption data on family members in the Panel Study of Income Dynamics (PSID) to test the implication of the altruism model that family members—including parents and their adult, non-coresident children—pool their incomes and, thus, "the distribution of consumption is independent of the distribution of resources" (Altonji et al. 1992, 1177). We referred to this as the income-pooling restriction. The results strongly reject this restriction. In a similar vein, Altonji et al. (1997) employ a test of the magnitudes of the derivatives of transfer amounts with respect to the incomes of the parent and child. As noted earlier, another prediction of the altruism model is that a one-dollar increase in the income of the parent (donor) accompanied by an identical decrease in the income of the child (recipient) will be met by a one-dollar increase in transfers (i.e., the transfer-income derivative restriction). Altonji et al. (1997) find that although the effects of an increase in the parent's income are in the predicted direction, the magnitudes are far too small to be consistent with altruistic behavior. In short, the data do not appear to support the strict implications of the economic version of the altruism model.

While the results from these direct tests cast doubt on the validity of altruism as the primary motive for transfers between family members, implicitly suggesting a greater role for the exchange motive, a closer look at these studies illustrates inherent difficulties in devising credible tests of such models. We briefly note some of these difficulties.

First, the data requirements for conducting such tests and distinguishing between models are daunting. One must have data on transfers between parents and children (or donors and recipients), as well as their incomes, and/or measures of consumption for both parties. Only a few data sources meet these requirements, and many only interview one generation, relying on that generation's "proxy" reporting for information on the other generation's income and characteristics.

Second, as Cox (1987) notes, data on both the existence and the amount of a transfer are necessary, at the very least, as the altruism and exchange models predict that changes in the recipient's (child's) income will have the same effect on the *probability* of a parental transfer but with potentially different effects on the magnitudes. Few data sets provide information on the incidence and amounts of parental transfers, and such measurement is prone to error.

Third, almost all strategies for distinguishing between altruistic and exchange motivations for intergenerational transfers are restricted to financial transfers. But, as the preceding sections made clear, transfers can be made in various currencies and at different times. A parental investment in a child's schooling, for example, could be repaid in home health care decades later. The data requirements for such examinations are extraordinary, requiring time series data on family transfers and measurement of transfers of time, cash, coresidence, and goods. No one data source meets all of these requirements.

Finally, these tests either presume that the incomes of parents and children are exogenous with respect to transfer decisions or devise estimation strategies that account for the endogeneity of income. It is difficult to believe that children do not respond, in some way, to the prospect of receiving support from a parent, perhaps by being more selective in choosing a job or forgoing extra effort at work. Benefits received from public transfer programs depend directly on the amount of other income received, including transfers. Finally, concerns inevitably exist with respect to the robustness of methods to control for endogeneity, suggesting that unbiased estimates of the income effects are difficult to obtain.

In short, while there are important theoretical distinctions between exchange and altruistic motives for intergenerational transfers, devising credible ways to distinguish between them empirically remains an ongoing challenge. However, two recent studies represent promising new directions for assessing alternative models of intergenerational transfers.

One avenue is to use direct reports from parents about their motives for transferring resources to their children. For example, Light and McGarry (2004) use responses from the National Longitudinal Surveys (NLS) of Mature Women and Young Women about the motives behind planned bequests to children, along with detailed information on how respondents plan to divide their estates among their children. In essence, Light and McGarry use parents' responses to direct questions about motive to supplement more conventional data on (planned) bequests and children's attributes to assess the relative importance of altruism and exchange. At the same time, self-reported information on transfer motives must be interpreted with caution. Responses to such questions may represent ex post rationalizations of behavior rather than true, underlying motivations. Nonetheless, the use of direct measures of parents' motivations for transfers represents a promising approach to devising more informative strategies for distinguishing between alternative theories of such transfers.

A related, but distinct, strategy involves using direct measures of family members' preferences concerning altruism toward kin and "trust" between family members with measures of within-family transfers. Social psychologists have a long history of developing such measures and, more recently, economists have extended this work by formulating "incentivized games" in which subjects—usually college students in laboratories—are given "endowments" of money that they allocate between themselves and another subject. How they allocate their endowments provides a measure of the subject's altruistic preferences. In a recent paper, Hamoudi and Thomas (2006) present results from a field experiment using families from the Mexican Family Life Survey (MxFLS) in which the subjects play these and other games. In this study, members of MxFLS households played trust games with members of their families, other members of their village, and strangers from distant villages. Using family members' allocation of their endowments in these various games as measures of altruism, Hamoudi and Thomas (2006) analyzed the relationship between altruism and various intergenerational transfers, such as whether adult children coresided with their parents, the probability of adult children receiving financial transfers, and indicators of the health status of children in the family. While this study does not propose explicit strategies for distinguishing between altruism and exchange motives, it provides an excellent illustration of how preferences, such as altruism, might be measured in the field and combined with survey data on transfers to improve our understanding of what motivates intergenerational transfers.

Changing Contexts and Intergenerational Support

Intergenerational transfers obviously do not occur in a vacuum but depend on the prevailing demographic, political, economic, and social conditions. Social norms influence how generations relate to one another, laws govern the exchange of financial resources through taxes and obligatory support, and economic institutions, such as public transfer programs, interact with familial support. In our attempt to understand intergenerational familial ties, we must view patterns and trends with an eye toward the environment in which the agents act.

The Changing Demographic Context

The patterns described in the preceding section are influenced by the demographic environment in which the agents function, an environment that is changing rapidly. America and the developed world face an aging of the population due to increases in life expectancy and declines in fertility. In the United States, the population age 65 and over is projected to increase from 12 percent in 2003 to 20 percent in 2030 (He et al. 2005). Total fertility rates now hover around 2.0, a figure just below the replacement rate of 2.1 (Bramlett and Mosher 2002), which suggests that future generations of elderly are likely to have fewer children on whom they can rely for care.

Along with having fewer children, women are more likely to work outside the home and earn their own incomes (Casper and Bianchi 2002).

As we noted previously, various studies have shown that income in the hands of the mother rather than the father results in different spending patterns, with mothers appearing to direct more resources to children. At the same time, more children have working mothers and spend at least part of their preschool lives in some form of nonparental child care. Other family members, such as grandparents, may provide this care, potentially strengthening family ties. Working women also are less likely to be able to provide care for an elderly parent. Because women have been the primary caregivers, this trend could imply a shift to a more equal division of caregiving between sons and daughters or to the use of more paid care.

Less widely discussed are other changes affecting the composition of the family. Children are increasingly likely to be born outside marriage, with the percentage of children born to unmarried mothers increasing from 3.8 percent in 1940 to 35.7 percent in 2004 (Ventura and Bachrach 2000; Hamilton et al. 2005). Children born to single mothers may have weaker ties to their fathers and paternal grandparents, a situation that could be offset by stronger ties to maternal kin, particularly their maternal grandmothers (Nelson 2006; Bianchi 2006). The rise in cohabitation further complicates the effect of out-of-wedlock births. In recent years, approximately 40 percent of nonmarital births were to cohabiting couples (Bumpass and Lu 2000), suggesting that the father may be very much in the picture early in children's lives even if the parents are not legally married.

Divorce probabilities also remain at approximately 50 percent but are even higher for some groups, such as blacks and less educated individuals (Raley and Bumpass 2003). Divorce is likely to put greater distance between fathers and their children and will likely curtail contact with children even when those children become adults (Cooney and Uhlenberg 1990).

Finally, cohabitation, as a precursor or alternative to legal marriage, has become increasingly common—not only among young adults but also among older persons (Waite 1995; Bumpass and Sweet 1989, 1995). This phenomenon increases the likelihood that children will have "quasi" step-grandfathers and grandmothers as well as the probability that adult children will interact and perhaps incur obligation to (or support from) the partners of their elderly parents late in life (Hagestad 2000).

A direct consequence of these trends in fertility and alternative unions is an enormous growth in step- or blended families, with a substantial increase in the percentage of children who have experienced a step-family.

While the rise in step-families means individuals have more familial connections, these ties are likely to be weaker and less clearly defined than those with biological kin (Ganong and Coleman 1999). How these changes affect familial support is still an open question.

All these factors—increased life expectancy, lower fertility, less specialization of women in the home, and more family disruption—combine to alter greatly the context for intra- and intergenerational caregiving and exchange.

Familial Support and Public Policy

Along with changes in demographics, changes in social welfare programs and legal institutions are likely to affect intra- and intergenerational ties and interactions. For example, the United States just marked the tenth anniversary of welfare reform, which brought sweeping changes to the provision of public support for low-income families. The future will necessarily bring substantial changes to the Social Security, Medicare, and Medicaid programs as the country struggles with its aging population and rising health care costs. How these changes are implemented and how families respond will in large part determine the success of these policies.

The Policy Environment

Public policy can affect family ties directly by mandating support between family members. The legal requirement for parents to support a child to adulthood and court-ordered child support payments are examples of such policies. Perhaps surprisingly, the laws governing these family obligations have changed over time, and the changes have sometimes reduced and sometimes increased family responsibilities. The former Old Age Assistance programs (OAA) operated by individual states often contained "relative responsibility" clauses that required adult children to provide support for their elderly parents. When necessary, court action could enforce this requirement. These relative responsibility rules were eventually omitted from the federal Supplemental Security Income program (SSI), which replaced OAA. More recently, welfare reform legislation has redirected policy toward encouraging greater reliance on family, with requirements that single underage mothers live with a parent or guardian if they are to receive public support. States also have increased efforts to ensure that noncustodial parents make required child support payments and have changed strict rules that cut public support dollar for dollar with child support payments.

The effects of many of these changes in public policy on the incidence and intensity of family transfers seem obvious at first blush. For example, by increasing a recipient's resources, public transfers seem to displace or "crowd out" familial assistance. Yet, on closer inspection, the effects are less clear. As we have noted, the altruistic and exchange models make different predictions about how changes in the donor's or the recipient's income affect the incidence and amount of family transfers. In the next section, we discuss research that has attempted to tease out the effect of public policies on familial support.

Empirical Evidence

There is a growing body of research examining the relationship between changes in the generosity of public support programs and changes in familial transfers. Although the results are still far from conclusive, analyses of broad trends over time consistently point to a negative relationship between public support programs and family transfers—that is, there is evidence of crowding out. However, at the same time, analyses of individual public programs have found little, if any, evidence of such crowding.

Consider the effect of the expansion and increases in the generosity of the Social Security program. There is compelling evidence that the growth of the Social Security program during much of the 20th century led to an enormous decline in the propensity of the elderly to live with adult children (McGarry and Schoeni 2000; Michael, Fuchs, and Scott 1980; Schwartz, Danziger, and Smolensky 1984). Other work suggests that recent cutbacks in public support may have similarly affected living arrangements with low-income mothers becoming increasingly likely to reside with a cohabiting partner or family member throughout the 1990s as welfare benefits were being reduced (Haider and McGarry 2006).

In contrast to these significant effects on living arrangements, studies examining crowding out of cash transfers have failed to find evidence of such a trade-off. Rosenzweig and Wolpin (1994) find that increases in income from public-assistance programs affect cash transfers from parents to children to the same extent as increases in the child's earned income, but that the responsiveness of parental transfers to changes in either source of income is small. Altonji et al. (1997) investigate the responsiveness of parental transfers to a child's income regardless of source and also find that changes in transfers are on the order of pennies on the dollar, again suggesting that the amount of crowding out is likely to be small. Recent work examining the potential crowding out of familial assistance by the unemployment insurance program, however, finds much greater responsiveness, with a dollar of unemployment insurance reducing family support by approximately 40 cents (Schoeni 2002). This result is far from a complete crowding out by public assistance but is obviously an important effect when considering the recipient's well-being.

The responsiveness of private caregiving to the public provision of care seems to fall somewhere in between that estimated for living arrangements and that for cash transfers. Pezzin, Kemper, and Reschovsky (1996) find little, if any, effect of free (or very low cost) home health care for the infirm elderly on the hours of assistance informal caregivers provide. However, the study did find relatively large effects on the chance that the elderly individual lived independently instead of in a shared household or a nursing home.

Taken together, these results suggest that public programs do not completely replace cash transfers among family members but may affect other dimensions of assistance, particularly shared living arrangements. They also demonstrate that changes in public programs likely affect a broader set of individuals than those the specific legislation targets. The growth of Social Security has freed many adult children from the need to provide for elderly parents and, in this sense, also serves as a transfer program to the young. Medicaid, which covers the cost of much nursing home care, similarly relieves the children of poor elderly persons from the obligation of paying for a parent's care or providing it themselves. In this case, if the elderly individual is still receiving care, the transfer is largely one to the younger generation. Medicare works similarly. By providing a large transfer to the elderly who are receiving benefits valued at much more than was paid into the program, it frees up resources for the elderly to use in other forms of consumption. Some of these resources may eventually be bequeathed or given as inter-vivos gifts to their children.

Finally, we note that even if public programs do crowd out family support through a particular currency, families may respond by changing the type of assistance provided. For example, a child whose parent becomes eligible for Medicaid coverage of home health care may reduce the time she spends caring for the parent but increase financial transfers or gifts to the parent, perhaps in response to an increase in the time the child can spend in the labor market. These interactions are obviously extremely complicated, and assessing their relative importance places tremendous demands on the data. However, if we are to create a complete picture of familial assistance, we must consider the interaction between public and private support in not just one, but in many dimensions.

Conclusions

As we have noted, the changing demography of U.S. families raises new questions about relationships within and between generations. In many cases, these changes are likely to be a double-edge sword. For example, while increases in life expectancy mean more multigeneration families and thus an extended kin network, the concurrent declines in fertility mean fewer children on whom elderly individuals can rely for support, as well as fewer siblings with whom a child can share parental caregiving responsibilities (Bengtson 2000). Divorce and nonmarital childbearing distance children from their biological fathers (Cooney 1994; Pezzin and Schone 1999) but lead to new types of kin relationships formed by cohabitation and remarriage, and thus, to increases in the number of family members who could provide support (Wachter 1998). Changes in women's labor force participation and expectations about greater equity in women's and men's family responsibilities also alter the costs of providing care and possibly ideas about who is a preferred caregiver.

These changes pose challenges to families and will likely lead to shifts in the behavior patterns we are accustomed to seeing. Observing how families adapt to these new environments may provide the research community with a powerful tool to deduce the motives behind family ties. For example, stepchildren do not have biological ties to a stepparent. Whether stepparents invest in these children, provide for them financially, or receive care from them will help us identify the importance of the evolutionary model. Changes in the opportunity cost of a daughter's time will similarly help us assess the role of exchange in family transfers.

Not only are families changing, but the data we have to analyze these relationships are growing. In the past several decades, we have seen substantial investment in new data sets—such as the Health and Retirement Study, which focuses on older Americans, and the 1997 National Longitudinal Survey (NLS97)—as well as the continuation of other surveys, such as the Panel Study of Income Dynamics (PSID) and other National Longitudinal Survey (NLS) cohorts, which provide rich data on inter-generational family relationships. New surveys in other countries—such as the Family Life Surveys in several developing countries (Malaysia, Indonesia, and Mexico) and the Generations and Gender project in Europe—are helping us understand how families behave in different economic and social environments. These surveys continually provide new and better quality data and help researchers explore complicated family relationships. The recent surge across disciplines in articles examining familial transfers is evidence of the importance of newly available data.

Despite this progress, we believe there is still substantial scope for improving the measurement of transfers in survey data. Surveys, such as the PSID, which by their nature provide a long panel and links to many, if not all, members of the immediate family, could prove enormously useful were they to improve their measures of transfers and the nature of other interactions between family members. Similarly, the Health and Retirement Study (HRS)—which contains relatively complete information on time help, cash transfers, and co-residence and information on all children and caregivers—could easily be improved if the sample design were altered so that the younger cohorts included children of the older respondents. This overlapping cohort design would permit an examination of transfers from both donors' and recipients' perspectives.

Theory and research on relationships involving repeated exchanges, such as those between parents and children, would benefit from attention to how changes in socio-emotional health and cognitive processes (e.g., memory) affect transfers and caregiving decisions (Carstensen and Hartel 2006). Unfortunately, prospective longitudinal data with information on cognitive, social, and economic characteristics of individuals and their families are extremely rare. A prominent exception is the Wisconsin Longitudinal Survey (WLS), which has followed high school graduates for 50 years. Yet like the HRS, it lacks essential information about both sides of parent-child or grandparent-grandchild relationships. Only the children themselves can report the quality of their relationships with their parents, their perception of what parents have given them as a gift or a loan, and what they think they owe their parents as good children. Conclusions drawn from this study also are somewhat limited by the unique nature of the sample and its lack of representativeness of the larger U.S. population.

Obtaining reports about family relationships from more than one family member raises issues beyond the costs of survey time and money, particularly the difficulty involved with dealing with conflicting reports. Studies suggest parents and children report different information. For instance, Goldscheider, Thornton, and Yang (2001) find that mothers expect to give less for college than children expect to receive. Goldscheider and Goldscheider (1993) showed that young-adult children and parents both estimated that children would move out sooner than they did—but parents' estimates were closer to the actual timing of the move than children's. Parents and children also differ in their reports about the amounts of transfers (Freedman et al. 1991), although donors are more likely than recipients to report a transfer. Research using external validation criteria may improve question wording to elicit responses with greater accuracy. Of particular concern for theories about caregiving to older parents is the finding from a small Midwestern study that adult children describe their parents as being in worse health than their parents report (Cicirelli 2000). Children's understanding of their parents' needs and resources is an important component of dynamic models of caregiving.

A more serious concern for studying intergenerational processes is that studies that interview multiple respondents in the same family have greater success interviewing family members with whom the original respondent has a good relationship than those with whom the respondent has a poor relationship. Response rates for additional family respondents also are higher when they live with the original respondent than when they live in separate households (Dykstra et al. 2004). Methodological work to learn more about the reasons for other family members' non-participation—the original respondent's refusal to provide contact information, inadequate contact information for the second family member, or that person's refusal to participate—will help investigators develop ways to reduce this type of bias.

Combining information about family members who live together as well as those who live apart is a difficult enterprise for conceptual as well as practical reasons. Family members who live together share time and material resources. Coresidence facilitates frequent interaction, which has the benefits of intimacy and more effective monitoring of adults or children who need care, but coresidence also entails a loss of privacy. Family members who live apart also may transfer money, make payments to third parties on behalf of their kin (e.g., paying medical bills), and devote time to providing care. But figuring how to compare within-household to between-household transfers has posed difficulties in studies of nonresident fathers' participation in childrearing and in studies of relationships between parents and adult children. The meanings of behaviors sometimes depend on the setting in which they occur. For instance, having a casual conversation about a grade on a school project or a medical test has less importance and may communicate information more effectively among those who live together because the situation is less stressful than if the conversation occurs between people who do not see each other every day. Similarly, quantifying the resources transferred within the household is difficult because some of what is shared are public goods, and because the costs and benefits of the loss of privacy are evaluated on a different, and hard-to-determine, metric than financial transfers.

Efforts to learn more about what family membership means to individuals and how this meaning is negotiated would benefit from a closer collaboration between ethnographic and survey researchers. Ethnographic studies of the process in which information is transmitted about what is and what is not desirable can help survey researchers do a better job of developing questions about kin obligations in families with complex biological and social ties. For instance, Linda Burton (2006) is studying kinship networks with complicated social ties and social networks in which one or both members of a couple have biological children with other partners and care for other children. Children in these networks ask their adult caregivers how they are related to the other children. The contexts in which children pose these questions and how the questions are answered provide a unique opportunity to study how children learn about who is in their family and what they can expect from them.

Understanding intergenerational relationships in U.S. families requires a recognition of new types of families, the dynamic policy environment, and a willingness to draw on insights about intergenerational relationships from research in other countries. Although our discussion has focused on economic and sociological perspectives, theory and research on intergenerational relationships in those fields would benefit from integration with insights on the processes of human development and attachment. These difficult challenges for researchers parallel the complex challenges of contemporary families that care for their members, exchange resources to enhance members' well-being, and struggle to adapt to changes in their social, political and familial environments.

NOTES

This chapter was prepared for the 2006 Penn State Symposium on Family Issues, "Caring and Exchange within and across Generations," October 4–5, State College, Pennsylvania. Authors are listed in alphabetical order. We are grateful to Gideon Lukens for research assistance and to the National Institute of Child Health and Human Development (NICHD) for financial support through contract number N01-HD-3-3354. This project also benefited from the resources of the California Center for Population Research and the Maryland Population Research Center, both of which receive core support from NICHD. We thank the other authors in this volume and the conference organizers for helpful comments.

1. Adverse selection refers to the phenomenon where those who are at higher risk, in ways unknown to the insurer, are more likely to purchase coverage. Because the insurer is unaware of the higher risk (or simply unable to price the policy based on this), the risky individual gets a good deal. In the annuity market, those who purchase annuities live significantly longer than those who do not buy this type of insurance. This selection increases the cost of the insurance and may make it an unattractive option for many.

Moral hazard refers to the situation where an insured party alters her behavior because she is covered by insurance. An individual who loses a job may search less intensively for a new job because of unemployment insurance. Parents might be better positioned to monitor behavior than a private provider of unemployment insurance.

2. For instance, some evidence suggests older mothers prefer children to provide help with such tasks as grocery shopping and financial help but that they are willing to have non–family members provide personal care (Brody and Schoonover 1986).

3. More specifically, the model predicts that if a parent is making transfers to say, each of her two children, then the marginal utilities of consumption will be equalized across children.

4. Other research examines various forms of emotional support. We readily acknowledge the importance of attachment and emotional ties, but focus here on the more readily quantified types of support in demographic studies.

5. This contrasts with conclusions in earlier work that changes in attitudes were the primary factors driving the move to independent living (Ruggles 1994; Kobrin 1976).

6. Thomas (1990) shows that greater unearned income in the mother's hands results in more nutrient intake by children and greater survival probability for children than income in the father's hands. Similarly, Lundberg, Pollak, and Wales (1997) show that when welfare benefits are given to the mother rather than the father, more money is spent on children (but see Hotchkiss 2005).

7. This lack of income pooling does not mean that individuals are not altruistic or that they do not share to some extent. The altruism model allows the donor to value her own utility more than that of the recipient.

8. In a sample of individuals age 70 and over, just over 13 percent of primary caregivers were paid for their time (McGarry 1998).

9. Studies examining caregiving typically begin by defining a sample of needy elders—those having difficulty with what are termed activities of daily living, or ADLs, which include dressing, bathing, feeding, toileting, getting in and out of bed, and walking across a room. IADLs (instrumental activities of daily living) include such tasks as cooking, managing money, and using a telephone.

10. Very few studies examine the magnitude and explanations for transfers between siblings. For valuable exceptions, see White and Riedmann (1992) and Eriksen and Gerstel (2002). We know of no work that examines transfers between more distant relatives, such as aunts and uncles and their nieces or nephews. Some surveys have attempted to measure transfers from "anyone outside the household," but these typically find such transfers are rare.

11. The remainder was transferred through financial instruments, such as life insurance policies and trusts.

12. Of course, inter-vivos transfers can be made in many years, while bequests are made just once, so the total transferred between the two methods may look very different from the annual figures.

REFERENCES

Alderman, H., Pierre-Andre Chiappori, Lawrence J. Haddad, John Hoddinott, and Ravi Kanbur. 1995. "Unitary versus Collective Models of the Household: Is It Time to Shift the Burden of Proof?" *World Bank Research Observer* 10(1): 1–19.

Altonji, Joseph, Fumio Hayashi, and Laurence Kotlikoff. 1992. "Is the Extended Family Altruistically Linked? Direct Tests Using Micro Data." *American Economic Review* 82(5): 1177–98.

———. 1997. "Parental Altruism and Inter Vivos Transfers: Theory and Evidence." *Journal of Political Economy* 105(6): 1121–66.

Andreoni, James. 1989. "Giving with Impure Altruism: Applications to Charity and Ricardian Equivalence." *Journal of Political Economy* 97: 1447–58.

Antonucci, Toni C. 1990. "Social Supports and Social Relationships." In *Handbook of Aging and the Social Sciences,* 3rd ed., edited by R. H. Binstock and K. George (205–26). New York: Academic Press, Inc.

Bandura, Albert. 1977. "Self-Efficacy: Toward a Unifying Theory of Behavior Change." *Psychological Review* 84: 191–215.

Becker, Gary S. 1974. "A Theory of Social Interactions." *Journal of Political Economy* 82(6): 1063–93.

———. 1991. *A Treatise on the Family.* Cambridge, MA: Harvard University Press.

Bengtson, Vern L. 2000. "Beyond the Nuclear Family: The Increasing Importance of Multigenerational Bonds." *Journal of Marriage and the Family* 6: 1–16.

Bergstrom, Theodore C. 1997. "A Survey of Theories of the Family." In *Handbook of Population and Family Economics,* vol. 1, edited by Mark R. Rosenzweig and Oded Stark (21–79). New York: North-Holland.

Bernheim, B. Douglas, Andrei Schleifer, and Lawrence Summers. 1985. "The Strategic Bequest Motive," *Journal of Political Economy* 93(6): 1045–76.

Bianchi, Suzanne M. 2006. "Mothers and Daughters 'Do,' Fathers 'Don't Do' Family: Gender and Generational Bonds." *Journal of Marriage and the Family* 68(4): 812–16.

Blau, Peter M. 1964. *Exchange and Power in Social Life.* New York: Wiley.

Boaz, R. F., J. Hu, and Y. Ye. 1999. "The Transfer of Resources from Middle-Aged Children to Functionally Limited Elderly Parents: Providing Time, Giving Money, Sharing Space." *The Gerontologist* 39(6): 648–57.

Bramlett, Matthew D., and William D. Mosher. 2002. "Cohabitation, Marriage, Divorce, and Remarriage in the United States." *Vital and Health Statistics* 23(22).

Brody, Elain M., and Clair B. Schoonover. 1986. "Patterns of Parent-Care when Adult Daughters Work and when They Do Not." *Gerontologist* 26(4): 372–81.

Bumpass, Larry L., and H. H. Lu. 2000. "Trends in Cohabitation and Implications for Children's Family Contexts in the United States." *Population Studies* 54: 29–41.

Bumpass, Larry L., and James A. Sweet. 1989. "National Estimates of Cohabitation." *Demography* 26:615–25.

———. 1995. "Cohabitation, Marriage, and Nonmarital Childbearing and Union Stability: Preliminary Findings from NSFH2." National Survey of Families and Households Working Paper No. 65. Madison: University of Wisconsin, Center for Demography and Ecology.

Burr, Jeffrey A., and Jan E. Mutchler. 1999. "Race and Ethnic Variation in Norms of Filial Responsibility among Older Persons." *Journal of Marriage and the Family* 61(3): 674–87.

Burton, Linda. 2006. "Great Divides: The Changing Organization of Marriage and Consensual Unions." Presentation at the annual meeting of the American Sociological Association, Montreal, Quebec, August.

Caldwell, John C. 2005. "On Net Intergenerational Flows: An Update." *Population and Development Review* 31(4): 721–40.

Carstensen, Laura L., and Christine R. Hartel, eds. 2006. *When I'm 64.* Washington, DC: National Academy Press.

Casper, Lynne M., and Suzanne M. Bianchi. 2002. *Continuity and Change in the American Family.* Thousand Oaks, CA: Sage Publications.

Casper, Lynne M., and Kenneth R. Bryson. 1998. "Coresident Grandparents and Their Grandchildren: Grandparent Maintained Families." Washington, DC: U.S. Census Bureau.

Cherlin, Andrew J. 1978. "Remarriage as an Incomplete Institution." *American Journal of Sociology* 84(3): 634–50.

Chiappori, Pierre-Andre. 1988. "Rational Household Labor Supply." *Econometrica* 56(1): 63–89.

Choi, Namkee G. 2003. "Coresidence between Unmarried Aging Parents and Their Adult Children: Who Moved in with Whom and Why?" *Research on Aging* 25(4): 384–404.

Cicirelli, Victor G. 2000. "An Examination of the Adult Child's Caregiving for an Elderly Parent." *Family Relations* 49(2): 169–75.

Cohen, Phillip N., and Lynne M. Casper. 2002. "In Whose Home? Multigenerational Families in the United States, 1998–2000." *Sociological Perspectives* 45(1): 1–20.

Cook, Karen S., and Eric Rice. 2003. "Social Exchange Theory." In *Handbook of Social Psychology,* edited by J. Delamater (53–76). New York: Kluwer.

Cooney, Teresa. M. 1994. "Young Adults' Relations with Parents: The Influence of Recent Parental Divorce." *Journal of Marriage and the Family* 56:45–56.

Cooney, Teresa, and Peter Uhlenberg. 1990. "The Role of Divorce in Men's Relations with Their Adult Children after Mid-Life." *Journal of Marriage and the Family* 52(3): 677–88.

Costa, Dora, 1997. "Displacing the Family: Union Army Pensions and Elderly Living Arrangements." *Journal of Political Economy* 105(6): 1269–92.

———. 1999. "A House of Her Own: Old Age Assistance and Living Arrangements of Older Nonmarried Women." *Journal of Public Economics* 72(1): 39–59.

Couch, Kenneth A., Mary C. Daly, and Douglas A. Wolf. 1999. "Time? Money? Both? The Allocation of Resources to Older Parents." *Demography* 36(2): 219–32.

Coward, Raymond T., and Jeffrey W. Dwyer. 1990. "The Association of Gender, Sibling Network Composition, and Patterns of Parent Care by Adult Children." *Research on Aging* 12(2): 158–81.

Coward, Raymond T., S. L. Albrecht, and A. Shapiro. 1996. "The Perceptions of Elderly Parents about the Possibility of Discontinuing their Coresidence with Adult Children." *Research on Aging* 18(3): 325–48.

Cox, Donald. 1987. "Motives for Private Income Transfers." *Journal of Political Economy* 95(3): 508–46.

———. 1990. "Intergenerational Transfers and Liquidity Constraints." *The Quarterly Journal of Economics* 105(1): 187–217.

Cox, Donald, and Oded Stark. 2005. "On the Demand for Grandchildren: Tied Transfers and the Demonstration Effect." *Journal of Public Economics* 89: 1665–97.

Dykstra, Pearl A., Matthijs Kalmijn, Trudie C. M. Knijn, Aafke E. Komter, Aart C. Liefbroer, and Clara H. Mulder. 2004. "Codebook of the Netherlands Kinship Panel Study: A Multi-Actor, Multi-Method Panel Study on Solidarity in Family Relationships, Wave 1." NKPS Working Paper no. 1. The Hague: Netherlands Interdisciplinary Demographic Institute. http://www.nkps.nl/NKPSEN/nkps.htm.

Eriksen, Shelly, and Naomi Gerstel. 2002. "A Labor of Love or Labor Itself." *Journal of Family Issues* 23(7): 836–56.

Finch, Janet. 1989. *Family Obligations and Social Change.* Cambridge: Polity Press.

Freedman, Vicki A., Douglas A. Wolf, Beth J. Soldo, and Elizabeth H. Stephen. 1991. "Intergenerational Transfers: A Question of Perspective." *The Gerontologist* 31(5): 640–47.

Gale, William G., and John K. Scholz. 1994. "Intergenerational Transfers and the Accumulation of Wealth." *Journal of Economic Perspectives* 8(4): 145–60.

Ganong, Lawrence H., and Marilyn Coleman. 1999. *Changing Families, Changing Responsibilities: Family Obligations Following Divorce and Remarriage.* Mahwah, NJ: Lawrence Erlbaum.

Goldscheider, Frances, and Calvin Goldscheider. 1993. "Whose Nest? A Two Generational View of Leaving Home during the 1980s." *Journal of Marriage and the Family* 55(4): 851–62.

Goldscheider, Frances K., and Leora Lawton. 1998. "Family Experiences and the Erosion of Support for Intergenerational Coresidence." *Journal of Marriage and the Family* 60(3): 623–32.

Goldscheider, Frances, Arland Thornton, and Li-Shou Yang. 2001. "Helping Out the Kids: Expectations about Parental Support in Young Adulthood." *Journal of Marriage and Family* 63(3): 727–40.

Hagestad, Gunhild O. 2000. "Intergenerational Relationships." Paper prepared for the Gender and Generations Programme. New York: United Nations, Economic Commission for Europe/Population Activities Unit.

Haider, Steven J., and Kathleen McGarry. 2006. "Recent Trends in Income Sharing among the Poor." In *Working and Poor: How Economic and Policy Changes Are Affecting Low-Wage Workers,* edited by Rebecca Blank, Sheldon Danziger, and Robert Schoeni. New York: Russell Sage Press.

Hamilton, B. E., S. J. Ventura, J. A. Martin, and P. D. Sutton. 2005. "Preliminary Births for 2004." Hyattsville, MD: National Center for Health Statistics. http://www.cdc.gov/nchs/data/hestat/prelimbirth04_tables.pdf.

Hamoudi, Amar, and Duncan Thomas. 2006. "Do You Care? Altruism and Inter-Generational Exchanges in Mexico." CCPR Working Paper 008-06. Los Angeles: California Center for Population Research, University of California–Los Angeles.

He, Wan, Manisha Sengupta, Victoria Velkoff, and Kimberly DeBarros. 2005. *65+ in the United States: 2005.* Current Population Reports Special Studies no. P23-209. Washington, DC: U.S. Government Printing Office.

Henretta, John C., Martha S. Hill, Wei Li, Beth J. Soldo, and Douglas A. Wolf. 1997. "Selection of Children to Provide Care: The Effect of Earlier Parental Transfers." *Journal of Gerontology* Series B, 52B, 110–19.

Hernandez, L., 1989. "Nonfamily Living Arrangements among Black and Hispanic Americans." In *Ethnicity and the New Family Economy: Living Arrangements and Intergenerational Financial Flows,* edited by F. Goldscheider and C. Goldscheider (17–37). Boulder, CO: Westview Press.

Hofferth, Sandra L. 1984. "Kin Networks, Race, and Family Structure." *Journal of Marriage and the Family* 46(4): 791–806.

Hogan, Dennis P., and David J. Eggebeen. 1995. "Sources of Emergency Help and Routine Assistance in Old Age." *Social Forces* 73(3): 917–36.

Homans, George C. 1961. *Social Behavior and Its Elementary Forms.* New York: Harcourt, Brace and World.

Hotchkiss, Julie. 2005. "Do Husbands and Wives Pool their Resources? Further Evidence." *Journal of Human Resources* 40(2): 519–31.

Kobrin, Frances. 1976. "The Fall in Household Size and the Rise of the Primary Individual." *Demography* 13:127–38.

Kotlikoff, Laurence, and Avia Spivak. 1981. "The Family as an Incomplete Annuities Market." *Journal of Political Economy* 89: 372–91.

Laditka, James N., and Sarah B. Laditka. 2001. "Adult Children Helping Older Parents: Variations in Likelihood and Hours by Gender, Race, and Family Role." *Research on Aging* 23(4): 429–56.

Lawler, Edward J., and Jeongkoo Yoon. 1998. "Network Structure and Emotion in Exchange Relations." *American Sociological Review* 63: 871–94.

Lee, Ronald. 1997. "Intergenerational Relations and the Elderly." In *Between Zeus and the Salmon: The Biodemography of Longevity,* edited by Ken Wachter and Caleb Finch (212–33). Washington, DC: National Academy Press.

Light, Audrey, and Kathleen McGarry. 2004. "Why Parents Play Favorites: Explanations for Unequal Bequests." *American Economic Review* 94(5): 1669–81.

Logan, John R., and Glenna D. Spitze. 1996. *Family Ties: Enduring Relations between Parents and Their Grown Children.* Philadelphia, PA: Temple University Press.

Lundberg, Shelly, Robert Pollak, and Terence Wales. 1997. "Do Husbands and Wives Pool Their Resources? Evidence from the United Kingdom Child Benefit." *The Journal of Human Resources* 32(3): 463–80.

Mason, Karen Oppenheim. 1983. "Norms Relating to the Desire for Children." In *Determinants of Fertility in Developing Countries,* vol. 1, edited by Rodolfo A. Bulatao and Ronald D. Lee (388–428). New York: Academic Press.

———. 1991. "Multilevel Analysis in the Study of Social Institutions and Demographic Change." In *Macro-Micro Linkages in Sociology,* edited by Joan Huber (223–30). Newbury Park, CA: Sage Publications.

McElroy, Marjorie B., and Mary Jean Horney. 1981. "Nash-Bargained Household Decisions: Toward a Generalization of the Theory of Demand." *International Economic Review* 22(June): 333–49.

McGarry, Kathleen. 1998. "Caring for the Elderly: The Role of Adult Children." In *Inquiries in the Economics of Aging,* edited by David A. Wise (133–63). Chicago: University of Chicago Press.

———. 1999. "Inter vivos Transfers and Intended Bequests." *Journal of Public Economics* 73(3): 321–51.

McGarry, Kathleen, and Robert Schoeni. 1995. "Transfer Behavior in the Health and Retirement Study." *Journal of Human Resources* 30(supplement): S184–S226.

———. 1997. "Transfer Behavior within the Family: Results from the Asset and Health Dynamics Study." *Journals of Gerontology* 52B: 82–92.

———. 2000. "Social Security, Economic Growth, and the Rise in Elderly Widows' Independence in the Twentieth Century." *Demography* 37(2): 221–36.

Michael, Robert T., Victor R. Fuchs, and Sharon R. Scott. 1980. "Changes in the Propensity to Live Alone: 1950–1976." *Demography* 17(1): 39–56.

Molm, Linda, Nobuyuki Takahashi, and Gretchen Peterson. 2000. "Risk and Trust in Social Exchange: An Experimental Test of a Classical Proposition." *American Journal of Sociology* 49:98–121.

Nelson, Margaret K. 2006. "Single Mothers 'Do' Family." *Journal of Marriage and Family* 68(4): 781–95.

Nock, Steven L. 1995. "A Comparison of Marriages and Cohabiting Relationships." *Journal of Family Issues* 16(1): 53–76.

Pebley, Anne, and Laura L. Rudkin. 1999. "Grandparents Caring for Grandchildren: What Do We Know?" *Journal of Family Issues* 20(2): 218–42.

Pezzin, Liliana E., and B. S. Schone. 1999. "Parental Marital Disruption and Intergenerational Transfers: An Analysis of Lone Elderly Parents and Their Children." *Demography* 36:287–97.

Pezzin, Liliana, Peter Kemper, and James Reschovsky. 1996. "Does Publicly Provided Home Care Substitute for Family Care? Experimental Evidence with Endogenous Living Arrangements." *Journal of Human Resources* 31(3): 650–76.

Pollak, Robert, 1984. "Tied Transfers and Paternalistic Preferences." *American Economic Review* 73:1023–35.

Pollak, Robert A., and Susan Cotts Watkins. 1993. "Cultural and Economic Approaches to Fertility: Proper Marriage or Mésalliance?" *Population and Development Review* 19: 467–96

Raley, R. Kelly, and Larry Bumpass. 2003. "The Topography of the Divorce Plateau: Levels and Trends in Union Stability in the United States after 1980." *Demographic Research* 8(8): 245–60. http://www.demographic-research.org/volumes/vol8/8/8-8.pdf.

Rossi, Alice S., and Peter H. Rossi. 1990. *Of Human Bonding: Parent-Child Relations across the Life Course.* New York: Aldine de Gruyter.

Rosenzweig, Mark R., and Kenneth I. Wolpin. 1994. "Parental and Public Transfers to Young Women and Their Children." *American Economic Review* 84(5): 1195–1212.

Ruggles, Steven. 1994. "The Transformation of American Family Structure." *American Historical Review* 99(1): 103–27.

———. 2005. "The Decline of the Multigenerational Family in the United States, 1850–2000." Minneapolis: Minnesota Population Center, University of Minnesota.

Schoeni, Robert F. 1997. "Private Interhousehold Transfers of Money and Time: New Empirical Evidence." *Review of Income and Wealth* 43(4): 423–48.

———. 2002. "Does Unemployment Insurance Displace Familial Assistance?" *Public Choice* 110(1–2): 99–119.

Schwartz, Saul, Sheldon Danziger, and Eugene Smolensky. 1984. *The Choice of Living Arrangements by the Elderly.* Madison: University of Wisconsin–Madison, Institute for Research on Poverty.

Silverstein, Merrill. 2005. "Social Exchange Theory." In *Sourcebook of Family Theory and Research,* edited by V. L. Bengtson, A. C. Acock, K. R. Allen, P. Dilworth-Anderson, and D. M. Klein (407–10). Thousand Oaks, CA: Sage.

Smith, Herbert L. 1989. "Integrating Theory and Research on the Institutional Determinants of Fertility." *Demography* 26: 171–84.

Spitze, Glenna, and John R. Logan. 1990. "Sons, Daughters, and Intergenerational Social Support." *Journal of Marriage and the Family* 52(2): 420–30.

Spitze, Glenna, John R. Logan, Glenn Deane, and Suzanne Zerger. 1994. "Adult Children's Divorce and Intergenerational Relationships." *Journal of Marriage and the Family* 56(2): 279–93.

Szinovacz, Maximiliane E., and Adam Davey. 2005. "The Familial Context of Caregiving: Flexibility in the Division of Care among Adult Children." Paper presented at the annual scientific meeting of the Gerontological Society of America, Orlando, Florida, November 20.

Thomas, Duncan. 1990. "Intra-Household Resource Allocation: An Inferential Approach." *The Journal of Human Resources* 25(4): 635–64.

Ventura, Stephanie J., and Christine A. Bachrach. 2000. "Nonmarital Childbearing in the United States, 1940–99." *National Vital Statistics Reports* 48(16). http://www.cdc.gov/nchs/data/nvsr/nvsr48/nvs48_16.pdf.

Wachter, Kenneth W. 1998. "Kinship Resources for the Elderly: An Update." Unpublished manuscript, Department of Demography, University of California, Berkeley. http://www.demog.berkeley.edu/~wachter/WorkingPapers/terrace.pdf.

Waite, Linda J. 1995. "Does Marriage Matter?" *Demography* 32:483–507.

White, Lynn K., and Agnes Riedmann. 1992. "When the Brady Bunch Grows Up: Step/Half- and Fullsibling Relationships in Adulthood." *Journal of Marriage and the Family* 54(2): 197–208.

Wilhelm, Mark. 1996. "Bequest Behavior and the Effect of Heirs' Earnings: Testing the Altruistic Model of Bequests." *The American Economic Review* 86(4): 874–92.

Zissimopoulos, Julie. 2001. "Resource Transfers to the Elderly: Do Adult Children Substitute Financial Transfers for Time Transfers?" RAND Working Paper Series 01-05. Santa Monica, CA: The RAND Corporation.

2

Are We Asking the Right Questions on Intergenerational Ties?

Rebeca Wong

Transfers of privately owned resources are common across generations of extended families, and they are often used by researchers to reflect intergenerational ties. In the United States, the transfers usually flow from parent to child regardless of age, although the type of transfer and intensity of the flow varies by the circumstances of donors and recipients, such as their stage in the life cycle or their economic status. The study of these intergenerational family ties has received attention mostly within discussions of the likely effect of public transfers. The argument is that if we understand the nature of family transfers, then we can potentially assess who is likely to benefit more or less from social programs, such as assistance for higher education, child tax credits for families with young children, low-income assistance programs, or Social Security and Medicaid programs.

Chapter 1, by Bianchi, Hotz, McGarry and Seltzer, presents an overview of the approaches different disciplines use in the study of intergenerational ties and the reasons for such relationships. The focus is on ties between adult children and their parents. The chapter provides also a summary of what is known empirically about these relations, and the changing demographic context and what it implies for intergenerational ties. Their chapter concludes with a discussion of future directions of study and the data needed to support such research. Indeed, this is a paramount undertaking, and the authors accomplished the goals of the chapter quite well.

In *theoretical approaches,* the authors make a major contribution to this literature by merging particularly the economic and the sociological literatures—how these two disciplines approach the study of inter vivo transfers. One comes away with the sense that economics has focused on the *motivation* for transfers, and sociology on the *social bonds* that either motivate the transfers or result from these transfers.

Focusing first on the interest for discovering the motivation, the authors make a convincing case that testing empirically for the motivation of transfers has been a daunting and almost impossible task. This is because the phenomenon includes several dimensions: members of two or more generations, a variety of currencies for transfers (money, time, in-kind, and coresidence), multiple directions of flows, and the timing across the life cycle (and beyond) in which transfers occur. Indeed, trying to infer motivation from transfers observed over a relatively short period of time, on a phenomenon that could unravel over the lifetime of several generations, can be challenging and limited in scope. In economic terms, we can assume that the preferences for transfers are stable; that is, individuals are inclined to be involved, sometimes as a donor, sometimes as a recipient. The transfer may not even be directly to the person but to a family member of the target person, and the transfer may or may not have been recent or even during the target person's lifetime. Family transfers can be motivated for exchange, altruism, a warm glow, a demonstration, insurance, norms, evolutionary reasons, or any combination of the above and other reasons. As the authors state, not one of these reasons likely explains all behaviors, but rather they *all* likely play a role at different times over the life cycle, over long periods that may include one's lifetime and beyond. With these principles in mind, we can talk of the variables that can help us proxy the shape or strength of such preferences (previous transfer activity or obligation, altruism, warm glow, etc.). Research that empirically tests these various motivations now shows that they exist. Even if isolating or separating the motives for transfers is difficult, we need to acknowledge that these reasons shape an individual's preferences for intergenerational ties.

Chapter 1 makes an emphasis that seems particularly appealing. We need to build the theory, acting on the premise that there are a myriad of motivations for the intergenerational ties, and add the circumstances (individual, family, social network, and broader context) that facilitate or impede the transfers. It would be useful to move forward with a theoretical framework that indicates or stipulates "universal trends" that should hold across cultures and socioeconomic groups. Chapter 1 falls short of telling us, for example, which predictions are common across the different theoretical approaches, and this could be a good starting point. The chapter points toward a theory that includes various generations, times over the life cycle, currencies, and directions of flows. As the authors mention, several advances have been made on this theoretical front, but these advances seem isolated and fail to integrate all of the considerations now widely acknowledged.

Are We Asking the Right Questions?

A major gap in both the economic and sociological literature is that, empirically, we have focused on the study of *observed* or *active* transfers to infer generational ties or social bonds. There is a conceptual problem with this approach because an *inactive* link among people may also constitute part of the social bonds that tie them and may affect the way people behave and plan. Researchers may miss a large fraction of what determines people's behavior by focusing only on active links. In particular, the vast majority of social links may be dormant among healthy people of preretirement age or those who have had no major health problems or disabilities. But their behavior and plans may very well take into account this potential network.

Thus, part of this empirical research needs to be framed in the realm of *latent* inter-generational ties, that is, the potential or dormant family support. Furthermore, research needs to focus on how latent ties are associated with the well-being of those involved. We need to answer such questions as the following:

- What affects individual behavior and well-being? Is it the active transfers only or is it the potential or latent safety net as well?
- If transfers are inactive between two people, do they view the social bonds that tie them to be weak?
- Do people involved in active transfers feel more satisfied with the social bonds around them than those that have a large safety net but are not actively involved in transfers? Do they feel more secure? Better prepared to face uncertainties and emergencies?
- Do latent ties affect people's mental health in positive ways?
- Are people with latent ties less likely to engage in poor health behaviors than those who lack latent ties?

The emphasis on perceptions is important; the mere perception of a safety net may affect how people behave and plan for their future. In other words, whether they *perceive* that someone would support them *if* they were in need may affect how they plan—not necessarily whether someone actively helps or has helped them in the past. The literature has focused on the active net measured by observed transfers and has given little importance to the latent net and the corresponding sense of security that may derive from this dormant presence. To draw a similarity using insurance jargon, economists and sociologists researching intergenerational ties have focused mostly on the insurance claims and not on the availability of insurance. We need to consider asking the right questions to capture this concept, such as a *perceived* sense of security regarding family support in case of immediate need.

On the empirical analyses and what is known about intergenerational transfers, the chapter also makes a contribution in summarizing the findings in the literature. However, how little we know about the *dynamics* of transfers is surprising; we ought to know more about these patterns (entries and exits and why) and the joint determination of movements, given the data that have been collected in the United States over a long period.

In the event of future demographic changes, we need to get a sense of the current importance of active transfers. Then we need to know if the potential safety net is relevant. For example, if the evidence indicates that strong bonds (and not necessarily observed transfers) exist regardless of family size, among step- and biological families, and among people who worked all their lives and those who did not, then we have less to worry about in the sense that these are the demographic changes that could impact intergenerational ties. What does research show regarding how these changes are associated with active transfers, and with the latent safety net? In a review of the empirical evidence, it would be useful to spell this out more specifically. The most critical area to understand is the importance of women's care-giving role and the consequences of more women participating in the labor market and being unable to provide care in the future.

The discussion in the chapter of possible *future approaches* seems appealing, although it could be more specific or targeted. For example, the authors could integrate their discussion of how the Health and Retirement Study or the Panel Study of Income Dynamics could improve its information gathering with previous discussions about observing various points over the lifetime. The authors could integrate this discussion with their arguments on using external validation, innovative ways of measuring motivation for exchanges, a need to collaborate with ethnographic researchers, and conflicting reports by different respondents. I echo the authors' concern that we ought to be willing to draw from insights based on research on other countries, but again, this is not specific enough. What hypotheses or tests would cross-national comparisons enable, for example? What specific insights could we gain?

To illustrate, I would like to provide an example. Among families in Mexico, monetary transfers flow generally from adult children to parents, whereas the flow tends to be from parents to children in the United States. This particular Mexico–United States comparison has been enabled recently by the availability of survey data from the Mexican Health and Aging Study (MHAS), which is comparable to the Health and Retirement Study in the United States. Adults age 50 and older in Mexico report that they are more likely to receive monetary help from their children (54 percent) than to give help to their children (20 percent) in a two-year period (Wong and Higgins 2007). Over the life cycle from middle to old age, receiving help from children becomes increasingly dominant over giving (Wong and Espinoza 2004). Figure 1 plots the estimated propensities to give help to children, and to receive assistance from children, controlling for living arrangements and demographic, economic, and health factors.[1] The patterns of intergenerational transfers indicate that the propensity to receive help rises and to give help drops with older age, in particular beyond age 70. Also, the propensity to receive economic help increases the most with age, and the propensity to give economic help drops the most. These age gradients are similar for men and women and across living arrangements.

The differences in giving patterns between Mexico and the United States could provide insights into the cultural norms of intergenerational ties. However, while the propensity to help parents is higher in Mexico, we need to be cautious in inferring that this is mostly due to a different culture of giving. While the overall propensity to give help to children and to receive help from children is similar in two cross sections (the 2001 and 2003 waves of the MHAS), the dynamics of the phenomena in Mexico reveal quite a bit of activity; older adults enter and exit the help system. Families do not remain in a state of continuously giving and receiving help, as a cultural norm would indicate (Wong and Higgins 2007). Holding socioeconomic and demographic factors constant, monetary transfers

Figure 2.1. Propensity to Give and to Receive Economic and Noneconomic Assistance, Adults Age 50 and Older in Mexico

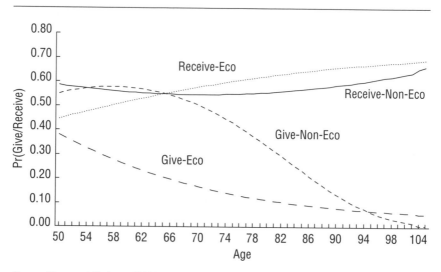

Source: Wong and Espinoza (2004), using data from the Mexican Health and Aging Study 2001.

Notes: Intergenerational transfers refer to those in the two years prior to the survey by older adults, giving or receiving help to or from their children and grandchildren. Economic help refers to money or in-kind transfers worth at least 5,000 pesos (approximately $500) over the past two years. Noneconomic help refers to time-transfers of at least an hour a week with care-giving or chores over the past two years. The estimated probability is obtained using probit regression, controlling for economic, demographic, and health factors.

respond largely to economic factors, and time-help (assistance with caregiving or chores) is associated with health shocks. Thus, the family transfers system of older adults with their children responds largely to economic and health needs just as in the United States.

In trying to understand why the transfer flow is mostly from children to parents, we need to understand the historical context of the cohorts under study. The current elderly in Mexico have children whose education is dramatically higher compared with their parents' education, and the number of children that the elderly in Mexico have is high compared with the elderly in the United States. Thus, the stage of the demographic transition and the relative economic standing of the generations, rather than cultural differences, may explain the different patterns of inter-generational transfers between Mexico and the United States. Cross-national comparisons need to be driven by research hypotheses that account for the different stages of transitions and the historical context of institutions as well as cultural differences.

In summary, chapter 1 makes a solid contribution in reviewing a topic that is complex not only theoretically but empirically. Moving beyond what the current literature has done is timely and needed, and the paper accomplishes this as well. How the questions raised could be rephrased to capture potential ties, which may affect people's economic and health behaviors, should be discussed. I argue that we need to focus on not only the active transfers within families but the sense of a safety net that families have. The *latent safety net* may be more important than the transfers received or given in determining people's behaviors and plans. If people behave according to their sense of security and not their active transfers, then policy recommendations may be better designed and guided to capture this conceptual difference. Notwithstanding these comments, chapter 1 also makes an important contribution by formulating a blueprint of a multidisciplinary research agenda for intergenerational ties.

NOTE

This chapter was originally prepared for the 2006 Penn State Symposium on Family Issues, "Caring and Exchange within and across Generations," October 4–5, State College, Pennsylvania.

1. Demographic controls are sex, age, education, urban/rural residence, residence in high-migration states, ever a U.S. migrant, number of living children, children's schooling, and number of children currently in the United States. Economic controls include individual net worth, current employment, and household consumer durables. Health controls include problems with activities of daily living, problems with instrumental activities of daily living, and self-reported global health. The plots correspond to the probability of giving and receiving monetary and in-time help over the two years prior to the survey using probit regressions.

REFERENCES

Wong, Rebeca, and Monica Espinoza. 2004. "Intergenerational Assistance in Middle- and Old-Age in Mexico: Life Cycle Stages in a Developing Economy." Paper presented at the Population Association of America Meetings, Boston, MA.

Wong, Rebeca, and Monica Higgins. 2007. "Dynamics of Intergenerational Assistance in Middle- and Old-Age in Mexico." In *The Health of Aging Hispanics: The Mexican-Origin Population,* edited by J. L. Angel and K. E. Whitfield (99–120). New York: Springer Publishing Co.

3

Intergenerational Ties

What Can Be Gained from an International Perspective?

Francesco C. Billari and Aart C. Liefbroer

I n this chapter, we argue for the importance of adopting an international comparative perspective in the study of intergenerational ties. We take chapter 1 as a starting point. However, while Bianchi and coauthors point out the importance of taking contexts into account by stating that "understanding intergenerational ties requires theory about individuals' motivation for behavior as well as an appreciation of the larger context that surrounds generational interaction," they do so mainly by focusing on medium- to long-term changes within the United States. Our discussion emphasizes the need for taking other contexts seriously and focuses on the usefulness of an international comparative perspective. Within such a perspective, the larger context includes cultural, economic, and institutional variation at the international level. This is a particularly fruitful perspective, not just because the strength and nature of intergenerational ties may depend on the context, but because motivations, rewards, and the determinants of individual behavior might explicitly interact with the context as well. This potential micro–macro interaction also makes a cross-contextual perspective fundamental when context is not the primary focus of research.

In our opinion, research based on a single national setting might be weaker in stimulating alternative theories of behavior, or might not lead to empirical observations that point to different types of individual-level determinants of behavior. Our discussion of the usefulness of comparative research focuses on Europe, mainly because, unfortunately, few current comparative studies include the United States.

The first section of this chapter comments on theoretical approaches to understand intergenerational ties. The second section reflects on the types of ties to be distinguished. The third, and longest section, takes up the importance of contexts in understanding intergenerational ties and focuses heavily on the gains to be made from taking an international comparative perspective. A short discussion of the implications for future research is provided in the fourth section.

Theoretical Approaches to Understanding Intergenerational Ties

A major strength of chapter 1 is its extensive and insightful discussion of different theoretical approaches to understand intergenerational ties. First of all, Bianchi and colleagues show that, despite differences in language and mathematical rigor, approaches in economics, sociology, anthropology, and psychology have much in common. This understanding facilitates the diffusion of knowledge across disciplines. A second key asset of chapter 1 is its emphasis on the fact that more than one type of motivation often drives intergenerational exchanges. The importance of the authors' suggestion that both exchange and altruism, or reciprocity and care, are important in understanding exchanges can hardly be overstated, as it opens avenues to study the conditions under which either motivation is more or less important. Such an approach is more useful than one that presents exchange and altruism as mutually exclusive motivations.

Sociologists emphasize that societal norms about filial and parental obligations can act as bases of altruistic behavior between parents and children. However, the strength of such normative obligations in modern societies has been a topic of debate. Recent societal change has been interpreted both within demography (e.g., Lesthaeghe 1995; Van de Kaa 1987) and sociology (e.g., Giddens 1992; Beck and Beck-Gernsheim 2002) as driven by processes of secularization, individualization, and modernization. One of the main arguments in the theoretical discourse about the changes in young adulthood is that individual control has increased and that young adults are less dependent on normative constraints that institutions like the family and the church impose. Social norms, therefore, might be losing their importance as a regulatory device in the life course. If so, weakening norms of family obligations may decrease altruism as a motive for intergenerational support.

A counterargument can be found in the life-course literature, which emphasizes the importance of social norms as regulatory mechanisms during the life course. Some of these norms relate, for instance, to coresidence: what is the appropriate time to leave the nest? Is there an age after which young adults ought not to return home? Settersten and Hagestad (1996) document such age norms in the United States. Nock et al. (this volume) interpret the choice to support relatives in need as arising from the presence of social norms. Are these social norms around?

Cross-national comparative research is a promising approach to studying the "survival" of norms of family obligation in an individualizing world and can help researchers identify factors that influence the strength and persistence of such norms. Combined data from the European Values Study (EVS) and the World Values Study (WVS) can help us grasp the importance of this topic in the study of intergenerational ties. In this dataset, questions have been posed both on the obligations parents have toward their children and on the obligations children have toward their parents.

Figure 3.1 presents the percentage of persons that agree with the statement "Parents' duty is to do their best for their children even at the expense of their own well-being" for selected countries in 1981, 1990, and 1999. This figure documents two facts. First, in a number of Western countries, during the past two decades, feelings of parental obligation have increased rather than decreased. Agreement with the statement about parents' duty has risen on average from 63 percent in 1981 to 70 percent in 1999. Second, cross-country differences have diminished (the cross-country standard deviation has decreased from 10.8 to 8.0). These findings suggest that altruism in favor of children is increasingly becoming a basic social norm across several societies.

The picture is rather different when we look at feelings of filial obligation (figure 3.2). Although the EVS/WVS statement ("Regardless of what the qualities and faults of one's parents are, one must always love and respect them") is less related to support than the one on parental obligations, it still illuminates interesting differentials. Figure 3.2 shows no clear trend over time (the cross-country average is 61.2 percent in 1981 and 60.7 percent in 1999), and cross-country differences are relatively stable, with the cross-country standard deviation rising from 15.0 to 17.2. Nordic countries, Germany, and the Netherlands are persistently

Figure 3.1. Share of Respondents Who State that "Parents' duty is to do their best for their children even at the expense of their own well-being"

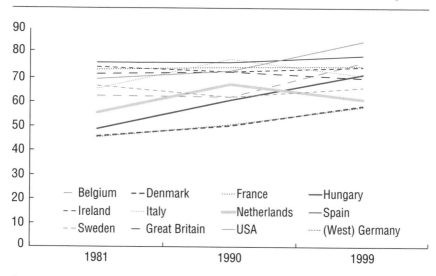

Source: Authors' analysis of data from World Values Survey, http://www.worldvaluessurvey.org/.

below 50 percent. Italy and Spain are persistently above 70 percent, with the United States very close to that.

Several conclusions can be drawn from these findings. First, norms about family obligations are widely shared within modern, individualized societies. Second, the norms of parents' obligations seem to have become stronger since 1981, whereas filial obligations remain about the same level. Third, a wide variety in the strength of such norms exist across modern societies. A challenge of research in this area is to account for these differences.

How to Conceptualize Intergenerational Ties?

Bianchi and coauthors discuss empirical research related to three types of ties: coresidence, transfers of time and caregiving, and financial support. Although these ties obviously are important, we feel that their chapter could have benefited from a more general reflection on the types of ties between parents and their adult children. We suggest that at least three aspects of intergenerational ties warrant attention: the proximity of

Figure 3.2. Share of Respondents Who State that "Regardless of what the qualities and faults of one's parents are, one must always love and respect them"

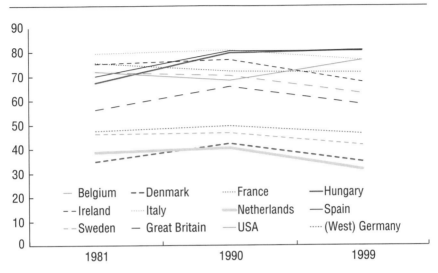

Source: Authors' analysis of data from World Values Survey, http://www.worldvaluessurvey.org/.

parents and adult children, the level and type of contact between parents and children, and the exchange of support between parents and children.

Proximity

Coresidence of parents and adult children is a key issue for research, as coresidence not only facilitates other types of support, but is itself an indicator of support and perhaps of the prevalence of specific norms. Nevertheless, seeing coresidence in a dichotomous fashion may prevent detecting trends that could become crucial in new developments, especially in light of population aging. A view on proximity, rather than coresidence, could more fruitfully orient research on intergenerational ties. An adult child, for instance, might decide not to move to a different city in order to live close to an elderly parent who is needy or who could become needy. At the same time, proximity is strongly related to types of support that ask for a regular time contribution. Also power relationships might guide proximity, which is consistent with exchange models of intergenerational ties—for instance, when parental financial assistance is crucial in getting access for adequate housing, parental help may be conditioned on the proximity of the young adult's residence (Tomassini et al. 2003).

Figure 3.3 documents the extent to which children of adults (with at least one child) older than 50 years coreside with their parents in European countries where the SHARE survey was conducted (Hank 2007). It shows whether the nearest living child is coresiding, lives within 25 kilometers of the parents, or lives more than 25 kilometers away. The typical "latest-late" pattern of transition to adulthood prevailing in Southern Europe (Billari et al. 2001; Billari 2004) is clearly visible: in Greece, Italy, and Spain, the majority of older adults have a coresident child. Although coresidence is less common in other countries, most parents still have at least one child who lives nearby and could provide support, though with considerable cross-nation variation: in Denmark, France, and Sweden, more than 20 percent of parents do not have a child within 25 kilometers (about 15.5 miles).

Figure 3.3. Proximity to Nearest Living Child, Individuals Age 50 and Older

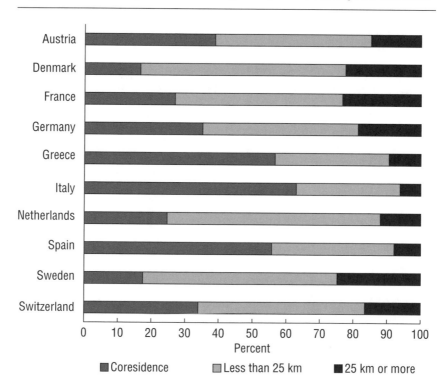

Contact

Another important dimension of intergenerational ties is how often parents and children have contact and what the content of this contact is. Frequency of contact, like proximity, conditions other types of ties. For instance, if parents and children have no or only very infrequent contact, the odds that they will exchange support diminish. Again, there is a wide cross-national variation in frequency of contact, as figure 3.4 shows. Figure 3.4 mirrors the pattern observed in figure 3.3. Unavoidably, coresident kin are likely to have daily contact with each other. Figure 3.4 also gives some interesting hints concerning norms of filial obligation. Although these norms were rather weak in the Nordic countries and the Netherlands (see figure 3.2), weekly contact between parent and children

Figure 3.4. Frequency of Contact with Most Contacted Child, Individuals Age 50 and Older

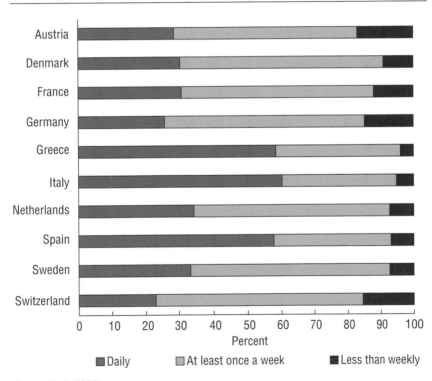

Source: Hank (2007)

in these countries is still relatively high compared with countries like Austria, France, Germany, and Switzerland, where more than 10 percent of adults have less than weekly contact with their children. However, research should not just focus on the frequency of contact but on the type of contact (face-to-face, phone, mail, e-mail, etc.) and on the kinds of activities parents and children perform together.

Support Exchanges

Bianchi and colleagues focus on two types of support exchanges, time assistance and financial assistance. While these types of support are important, other types may be important as well. For instance, emotional support may be at least as important in influencing the well-being of parents and children, and the fact that it is a more subjective type of support than time or money does not imply that it is difficult to measure. In addition, in a complex society, informational support (e.g., how to pick one's way in bureaucracies and how to gain access to welfare arrangements) and social network support (e.g., using family members' ties to enhance one's labor market prospects) are important types of support. Finally, our understanding of financial assistance can gain a lot from using a cross-national perspective that accounts for welfare state arrangements (see Nock et al., this volume). Future trends in pension systems might affect opportunities for financial transfers. Therefore, we could learn a lot about future trends in financial transfers in the United States by studying European countries that exhibit an older age structure.

Contextual Variation

Chapter 1 pays a lot of attention to contextual variation in intergenerational ties. We welcome this emphasis, but would like to suggest that the study of intergenerational ties could profit from an even stronger intercultural and international focus.

Migration

Bianchi and colleagues emphasize that population aging, as influenced by lower fertility and longer lives, and family dynamics will clearly affect intergenerational ties. We agree with the emphasis the authors put on these demographic dynamics. What surprises us, however, is that they do not pay attention to another major aspect of the new demography (Vaupel 2000) that will affect intergenerational ties—high migration.

Most Western countries have witnessed a large increase in migration during the past decades of the 20th century. This increase in residential mobility and international migration is likely to become a key factor within the changing demographic context that may have an important impact on intergenerational ties. Increases in international migration have changed the population composition of most Western countries, with a rise in the share of foreign-born residents: according to the UN Population Division, in 2005, 9.5 percent of people in the more developed regions of the world were born outside their country of current residence. The United States is the country with the largest migrant stock (more than 38 million immigrants, or 12.9 percent of the total population). Similarly, the share of U.S. citizens who reside outside their state of birth has risen over the long run, although people of the same age do not necessarily show an increasing propensity for internal migration (Berrie 2006). In Europe as well, an increasing proportion of the population is either foreign-born or is born to parents who were born outside their country of residence.

These migration patterns affect intergenerational ties in at least two ways. First, they will increase transnational ties. Long-distance ties may nevertheless be strong, given that family members in the countries of origin depend on (financial) transfers from family members in Western countries, and that family members in the countries of destination may want to keep the option of returning to their country of origin open. Second, the many migrants from countries with different family and cultural systems (Kagitcibasi 2005) will lead to increased diversity in norms of family obligation and, thus, to increased diversity in family ties within Western societies. These considerations strongly suggest that high migration is part of the changing demographic context that will shape intergenerational ties in coming decades.

Welfare and Public Policy: Can the United States Be Understood without an International Comparison?

It is hard to understand the role of policies within a U.S. context only, given that variation in public policies is constrained within the institutional setting of a single country. International comparative research offers a more fruitful approach to understanding the interplay between policies and intergenerational ties, because institutional settings can vary between countries. At least two promising avenues of research can be distinguished. First, one could formulate detailed hypotheses about the relation between specific welfare-state arrangements (e.g., the availability of universal and free medical care) and the provision of support from children to parents. A major obstacle in testing such hypotheses is that collecting high quality data on specific welfare-state arrangements is not an easy task. Contextual databases, like the one developed within the Generations and Gender Programme (GGP), could help bridge this gap. Second, one could test more general hypotheses by focusing on differences in support exchanges between sets of countries classified on the basis of a welfare-related criterion. A very popular example of such a classification is the welfare-regime classification Esping-Andersen developed (e.g., 1999). In his view, three or four different types of welfare state regimes can be distinguished based on the roles the government, the market, and the family play in providing welfare to a country's citizens. Esping-Andersen first developed a classification with three different welfare regimes: social democratic welfare regimes, typical of Nordic Europe; liberal market welfare regimes (such as the United States and the U.K.); and conservative continental welfare regimes (e.g., France and Germany). However, others (Ferrera 1996; Mayer 2001; Trifiletti 1999) proposed a fourth, "familialistic" (Southern European) welfare regimes (e.g., Italy and Spain). The configuration of the welfare regime has important consequences on life-course choices, as each regime shapes expectations on intergenerational ties differently. For instance, one could test the "crowding out" hypothesis by focusing on the support provided between parents and children in different welfare regimes. If the crowding out hypothesis is correct, intergenerational support in social democratic welfare regimes should be lower than in familistic welfare regimes.

Of course, in the long run, developments in welfare regimes are not exogenous (Mayer 2001). For instance, whether a society encourages young adults to attend higher education at universities with on-campus accommodation or local universities where young adults and their parents can coreside for longer periods partly depends on the prevailing views of intergenerational relationships. The causal link is then from the cultural framework to the institution, which means that in a longer causation chain, long-term cultural differences explain a substantial part of the differences in family and social policies (Pfau-Effinger 1999). In addition, economic developments also influence welfare arrangements.

This attests to the fact that economic, cultural, and institutional factors influence intergenerational ties, and that, ideally, all three factors should be taken into account simultaneously.

Welfare regimes mediate individual-level incentives and propensities, and the individual-level determinants of intergenerational support are certainly mediated by welfare. The social democratic welfare regime, for instance, uses an individual perspective as a guide: a young adult or an elderly person has to be eligible for public support independent of his or her family situation. The worry that public support might crowd out family support is not particularly important in this context. On the contrary, assumptions of family support may guide the provision of public support, as in a "familialistic" welfare regime. For example, in Poggibonsi (Tuscany), a parent who has a grandparent residing in the same municipality is given lower priority in being granted access to public child care.

New Data for Comparative Studies

To allow for comparative analysis, internationally comparable data are needed. Collecting such data requires a huge effort in many areas: increasing investment in fund raising, as funding obtained from multiple national-level entities has to be coordinated and available according to a schedule; harmonizing sampling procedures, including defining the population under study (e.g., deciding whether to include people living in institutions); preparing and implementing a questionnaire, which includes creating common definitions and translating subjective questions and items; and deciding how collected data may be used, as procedures to release data in the public domain may differ across countries. In what follows, we outline three projects that have been going on mostly in Europe, all including data collection on intergenerational relations.

The Survey of Health, Ageing, and Retirement in Europe

The 2004 Survey of Health, Ageing, and Retirement in Europe (SHARE) is modeled closely after the U.S. Health and Retirement Study (HRS).[1] It is the first comparative study that combines extensive information on the socioeconomics status, health, and family relationships of older adults. The results of the first wave are already available (see Börsch-Supan et al. 2005). Release 1 of the data contains information on some 22,000 individuals age 50 and older from 15,000 households in 10 European countries (Sweden, Denmark, Germany, the Netherlands, France, Switzerland, Austria, Italy, Spain, and Greece). Some of the results have been used in the previous part of this chapter.

The European Social Survey

The European Social Survey (ESS), partially inspired by the U.S. General Social Survey, aims at charting and explaining the interaction between Europe's changing institutions and the attitudes, beliefs, and behavior patterns of its diverse populations. Implemented in more than 20 countries, the ESS makes a considerable methodological effort to ensure international comparability. The ESS is a repeated cross-sectional, cross-country survey. In its third wave, in 2006, a rotating module on the "timing of life" (Billari et al. 2006) will focus on life course issues related to intergenerational ties, such as the following: To what extent do citizens perceive the life course as a structured sequence of stages, and which events mark the transition from one stage to the other? Do social norms concerning the life course exist, and if so, to what extent are these norms supported by sanctions if people transgress the norms? What are the expectations and capacities of citizens concerning life course planning? Important intergenerational topics that are part of this module concern the timing of leaving the parental home and the role family and the state will play in securing adequate living conditions during old age.

The Generations and Gender Programme

The Generations and Gender Programme (GGP) is a combination of comparative national surveys (Generations and Gender Surveys [GGS]) and contextual databases (designed to complement the micro-level data with macro-level information on policies and aggregate indicators), coordinated by the United Nations Economic Commission for Europe (http://ggp.unece.org). The GGS is a panel survey on persons age 18 to 79, with a particular emphasis on intergenerational and gender relationships (Vikat et al. 2007). Different from surveys, such as SHARE, that focus on older persons, the GGS provides both the parent's and the child's perspective. Items in the questionnaire provide information on coresidence (with additional information on proximity between parents and children), support given and received (including childcare, personal care in daily activities, and emotional support), and monetary transfers and inheritance. Using an ego-centered, social-network approach, ties with kin are covered extensively and are not limited to parent–child (or step-parent–step-child) dyads. The complexity, and the resulting high costs, of the survey means fewer countries participate in the GGS compared with projects such as the ESS. Nevertheless, the GGS provides unique (and simultaneous) information on key aspects of intergenerational relationships. The contextual database also provides valuable information on the changing context of intergenerational ties.

Implications for Future Research

In this chapter, we underlined the gains that can be made from adopting an international comparative perspective in the study of intergenerational ties. The main message is that contextual variability is fundamentally important for advancing knowledge on the subject. A comparative approach helps us (1) formulate and test general theories on intergenerational ties (emphasizing, in particular, the importance of micro–macro interactions between contexts and individual motivations and constraints); (2) improve the way ties are measured; and (3) understand ties in a world increasingly influenced by migration. In addition, the challenges of international comparative research might push innovative projects. Cooperation between U.S. scholars and scholars from other Western countries would help them obtain cross-national comparable data and understand trends occurring throughout the Western world.

NOTES

Paper prepared following the 2006 Penn State Symposium on Family Issues, "Caring and Exchange within and across Generations" October 4–5, State College, Pennsylvania. Address correspondence to francesco.billari@unibocconi.it.

1. For more information on SHARE, see http://www.shareproject.org.

REFERENCES

Barber, Jennifer S. 2000. "Intergenerational Influences on the Entry into Parenthood: Mothers' Preferences for Family and Nonfamily Behavior." *Social Forces* 79(1): 319–48.

Berrie, Joseph P. 2006. "Internal Migration." In *Historical Statistics of the United States, Millennium Edition*, edited by Susan B. Carter, Scott Sigmund Gartner, Michael R. Haines, Alan L. Olmstead, Richard Sutch, and Gavin Wright. Cambridge, U.K.: Cambridge University Press.

Billari, Francesco C. 2004. "Becoming an Adult in Europe: A Macro(/Micro)-Demographic Perspective." *Demographic Research,* Special Collection 3 (Article 2): 13–44. http://www.demographic-research.org/special/3/2/.

Billari, Francesco C., Dimiter Philipov, and Pau Baizán. 2001. "Leaving Home in Europe: The Experience of Cohorts Born around 1960." *International Journal of Population Geography* 7(5): 339–56.

Billari, Francesco C., Gunhild O. Hagestad, Aart C. Liefbroer, and Zsolt Spéder. 2006. "The Timing of Life: The Organisation of the Life Course in Europe." Documentation for a rotating module in the European Social Survey, unpublished manuscript.

Börsch-Supan, Axel, Agar Brugiavini, Hendrik Jürges, Johan Mackenbach, Johannes Siegrist, and Guglielmo Weber, eds. 2005. *Health, Ageing and Retirement in Europe: First Results from the Survey of Health, Ageing and Retirement in Europe.* Mannheim, Germany: Mannheim Research Institute for the Economics of Aging. http://www.share-project.org.

Esping-Andersen, Gøsta. 1999. *Social Foundations of Postindustrial Economies.* Oxford: Oxford University Press.

Hank, Karsten. 2007. "Proximity and Contacts between Older Parents and Their Children: A European Comparison." *Journal of Marriage and Family* 69(1): 157–73.

Kagitcibasi, Cigdem. 2005. "Autonomy and Relatedness in Cultural Context. Implications for Self and Family." *Journal of Cross-Cultural Psychology* 36(4): 403–22.

Knijn, Trudie C. M., and Aart C. Liefbroer. 2006. "More Kin than Kind: Instrumental Support in Families." In *Family Solidarity in the Netherlands,* edited by Pearl A. Dykstra, Matthijs Kalmijn, Trudie C. M. Knijn, Aafke E. Komter, Aart C. Liefbroer, and Clara H. Mulder (89–104). Amsterdam: Dutch University Press.

Mayer, K. U. 2001. "The Paradox of Global Social Change and National Path Dependencies: Life Course Patterns in Advanced Societies." In *Inclusions-Exclusions,* edited by Alison E. Woodward and Martin Kohli (89–110). London: Routledge.

Pfau-Effinger, Birgit. 1999. "Change of Family Policies in the Socio-Cultural Context of European Societies." *Comparative Social Research* 18: 135–59.

Settersten, Richard A., and Gunhild O. Hagestad. 1996. "What's the Latest? Cultural Age Deadlines for Family Transitions." *The Gerontologist* 36: 178–88.

Tomassini, Cecilia, Douglas A. Wolf, and Alessandro Rosina. 2003. "Parental Housing Assistance and Parent-Child Proximity in Italy." *Journal of Marriage and the Family* 65: 700–15.

Vaupel, James W. 2000. "Longevity and Fertility: How are the Industrial Countries Aging? Are Our Projections Reliable?" Paper presented at the Center for Strategic and International Studies conference, "The Graying of the Industrial World: A Policy Conference on Global Aging," Washington, D.C., January 25–25.

Vikat, Andres, Zsolt Spéder, Gijs Beets, Francesco C. Billari, Christoph Bühler, Aline Désesquelles, Tineke Fokkema, Jan M. Hoem, Alphonse L. MacDonald, Gerda R. Neyer, Ariane Pailhé, Antonella Pinnelli, and Anne Solaz. 2007. "Generations and Gender Survey (GGS): Towards a Better Understanding of Relationships and Processes in the Life Course." *Demographic Research* 17(14): 389–440. http://www.demographic-research.org/volumes/vol17/14/.

4

Developing Interdisciplinary Approaches to Study Intergenerational Relationships

Melissa Hardy

Intergenerational relationships—their distinctiveness, prevalence, strength, and importance—is a good example of the type of interdisciplinary topic often examined in research literature on aging and development. That said, practical attempts to bridge disciplines often lead to a simple juxtaposition of perspectives. Researchers from different fields define research projects that reflect the conceptual and methodological frameworks of their individual disciplines. Once projects are completed, researchers may discuss their results and what they've learned, but such findings are often viewed as more persuasive by those within the given perspective than outside it. Further, this type of approach does not allow us to investigate directly the competing or (perhaps) complementary nature of the different perspectives, nor does it necessarily help us appreciate how a more formal integration of different perspectives might enhance our understanding.

In chapter 1, Bianchi, Hotz, McGarry, and Seltzer tackle the notion of interdisciplinarity in the study of intergenerational relationships. By reviewing a range of relevant theories and empirical findings from different disciplines, particularly sociology and economics,[1] they take several useful steps toward building an interdisciplinary bridge. Although psychological theories are not an explicit part of their review, the fit between psychology and economics has been pursued in other areas through experimental research, particularly decision theory; however, the fit between sociology and either of these sister social sciences has been more resistant to melding, and that resistance persists despite the recognition that the three disciplines share scientific interests. Indeed, sections within the American Sociological Association include "economic sociology," "social psychology," and "political economy of the world system"; divisions in the American Psychological Association include "personality and social psychology" and "the psychological study of social issues"; and topics in the American Economics Association's *Journal of Economic Literature* (and annual meetings) include "cultural economics/economic sociology" and "social norms/social capital/social networks." If disciplines could easily connect by tackling similar subjects, economic sociology from either the economics side or from the sociology side would look similar. But disciplines differ, in part, because they view phenomena through distinct lenses. In tightening their focus to interdisciplinary relationships, Bianchi and colleagues ask what "family economics" and "sociology of the family" say to each other. If we hold aside the organizational features of colleges and universities that tend to reinforce disciplinary boundaries and instead focus on attempts to translate concepts and terminology from one discipline's language to another's, perhaps we can begin to answer the question, why is working across disciplines so difficult?

Because psychology and microeconomics focus on the individual and his or her actions, both explore cognitive dimensions of behavior—motivations, preferences, incentives, expectations. The economic notion of "utility" adds a strategic dimension to behavior: we act in ways that enhance our sense of well-being. Sociology is more concerned with how actions, behaviors, and lives in general are socially linked. Certain social situations can cue specific social behaviors as behavior patterns become normative for those occupying specific roles. Although people may perform these roles in their own styles, certain empirical regularities in their actions will be noticeable. An economist may be interested in identifying changes in benefits or costs that may alter the utility associated with a particular behavior in a given situation. A sociologist may be interested in how a person's behavior varies from one social context to another as well as how different people may behave in different ways in a shared social context. But the more fundamental difference between the two disciplines involves their underlying theories of behavior. Is behavior highly individualized or is behavior social? If we assume it is highly individualized, then how do we think about "collective" behaviors—how do we move from the individual to the group? If we believe all behavior is social, then how do we understand human agency—how do we move from the group to the actions of single members of the group?

An individualized theory of behavior views the individual as we would view a ship-in-a-bottle. We imagine an autonomous subject, a distinct and self-contained agent who can be in any social context, move seamlessly from one situation to another throughout the day, and yet retain his or her essential self, separate from those contexts (Hazelrigg 1995, 2000). Each environment—the grocery store, the doctor's office, the pharmacy, the gas station—is unaffected by the presence or absence of that person on that day. Although she may have pleasant (or unpleasant) interactions in these places, her experiences will generally be small enough that she emerges from each exchange as the same person. For many behaviors, such as those involving commerce and everyday interactions, this understanding of how people behave "in" different social contexts is sufficient.

But other aspects of social context are already integral to a person's self-consciousness and can affect perception and interpretation. Such aspects are usually permanent, or long lasting, because they involve major parts of one's culture, subculture, or social status—from language, which is intensely contextual, to educational achievement, to family status; the deeper the integration, the more resistant to change this overall interpretive context becomes. Relevant aspects of this social context involve learned behaviors, norms of interactions, assertiveness versus deference, and certain routines that people use when under stress or when facing difficult decisions. From this perspective, social relations are organic rather than simply contractual.

From a psychologist's point of view, these long-lasting, integrated aspects of consciousness are part of an individual's personality. From a sociologist's point of view, this integrated type of social context is part of one's sense of self and always involves social groups—not merely the groups of people one drifts through while performing everyday tasks, but relationships with people more deeply integrated in self-identity. These groups vary on a number of dimensions. They involve different people, though some people may be members of multiple networks; they involve different formal and informal obligations, such as legal rights; and they may influence different types of decisions a person typically makes—such as where to live, whom to marry, or what kind of car to drive. Thinking of people as embedded in sets of social relations is helpful; as nodes in a network, they can serve as resource for others in the network or they can call on others for information, advice, or assistance as needed. Because sociology's emphasis on social relationships elevates the importance of social groups involved in shaping behavior, sociologists must identify which groups matter, how these groups are constituted, and how membership in a group can shape people's perceptions of the world and their actions in it.

How Is a Family Distinct?

Within sociology, the family merits special consideration as a social group. Defined as a fundamental institution of social organization, the family is centrally involved in socialization, education, childhood and adolescent development, social control, and social support. Family members are interconnected, but are they interconnected in a unique way? What is it about intergenerational relationships that make them worthy of special attention? Sociology defines the family as an example of a primary group—a group distinguished by its small size and members who share close ties. By definition, these groups are not ephemeral; they persist. Members are concerned for one another, they have a shared culture, and they spend a lot of time together. This cohesion often produces habituated patterns of behavior—predictable styles of interaction, the routine performance of specific roles, an understanding of other members' strengths and weaknesses, and a sense of solidarity. Although families are not the only examples of primary groups, the presumption is that one would have allegiance to few such groups because of the demands such groups make. Families face constraints in what they can do for themselves and what they can purchase from the market, and they must often decide how to allocate their resources. How do they make these decisions? These are the practical questions that the "new" family economics attempts to answer.

The new family economics defines the household as the basic unit of consumption and home production. As a producer of goods, the family is less important now than in the past, but it remains central to the production of services. Building on the premise in Becker (1991) that market exchange provides an appropriate model for family relationships, research in this genre emphasizes individual action and assumes that individual behavior is dominated by attempts to maximize utility under a linear budget constraint. If people behave in ways that improve their well-being (utility), does placing that behavior within a family context require any theoretical adjustments?

By analyzing family decisionmaking within the context of household production and distribution functions, the household (or family) becomes a system whose actors belong to multiple generations. The family maximizes its well-being balancing household production and consumption functions. Both functions face constraints: household production faces a time constraint, and household consumption faces an income constraint. Extending this framework to more than two generations (beyond the nuclear family) introduces the intergenerational dimension to family decisionmaking. Transfers of money from grandparents to parents and grandchildren can increase the nuclear family's capacity for consumption. Transfers of time from grandparents to parents and grandchildren can substitute for the household production in which parents and their children must engage or for services that they would otherwise have to purchase. If we change the direction of the transfers, then adult children subsidize their elder parents' consumption and take care of household chores or provide care.

How spouses allocate time to household production and market work is jointly determined, with the value of each person's time being a major consideration. Studies of home production have used relative wage rates to explain the often unequal distribution of household chores. What economists explain through utility maximization and equilibrium points, sociologists attribute to institutional arrangements, norms, and values.

This difference in explanations illustrates a difference in focus: economists focus on predicting behavior, and sociologists focus on understanding why the behavior occurs. Economic models of behavior are largely silent on motivations, linking them to preferences without explaining how these preferences have been produced. Becker's (1991) treatise on family behavior pushes preferences far into the background. Behavior that sociologists view as consistent with family roles, responsibilities, and obligations, economists place in the more generic category of economic activity. Although economists acknowledge the notion of obligation, the formation and persistence of obligations depends on whether they are consistent with maximizing behavior. Economists therefore argue that institutional arrangements (or culture or social structures) have no independent effect on behavior; sociologists disagree.

Within that context, for example, the head of the household can make the decisions, either in a paternalistic regime where decisions are made in the family's "best interest" or under Becker's assumption of an altruistic head. Presumably, other family members may express their opinions or introduce relevant information, but the final decision rests with a single person. Becker's approach acknowledges the family as a special category of group by defining the utility functions of family members as inter-related: the well-being of family members is a function of how the family as a whole fares. The household head must make decisions to maximize the utility of the household. Becker explains how a single utility function can characterize a multiperson household by introducing an altruistic household head, responsible for a single sense of well-being. As an altru-istic household head, his or her sense of personal well-being is enhanced by the improved well-being of other family members (i.e., the head obtains utility from other members' consumption). This definition of altruism maintains the individual focus, since the decisions made remain within a self-maximizing strategy.

Alternatively, the collective approach to decisionmaking suggests some kind of group process that leads to an outcome. How the process unfolds and how individual preferences are combined to produce a single "family" decision are interesting questions to consider. One approach to collective decisionmaking suggests that a bargaining model is appropriate. Negotiation allows family members to define a situation that all find acceptable. Siblings might trade chores; parents might increase a child's allowance in exchange for additional responsibilities. Regardless of the outcome, as long as the exchange is voluntary, all members' well-being should increase as a result of the trade. Once a choice is made, one can reconstruct what must have been operating for the different family members' competing interests to have been resolved as they were. But can we predict the outcome on the basis of individual-level information?

For many sociologists, dividing responsibility for household tasks involves more than assigning chores to the person whose time is least val-ued in the labor market. Many families view cooking, cleaning, laundry, yard-work, trash, home maintenance, repairs as well as child care, sick care, and, in a growing proportion of families, elder care as tasks they per-form for one another—the way they contribute to their family. While the "household" is the living arrangement for a family, the "family" is more than that living arrangement and different from a special case of a firm, with management and labor positions. When assigning chores to their children, parents generally strive for fairness while noting differences in age, gender (perhaps more than they should), and other talents or outside demands on their children's time (e.g., homework, lessons, practice). Some families offer rewards (e.g., allowances, verbal praise) in exchange for performing chores, and some also impose penalties (e.g., restrictions, verbal reprimands) if chores are neglected. But family counseling literature discourages pairing allowances with chores, since it individualizes the behavior, making the process like an exchange of labor for wages. Sociologists might view these actions as an exercise in social solidarity, an opportunity to teach children the responsibilities of citizenship (and internalize the notion that belonging to certain beneficial groups carries an expectation that one helps with the group's work), a lesson in how contributing to a common goal—the family's well-being—can enhance a sense of self-worth and accomplishment.

Sociologists tend to read the translation of economic theory into statistical utility models that predict behavior as imposing a self-centered hedonism as the central value people endorse through their actions. Therefore, an altruism motivated by self-interest seems contradictory and substituting commercial exchange for a morality of reciprocity turns affection and a sense of mutual obligation that bind a family together into self-centered calculations for individual advantage. But if economics is interested in actions and not motivations, the *reasons* people make choices are irrelevant. As long as they act *as if* they were maximizing utility, the model works as a predictor of outcomes. To argue the importance of social effects, sociologists must find ways to demonstrate these effects and distinguish them from nonsocial effects.

Social Effects

Sociologists want to understand the mechanisms through which society affects individual behavior, which is another way of asking about the motivations behind actions. Motivations are deeply internalized. As Alfred Schutz (1962; 1967) argued, "in order to" motives are clearly different from "because of" motives; individual actors may not even be aware of their motivations, but after the fact, they can explain their actions as being consistent with motivations they now impute to their behaviors. And as any lawyer will attest, proving intention is difficult and relies on persuading a judge or jury that the outcome was the goal that motivated the behavior in the first place.

While sociologists hypothesize that society—as a combination of institutional arrangements, culture, and social structures—affects individuals in many ways, economists tend to see society's influence in a more limited way, as constraints on opportunities, for example. Economists view such central sociological concepts as "norms" and "reference groups" not as important endogenous processes but as spurious processes that within-person assessments can explain. Empirically demonstrating these specific social effects requires careful measurement and methods of analysis that distinguish between conceptually distinct but empirically challenging endogenous and exogenous effects. Outcome data cannot reveal the structure of social effects unless they are combined with substantial prior information (Manski 1993).

We can discuss these differences in concrete terms by addressing the choices of adult children to provide care for an elder parent. Bianchi and colleagues, in chapter 1, provide a review of what we know empirically about caregivers. Here we focus on the social and nonsocial effects following Manski's framework (see, e.g., Manski 1993, 31) and denoting social effects as

- endogenous effects, where an adult child is more likely to provide care when providing care is common within his or her reference group, and
- contextual (exogenous) effects, where an adult child's propensity to provide care varies with the distribution of background characteristics of the reference group.

In contrast, we classify nonsocial effects into

- ecological effects, where adult children in the same reference group tend to behave similarly because they face similar institutional environments, and
- correlated individual (endogenous) effects, where adult children in the same reference group tend to behave similarly because they have similar individual characteristics.

To further the example, we could assume that the reference group is the extended family or members of the same religious community. We could identify an endogenous effect if an adult child (with surviving parents) is more likely to care for an elderly parent when other adult children within the extended family routinely become caregivers for their parents. There is a contextual effect if (other things being equal) the likelihood of being a caregiver varies with the socioeconomic composition of the extended family members. We define an ecological effect when members of the same family behave in similar ways because they are products of the same socialization experience. Correlated individual effects occur when family members share background and socioeconomic characteristics, and these characteristics influence the likelihood of being a caregiver.

Sociologists are particularly interested in endogenous effects since they suggest behavioral processes governed by imitation (or modeling), conformity, and compliance with normative expectations. Further, endogenous effects can generate a social multiplier effect; contextual effects cannot. Estimating exogenous effects is more straightforward. Estimating endogenous effects requires more information, since the relationship between the outcome and the factor that influences the outcome is embedded in a system of relationships that jointly determine the outcome and the factor. Our typical approach—seeing what happens to the distribution of outcomes when we change the value of the factor—does not work; we cannot change the value of the factor without simultaneously changing the outcome.

Subjective Factors

Sociology has traditionally been interested in what people are thinking— their opinions, attitudes, values, and beliefs. Economics also acknowledges the role of subjective factors, such as preference hierarchies and expectations, in shaping behavior. While a sociological approach to studying subjective phenomena is to ask respondents to report their attitudes, values, preferences, and beliefs, economists distrust survey data from individuals, especially subjective data. They argue that people's responses are unreliable. Instead, they infer subjective phenomena from data on opportunities and choices, assuming that the choices people make reveal their preferences. Sociologists, in contrast, have developed a vast statistical methodology on how to assess reliability.

Studying the subjective aspects of behaviors again moves us into the realm of motivations: why are daughters more often the caregivers? Is it because quality care is not available or affordable, because they *believe* that quality care is not available or affordable, because they want to provide the care themselves, or because they believe they *should* provide the care themselves?

The first of these four reasons is an objective condition. Quality care is expensive, and not all families can afford the cost. The second reason is based on perception, leaving open the question of the objective situation. Also at issue here is whether the quality of care is ever "good enough" by some people's standards. The third response suggests a voluntary choice but leaves open the question of whether the arrangement is what the elderly parent wants. It also fails to address the underlying motivation or whether the person offering care expects to gain some sort of advantage. The fourth reason is based on morality, suggesting a sense of moral obligation, perhaps a promise made, or a belief that providing care for an ill parent is part of the role of an adult daughter.

One research area that makes clear how little we understand about each other's preferences is end-of-life care. One option for advance directives is naming a health care proxy. Although some proxy situations ask the decisionmaker to use a "best interest" criteria (e.g., a legal instrument such as the power of attorney), a health care proxy is to operate under "substituted judgment." The first criterion requires treatment decisions that make certain assumptions about what is best for someone. On occasion, a parent's treatment decision is ruled as not being in a child's best interest (e.g., when the parents hold a religious belief that leads them to refuse treatment when physicians believe they can save the child). The second criterion requires that treatment decisions be made on the basis of the patient's preferences, whatever they may be. If a health care proxy argues that treatment should be withheld or ended, the assertion that he or she is acting in accordance with the patient's wishes is viewed with skepticism unless other people or documents can verify that position. Thinking about being asked to act as someone's health care proxy helps one understand the complexity of the task and the responsibility associated with this position of trust: how sure can we be that we are making the same choices the patient would make? But this example also suggests that our willingness to believe that it is possible to "know" someone's mind is substantially reduced when the values attributed to this person conflict with our own.

Final Thoughts

Although there are substantial and fundamental differences between economic and sociological approaches to intergenerational relationships, opportunities for creative collaborations are also apparent (Hannan 1982).

Sociologists appear to start from complexity, theorizing connections among individual behaviors and institutions and social structures; when testing how this system operates, sociologists face limitations in their ability to measure the concepts they theorize and model the processes they hypothesize. In contrast, economists start with relative simplicity, individual behaviors, and exogenous factors woven together with strong theoretical assumptions; they apply sophisticated quantitative techniques to estimate their models. Somewhere in the middle is an approach that relaxes some of the exogeneity assumptions of economics, allowing researchers to explore institutional structures and how they shape and are shaped by individual behavior.

NOTES

Prepared for the 2006 Penn State Symposium on Family Issues: "Caring and Exchange Within and Across Generations," October 4–5, State College, PA.

1. In this and the following discussion, "economics" refers to microeconomics, the specific branch of economics being referenced.

REFERENCES

Becker, Gary S. 1991. *A Treatise on the Family*. Cambridge, MA: Harvard University Press.

Hannan, Michael T. 1982. "Families, Markets, and Social Structures: An Essay on Becker's *A Treatise on the Family*." *Journal of Economic Literature* 20 (March): 65–72.

Hazelrigg, Lawrence E. 1995. "Cultures of Nature: An Essay on the Production of Nature." Gainesville, FL: University of Florida Press.

———. 2000. "Individualism." In *Encyclopedia of Sociology*, 2nd ed., edited by Edgar Borgatta and Rhonda Montgomery (1301–8). New York: MacMillan.

Manski, Charles. 1993. "Identification Problems in the Social Sciences." *Sociological Methodology* 23: 1–56.

Schutz, Alfred. 1967. *The Phenomenology of the Social World*. Evanston, IL: Northwestern University Press.

PART II
Explaining Change and Variation in Intergenerational Caregiving and Exchanges

5

Intergenerational Caregiving and Exchange

Economic and Evolutionary Approaches

Donald Cox

What factors explain change and variation in intergenerational caregiving and exchange? I broach this large and vital question with some narrower ones: How does economics contribute to our understanding of intergenerational transfers? How about evolutionary biology and related fields? How does the integration of evolutionary thought into economics and other social sciences contribute to our understanding of family behavior? What prospects for further cross-fertilization lie ahead?

Understanding how families tick has become all the more pressing in recent decades, as rising rates of divorce, remarriage, and nonmarital childbearing threaten to weaken ties that sustain economic dependents, both young and old. The tug of parental altruism, for instance, might on average be weaker for stepparents than for biological parents. Likewise, adult stepchildren might lack strong ties to either stepparents or biological parents that they lived with briefly or not at all (e.g., Lundberg and Pollak 2007). Consider another trend, women's education and work patterns, which have become more similar to men's life course patterns. As rising workplace demands compete for women's time for family, how much can we count on men to pick up the slack?

Conventional economic approaches to the family have both strengths and weaknesses for analyzing transfers and investments of money, time, and care. A key strength of economics is its exacting logic and carefully considered evidence concerning the effects of incomes and prices on

81

private transfer behavior. A lingering weakness is the discipline's lack of a coherent framework for grappling with other pertinent variables, such as gender and age effects that remain after accounting for economic forces. While the discipline can draw upon a refined body of work on human capital investment to analyze, for example, *economic* incentives to educate sons versus daughters, it has little to say about differential treatment of the two *just because they are sons or daughters.* Likewise, while economics has plenty to say about how, for instance, male–female wage differences affect fathers' versus mothers' incentives to care for children, it has little to say about fatherhood versus motherhood per se, except to consign them to the rubric of "preferences."

Accordingly, I explore the possibility that economics might profitably borrow well-established insights from evolutionary biology (as well as evolutionary thought from other disciplines) to sharpen predictions concerning age, relatedness, and gender, such as differences in how maternal and paternal grandparents treat their grandchildren, just because they are from one side of the family or the other.

Indeed, evolutionary thought has been percolating within economics (and sociology) for some time, and I explore ways to build on these insights. To this end, I present the beginnings of a case study that addresses the problem of how paternity uncertainty might affect the propensity of maternal versus paternal grandmothers to care for children.

The case study usefully demonstrates possible advantages and potential pitfalls that can bedevil empirical work on evolutionary hypotheses. A key strength of the evolutionary approach, I contend, is its potential for illuminating novel behavioral pathways in family behavior, such as the maternal/paternal distinction referenced above. A key challenge is distinguishing biological from nonbiological crosscurrents, such as purely economic or social forces that arguably operate independent of biology. Such challenges are well evidenced by the many instructive difficulties that emerge from my descriptive work; while evolutionary thinking suggests new partial correlations that might be fruitfully explored, such correlations cannot settle the deeper questions of biological causes of familial transfers. (Further, some descriptive results point up novel pathways, but others appear counter to the evolutionary approach.)

Accordingly, I take a further step by thinking about how a more rigorous empirical framework might be crafted, and what sort of data might be required to implement it. Though the case itself is narrowly focused, it is useful for illustrating general points concerning empirical work on evolutionary forces in intergenerational transfers. A paradoxical upshot is that in trying to estimate *biological* influences, it can be useful to have information on *cultural* forces and to think hard about what generates and sustains practices, customs, and traditions that impinge on gender and age-related determinants of intergenerational transfers.

How an Evolutionary Perspective Might Refine Economic Analyses of Intergenerational Transfers—Thought Experiments

To illustrate the strengths, as well as possible limitations, of economics for explaining and predicting trends in intergenerational transfers and care—and to explore possible synergies between economics and evolutionary thought—I begin with a thought experiment. Turn the clock back, say, three or four decades, and imagine that, as an economist constrained by the current state of the art, you have been asked to forecast trends in the time women will spend in home production (i.e., time spent caring for children, in household chores, and the like). The forecasting scenario is an assumed rising path of women's market earning potential—a fair description of what happened—and your task is to predict what was referred to in those days as women's "home time." This variable is germane to intergenerational transfers, for it encompasses time spent caring for children (as well as dependent elders).

So, what would have been your answer? The economics literature at the time would have served you well, for you would have predicted that women's home time would fall. Do not be misled by this simple-looking answer. Even as early as the late 1960s, economic theory generated sophisticated insight on the allocation of time (e.g., Becker 1965). A crucial insight, developed by Lewis (1968) and refined by Ben-Porath (1973), was that women's time allocation is apt to be more responsive to wage changes than men's because the decision of whether to work is more sensitive to wages than the decision of how many hours to work for someone already in the labor force.[1] More recently, such as in the early 1980s, our hypothetical economist could tap into a greater body of knowledge, including empirical estimates pertinent to the above-mentioned theory (e.g., Heckman and Macurdy 1980). Armed with this knowledge, he or she could have made predictions about, for instance, the relative responsiveness of husbands' versus wives' home time based on trends in sex-based wage differentials.

But our economically savvy prognosticator might not have been able to nail every detail about how trends in home time eventually played out. For example, recent evidence indicates that, while women's home time has declined as economic reasoning predicted, some components have fallen less than others (Bianchi 2000; Bianchi et al. 2000). In particular, women's allocation of time to child care has not fallen apace with other nonmarket uses of time. To quote Bianchi (2000, 402), "in our amazement at how rapidly women's market work has trended upward in the United States, we may have failed to appreciate how much working mothers do to protect investment in children even as they enter the paid labor force."

Bianchi's findings are consistent with earlier ones recounted in Gronau's (1986) survey. But they do not emerge naturally from standard economic models of home production—a state of affairs consistent with the discipline's longstanding focus on the effects of prices and incomes on behavior. While economists might differentiate between child care and, say, vacuuming on the grounds that the former constitutes long-term investment (but not the latter, no doubt to the dismay of many), they would be wary of taking a stand on which of the two activities people would prefer. Some research has made forays into the endogenous formation of preferences (e.g., Becker and Mulligan 1997), but economists tend to be cautious about making assertions regarding preferences.[2] This approach entirely (and reasonably) accords with the objectives of the discipline.

However, the evolutionary perspective *does* say something about, for instance, the expected relative weights of child care versus other aspects of home time in the utility functions of mothers and fathers. A central issue in this chapter is whether this perspective can usefully complement standard economic approaches.

Not that evolutionary thinking has a monopoly on preference-related issues in family behavior. One need only consult Bianchi's (2000) paper, and the references cited therein, to see that disciplines like sociology have lots to say about gender-based preferences and norms connected with the myriad activities of family life.[3] Further, ideas already entrenched in the social sciences might well render evolutionary considerations superfluous. I hope this chapter stimulates discussion and debate concerning such questions. (Though, for the most part, I will limit my social-science-related discussion to economics.)

I suggest the existence of what biologists call "hybrid vigor": that the cross-fertilization of economic and evolutionary approaches might contribute to a new perspective greater than the sum of its parts. My main message is one of cautious optimism: that combining economic and evolutionary thinking is worth pursuing. Indeed, several economists have for some time been doing just that, and I will note progress (mainly on the theoretical front) made thus far. And while I will mostly stick to economics, I will point out a few highly illuminating studies by sociologists, demographers, and anthropologists who have investigated (and sometimes rejected) evolutionary hypotheses.

To return to our thought experiment: I contend that evolutionary thinking would have sharpened our hypothetical economist's decades-old prediction about the connection between trends in women's wages and time spent in child care versus, say, time spent in volunteer work or in household chores, for the simple reason that biology predicts that a parent's time with a child is qualitatively different from time with, say, a lawn mower. A reasonable response might be that this "prediction" merely belabors the obvious. So an important order of business will be to consider nonobvious evolutionary pathways.

But first, reflect on another thought experiment, this time in the here and now. Consider a member of the so-called "sandwich generation"—someone (most often a woman) who juggles the competing demands of child rearing and elder care while at the same time contending with the demands of market work. Imagine a case where an extra hour of care would confer exactly the same marginal utility (from the recipient's perspective) for both the child and the elder. Indeed, invoke any other assumption in order to ask, all else equal, if this woman's time budget exogenously shrunk because of, say, unexpected work demands, which dependent would experience a larger reduction in care? Evolutionary biology predicts that the elder would take the bigger hit. While such a prediction may not necessarily prove correct, it shows that evolutionary-based theory treads where economics normally does not, by going out on a limb regarding the likely relative weights accorded child versus elder within the woman's utility function. Later discussion, which draws upon standard evolutionary biology, elaborates reasons why.

Economics of the Family: Achievements and Challenges

A central achievement of family economics in the past three decades has been the addition of insights about a leading intellectual and policy concern—the problem of "crowding out," that is, the possibility that expansions of public income transfers might merely supplant private transfers. If my indigent grandmother becomes frail, and Medicaid benefits foot the bill for nursing home care, my mother's caregiving burden (which might have entailed taking her into her own home and providing informal care) is thus eased.

Crowding out impels policymakers and others to look at public transfers in a dramatically different light than a simple accounting of taxpayers and beneficiaries would imply. If crowding out is empirically important, then arguably my grandmother benefits little from Medicaid, since she would have gotten shelter and care regardless. Indeed, the true beneficiary is my mother, whose obligation to provide care is reduced. Further, crowding out can conceivably affect any public transfer program, including public transfers from the old to the young in the form of, say, public education or debt-financed fiscal policy.[4]

Not that crowding out emerges from every approach—far from it. For instance, while Becker's (1974) model (in which a donor's unvarnished altruism motivates private transfers) implies crowding out, the exchange models of Bernheim, Shleifer, and Summers (1985) and Cox (1987), in which private transfers are part of a quid pro quo, do not.[5] (For a detailed discussion of alternative models of private transfers, see chapter 1.)

Crowding out emanates mostly from income effects due to shared budget constraints. In a family made up of just my altruistic (and richer) mother and me, she implicitly decides how much we each consume by giving me money. Suppose the government taxes her and gives me the proceeds. Since neither our aggregate income nor her preferences have changed, our respective consumption levels will remain the same. What *does* change is her private transfer, whose reduction mirrors, dollar for dollar, the increase in the government's tax and subsidy. (To see why this does not generally happen in the exchange model, imagine that my mother's transfer springs not from altruism but is instead a payment for some nonmarket services that I provide, such as care or attention.)

The possibility of large income effects from crowding out galvanized the empirical literature on intergenerational transfers, spawning several studies of what have become known as "transfer derivatives," that is, the responsiveness of private transfers to incomes (e.g., Cox and Rank 1992; Altonji, Hayashi, and Kotlikoff 1997). Empirical research for the United States has revealed that transfer derivatives tend to be rather small, so the apparent specter of crowding out has receded.[6]

Not all of the economic literature on private transfers has placed such exacting focus on income effects. For instance, the work of Ronald Lee (e.g., Lee 1997) has followed earlier work in demography by concentrating on age and generational patterns in familial transfers. Indeed, age and gender effects in empirical studies of the economics of private transfers are fruitful directions for further research.

A recent paper emblematic of these crossroads is Duflo's (2003) study of expanded pensions in South African families. At apartheid's end, the South African government greatly expanded old age pensions, many of which were paid to grandparents living with their grandchildren. Duflo investigated whether grandchildren reaped any nutritional benefits from their grandparents' increased incomes, giving painstaking attention to the fact that the quarter of African children who lived with a pensioner were not randomly assigned, as in a controlled experiment.[7] This careful attention to the daunting problems of making causal inferences is a key strength of empirical work in economics. And, like many previous economic studies, the main objective was estimating income effects in the provision of intergenerational transfers.

But the study's most exciting results were not just about income effects but *demographic* patterns, because, as it turned out, the strongest estimated intergenerational connection was between maternal grandmothers and their granddaughters. As I argue in Cox (2007), this is, I think, where standard economics comes up short, for the discipline offers little for understanding the impact of maternal grandmother-hood or granddaughter-hood. Longstanding fundamentals from evolutionary thought can aid researchers in coming to grips with such variables. Indeed, evolutionary thinking has become increasingly integrated into economic approaches to the family.

Emerging Evolutionary Thought in Economics (and Sociology)

Biological considerations play a key role in Gary Becker's early research on economics of the family, which culminated in his monumental *A Treatise on the Family*, first published in 1981. This work, as well as updated material appearing in 1991, is replete with references to, and analyses of, biological underpinnings of familial behavior. Becker notes intellectual debts to the analyses of R. A. Fisher, Edward Wilson, Richard Dawkins, and several other pioneering thinkers in the field of evolutionary biology. (Still, Becker was concerned first and foremost with economic forces, and ensuing empirical work paralleled this emphasis.)

Theodore Bergstrom has written several papers that use and extend ideas from evolutionary biology and combine them with economic reasoning to study family behavior (e.g., Bergstrom 1996). An analysis of a longstanding biological theory of preferences of sons versus daughters—the so-called Trivers-Willard hypothesis, which I will discuss in more detail later—was published in a leading economics journal (Edlund 1999). That year saw the publication—this time in a leading sociology journal—of an empirical investigation of the same hypothesis (Freese and Powell 1999).[8]

Aloysius Siow (1998) has explored the implications of male–female differences in reproductive lifespan for gender roles in the labor market. Robert Willis's (1999) theory of out-of-wedlock childbearing recognizes the distinct problems and incentives faced by men versus women. Anne Case, I-Fen Lin, and Sara McLanahan (2000) have measured the strength of genetic ties for the nurturing of biological versus nonbiological children.

But there is much to be done to investigate evolutionary-based forces that might impinge on familial caregiving and exchange, particularly on the empirical front. However, before going further in empirical directions, it is essential to understand the earliest and most fundamental biological underpinnings of family behavior.

The Roots of Biological Basics in Family Behavior— Hamilton's Rule

Which should we expect to be stronger, a mother's altruism toward her young son, or an adult son's altruism toward his elderly mother? Might we expect mothers to be more solicitous toward their children than fathers? How about maternal versus paternal grandmothers? How much might we expect sons to be treated differently than daughters, purely because of their sex? What about altruism toward stepchildren, adopted children, and foster children?

Note that these questions are concerned with issues such as relatedness, age effects, and gender effects per se: mothers versus fathers, sons versus daughters, old versus young, and the discussion that follows contains the underpinnings for a biological approach. What is now known as Hamilton's rule—derived by biologist William D. Hamilton over 40 years ago (Hamilton 1964)—and its offshoots (mainly those of Robert Trivers and his collaborators) form the theoretical underpinnings of evolutionary-based familial altruism. Judiciously applied, the biologically based approach shares the strengths of well-executed economic theory in that it is parsimonious and can generate counterintuitive and falsifiable predictions.

Hamilton's rule contains elementary but powerful logic for explaining familial altruism.[9] Before getting to details, a couple of preliminary remarks are in order. The ensuing material might well strike some as an excursion into unfamiliar and perhaps irrelevant territory for a couple of reasons. First, in the interest of pedagogy, it begins with examples from animal behavior. Second, it is founded upon decidedly hypothetical entities— genes that impel kin to assist one another. Accordingly, I must relate these seemingly other-worldly constructs to empirical research aimed at explaining caregiving and exchange within families made up of conscious, thinking human beings.

A short excursion into this stylized and perhaps unfamiliar realm delivers simple logic—the analytics of which go no further than simple arithmetic—that has for some time been regularly harnessed in several subfields of evolutionary thought (including branches that deal with human behavior) to explain assistance among kin. I hasten to add that I am in no way attempting to argue that the reasoning below is *correct* (indeed, later I will point out reasons for skepticism; no doubt you could add your own). I merely wish to convey the evolutionary logic. Beginning with animal behavior, I will proceed to human behavior.

But first, consider a member of a different species—a sterile honeybee who just sacrificed its life to defend its hive by stinging an intruder. Such behavior puzzled Charles Darwin, whose theory of evolution by natural selection predicted that organisms whose makeup enables them to both survive and reproduce would be the ones that prevail in nature. Our hapless bee has succeeded in doing neither!

Hamilton solved the problem by approaching it not at the level of the individual animal, but at the level of the *gene*. Imagine that there exists a "helping gene," which governs an animal's altruistic behavior. (And imagination is clearly required because no such thing exists; nonetheless, this hypothetical gene is a useful pedagogical tool.) Imagine, too, that the Darwinian dictum of "survive and reproduce" applies not at the level of the individual animal, but at the level of this gene.

For instance, suppose that a watchful squirrel spies a deadly predator poised to eat three of his brothers.[10] Suppose that by crying out, our hero gets eaten but saves his kin. How do things look from a "gene's eye view"?

For any one of his brothers, there is a 50-50 chance—owing to sexual reproduction—that the identical gene resides within him. (Those odds are due to sexual reproduction. Like in a game of matching pennies, our hero's gene would be the same as a brother's if both inherited the gene from their father *or* if both inherited it from their mother—probabilities that sum to 50 percent.) Since there are *three* imperiled brothers, the *expected value* of our hero's helping gene that resides in the potential victims is 3×0.5, or 1.5. Issuing a warning cry dooms his *own* helping gene, but allows a greater number of *identical* genes to survive within rescued relatives.

Accordingly, a gene that impelled the sentinel squirrel to issue a suicidal warning cry to save the lives of three (or four, or five, etc.) siblings would tend to *spread*. That is how Hamilton solved the problem of the honeybee's sacrificial labors. From the *gene's* perspective, sterility and the suicide of the body in which the gene resides need not be an evolutionary dead end—so long as the body in question takes actions that encourage the survival and proliferation of identical genes residing in *other* bodies.

More generally, a "helping gene" will spread if it impels an animal to make sacrifices on behalf of sufficient numbers of relatives of sufficient genetic closeness.[11] Denote the cost of the altruistic act to the donor by C, and benefits of the act to the recipients by B. Let r denote the coefficient of relatedness, that is, the chances that donor and recipient share the same helping gene. Hamilton's rule stipulates that the donor provides help if

$$rB > C. \tag{1}$$

In our example, B and C are counted in terms of lives saved. More generally, evolutionary biologists characterize these terms as "fitness," a catch-all term that refers to one's reproductive success. *Inclusive fitness* (also known as *extended fitness*) includes one's own fitness plus that of other relatives, down-weighted by the appropriate value of r. In the example above, the heroic squirrel's helping gene impels the squirrel to undertake an altruistic sacrifice that, when all is said and done, enables the gene to proliferate more widely through helping gene replicas that likely reside within the bodies of kin.[12]

Another way to grasp the metaphorical nature of the "helping gene" is to consider a similar construct from economics—the so-called "Walrasian auctioneer": a hypothetical character who helps markets reach equilibrium by calling out prices and collecting information about desired quantities supplied and demanded, but forbidding transactions from occurring until these two quantities are equal. This is not how the world really works, obviously, and the details of how markets equilibrate is the subject of ongoing, cutting-edge economic research. Still, this hypothetical auctioneer is a convenient device for addressing basic questions about markets. Likewise, though the details of mechanisms that might facilitate biologically based kin assistance remain at the frontier of evolutionary biology, the "helping gene" serves as a convenient device for understanding the rudiments of the biology of assistance among kin.[13] Like simple supply and demand analysis, then, Hamilton's kin selection theory can generate benchmark explanations and predictions. Though neither theory covers every link in the causal chain, they can generate testable implications nonetheless.

For instance, let's return to the issue of sterility, only this time within a context pertinent to our own species. Consider that menopause imposes sterility upon (usually female) humans—hence the prediction that its onset should spur increased altruistic behavior toward kin. Indeed, some behavioral ecologists have advanced the idea that menopause itself—rare among mammals—is an adaptation for facilitating investment in children (Hawkes, O'Connell, and Blurton Jones 1997).

Menopause is but one example of the inherent, age-related asymmetries in altruistic sentiments implied by Hamilton's rule. Though human relatedness is symmetric (r is 0.25 between grandmother and granddaughter from either's point of view), extended fitness is likely not because the grandmother will have passed her reproductive potential long before her granddaughter. So elders would feel more altruistic toward younger kin than vice versa. Put aside for now considerations of income; Hamilton's rule is best conceptualized as a tool for coming to grips with utility weights that grandmother and granddaughter assign to one another's well-being. If each had the same resources, Hamilton's rule would predict that, all else equal, the grandmother is more likely to give to the granddaughter than the reverse.

Biological Basics and Elder Care

Economists sometimes postulate models of "two-sided altruism" between generations, whereby, for whatever reason, children care about their parents' well-being (sometimes in equal or approximately equal measure) as parents care about their children's. Though such a model might be appropriately convenient for certain questions, economists should nonetheless be aware that the specifications are, strictly speaking and per the preceding discussion, at odds with biologically based thinking.

Of course, there is likely much more to altruism than biology, but this is all the more reason to probe its biological nature, so as to throw into sharp relief alternative—perhaps culturally based, perhaps stronger— crosscurrents that impinge upon familial preferences. For instance, Bergstrom (1996) and Cox and Stark (2005) emphasize the social forces that might impel transfers from young to old. (Indeed, this direction of transfers predominates in many parts of the developing world, where kin networks provide the sole source of old-age support [e.g., see Cox and Fafchamps 2008].) For instance, Cox and Stark posit a "demonstration effect," whereby a parent desirous of eventual care from her child will provide for a grandparent in order to display, and thereby instill, the appropriate caregiving norms in the child. A vast related literature in sociology, social gerontology, and demography addresses the normative, social, cultural, and emotional factors that impinge upon the care of elderly by adult children (see Silverstein, Parrott, and Bengtson [1995] and the citations therein as well as chapter 1, this volume).

Nonetheless, I wish for now to put these other forces aside to focus on evolutionary biology's implications for the generational directions of trans- fers. The anthropological work of Kaplan and his coauthors for traditional societies reveals patterns consistent with Hamilton's rule in that transfers from old to young outweigh flows in the opposite direction. Elderly women, for example, tend to produce more food than they consume, thus gen- erating a surplus for younger household members (Kaplan 1994).

A fair criticism of such evidence is that it might not be so relevant for a developed country such as the United States. A controversial counter- argument from evolutionary quarters is that the traditional context, far from being irrelevant, might be advantageous for coming to grips with the underpinnings of the psychology of utility functions. A key tenet of evolutionary psychology, for instance, is that our preferences and pro- clivities are artifacts of our early hunter-gatherer history. If so, then current hunter-gatherer groups might prove useful for homing in on early origins that helped determine what our present-day preferences look like.

Much of the controversy surrounding the use of current traditional settings as a guide to evolutionary conditions is that, either because of marginalization from other cultures or, conversely, integration with other societies, traditional settings may not accurately reflect early evolutionary conditions. Evolutionary psychologists prefer to counter these criticisms by pointing to the timelessness of the essential human condition (women were always the sex that bore children, people have always gotten hungry and tired, and so forth).

Nonetheless, most would agree that both the invention of agriculture and manufacturing were ostensibly juggernauts for upsetting the traditional steady states. If for no other reason, then, it would be all the more critical to consider Lee's (1997) summary of age-related patterns of intergenerational transfers in industrial and agricultural economies. Lee finds that, in the former, resources also flow from old to young, consistent with biological considerations. But in the latter, Lee finds that transfers can flow in the opposite direction. He argues that such reverse flows can still be consistent with the dictates of evolutionary forces if they support and maintain farm-specific knowledge residing within the elderly, which can confer benefits upon children.

Still, what are we to make of the many instances in which adult children care for frail and perhaps indigent elderly, who can offer no fitness-related benefits in return? A diehard evolutionist might argue that such altruism could be an adaptive trait that springs from some all-purpose, sincere, and ingrained propensity to be nice, which in turn facilitates a person's ability to trade with other people, including nonrelatives. Maybe, but unless this line of thought helps us answer other questions too, I would be inclined to propose a simpler assessment—namely, that such behavior constitutes a puzzle for the theory, and that we might look outside biology (perhaps to the culture-related considerations referenced earlier) to gain traction on the problem.

Puzzles are not bad things to collect; indeed, the hallmark of a good theory is to distinguish puzzles from non-puzzles. I would be inclined to compile a "big book of puzzles," and, once the list grows long enough, support a full frontal assault upon the entire panoply of anomalies, rather than patching them up in a piecemeal fashion.

The basic biological insight that altruism should exhibit generational lopsidedness points to several intriguing approaches to studying elder care. For instance, an evolutionary perspective on a living will, whereby a person contracts to limit expenditures for prolonging his or her life, is that it might constitute an adaptive measure for increasing one's inclusive fitness. One implication is that adult children of elders who themselves have young children should be more sanguine about a parents' signing a living will than (say) their childless siblings. Or, consider depression among the elderly. Might this illness be a "strategy" for eliciting transfers from otherwise recalcitrant kin, as, for instance, Hagen (2003) suggests? Such speculations make clear that an evolutionary view can stimulate new ways of thinking about issues associated with elder care.

Biological Basics and the Care of Children

One of the most noteworthy advances in the economics of the family is the research program on household bargaining (e.g., McElroy and Horney 1981) and the collective model of the household, originating in the work of Chiappori (1988, 1992). The key innovation of these approaches is that they offer ways of thinking about how the distinct preferences and constraints of husbands versus wives affect allocation of resources within the household and the care of, and investments in, children in particular. This advance in the logic of household decisionmaking, a step beyond the mostly single-decisionmaker models of, say, Becker (1974), spawned dozens of empirical studies aimed at gathering evidence about how the separate interests and constraints of fathers and mothers affect children's well-being.

The results? Nearly every study (and there are now dozens) shows that putting more money in the hands of mothers relative to fathers redounds to the benefit of children. Emblematic is the investigation by Lundberg, Pollak, and Wales (1997) of a change in the way the United Kingdom disbursed its child benefit payments in the late 1970s, switching from payments funneled via primary earners (and hence husbands) through the income tax to one that paid mothers directly. Consistent with the idea that who gets the money matters (as would be the case, say, with household bargaining), the program change altered household expenditure patterns. Importantly, and tellingly, children did better after the change. The same pattern has been found in study after study of intrahousehold allocation (for instance, as surveyed by Strauss and Thomas [1995] and Haddad, Hoddinott, and Alderman [1997]). Though none of these are as compelling as that of Lundberg, Pollak, and Wales (who availed themselves of a "natural experiment," thus finessing the problem of endogeneity of individual income and wealth), the consensus is striking: children do better by their mothers than by their fathers.

These methodological advances and ensuing related evidence point up both a limitation of economics and an opportunity for pursuing evolutionary-based ideas to further this literature. The limitation is that, seeing how standard economics is not about (and probably *should not be* about) things like the nature of motherhood, the results are cast in a mostly gender-neutral "person 1, person 2" framework. The language used to describe the results is indicative of the (necessarily) gender-neutral approach inherent in economics. They are cast either in terms of the language of budget constraints (as in, e.g., "the rejection of 'common pooling' of resources") or in genderless verbiage concerning utility functions (as in "rejection of the 'common preference' model").

Peculiar as this phraseology might sound to noneconomists, it makes perfectly good sense, in that economics is about wants and desires (from wherever they spring, we care not) bumping up against limited budgets. Hence, the discipline is—at least traditionally and most of the time rightly—focused on prices and incomes, rather than, say, the wellspring of maternal solicitude.

However, and by way of preview, evolutionary biology is, at least partly, about the nature of those and other preferences. Hence, melding insights from economics with those of biology could advance our understanding of the family. A key bottom line is that evolutionary considerations imply that maternal altruism is stronger than paternal altruism and, accordingly, that maternal grandmothers would be more altruistic toward grandchildren than paternal ones. Such considerations also point to potential conflict between mothers and fathers over quality and quantity tradeoffs in decisions to produce and invest in children.

Biological considerations point to other results (elaborated upon below) that concern investments in children. Kin selection theory is a theory about *nepotism:* accordingly, stepchildren and other nongenetically related children would be expected to garner less parental transfers than genetically related children. In addition, and perhaps less obviously, biological considerations imply that favoritism of sons versus daughters can depend on the parental family's socioeconomic rank within the community, in places where the marriage market is not strictly monogamous.

But first, what are the relevant biological basics? Most important are the enormous physical and emotional costs that producing a child imposes upon women. These costs are large both in the absolute and relative to the costs that men incur. Even under the most felicitous circumstances imaginable, childbearing poses risks to a woman's physical and mental health. In contrast, the minimum costs a male must incur to get his genes into the next generation are trivial. Such disparity implies that mothers and fathers would apply different weights to quality and quantity tradeoffs in fertility, with mothers favoring quality, and fathers, quantity. While a man can—in principle, at least—"go forth and multiply," a woman can only "go forth and add."

Trivers (1972) was the first to point out the inherent conflict over quality and quantity tradeoffs between males and females. Biological considerations imply that a woman's route to advancing extended fitness entails tending to the "intensive margin," by securing the resources to provide for their offspring. While men have biological incentives to invest too, they can also advance their extended fitness via the "extensive margin," that is, by reproducing with additional mates. Reproductive effort consists of both investing in *existing* offspring and producing *new* offspring, and men benefit more than women from the latter. A further "biological basic"—one I will discuss in detail below—is that while a mother can be certain about her genetic relatedness to her child, a father might not be. A straightforward generalization of Hamilton's rule implies that maternal altruism would be stronger than paternal altruism for this reason.[14]

The Trivers-Willard Hypothesis

I will return to the issue of fathers versus mothers in more detail below, but before doing so, consider another gender-related issue concerning parent-to-child transfers that the evolutionary literature addresses: the favoritism of sons versus daughters. Such favoritism has been examined through an evolutionary lens, via the so-called Trivers-Willard hypothesis (Trivers and Willard 1973). Before getting to the details, let me note a reason for including it in this chapter—namely, that the hypothesis receives vanishingly *little* support in the United States (Keller, Nesse, and Hofferth 2001). Indeed, Freese and Powell (1999) find some evidence *against* the hypothesis.

If an idea appears to hold little water, why bother discussing it in this chapter? A primary reason, to quote from the opening text of Freese and Powell (1999, 1704), is this: "While some dismiss sociobiological theories as untestable, post hoc explanations, this article argues that sociologists should instead increase their efforts to identify and engage those theories that have novel empirical implications." Accordingly, an exceedingly valuable lesson from their study is that it helps debunk the longstanding canard that evolutionary-based theories are little more than "just-so" stories—

after-the-fact contrivances for putting an evolutionary spin on any and all behavior. On the contrary, as Freese and Powell point out, the Trivers-Willard hypothesis is indeed testable and falsifiable. What's more, it receives a rather sound drubbing in some of their empirical work, which concerns parental investments in children in the United States.

Just what *is* the Trivers-Willard hypothesis? The idea has to do with how parents might favor the production of, and investment in, sons versus daughters, and how such favoritism might vary with parental socio-economic status. Consider this scenario: You are from the poorest family in your community; you can have only one child; you can choose the sex of the child; and the marriage market is somewhat polygynous, with wealthy males getting more than their fair share of wives. One more thing, and here's where biology enters in: you are concerned only about your extended fitness.

Would you prefer a girl or a boy? Because of his impoverishment, a son might never attain the wherewithal to get a date, never mind produce grandchildren. But a poor daughter could produce grandchildren either within a monogamous or polygynous union. She might advance her socio-economic status via marriage (so-called hypergamy). Conversely, were you the richest parent, you would prefer a son since his wealth would enable him to produce many grandchildren, perhaps by more than one mate.

Though Trivers and Willard proposed their theory to explain sex ratios at birth, it can just as well explain parental investments in children, a point made not only by Freese and Powell (1999) but by Edlund (1999) in one of the few papers in economics to reference the Trivers-Willard hypothesis.

As my exposition of the hypothesis suggests, it is fitting for extreme situations. Indeed, in Cox (2007), I cite two case studies, one dealing with the extremely poor and the other dealing with the rich. But they do not pertain to developed countries, and are in any event selected merely to illustrate that something looking like Trivers-Willard effects *have* been uncovered for some instances. Whether a meta-study, even one that encompasses extreme settings, would necessarily produce similar findings is of course another question. But even if such patterns were to be discovered, they are likely far less relevant for advanced economies, such as that of the United States.[15]

References to Trivers-Willard effects are rare in economics. (For instance, Duflo [2003] does not refer to them, though it could be argued that the end of apartheid, and possibly reduced social stratification, could perhaps open new doors for female hypergamy, and thus encouraged grandmothers to favor granddaughters.) One exception is Edlund's (1999) insightful paper, which points out the possibility for deleterious long-run effects on the status of women. If a wife's power within marriage is influenced by her parent's wealth, a system in which low-income families provide brides for the sons of high-income families would perpetuate weak bargaining power of wives. A vicious cycle would emerge if, as the work of Thomas (1994) suggests, this weakness in turn limits a mother's ability to invest in daughters.

Applied development economists have produced a spate of studies comparing the treatment of sons versus daughters around the world (reviewed in, for example, Behrman 1997 and Strauss and Thomas 1995). But little evidence exists on the interaction of, among other things, the family's socioeconomic status within the marriage market, the inherent polygynousness of marriage systems, or sex-specific patterns in exogamy and inheritance of status.

Stepchildren—Evolutionary Considerations

A straightforward implication of Hamilton's rule is that children will fare less well in the care of stepparents than with biological parents. (Of course, as always, nonbiological explanations, perhaps complementary, perhaps competing, exist as well [e.g., Cherlin 1978]. But for now, let's stick to considerations of evolutionary biology; I'll have more to say about institutions and culture later on.)

A famous book, *Homicide,* by evolutionary psychologists Martin Daly and Margo Wilson (1988), documents rather striking differences in the rate of child abuse experienced by children living with two genetic parents versus those living with one genetic parent and one stepparent. The latter were found to be about forty times more likely to suffer physical abuse, even after adjusting for potentially confounding characteristics, such as the family's socioeconomic status. Differentials in child murder rates were found to be even more pronounced.

More recently, Case, Lin, and McLanahan (2000) investigated the less dramatic but equally vital connection between step-household status and child nutrition and found that, in both U.S. and South African survey data, there is reduced spending for food in households where a child is being raised by a nonbiological mother. The concordance of findings between countries is noteworthy in that genetic influences appear robust across environments with vastly different living standards and household structure.

Case, Lin, and McLanahan's (2000) findings are mirrored in research concerned with intergenerational transfers in the opposite direction, that is, the provision of resources and care to elderly parents by adult children. For instance, Ganong and colleagues (1998) found that perceived obligations to provide assistance to elderly kin were stronger if the elder in question was a biological parent than a stepparent. Pezzin and Schone's (1999) analysis of the Assets and Health Dynamics of the Elderly (AHEAD) data indicates that child-to-parent assistance of money, care, and shelter to lone elderly are significantly lower for elders with only stepchildren compared to elders with biological children.

Pathways, Problems, and a Prolegomenon: A Case Study of Paternity Uncertainty and Grandparental Care of Children

How can we add to our empirical knowledge of the relevance of biological forces for intergenerational transfer behavior? What are the strengths and weaknesses of the biological perspective? What progress can we make in inferring biological pathways with available data? What sort of deficiencies might bedevil data in addressing questions concerning biological forces in the provision of familial care? What do we wish we knew that we do not know? Could such wishes feasibly be fulfilled?

I broach these questions with a specific example: the problem of assessing the impact of paternity uncertainty on the provision of care to children. In particular, the question is this: does the propensity to care for grandchildren differ between *maternal* grandmothers (who, except under unusual circumstances, can always be sure that the grandchild is a genetic relative) versus *paternal* grandmothers (who, unlike their maternal counterparts, might harbor some doubt)? The empirical work represents only initial steps toward addressing the question. The preliminary (indeed, tentative) nature of the work has a distinct advantage for addressing the questions above. The initial foray raises fundamental questions, such as the following: Would it ever be possible to distinguish between biological forces and the more standard determinants emphasized in the social sciences, such as cultural norms or market prices? Indeed, do initial findings portend any sort of light at the end of the tunnel for parsing the biological from the nonbiological? Further, would such an attempt even make sense in light of what we know about the interplay between biological and, say, cultural forces? What might a workable methodological design look like? What sort of data resources would be needed to implement it?

Before getting into the details, here is my take on the "bottom line" of the foregoing exercise:

- The empirical example below demonstrates that a biological perspective can illuminate novel behavioral pathways concerning the intergenerational provision of care to children.
- However, nonbiological explanations exist for each and every correlation that arises from my descriptive empirical investigation of these pathways.
- Despite the preliminary nature of the descriptive results, some nonetheless appear to constitute rather strong evidence *against* the paternity uncertainty hypothesis.
- Nonetheless, I contend that further work is worth pursuing and outline a framework that could advance the empirical enterprise from mere description to the estimation of a causal model.
- Finally, though, such estimation would require information beyond the data at hand. And my example contains an ironic postscript: the needed information would be of a *cultural* rather than a biological nature.

Why Study Paternity Uncertainty?

I have several reasons for using paternity uncertainty to illustrate how empirical work in the economics of the family might broach biological considerations. First, as a matter of logic, at least, paternity uncertainty is a bona fide "biological basic": a woman is always certain of her genetic relatedness to her newborn, but it is nearly always possible, in principle at least, for a man to harbor a flicker of doubt.[16] Second, evolutionary literature gives a lot more emphasis to paternity uncertainty than economics literature does.[17] In contrast, while references to paternity uncertainty have appeared in economics literature, the issue hardly qualifies as a conceptual foundation of studies of economics of the family.

Third, the topic can aptly be characterized as "high-risk, high-return," and thus an area where fruitful discoveries might lurk. Fourth, the topic demonstrates how biologically based thinking can forge links between seemingly disparate variables (such as maternal-paternal differences in grandmothers' child care and parental work-related travel). Part of any theory's appeal rests in its ability to connect seemingly distant dots (even if, upon reflection, more ordinary explanations come to the fore).

Fifth, the example below implicates three generation members rather than the more standard two (i.e., the archetypical parent–child dyad.) Sixth, the case study's daunting conceptual and measurement problems are familiar territory in economics, where inferences must be made concerning behavior difficult or impossible to measure directly. For instance, most studies of labor market discrimination by race or sex employ datasets lacking direct measures of such bias, which instead must be inferred by indirect means. Indeed, below I show how one might borrow profitably from well-established empirical models in labor economics to address questions of paternity uncertainty.

Seventh, the example below arguably comes close to exhausting what can be learned from commonly available datasets; thus, it provides a useful segue into discussion of future data needs. Eighth, and finally, the subject of paternity uncertainty is fraught with daunting ethical and human-subjects concerns. Accordingly, it throws into sharp relief the tension between efforts to further our knowledge of family behavior and the exigencies of respecting the rights and concerns of survey respondents.

With these considerations in mind, let's now back up and turn to a description of data from a well-known and extensively used resource, the National Survey of Families and Households (NSFH).

A "Grandparental Gambit" and the Raw Numbers

Using data on fathers and mothers to assess influences of possible paternity uncertainty on child care would no doubt founder in light of other, more straightforward (not to mention more powerful) forces, such as the familial division of labor Becker and others espouse. Accordingly, I back up a generation to consider grandparents—specifically, grandmothers. Comparing paternal versus maternal grandmothers attenuates the apples-and-oranges quality of father–mother comparisons. But this "grandparental gambit" by no means finesses the problem of gender-based division of labor. If, for whatever reason, my wife assumes most of the responsibility for child care, she is more likely to feel comfortable asking her own mother to baby-sit rather than asking mine. Accordingly, finding an unconditional maternal–paternal advantage in grandmotherly care arguably proves little about any supposed connection between paternity uncertainty and investment in children.[18]

The empirical work that follows is purely descriptive: a set of correlations and partial correlations, no more. Discussion of these in connection with paternity uncertainty entails implicit warnings of caveat emptor. The goal is to assess whether the hypothesis is worth pursuing further. For instance, finding that all care is provided by paternal grandmothers would cast immediate doubt upon the paternity uncertainty hypothesis, while finding a maternal advantage would merely signal that further analysis may be worthwhile.

Where do the raw numbers come from? What do they show? My jumping off point is a set of simple descriptive exercises from earlier work (Cox 2003) where I found, in a variety of data sources (the Health and Retirement Study, a special module on grandparenting from the second wave of the National Survey of Families and Households [NSFH-2], and the Relatives and Friends Help Module of the Panel Study of Income Dynamics) that maternal grandmothers exhibit substantially more contact with, care of, and emotional closeness to grandchildren (Cox 2003, 183–86). For instance, in the NSFH-2 data, I found that, compared with paternal grandmothers, maternal grandmothers had 35 percent more sleepovers with grandchildren and 22 percent more visits with them. To avoid disparities that might arise because of the aftermath of divorce, I included only respondents whose daughters or sons are not single parents.[19] But besides this simple adjustment, I did little to address obvious possible confounding factors that could be associated with these rudimentary trends.

Clearly, commonsense and straightforward explanations for these differentials exist. Maternal grandmothers tend to be younger and healthier than paternal grandmothers, for instance, and considerations like these could account for some or all of the disparity. Further, such factors as geographic distance or socioeconomic and demographic attributes of family members could enter the picture.

Accordingly, the descriptive work below explores maternal–paternal differences in grandmotherly care, but this time conditioning on a variety of covariates ostensibly implicated in such differentials. Such conditioning points to narrower differentials, suggesting—not surprisingly—that raw numbers alone paint an incomplete and possibly misleading picture of maternal–paternal differences in grandmotherly care.

My measure of grandmotherly care, from the second wave of the NSFH, is an indicator of whether respondent husbands and wives received help with child care from their mothers during the month before the survey. This parent-centric measure can thus be linked to characteristics of each generational member, enabling me to control for a comprehensive a set of family characteristics.[20]

The sample is made up of married respondents with children at home, with non-co-residing grandmothers on both sides of the family. For reasons explained below, I focus on marriages intact since the first wave of the survey, undertaken five years earlier.[21] Finally, I restrict the sample to observations with usable information for all of the measures included in the estimates in table 5.1 (including answers to a self-enumerated questionnaire about marriage administered separately to each spouse in the first wave).

The unconditional means indicate a maternal advantage: 43 percent of maternal grandmothers provided child care in the previous month compared with 35 percent of paternal grandmothers, a statistically significant disparity that the first panel of figure 5.1 depicts. But the "conditional" disparity, generated by the bivariate probit estimates from table 5.1 and depicted in the rightmost panel in figure 5.1, is much smaller—a little over 3 percentage points (compared with more than 8 percentage points in the unconditional comparison) and not statistically significant at conventional levels. The conditional disparity is calculated by evaluating predicted care using entire-sample means for the covariates entered in the regression in table 5.1. (For example, one of the covariates is grandmother's age. The mean age used in generating the rightmost bars in figure 5.1 is the average age of all grandmothers.)

The covariates in table 5.1 make up many parent-level characteristics (such as earnings, individual labor force status, age, and number of siblings) as well as attributes of grandmothers (including age, health, and geographic distance, with like characteristics of in-laws) and grandchildren (the number of biological children and stepchildren grouped by age).

To repeat the caveats above, table 5.1's results are most aptly couched in terms of correlations and partial correlations.[22] With these caveats (hopefully) firmly established, I push the descriptive analysis further by discussing covariates that could be implicated in paternity uncertainty. At the risk of overkill, I hasten to add that they may have little to do with such uncertainty. To avoid a patchwork quilt of conjectures and qualifications, let's consider biological and nonbiological perspectives in turn.

Table 5.1. Receipt of Child Care from Grandmothers

Bivariate probit analysis: Child care provided by maternal versus paternal grandmothers

Wave 1 marriage/sex attitudes and work travel included

Dependent variable: Received child care last month (1 = Yes, 0 = No)

	Maternal Side (wives)			Paternal Side (husbands)		
	Marginal effect	Asymp. t-val.	Variable mean	Marginal effect	Asymp. t-val.	Variable mean
Current earnings (1,000s)	0.001	0.76	56.223	0.000	0.04	56.223
Permanent income (1,000s)	0.000	−0.44	52.242	0.000	−0.14	52.242
Full-time worker	0.016	0.38	0.381	0.094	1.57	0.798
Part-time worker	0.014	0.35	0.338	0.158	2.00	0.132
Age	−0.027	−4.37	35.564	−0.006	−1.18	37.668
Black	0.102	1.34	0.050	0.003	0.05	0.054
Hispanic	0.152	1.62	0.036	−0.168	−2.15	0.041
Number of siblings	−0.021	−3.09	3.400	−0.018	−2.85	3.436
Not first marriage	0.007	0.14	0.154	−0.035	−0.76	0.153
Not spouse's first marriage	−0.002	−0.03	0.153	0.049	0.98	0.154
Number of biological children age 0–4	0.096	3.68	0.576	0.083	3.55	0.564
Number of biological children age 5–12	0.064	3.34	1.010	0.047	2.70	0.976
Number of biological children age 13–18	−0.101	−3.43	0.450	−0.161	−4.91	0.397
Number of stepchildren 0–4	0.230	2.28	0.021	0.183	2.43	0.024
Number of stepchildren 5–12	0.064	1.13	0.04	−0.051	−1.24	0.081
Number of stepchildren 13–18	−0.096	−1.26	0.035	−0.044	−0.86	0.090
Spouse variables						
Spouse's age	−0.003	−0.60	37.668	−0.005	−0.86	35.564
Spouse full-time worker	0.014	0.22	0.798	0.073	1.88	0.381
Spouse part-time worker	−0.050	−0.67	0.132	0.003	0.08	0.338
Parental variables						
Mother's age	0.007	2.45	61.431	−0.001	0.36	63.323
Per capita income (1,000s)	0.003	0.86	14.963	−0.002	−0.48	14.418
Distance from mother (100s of miles)	−0.044	−8.93	3.630	−0.014	−5.61	3.950

Table 5.1. *(Continued)*
Bivariate probit analysis: Child care provided by maternal versus paternal grandmothers
Wave 1 marriage/sex attitudes and work travel included
Dependent variable: Received child care last month (1 = Yes, 0 = No)

	Maternal Side (wives)			Paternal Side (husbands)		
	Marginal effect	Aymp. t-val.	Variable mean	Marginal effect	Aymp. t-val.	Variable mean
Mother alone	−0.047	−0.75	0.250	−0.034	−0.58	0.310
Parents together	−0.034	−0.74	0.591	0.060	1.35	0.558
Parent in bad health	−0.122	−3.07	0.185	−0.144	−3.93	0.177
In-law variables						
Mother-in-law's age	0.003	1.07	63.323	0.000	0.12	61.431
Per-capita income (1,000s)	0.000	0.04	14.418	0.003	0.98	14.963
Distance from mother-in-law (100s of miles)	−0.004	−1.92	3.950	−0.007	−2.76	3.630
Mother-in-law alone	−0.036	−0.57	0.310	0.068	1.12	0.250
Parents-in-law together	−0.019	−0.40	0.558	0.040	0.98	0.591
Parent-in-law in bad health	−0.040	−0.95	0.177	−0.064	−1.73	0.185
Attitudinal variables						
Strict attitude toward marriage	0.014	0.33	0.417	0.026	0.62	0.424
Spouse strict marriage	0.007	0.16	0.424	0.097	2.44	0.417
Middling marriage	0.010	0.23	0.328	−0.011	−0.28	0.381
Spouse middling marriage	−0.023	−0.52	0.381	0.076	1.93	0.328
Strongly disagree: overlook infidelity	0.179	2.93	0.500	−0.074	−1.52	0.363
Spouse str. disagree: overlook infidelity	0.072	1.29	0.363	0.020	0.36	0.500
Middling disagree: overlook infidelity	0.127	2.04	0.405	−0.121	−2.55	0.513
Spouse mid. disagree: overlook infidelity	0.042	0.81	0.513	0.027	0.47	0.405
Travel variables						
Travels 1–59 days for work	0.033	0.52	0.070	0.001	0.03	0.267
Travels 60+ days for work	0.083	0.47	0.009	−0.115	−1.95	0.062
Spouse travels 1–59 days	0.016	0.41	0.267	0.035	0.60	0.070
Spouse travels 60+ days	−0.005	−0.06	0.062	0.153	0.91	0.009

(continued)

Table 5.1. *(Continued)*
Bivariate probit analysis: Child care provided by maternal versus paternal grandmothers
Wave 1 marriage/sex attitudes and work travel included
Dependent variable: Received child care last month (1 = Yes, 0 = No)

	Maternal Side (wives)			Paternal Side (husbands)		
	Marginal effect	Aymp. t-val.	Variable mean	Marginal effect	Aymp. t-val.	Variable mean
Constant	0.794	1.44	1.000	0.71	0.97	1.000
Estimated correlation of unobservables			0.42			
Estimated standard error of correlation			0.06			
Observations			1,164			
Recipients	500				402	
Nonrecipients	664				762	
Log-likelihood			−1147.1			
Chi-squared			450.32			
Dependent variable mean	0.430					0.345

Source: Author's calculations from Waves 1 and 2 of the NSFH.

Note: Estimates from this table are used to construct figures 5.1–5.4.

Figure 5.1. Child Care from Grandmothers
Maternal versus paternal grandmothers
Unconditional versus conditional means

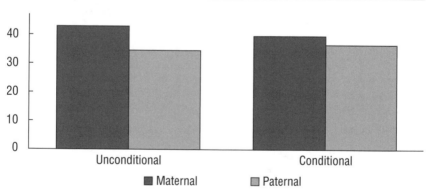

Source: Unconditional values from Wave 2 of the NSFH. Conditional child care calculated from table 5.1 estimates evaluated at sample means.

Note: The unconditional maternal advantage in child care is 8.4 percentage points. Conditional on the covariates in table 5.1, however, the estimated maternal advantage falls to 3.1 percentage points and is not significantly different from zero at conventional levels.

Included in the table 5.1 regressions is an attitudinal variable, collected in the first wave, concerning husbands' and wives' attitudes toward marriage, as reported privately in separate, self-enumerated questionnaires. I was drawn to this variable in light of the unique perspective on marriage advanced in some quarters within evolutionary biology: that marriage is tantamount to "mate guarding," wherein spouses monitor one another to safeguard against infidelity. The question asked how strongly respondents agreed or disagreed with the statement, "Marriage is a lifetime relationship and should never be ended except under extreme circumstances." The responses bore a statistically significant relationship to grandmotherly care in just one instance: paternal grandmothers were significantly more likely to provide care when their daughters-in-law reported a strict (as opposed to lenient) attitude toward the permanence of marriage (figure 5.2 and table 5.1).

This finding is consistent with the paternity uncertainty hypothesis, whereby only *one* of the grandmothers, the paternal one, would harbor concerns about the fidelity of only *one* of the spouses: her daughter-in-law. The point estimate is rather large: all else equal, the estimated probability of receiving paternal grandmotherly child care is 8.4 percentage points higher when the wife reported strict versus lenient attitudes.[23] The

Figure 5.2. Predicted Child Care from Grandmothers
Maternal versus paternal grandmothers
By wives' Wave 1 attitudes toward marriage

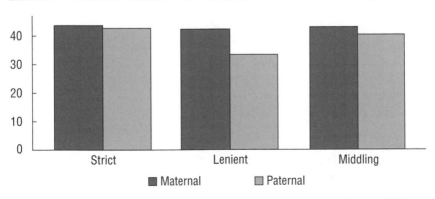

Source: Regression results from table 5.1, using information from Waves 1 and 2 of the NSFH.

Note: Respondent strictness concerning permanence of marriage is associated with higher care from paternal grandmothers relative to maternal grandmothers. Paternal grandmotherly care is 8.4 percentage points higher when wife's attitudes are strict versus when they are lenient.

8.4 figure refers to the difference between the paternal bars associated with the labels "strict" versus "lenient," and it is significant at nearly the 0.01 level. (But the difference between the maternal bar and the paternal bar within the lenient category [7.1 percentage points] is *not* significantly different at conventional levels, owing to imprecision in the estimation on the maternal side of the bivariate probit.)

Further, I find less solicitude from paternal grandmothers for households where the husband's work necessitates spending long periods away from home (figure 5.3). One interpretation of such absences is that they may be correlated with paternity uncertainty. The estimated effect is quite large (10.9 percentage points) and significant at the 0.05 level. (But the estimated difference between the maternal and paternal bars within the "60 days or longer" category for travel [13 percentage points] is significant only at the 0.13 level.)

Of course, there are other, arguably simpler explanations for the patterns depicted in figure 5.3. Maybe the propensity to travel is inversely related to altruism toward young children, and it is heritable too, so that mothers of traveling husbands tend to provide less care. Even more mundane: if standard family procedure is for me to call my mother to baby-sit and my wife to call hers, I might be apt to call upon my mother less

Figure 5.3. Predicted Child Care from Grandmothers
Maternal versus paternal grandmothers
By husbands' Wave 1 work travel

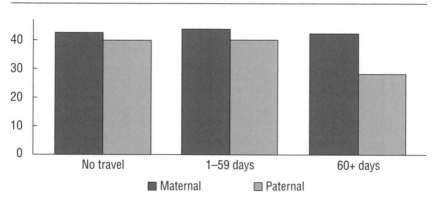

Source: Regression results from table 5.1, using information from Waves 1 and 2 of the NSFH.

Note: Paternal grandmotherly care is 10.9 percentage points lower when the husband travels 60 or more days out of the year compared to when he does not travel.

often if I'm always on the road. Still, despite obvious alternative explanations after the fact, the biologically based model illuminates novel pathways. I know of no standard theory from the social sciences that helps connect the dots between a parent's work-related travel, on one hand, and the paternal grandmother's transfers to grandchildren, on the other.

But to continue the theme of cautioning against reading too much into partial correlations, I return to figure 5.2 and the "marriage effect" on grandmotherly care. An alternative, nonbiological explanation might be that I discover that my mother-in-law is a wonderful babysitter, which fuels my appreciation for the joys of monogamy. (A countervailing consideration, though, is that the temporal sequence depicted in figure 5.2 runs in reverse of this alternative explanation—reported attitudes predate reported care by five years.)

My final descriptive finding concerns an NSFH wave 1 attitudinal variable that, on the face of it, gets closest to the heart of paternity uncertainty. Husbands and wives were asked about their attitudes regarding sexual infidelity: "Married couples ought to overlook isolated occasions of sexual unfaithfulness," and they were given a 1–5 Likert scale, ranging from "strongly agree" to "strongly disagree."[24]

Figure 5.4. Predicted Child Care from Grandmothers
Maternal versus paternal grandmothers
By couples' Wave 1 attitudes toward infidelity

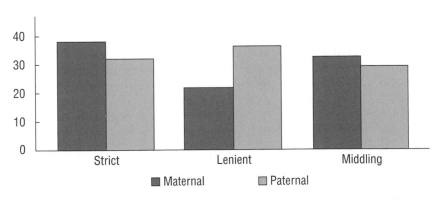

Source: Regression results from table 5.1, using information from Waves 1 and 2 of the NSFH.

Note: Respondent leniency concerning infidelity is associated with more care from paternal grandmothers relative to maternal grandmothers. There is a paternal advantage of 17.1 percentage points when the couple's attitudes are lenient, compared with a 7.1 percentage-point paternal deficit when the couple's attitudes are strict.

The estimated partial correlations (figure 5.4 and table 5.1) are the *opposite* of what I would have expected in light of considerations about paternity uncertainty. Sexual licentiousness should make paternal grandmothers chary of committing too much to grandchildren that might not be genetic relatives. Yet among couples in the lenient category, the estimated paternal–maternal difference is actually *positive;* indeed, it is quite large (17.1 percentage points) and significant at any popular level.

I formulated figure 5.4 to contrast the behavior of couples, rather than just wives, because of the ambiguous nature of the infidelity question. (Which spouse is presumed to be unfaithful? Who is doing the overlooking?) But restricting comparisons to attitudes of wives would alter the results little, since the strongest partial correlation in table 5.1 is between care maternal grandmothers provide and their daughters' attitudes concerning sexual infidelity.

A further step would be to think harder about what the infidelity variables might be picking up, such as differing norms among "traditional" versus "nontraditional" families, for instance. Might maternal grandmothers be less generous toward lax daughters, for fear that they might otherwise have to provide more child care than they wish? Such crosscurrents, arguably unrelated to paternity uncertainty, could be explored using additional attitudinal variables from the NSFH.

I prefer to use these anomalous findings as a springboard for discussion. First, anomalies spur progress. If they persist after more exacting scrutiny, then we must either refine the theory or abandon it; both paths can constitute progress. Second, the anomalous-looking partial correlations in figure 5.4 stand as an antidote to the aforementioned problem of "just-so"-story criticisms, wherein post hoc rationalizations render biologically based explanations immune to falsification. Should results similar to those in figure 5.4 be obtained within an exacting methodological design, rather than a descriptive exploration, the paternity uncertainty hypothesis would be rejected; the theory can indeed be falsified.[25]

Third, whatever the eventual reasons for the disparities in figure 5.4, I would not have uncovered them had I not been pondering paternity uncertainty. Perhaps more formal and painstaking work will shed further light on them in the future, as well as on those depicted in figures 5.2 and 5.3. Further, even if these explanations are rooted in nonbiological forces, a biological argument could ultimately lead to non-biologically related discoveries because biologically based thinking can flag variables that might otherwise be overlooked. And the parsimony from evolutionary thinking helps organize empirical exploration.

Before leaving the descriptive realm, I note one example of such a variable. It comes from the Fragile Families dataset, a survey of single mothers and (in 75 percent of the cases) fathers, taken soon after the birth of the child. One question asked of both fathers and mothers in the first wave concerned the *physical resemblance* of the child to parents and other relatives.

Two-thirds of the fathers reported that the child looked like them or relatives from their side of the family; the other third reported resemblance to the mother, the mother's side of the family, or some other answer (e.g., "looks like himself or herself"). In the second wave, conducted a year or more later, mothers were asked (in the case of non-coresident fathers) how many days during the past month the father spent with the child. I find statistically significant and large differences by self-reported resemblance, but intriguingly, only for fathers of boys (figure 5.5).[26]

What we make of such a finding, at this point, would constitute pure speculation. One could make a logical case for causality in either, both, or no direction. (For example, imagine that men who are intrinsically more altruistic also happen to be inclined to see themselves in their infant sons.) Notwithstanding daunting problems inferring causality, however, the focus on biological basics confers an advantage—even at the descriptive

Figure 5.5. Days Nonresident Fathers Spent with Child
Mother's reports of number of days in previous month
By father's self-reported perceptions of child's resemblance to him
And by sex of child

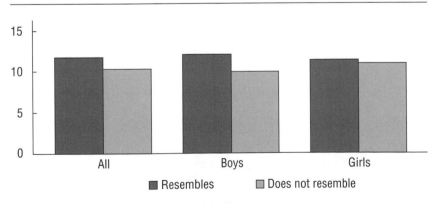

Source: First 2 waves of the Fragile Families dataset.

Note: A year or more after the birth of the child, nonresident fathers spent on average more days with children if they reported, in the first wave, that the child looked like them. But the discrepancy by resemblance only holds for boys.

stage—by pointing the way toward demographic variables of interest that more standard approaches might ignore.[27]

Beyond Description—Maternal/Paternal Differences in Grandparental Care

Put aside child care and other private transfers for a moment and consider an analogous question: How much of the difference in the wages of women and men is due to differences in qualifications and training? How much is due to labor market discrimination? Replace "wages" with "intergenerational transfers," "qualifications and training" by "resources and abilities," and "discrimination" by "paternity uncertainty." There are strong parallels, particularly with respect to paternity uncertainty and discrimination. Each is intangible, difficult to measure, and subject to alternative explanations. Feasible inferential paths are more likely to be indirect than direct.[28]

Consider, for example, the maternal grandmother's transfer equation

$$T_i = X_i \beta_m + \varepsilon_i, \tag{2}$$

where T_i is household i's maternal transfer received, X_i is a vector of explanatory variables, β_m is a vector of coefficients, and ε_i is a random component with mean 0. The maternal/paternal transfer differential is

$$D \equiv T_m - T_p = \Delta X \beta_m + \Delta \varepsilon \tag{3}$$

where the m and p subscripts refer to maternal and paternal averages and prefix Δ denotes the maternal/paternal difference in the subsequent variable Equation (3) states that the transfer differential can be decomposed into differences in measured attributes ΔX and residual differences $\Delta \varepsilon$. The latter term corresponds to the unexplained differential in the standard decomposition of gender differentials in wages.

Further, this simple model is subject to the same caveats that prevail in the wage discrimination literature. For instance, "unexplained" differences in transfers might come not from paternity uncertainty but from the omission of pertinent explanatory variables. Alternatively, the regressors might be affected by such uncertainty. As in wage discrimination, where "premarket" discrimination could affect schooling, the grandparents' propensity to make transfers could affect such variables as geographic distance. (Plus, even if the function were correctly specified, it would be subject to the familiar index number problem in which unexplained maternal/paternal differences in transfers depend on which values are used to standardize these differences.)

Adding Institutions to the Story

Even with a comprehensive set of explanatory variables and a correctly specified empirical model, a robust unexplained transfer differential need not have anything to do with paternity uncertainty. The word "unexplained" means exactly that.

Considering locales with different traditions and practices related to paternity certainty is one way to learn more about unexplained differences. Assume provisionally that traditions are exogenous and that communities reside in separate spheres. Examples from the developing world, though obviously remote from our immediate focus, are nonetheless pedagogically convenient. Imagine that community 1 has practices commonly associated with paternity certainty, such as the sequestration of women, whereas community 2 does not.[29]

Consider the maternal/paternal differential in transfers between these two communities using equation (3):

$$D_1 - D_2 = (\Delta X_1 - \Delta X_2)\beta_2 + \Delta X_1(\beta_1 - \beta_2) + (\Delta \varepsilon_1 - \Delta \varepsilon_2). \qquad (4)$$

The first term in (4) captures the contribution of between-community differences in maternal/paternal characteristics (community differences in the age disparity of maternal versus paternal grandmothers, for instance) to the intercommunity transfer gap. The second term captures how maternal/paternal differences in observed characteristics might have disparate influences on transfers between communities (e.g., maternal/paternal age disparity might matter more in one community than in another). The third term represents intercommunity differences in the unexplained differential. For example, suppose that the first community has a practice associated with the assurance of paternity. All else equal, such a practice should generate a lower maternal/paternal differential in the first community, and thus a negative unexplained differential in (4).

Again, refer to the wage differential analogy above. Blau and Kahn (1996) used estimates of (4) to make inferences about country-specific gender policies (Sweden's paternal leave policy, Australia's comparable worth policy) and their possible impact on gender–wage differences in those countries relative to gender–wage differences in the United States. Likewise, the problems and caveats associated with Blau and Kahn's interpretations carry over to this application as well.[30] In particular, the problem of policy endogeneity has a strong parallel with my suggested usage of traditions and community practices.

How Much of Tradition Is Really Exogenous?

Traditions, like government policies, do not spring up from nowhere but arise to solve problems. For example, Jewish dietary restrictions (kashrut) might have originated for ecological and health reasons (e.g., pigs were difficult for nomadic Israelites to raise in an arid climate, avoiding poisonous shellfish is healthy, and so on). Such practices might outlive their original purpose because they get co-opted to solve different problems, such as maintaining group identity or cohesiveness.

The problem of potential endogeneity of tradition can be described succinctly in terms of the above example: would kashrut be a valid instrumental variable for a study of the relationship between diet and health? Not likely, if such a hypothetical study were conducted in Biblical times. In an econometric study of health outcomes, the practice of kashrut would be correlated with error terms in any equation predicting healthiness. But if such a study were conducted today, kashrut might prove to be a valid instrument. I say "might," because even if the practice of kashrut had outlived its health-related impetus, the forces that sustain the practice could nonetheless also be correlated with health outcomes. So information about how and why traditions are maintained is also essential for substantiating their usefulness in identifying assumptions.

A parallel argument can be made in the context of intergenerational transfers. Refer to equation (4), and suppose that community 1, but not community 2, is characterized by the sequestration of wives. Five questions need to be answered: What are the functional origins of such sequestration? Are they still operative or defunct? If defunct, what forces sustain the practice? Can such forces credibly be assumed to be independent of error terms in the equation for intergenerational transfers? If so, are these forces nonetheless strong enough to be useful as instrumental variables?

These are difficult questions, and answering them requires a painstaking approach to the rather voluminous anthropological literature concerned with marriage practices and traditions.[31] Outside information from field studies, ethnographies, and the like is needed to address these interrelated questions. Such endeavors are inherently qualitative; no test statistic can be applied to evidence of this nature. Determining exogeneity is not mechanical, but a qualitative judgment call that requires an interdisciplinary approach.[32] The key task is to spell out precisely the conditions under which causal inferences can be made, versus describing correlations subject to multiple interpretations.

Nuances in the Logic of Paternity Uncertainty

Thinking harder about *why* paternity uncertainty might happen (tantamount to pondering why a woman might seek to have sexual relations with someone other than her long-term mate) can guide additional empirical tests. One theory, the "paternity confusion" hypothesis, proposed by Hrdy (1981) links paternity uncertainty with hardships imposed by poverty; two putative fathers may be better than one if one father's expected contribution is insufficient or at risk of drying up from, say, unemployment or incarceration.[33]

Hrdy's reasoning is consistent with the idea that upheaval in family life would be circumscribed by socioeconomic fault lines, and that trends in economic inequality would generate corresponding divergences in family life. Such considerations lead to a policy perspective diametrically opposed to the view that public income redistribution to the poor undermines "family values." Rather, the resultant economic security and nuclear-family norms emerge as complementary.

Data Needs

On the heels of the foregoing case study, my ensuing discussion of future data needs might seem odd because it concentrates on social and cultural information rather than biological data. Why? Though a list of intriguing biological indicators (most obviously, DNA-based information concerning relatedness) would be easy to construct, it would ignore the aforementioned realities of survey-based research. Such intrusive questions are ethically dubious and pose obvious human-subjects concerns. Moreover, as a practical matter, the research community depends on the vital (but fragile) goodwill of survey respondents to add to our knowledge of family behavior. Accordingly, when asking biologically based questions pertinent to family behavior, it is prudent to err on the side of caution.

This section's recommendations pertain to social, cultural, and community questions. As my case study indicates, these questions can contribute to our knowledge of biological bases for behavior. The basic template for such an enterprise is the "community questionnaire" that is standard in most of the World Bank's Living Standards Measurement Surveys (LSMS) for developing countries. These modules deal with questions of social and physical infrastructure, measures of social capital, and traditions, practices, and cultural mores endemic to the respondent's locale. Though early prototypes of such modules sometimes proved disappointing, recent incarnations are better (e.g., the community questionnaires in the Indonesian Family Life Survey).

Such initiatives have expanded outward into more refined questions about social capital and civic life. Why might such questions prove useful in a U.S. context? First, the recent work of Glaeser, Ponzetto, and Shapiro (2005) has shown that the United States is an exceedingly diverse cultural patchwork. Empirical evidence shows the "red state/blue state" cultural divide exists. Such cultural forces can impinge on biologically driven behavior, as the previous case study suggests. Moreover, the catchphrase "nature versus nurture" is mostly defunct—at least in the life sciences— and is headed for extinction in the social sciences too. Indeed, the two forces are mostly complementary. Such complementarity is self-evident: we have genes that build eyes because there is stuff to look at.

But second, consider how information about social capital helps us understand intergenerational transfer behavior in the following example. Return to the instance of "crowding out" referenced earlier in which a woman considers placing her indigent mother into nursing care funded by Medicaid. Suppose that, in checking out the various local nursing facilities where her mother might be admitted, she finds enormous heterogeneity in quality: some places are awful, some are marvelous, and she is not sure which place will have an available opening. The question of whether elder care will be provided by her or by Medicaid turns on which facility her mother can gain admission to.

Finally, suppose that her mother's admittance to a facility is dependent upon the woman's social or political connections. That is, a well-placed phone call to a local official or influential community member affects the chances of gaining access to a high quality facility. An example such as this casts the "crowding out" issue in a new light. Typically, standard economic models treat public income transfers as exogenous manna from heaven, to which family members react. But social capital considerations present novel and potentially important nuances. If family and community ties affect one's access to public transfers, a kind of "crowding in" emerges in which resourceful and altruistic kin help steer public monies toward their own dependent relatives. A primary theme in the economics of the family is that public and private transfers are substitutes. Empirical work indicates that extreme substitutability is not apparent in the data. A frontier would be to explore how the two kinds of transfer might complement one another, and community-based survey information, matched to individual household data, could help broach these issues.

Conclusion

Consideration of future data collection to learn more about what makes families tick suggests a twist on a central theme of this chapter: what factors *will help predict* change and variation in intergenerational caregiving and exchanges? Attention to biological basics is useful for contemplating future trends. Economists like to focus on exogenous forces for clarifying and organizing predictions. And from the standpoint of family behavior, biologically related changes in technology fit the bill for credible, exogenous drivers of trends in intergenerational transfers and other aspects of family behavior.

Just as, 50 years ago, assessing the Pill's impact on family life would have been impossible, likewise the technological developments in the offing present daunting challenges for would-be prognosticators. But we must sometimes speculate. What would happen, for instance, if DNA-based paternity tests were to become inexpensive and widespread? For the likely small fraction of cases where such tests might matter, fathers and children would probably be brought closer together. But a "mate-guarding" perspective might imply the opposite, a bizarrely counter-intuitive conclusion: fathers would no longer need to stick around so much to safeguard their paternity.

To continue speculating, what might happen if the artificial gestation of humans were to become feasible and cost-effective in the United States? While no "Manhattan Project" for such technology exists, nonetheless, rapid advancements in premature infant care are leading in the direction of such a possibility. What would the role of "biological basics" be then?

Finally, consider the twin technologies of geriatric medicine and the education of children. Much of the current rise in health care costs is technology driven, the result of new but expensive ways to prolong and enhance life in later years. Likewise, much of the rise in education costs is also technology related—but, paradoxically, driven by the *lack* of a technological means of lowering education costs. Education in the future will likely chug along the old-fashioned way: tutelage and coaching done face-to-face in groups.

How might such crosscurrents play out? How might biological basics matter? I imagine being well into my dotage, but happy and somewhat healthy, when one day I'm diagnosed with some awful, fatal disease—albeit one that can be cured at considerable expense, affording me an extra year of gratifying geezerhood. But here's the rub: the exigencies of economics dictate that by paying for the treatment, I must sacrifice one year of my granddaughter's college education. I can't vouch that I'd be thinking of Hamilton's rule (if indeed I would even remember it), but I know what it would predict. And, in case you hadn't heard of it before, now you do too. The relevance of such considerations is, I believe, a central question for our discipline.

NOTES

Prepared for the 2006 Penn State Symposium on Family Issues. I wish to thank the symposium organizers, in particular Suzanne Bianchi, Joe Hotz, Kathleen McGarry, and Judith Seltzer, for detailed and insightful comments on an earlier draft. Any remaining errors are mine alone. Financial support for this work was provided by a grant from the National Institute on Child Health and Human Development (R01-HD045637). The findings, interpretations and conclusions expressed herein are entirely my own and do not necessarily represent the views, opinions, or policy of the National Institutes of Health or of any other government agency.

1. For a succinct discussion of these points, see, for example, Heckman (1993).

2. In Gronau's words, "Whereas economists have little to contribute on the factors determining utility, they are comfortable with the analysis of prices" (1986, 300).

3. Further, that paper aptly conveys the complex array of crosscurrents impinging on trends in time spent in home production that this introductory discussion glosses over.

4. On this last example, the key reference is Barro (1974), but see also Becker (1974).

5. Indeed, exchange-related private transfers could actually *reinforce* rather than neutralize the effects of public income redistribution (Cox and Jakubson 1995).

6. The problem is far from having been rendered moot, however. For example, there is evidence to suggest that crowding out may be a viable concern in developing countries (e.g., Cox, Hansen, and Jimenez 2004 and Cox and Fafchamps 2008).

7. Duflo relies on the pronounced age requirements for the pension as a source of exogenous variation in the pension "treatment," but then goes further to address potential endogeneity problems by examining child height-for-weight outcomes *within* households, to check whether children born after the boost in pension benefits did better compared with their siblings born before pension reform.

8. See also Keller, Nesse, and Hofferth (2001) for related work, and Nielsen (1994) for an example of attention in sociology to evolutionary foundations of family behavior.

9. For more detailed discussion, see Cox (2007) and Cox and Fafchamps (2008). Or, better yet, consult Dawkins's (1976) superb and accessible explication of Hamilton's model and its immediate progeny.

10. My choice of species is deliberate, in light of supportive evidence for Hamilton's rule in Paul Sherman's (1981) study of Belding's ground squirrels (*spermophilus beldingi*), which demonstrated kinship's influence on the pattern of cooperation by (matrilineal) relatedness.

11. Eminent population geneticist J. B. S. Haldane is said to have claimed to be willing to lay down his life for at least two brothers or eight cousins.

12. If by now the "helping gene" story is straining your credulity, you are not alone; at this juncture, it is worth relating a passage from the work of biologist Robert Trivers (1985, 127–28):
> Some people object to kinship theory on the grounds that it has isolated an abstraction, "gene for altruism," and based the entire theory on this notion. Altruistic acts probably require many genes located at many different loci. After all, an altruist must have some means of measuring cost and benefit, some means of apprehending degrees of relatedness, and then be able to confer the benefit in question. How can this complicated phenomenon possibly be modeled by imagining a single gene for altruism and considering the condition under which it will spread? . . . But it is easy to show that the same analysis that applies to a single gene at a single locus also applies to genes located at many different loci.

13. Nonetheless, like all metaphors, one must be careful not to carry them too far. A literal reading of the helping-gene example would suggest a kind of genetic determinism; indeed, the word "genetic" sometimes connotes the inevitable, such as with genetic defects that lead to dreadful diseases like Huntington's chorea. No evolutionary biologist or behavioral geneticist would subscribe to such determinism. Genes code for proteins to build bodies that act and decide in the context of an environment, which, in the case of our species, nearly always includes a cultural milieu.

14. The evolutionary perspective lends insight into an economic study mentioned at the outset: the evidence of differential altruism between maternal and paternal grandmothers found in Duflo's (2003) study of South African pension reform. Related evidence in a different context was found by Sear and colleagues (2002), who examined the relationship between the availability of kin and child mortality in rural Gambia. Among grandparents, only one—again, the maternal grandmother—stood out as significant for influencing child mortality. Indeed, the availability of the maternal grandmother was found to be more important for child survival that even the child's father, despite the fact that the villages investigated were patrilocal. The loss of any kin from the father's side of the family did not matter for child mortality.

15. Further, even in the context of developing countries, there are forces arguably far more pressing than putative Trivers-Willard effects, such as the desire for old-age support (Nugent 1985) and sex differences in agricultural labor (Cain 1977). Further,

recent and controversial evidence on the incidence of hepatitis B and male-biased sex ratios (Oster 2005) suggests biological links other than, and distinct from, those Trivers and Willard propose.

16. The sequestration of women from practices like foot binding or *purdah* have been construed as attempts by males to monitor and control the sexual behavior of women (see, e.g., Hrdy 1999).

17. The *Handbook of Evolutionary Psychology*, for instance, casts paternity uncertainty as a key adaptive problem and conceptual foundation (Tooby and Cosmides 2005, 45) for understanding mating behavior (e.g., Campbell and Ellis 2005, chapter 14) and investment in children (e.g., Salmon 2005, chapter 17). In contrast, Becker's (1991) *Treatise on the Family* makes only passing reference to it (p. 48). Bergstrom (1996) refers to paternity confidence in traditional society in the context of a husband's decision to support his sister's versus his wife's children (p. 1923–24). There is a burgeoning literature on the establishment of paternity and child support in advanced economies (e.g., Argys and Peters 2001), and recent theoretical work on marriage places paternity uncertainty front-and-center in a theoretical analysis of marriage (Bethmann and Kvasnicka 2006). But references like these remain rare.

18. Euler and Weitzel's (1996) findings concerning differential solicitude reported by a sample of German respondents with four living grandparents, for example, have been construed by evolutionary psychologists as evidence for a connection between paternity uncertainty and investments in children: respondents reported higher average *gekummert* (i.e., solicitude or emotional concern) from maternal than paternal grandmothers, with paternal grandfathers scoring lowest. But the evidence fails to rule out alternative explanations based upon socioeconomic considerations.

19. The sample selection criteria for the respondent grandmothers were as follows: (1) they are grandmothers of biological grandchildren, (2) they either have grandchildren only by daughters or only by sons, and (3) they do not coreside with grandchildren.

20. Further, the NSFH is a well-established data resource with a long history of usage by sociologists, demographers, and economists.

21. The first wave of the NSFH was originally conducted for 13,017 households; nine of them were subsequently dropped for a sample of 13,008. There was rather large attrition between the first two waves (exactly 3,000 households).

22. Sometimes such descriptive analysis is mislabeled "reduced form." But table 5.1 is not the reduced form of anything, and, in particular, cannot be a tool for backing paternity uncertainty into an ever-shrinking corner, seeing how some of its regressors might themselves be affected by such uncertainty. Accordingly, I adhere to the "partial correlations" label.

23. I created these labels, where "strict" denotes choosing the highest value of the Likert scale (5) and "lenient" denotes choosing the lowest values (1–3).

24. For purposes of the estimations in table 5.1, I coded (and named) "strongly disagree" as "strict," "strongly agree" or "agree" as "lenient," and those in between ("disagree," "neither agree nor disagree") as "middling."

25. For related arguments, and similar (though more exacting) empirical evidence concerning a different biologically based theory—the Trivers-Willard hypothesis—see Freese and Powell (1999).

26. Though some biological models have been advanced to explain such sex-specific favoritism, considerably more progress has been made on understanding the economics of father-son and mother-daughter relationships within a social science perspective (notable recent work includes Lundberg and Rose 2002, 2003).

27. What's more—and by way of a type I error alert—the difference in the number of days non-coresident fathers spent with boy children who resembled them versus not (12 versus 10), depicted in the middle panel of figure 5 is on the cusp of statistical significance at conventional levels (estimated $t = 1.93$, p value = 0.055). Further, no other objective measure of attachment (propensity to marry or live together) bore a significant relationship to the father's report on child resemblance.

28. In Cox (2003), I provided an extensive review of current evidence concerning paternity uncertainty. Notwithstanding the spate of additions to this fast-paced literature since then (for a recent, extensive, and appropriately jaundiced review, see Anderson [2006]), my characterization of scientific knowledge concerning paternity uncertainty—that it is most aptly viewed as "X the unknown"—remains valid today. The subject is a minefield of sample-selection problems, human-subjects problems, urban legends, and plain old mistakes (Cox 2003). A possible silver lining, at least for learning about behavior, is that even mythology could prove empirically relevant if people act on perceptions rather than hard data. Still, the evidence strongly suggests that paternity uncertainty be conceptualized as an unobservable variable.

29. For discussions of these practices in the economics literature on family behavior, see Becker (1991, 48) and Posner (1992, 113).

30. These authors caution, for example, that the apparently favorable gender effects from Australia's comparable worth policy might actually be an artifact of missing information about trade unionism for that country.

31. For instance, examples of such studies for Malaysia and Indonesia include Banks (1976), Jones (1981), and Bowen (1995).

32. For examples of how qualitative evidence can be combined with economic reasoning and evidence, see Akerlof (1997).

33. For ethnographic evidence on American inner-city youth, for example, see Anderson (1993). Hrdy's is not the only proposed explanation for female infidelity. For a summary of alternative explanations, see Cox (2003).

REFERENCES

Akerlof, George A. 1997. "Social Distance and Social Decisions." *Econometrica* 65(5): 1005–27.

Altonji, Joseph G., Fumio Hayashi, and Laurence J. Kotlikoff. 1997. "Parental Altruism and Inter Vivos Transfers: Theory and Evidence." *Journal of Political Economy* 105(6): 1121–66.

Anderson, Elijah. 1993. "Sex Codes and Family Life among Poor Inner-City Youths." In *The Ghetto Underclass: Social Science Perspectives,* edited by William Julius Wilson (76–95). Newbury Park, CA: Sage Publications.

Anderson, Kermyt G. 2006. "How Well Does Paternity Confidence Match Actual Paternity?" *Current Anthropology* 47(3): 513–20.

Argys, Laura M., and H. Elizabeth Peters. 2001. "Interactions between Unmarried Fathers and Their Children: The Role of Paternity Establishment and Child-Support Policies." *American Economic Review* 91(2): 125–29.

Banks, David J. 1976. "Islam and Inheritance in Malaya: Culture Conflict or Islamic Revolution?" *American Ethnologist* 3(4): 573–86.

Barro, Robert J. 1974. "Are Government Bonds Net Wealth?" *Journal of Political Economy* 82(6): 1095–1117.

Becker, Gary S. 1965. "A Theory of the Allocation of Time." *Economic Journal* 75(299): 493–517.

———. 1974. "A Theory of Social Interactions." *Journal of Political Economy* 82(6): 1063–93.

———. 1991. *A Treatise on the Family.* Cambridge, MA: Harvard University Press.

Becker, Gary S., and Casey B. Mulligan. 1997. "The Endogenous Determination of Time Preference." *Quarterly Journal of Economics* 112(3): 729–58.

Behrman, Jere R. 1997. "Intrahousehold Distribution and the Family." In *Handbook of Population and Family Economics,* vol. 1A, edited by Oded Stark and Mark R. Rosenzweig (125–87). New York: Elsevier Science.

Ben-Porath, Yoram. 1973. "Labor-Force Participation Rates and the Supply of Labor." *Journal of Political Economy* 81(3): 697–704.

Bergstrom, Theodore C. 1996. "Economics in a Family Way." *Journal of Economic Literature* 34(4): 1903–34.

Bernheim, B. Douglas, Andrei Shleifer, and Lawrence H. Summers. 1985. "The Strategic Bequest Motive." *Journal of Political Economy* 93(6): 1045–76.

Bethmann, Dirk, and Michael Kvasnicka. 2006. "Uncertain Paternity, Mating Market Failure, and the Institution of Marriage." Berlin, Germany: Humboldt University.

Bianchi, Suzanne M. 2000. "Maternal Employment and Time with Children: Dramatic Change or Surprising Continuity?" *Demography* 37(4): 401–14.

Bianchi, Suzanne M., Melissa A. Milkie, Liana C. Sayer, and John P. Robinson. 2000. "Is Anyone Doing the Housework? Trends in the Gender Division of Household Labor." *Social Forces* 79(1): 191–228.

Blau, Francine D., and Lawrence M. Kahn. 1996. "Wage Structure and Gender Earnings Differentials: An International Comparison." *Economica* 63(250): S29–S62.

Bowen, John R. 1995. "The Forms Culture Takes: A State-of-the-Field Essay on the Anthropology of Southeast Asia." *Journal of Asian Studies* 54(4): 1047–78.

Cain, Mead T. 1977. "The Economic Activities of Children in a Village in Bangladesh." *Population and Development Review* 3(3): 201–27.

Campbell, Lorne, and Bruce J. Ellis. 2005. "Commitment, Love, and Mate Retention." In *The Handbook of Evolutionary Psychology,* edited by David M. Buss (419–46). Hoboken, NJ: John Wiley & Sons, Inc.

Case, Anne, I-Fen Lin, and Sara McLanahan. 2000. "How Hungry Is the Selfish Gene?" *Economic Journal* 110(466): 781–804.

Cherlin, Andrew. 1978. "Remarriage as an Incomplete Institution." *American Journal of Sociology* 84(3): 634–50.

Chiappori, Pierre-Andre. 1988. "Rational Household Labor Supply." *Econometrica* 56(1): 63–90.

———. 1992. "Collective Labor Supply and Welfare." *Journal of Political Economy* 100(3): 437–67.

Cox, Donald. 1987. "Motives for Private Income Transfers." *Journal of Political Economy* 95(3): 508–46.

———. 2003. "Private Transfers within the Family: Mothers, Fathers, Sons and Daughters." In *Death and Dollars: The Role of Gifts and Bequests in America*, edited by Alicia H. Munnell and Annika Sunden (168–97). Washington, DC: Brookings Institution Press.

———. 2007. "Biological Basics and Economics of the Family." *Journal of Economic Perspectives* 21(2): 91–108.

Cox, Donald, and Marcel Fafchamps. 2008. "Extended Family and Kinship Networks: Economic Insights and Evolutionary Directions." In *The Handbook of Development Economics*, vol. 4, edited by T. Paul Schultz and Robert Evenson. New York: Elsevier.

Cox, Donald, and George Jakubson. 1995. "The Connection between Public Transfers and Private Interfamily Transfers." *Journal of Public Economics* 57(1): 129–67.

Cox, Donald, and Mark R. Rank. 1992. "Inter-Vivos Transfers and Intergenerational Exchange." *Review of Economics and Statistics* 74(2): 305–14.

Cox, Donald, and Oded Stark. 2005. "On the Demand for Grandchildren: Tied Transfers and the Demonstration Effect." *Journal of Public Economics* 89(9–10): 1665–97.

Cox, Donald, Bruce E. Hansen, and Emmanuel Jimenez. 2004. "How Responsive Are Private Transfers to Income? Evidence from a Laissez-Faire Economy." *Journal of Public Economics* 88(9–10): 2193–2219.

Daly, Martin, and Margo Wilson. 1988. *Homicide.* New York: Aldine de Gruyter.

Dawkins, Richard. 1976. *The Selfish Gene.* Oxford: Oxford University Press.

Duflo, Esther. 2003. "Grandmothers and Granddaughters: Old Age Pension and Intrahousehold Allocation in South Africa." *World Bank Economic Review* 17(1): 1–25.

Edlund, Lena. 1999. "Son Preference, Sex Ratios, and Marriage Patterns." *Journal of Political Economy* 107(6): 1275–1304.

Euler, Harald A., and Barbara Weitzel. 1996. "Discriminative Grandparental Solicitude as Reproductive Strategy." *Human Nature* 7(1): 39–59.

Freese, Jeremy, and Brian Powell. 1999. "Sociobiology, Status, and Parental Investment in Sons and Daughters: Testing the Trivers-Willard Hypothesis." *American Journal of Sociology* 104(6): 1704–43.

Ganong, Lawrence, Marilyn Coleman, Annette Kusgen McDaniel, and Tim Killian. 1998. "Attitudes Regarding Obligations to Assist an Older Parent or Stepparent Following Later-Life Remarriage." *Journal of Marriage and the Family* 60(3): 595–610.

Glaeser, Edward L., Giacomo A. M. Ponzetto, and Jesse M. Shapiro. 2005. "Strategic Extremism: Why Republicans and Democrats Divide on Religious Values." *Quarterly Journal of Economics* 120(4): 1283–1330.

Gronau, Reuben. 1986. "Home Production—A Survey." In *Handbook of Labor Economics*, vol. 1, edited by Orley Ashenfelter and Richard Layard (273–304). New York: Elsevier Science.

Haddad, Lawrence, John Hoddinott, and Harold Alderman, eds. 1997. *Intrahousehold Resource Allocation in Developing Countries: Models, Methods, and Policy.* Baltimore: Johns Hopkins University Press.

Hagen, Edward H. 2003. "The Bargaining Model of Depression." In *Genetic and Cultural Evolution of Cooperation,* edited by Peter Hammerstein (95–124). Cambridge, MA: MIT Press.

Hamilton, William D. 1964. "The Genetical Theory of Social Behavior (I and II)." *Journal of Theoretical Biology* 7(1): 1–52.

Hawkes, Kristin, James F. O'Connell, and Nicholas G. Blurton Jones. 1997. "Hadza Women's Time Allocation, Offspring Provisioning, and the Evolution of Long Postmenopausal Life Spans." *Current Anthropology* 38(4): 551–77.

Heckman, James J. 1993. "What Has Been Learned about Labor Supply in the Past Twenty Years?" *American Economic Review* 83(2): 116–21.

Heckman, James J., and Thomas E. Macurdy. 1980. "A Life Cycle Model of Female Labor Supply." *Review of Economic Studies* 47(1): 47–74.

Hrdy, Sarah Blaffer. 1981. *The Woman That Never Evolved.* Cambridge, MA: Harvard University Press.

————. 1999. *Mother Nature: Maternal Instincts and How They Shape the Human Species.* New York: Ballantine Books.

Jones, Gavin W. 1981. "Malay Marriage and Divorce in Peninsular Malaysia: Three Decades of Change." *Population and Development Review* 7(2): 255–78.

Kaplan, Hillard. 1994. "Evolutionary and Wealth Flows Theories of Fertility: Empirical Tests and New Models." *Population and Development Review* 20(4): 753–91.

Keller, Matthew C., Randolph M. Nesse, and Sandra Hofferth. 2001. "The Trivers-Willard Hypothesis of Parental Investment: No Effect in the Contemporary United States." *Evolution and Human Behavior* 22(5): 343–60.

Lee, Ronald D. 1997. "Intergenerational Relations and the Elderly." In *Between Zeus and the Salmon: The Biodemography of Longevity,* edited by Kenneth W. Wachter and Caleb E. Finch (212–33). Washington, DC: National Academy Press.

Lewis, H. Gregg. 1968. "Participacion de la Fuerza Laboral y Teoria de las Horas de Trabajo." *Rev Facultad Ciencias Econ* (May–December 1968): 49–63.

Lundberg, Shelly, and Robert A. Pollak. 2007. "The American Family and Family Economics." *Journal of Economic Perspectives* 21(2): 3–26.

Lundberg, Shelly, and Elaina Rose. 2002. "The Effect of Sons and Daughters on Men's Labor Supply and Wages." *Review of Economics and Statistics* 84(2): 251–68.

————. 2003. "Child Gender and Transition to Marriage." *Demography* 40(2): 333–49.

Lundberg, Shelly, Robert A. Pollak, and Terrance J. Wales. 1997. "Do Husbands and Wives Pool Their Resources? Evidence from the United Kingdom Child Benefit." *Journal of Human Resources* 32(3): 463–80.

McElroy, Marjorie B., and Mary Jean Horney. 1981. "Nash-Bargained Household Decisions: Toward a Generalization of the Theory of Demand." *International Economic Review* 22(2): 333–49.

Nielsen, Francois. 1994. "Sociobiology and Sociology." *Annual Review of Sociology* 20: 267–303.

Nugent, Jeffrey B. 1985. "The Old-Age Security Motive for Fertility." *Population and Development Review* 11(1): 75–97.

Oster, Emily. 2005. "Hepatitis B and the Case of the Missing Women." *Journal of Political Economy* 113(6): 1163–1216.

Pezzin, Liliana E., and Barbara Steinberg Schone. 1999. "Parental Marital Disruption and Intergenerational Transfers: An Analysis of Lone Elderly Parents and Their Children." *Demography* 36(3): 287–97.

Posner, Richard A. 1992. *Sex and Reason.* Cambridge, MA: Harvard University Press.

Salmon, Catherine. 2005. "Parental Investment and Parent-Offspring Conflict." In *The Handbook of Evolutionary Psychology,* edited by David M. Buss (506–27). Hoboken, NJ: John Wiley & Sons, Inc.

Sear, Rebecca, Fiona Steele, Ian A. McGregor, and Ruth Mace. 2002. "The Effects of Kin on Child Mortality in Rural Gambia." *Demography* 39(1): 43–63.

Sherman, Paul W. 1981. "Kinship, Demography, and Belding's Ground Squirrel Nepotism." *Ecology and Sociobiology* 8(2): 251–9.

Silverstein, Merril, Tonya M. Parrott, and Vern L. Bengtson. 1995. "Factors That Predispose Middle-Aged Sons and Daughters to Provide Social Support to Older Parents." *Journal of Marriage and the Family* 57(2): 465–75.

Siow, Aloysius. 1998. "Differential Fecundity, Markets, and Gender Roles." *Journal of Political Economy* 106(2): 334–54.

Strauss, John, and Duncan Thomas. 1995. "Human Resources: Empirical Modeling of Household and Family Decisions." In *Handbook of Development Economics,* vol. 3A, edited by Jere Behrman and T. N. Srinivasan (1883–2023). Amsterdam: North Holland.

Thomas, Duncan. 1994. "Like Father, Like Son; Like Mother, Like Daughter: Parental Resources and Child Height." *Journal of Human Resources* 29(4): 950–88.

Tooby, John, and Leda Cosmides. 2005. "Conceptual Foundations of Evolutionary Psychology." In *The Handbook of Evolutionary Psychology,* edited by David M. Buss (5–67). Hoboken, NJ: John Wiley & Sons, Inc.

Trivers, Robert L. 1972. "Parental Investment and Sexual Selection." In *Sexual Selection and the Descent of Man: 1871–1971,* edited by Bernard Campbell (136–79). Chicago: Aldine.

————. 1985. *Social Evolution.* Reading, MA: The Benjamin/Cummings Publishing Company, Inc.

Trivers, Robert L., and Dan E. Willard. 1973. "Natural Selection of Parental Ability to Vary the Sex Ratio of Offspring." *Science* 179(4068): 90–92.

Willis, Robert. 1999. "A Theory of Out-of-Wedlock Childbearing." *Journal of Political Economy* 107(6, Part 2): S33–S64.

6

Do Bioevolutionary Forces Shape Intergenerational Transfers?
Detecting Evidence in Contemporary Survey Data

Merril Silverstein

P hylogenic theories such as those under the rubric of evolutionary biology give us much to consider for better understanding social patterns in the here and now. Donald Cox, in chapter 5, carves out intellectual space for bioevolutionary theories and offers a set of principles for explaining empirical regularities in intergenerational transfers that lay outside the theoretical scope of neoclassical economics, a field that tends to be neutral toward the intrinsic characteristics of the parties to a transfer. Standard economic theories that rely purely on the operational premise that intergenerational transactions are governed by market-like calculations have little to say about the role of demographic characteristics per se.

Despite evidence that reciprocity at least partially guides intergenerational transfers, the metaphor of the marketplace only goes so far toward explaining behavior in the family, a human grouping that has its very basis in genotypic resemblance. Compared to sociology, for instance, economics is agnostic about structural aspects of transfers, particularly those rooted in fundamental characteristics of sex and age, and the complex biological and cultural forces from which these structures have evolved and become reified. Sociologists have traditionally viewed social behaviors associated with biological endowments, particularly those of sex, as ascribed and made fully malleable by the social environment. Where economics may pay little attention to biological facts in and of themselves, sociology has traditionally eschewed biology, only recently considering its role in producing patterned social behavior.

Any theory linking social behavior and social structures to the selective pressures of bioevolution—the unintentional positive selection of adaptive genes—bears a high burden of proof. Competing theories that rely on more proximate causal factors can be tested in real time as social conditions change. By contrast, bioevolutionary explanations must rely on backward induction because only the end product of the process is observed. Underlying causes are fixed in history, presenting vexing epistemological questions about this metatheory. Is bioevolutionary theory falsifiable? Does it provide added value beyond more proximate explanations? Does reliance on teleological inference—where an effect is identified by its consequence—present risks for tautological, self-fulfilling conclusions?

Cox ably states the promise and pitfalls of bioevolutionary theory for social science inquiry; they will not be reviewed here. I tend to agree with his basic assessment and will suggest conditions under which bioevolutionary inferences can best provide leverage for explaining social patterns in transfer behavior. These conditions are premised on carefully specifying biological and social theories and their intersection, crafting well-articulated hypotheses that outline where the balance stands between biological and social/cultural influences, and having available data that are up to the task of detecting these influences and controlling for alternative explanations. At best, evidence for bioevolution in survey data will be indirect and speculative. With this modest goal, I suggest that bioevolutionary processes (1) are (sometimes) sufficient but (usually) not necessary to explain how transfer behaviors vary by basic biologically determined categories such as sex and age (and their social complements of gender and life-stage, respectively), (2) do a better job at explaining downstream than upstream transfers, (3) need to be considered within a life-span context where senders of transfers are also (or become) receivers, (4) may be obscured by institutional and cultural factors that need to be taken into account for biological factors to become observable.

A fundamental issue for researchers is that evolutionary outcomes are historical vestiges, shrouded by more proximate social and economic forces that have relegated human "instinct" to the background of human affairs—perhaps present but not particularly relevant. The incentives and constraints built into social institutions may trump biological characteristics in determining social behavior. Economic and ideological change, for instance, altered longstanding gender patterns in labor market participation in as little as one generation. Further, proximate causes of behavior are more open to empirical testing than more distal ones. Where proximate causes are dynamic and can be directly linked to observable outcomes, distal causes are fixed and only their faded outcomes are observable.

Biological explanations for social patterns rely on "essential" properties of biological life, two of the most basic being that (1) woman bear children and men do not and (2) life is finite. Although most examples in the social sciences focus on sex, some social-behavioral theories rely on the finiteness of life as a mechanism guiding social behavior. For instance, socioemotional selectivity theory (Carstensen, Fung, and Charles 2003) maintains that as we age, social action from midlife onward is increasingly shaped by the time we have left to live rather than the time we have lived. Therefore, humans increasingly choose to associate with others who provide them with the greatest emotional gratification as they age—a phenomenon observed with older adults as well as those with terminal diseases. From another vantage point, Tornstam's (2005) theory of gerotranscendence hypothesizes that a successful old age is one in which earthly possessions are divested for the benefit of younger generations. Both theories emphasize the strengthening of altruistic tendencies with approaching mortality.

Opportunities to view the evolutionary basis of social behavior are fewer in the developed world than they are in the less developed world. The welfare state has to some extent leveled the playing field between age groups through public programs that transfer large sums of money from younger to older generations, creating distortions in the net balance of intergenerational transfers that under evolutionary principles should favor the young (Lee 2000). Our best understanding of intergenerational transfers in their "pristine" state comes from studies of premodern, isolated societies that provide views of human nature unspoiled by the contrivances of modern society. These studies show that intergenerational resources tend to flow from older to younger individuals, an adaptive pattern that persists until quite late in the lives of those in older generation (Hill and Kaplan 1999).

Because evolutionary theory rests on the assumption that adaptive traits are transmissible, the residue of bioevolutionary processes may reside in contemporary behaviors, even if social and cultural forces obscure their detection. Below I present three disparate examples that use quantitative survey data to identify age and gender patterns of intergenerational transfers that are consistent with predictions based on bioevolutionary selection.

Simulating Bioevolutionary Outcomes Using Modern Equivalents

Contemporary studies documenting the extraordinary efforts of grandparents as caregivers for their grandchildren are consistent with theories from evolutionary biology positing that human longevity resulted from the favorable selection of able and altruistic grandparents who could better ensure the survival of their grandchildren (Hawkes et al. 1998). Indeed, grandparents who raise their grandchildren in response to parental crises and incapacities often do so at great cost to their material, physical, and psychological well-being (Minkler et al. 2000). The importance of downward transfers from grandparents has also been recognized under more ordinary circumstances, particularly in their provision of childcare to working parents (Cardia and Ng 2003). Direct transfers of money from grandparents to their grandchildren are not uncommon. A study of three-generation families in France found that one-third of grandparents provided a financial gift to at least one adult grandchild (Attias-Donfut 2003).

Bioevolutionary theories provide a lens through which we can examine the selflessness that grandparents demonstrate toward their grandchildren. Based on Hamilton's rule that the survival of genes, not people, drives behavior (Hamilton 1964), it can be inferred that grandparents are genetically predisposed to promote the quality and life-chances of their grandchildren as enabled by positively selected traits of altruism and longevity—a phenomenon known as the "grandmother effect" (Hawkes 2003). In evolutionary terms, grandmothers equipped with those two traits improved the likelihood that their grandchildren would survive to puberty (particularly in the event of maternal death) and, in the process, ensured the survival of their genes in subsequent generations.

One strategy for testing the grandmother effect with contemporary data is to rely on a modern parallel to the evolutionary story where the vulnerability of children caused by parental absence is assuaged by the resources of grandparents. Therefore, I examine how grandparents serve as second lines of defense to protect the well-being of grandchildren whose developmental success may be threatened by emergent fissures and fractures in the family. The structure of the family raising a child defines a host of social, economic, and psychological factors important for childrearing (Haurin 1992). Children in single-parent families are subject to less consistent parenting styles and less social control and supervision than are children in two-parent families (Astone and McLanahan 1991). Parental absence has serious adverse consequences for children, as a result of decreased parental monitoring, lack of parental role models, and fewer financial resources (Hetherington, Bridges, and Insabella 1998). Time and economic constraints faced by the custodial parent (typically the mother) explain the heightened risk of maladjustment among children in single-parent families (Amato 1994). In the current analysis, being raised in a single-parent or disrupted household is used to represent a family deficit that grandparents may move to fill.

Since grandparents commonly increase their involvement with grandchildren after marital disruption, with grandmothers in particular providing babysitting and emotional support (Gladstone 1988), the contributions of grandparents are captured by their role as confidants to their grandchildren. The benefit to grandchildren of confiding in grandparents is operationalized by the construct of self-esteem. Self-esteem in late childhood and adolescence tends to be positively correlated with aspirations, socioeconomic achievement, and psychological adjustment in adulthood—key markers of success in contemporary society.

Data used to examine social processes in grandparent-grandchild relations are from the National Survey of Families and Households (NSFH) (see Sweet, Bumpass, and Call 1988 for design and interview details). The NSFH began in 1987 as a nationally representative survey of 13,007 individuals. From 1992–94, the NSFH surveyed one child of the original respondents between the ages of 10 and 17 ($n = 1,324$). These children were asked questions about their relationships with up to four surviving grandparents. More than 95 percent of the children had at least one grandparent alive.

We considered three types of household structures within which children were mostly raised: intact two-parent household, stepparent household, and single-parent household. Children were asked how likely they would be to talk to one of their grandparents if they had a major decision to make or felt depressed or unhappy. Responses ranged on a five-point scale from "definitely wouldn't" to "definitely would." Children were also asked how close they felt to each of their grandparents on a scale ranging from 0 to 10, where 0 = "not at all close" and 10 = "extremely close." (This variable is the only one specifically about maternal and paternal grandmothers and grandfathers.) Three items from the Rosenberg Self-esteem Scale (Rosenberg 1979) measured self-esteem. Children were asked to rate their agreement with the following statements: "I am a person of worth";

"I do things as well as others"; "I am satisfied with myself." Responses ranged on a five-point scale from "strongly disagree" to "strongly agree."

We first examined emotional closeness to grandparents by the lineage/gender of the grandparent and whether grandchildren were from an intact or disrupted household (children from single-parent and step-parent households were combined due to sample size restrictions.) Results in figure 6.1 show that the percentage of relationships deemed extremely close was highest overall for maternal grandmothers, an expected result given the strong matrilineal tilt in American families. This result is also consistent with bioevolutionary theory based on the principle of paternity certainty. Furthermore, grandchildren from disrupted families are closer to their grandparents than those from intact families, and this gap is greatest with respect to maternal grandmothers. This pattern supports the hypothesis that maternal grandmothers are particularly salient for children facing adverse risks associated with parental absence.

Next, we examined the benefits to self-esteem that grandparents confer on their grandchildren by being available as confidants to them. Ben-

Figure 6.1. Percent of Grandchildren Who Feel Extremely Close to Grandparents, by Lineage and Gender of Grandparent and Household Structure of Grandchild ($N = 1,324$)

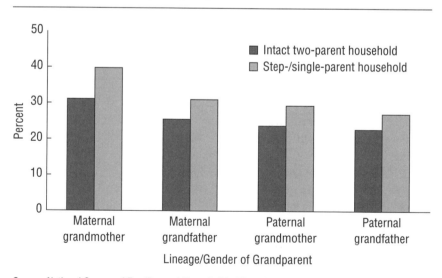

Source: National Survey of Families and Households, Wave 2 (see Ruiz and Silverstein [2007] for details).

efits were compared among grandchildren raised in intact, step, and single-parent households. We used structural equation modeling to ascertain the strength of the relationship between grandchildren's likelihood of confiding in grandparents and their self-esteem, controlling for grandchildren's age, race/ethnicity, and gender, their emotional closeness and amount of contact with grandparents, and their parents' household income and martial status. We note that the propensity to confide in grandparents is positively associated with the self-esteem of grandchildren, whereas neither emotional closeness nor in-person contact with maternal or paternal grandparents exert a significant influence (not shown). However, when the influence of confiding in grandparents on self-esteem is examined by the household structure of grandchildren, we found that the benefit was strongest among those who were raised in single-parent households (figure 6.2). These findings mirror a bioevolutionary process whereby grandparents enhance the successful development of grandchildren confronting the challenges presented by parental absence.

Figure 6.2. Standardized Coefficients of Self-Esteem Regressed on Confiding in Grandparents by Household Structure of Grandchild (*N* = 1,324)

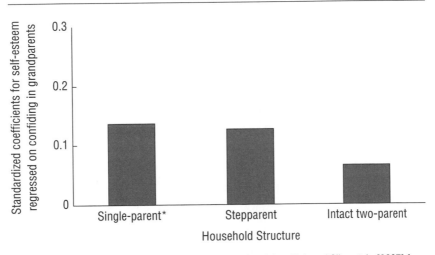

Source: National Survey of Families and Households, Wave 2 (see Ruiz and Silverstein [2007] for details).

*Signifies coefficient is statistically different from coefficient for children in intact two-parent households, *p* < .05.

Accounting for Bioevolution in the Presence of Oppositional Forces

Evolutionary selection is predicated on the principle that human action is directed toward maximizing the "inclusive fitness" of those whose genes one most shares. In chapter 5, Cox posits that since grandmothers are more certain that grandchildren borne by daughters are biological relatives compared to grandchildren sired by sons, maternal grandmothers will pay more attention to their grandchildren than will paternal grandmothers. He finds supporting evidence from U.S. national data, confirming the paternity-certainty hypothesis.

However, the theory of bioevolution carries with it the supposition of universality and as such offers many opportunities to be falsified. If one were to test the very same hypothesis of maternal advantage within a paternalistic society such as China, it would likely receive little affirmation. Predicting that grandparents in China would invest more in their maternal grandchildren would be absurd in a culture known for its strong preference for sons and their families. Theories of human capital would strongly predict a paternal tilt to investing in children where the farm labor of sons is important to the family economy. Further, rampant rural-to-urban migration of the working-age sons in China has left many young children left behind in rural villages to be cared for by their paternal grandparents. Investing in the families of migrant sons provides grandparents with financial compensation in the form of remittances, further reinforcing their willingness to care for paternal grandchildren (Silverstein, Cong, and Li 2006).

Suppose that paternal-certainty is one of several forces guiding grandparents' choices over which grandchildren to invest time and economic resources. If cultural and economic forces that favor investing in sons' families are sufficiently strong, then preferences for investing in daughters' families—perhaps present as predispositions—may be suppressed by more immediate and more practical considerations. Social scientists can address the problem by building models that include latent evolutionary triggers and their proximate suppressors.

If impulses to care for daughters' children have been countered by cultural precepts and economic imperatives that favor investing in sons, these impulses may still be detectable under specific conditions that render them relevant. This line of reasoning leads to intriguing speculations. Could filial piety required of sons be the means by which daughters-in-law are better monitored by their parents-in-law? Could the cultural demand that sons live near or with their parents be an evolutionary adaptation for assuaging doubt about the paternity of paternal grandchildren by keeping daughters-in-law close at hand?

Assume that frequency of contact with children is a reasonable indicator of the ability of parents to monitor their daughters-in-law. One might then expect that among sons and daughters seen frequently, grandparents would choose to provide more child care to their paternal grandchildren, but among sons and daughters seen infrequently, grandparents would choose to provide more child care to their maternal grandchildren. That is, a maternal tilt should emerge when infrequent monitoring of daughters-in-law increases doubt about the paternity of son's children, and a paternal tilt when frequent monitoring of daughters-in-law assuages that doubt.

The above proposition is tested with data from the Longitudinal Study of the Elderly in Anhui Province, China, a joint project of Xi'an Jiaotong University, China and the University of Southern California, Los Angeles. The study consists of a stratified random sample of 1,698 adults age 60 and over living in rural townships within the city of Chaohu in 2001. There are 1,421 grandparents in the sample with at least one grandchild 16 years older or younger. These grandparents provide an analytic sample of 4,289 parent-adult child dyads in which the adult child was the parent of at least one child age 16 or younger.

The study measured the contribution of grandparents to the care of their grandchildren as the frequency with which they had provided child care for the offspring of each adult child during the past year. Grandchildren were treated in family sets, grouped by the adult child who parented them. Thus, there is a single value of care for each set of grandchildren. This variable ranged from 0 to 6 (0 = "not at all," 1 = "seldom," 2 = "once per month," 3 = "several times per month," 4 = "at least once per week," 5 = "every day, but not for the entire day," and 6 = "every day, for the entire day"). Frequency of in-person contact with each adult child ranged from 0 to 6 (0 = "none," 1 = "several times per year," 2 = "once per month," 3 = "several times per month," 4 = "at least once per week," 5 = "several times per week," and 6 = "every day").

Figure 6.3 shows the total amount of grandchild care provided by grandparents to the families of their sons and daughters. As expected, such care is greater to the families of sons than to the families of daughters. Since in this rural, agricultural region of China, sons and daughters-

Figure 6.3. Average Care for Paternal and Maternal Grandchildren among Grandparents in Rural China ($N_{sets\ of\ grandchildren} = 4{,}287$; $N_{grandparents} = 1{,}411$)

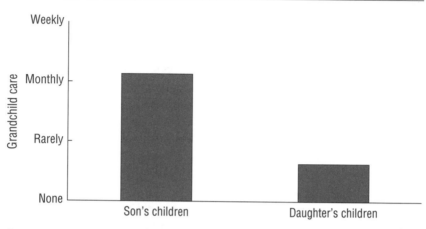

Source: Longitudinal Study of Older People in Anhui Province, China (see Silverstein, Cong, and Li [2006] for details).

in-law bear the primary responsibility for providing financial and instrumental support to older parents, investing in the families of sons would seem prudent for the practical benefits that sons and their wives provide.

Next we estimate how care for maternal and paternal grandchildren is influenced by the amount of contact grandparents have with their adult sons and daughters. Using fixed effects multiple regression, we found a statistically significant interaction between contact with adult children and their gender, after controlling for other characteristics of parent-adult child relationships (emotional closeness, geographic distance, money and instrumental support received), and characteristics of adult children (age, education). Figure 6.4 describes predicted values from this analysis, showing that the amount of care grandparents devote to their grandchildren is more sensitive to the amount of contact they have with their adult sons than with the amount of contact they have with their adult daughters. At the lowest amounts of contact, care is greater for the children of daughters than for the children of sons, but at the highest amounts of contact, the trend is reversed. This pattern is consistent with the paternity uncertainty hypothesis that grandparents' paternity doubts about the offspring of infrequently seen sons are stronger than the paternity doubts about the offspring of infrequently seen daughters. Thus, when monitoring the

Figure 6.4. Predicted Care for Paternal and Maternal Grandchildren among Grandparents in Rural China by Level of Contact with Adult Children ($N_{grandparents} = 1,411$; $N_{sets\ of\ grandchildren} = 4,287$)

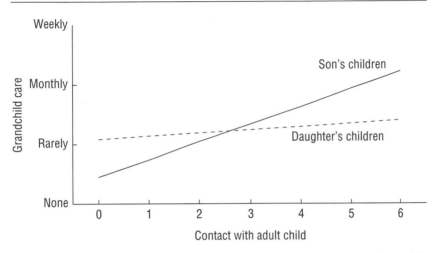

Source: Longitudinal Study of Older People in Anhui Province, China (see Silverstein, Cong, and Li [2006] for details).

Note: For contact with adult child, 0 = "none," 1 = "several times per year," 2 = "once per month," 3 = "several times per month," 4 = "at least once per week," 5 = "several times per week," and 6 = "every day." Predicted values are adjusted for the adult child's age and education level, geographic distance from the child, emotional closeness to the child, and receipt of household, personal, and monetary assistance from the child.

actions of children is most difficult, grandparents prefer to invest in the children of their daughters whose genetic relatedness to them can be virtually guaranteed. When monitoring the actions of children is easiest, grandparents are comfortable devoting resources to the children of their sons in keeping with tradition and patrilineal lines of succession.

Linking Bioevolutionary Processes across Life Forms

Why adult children provide transfers of time and money to their elderly parents would seem to have little basis in bioevolution because reproductive advantages are ostensibly not at issue as they for why parents' provide similar transfers to their children. Evolutionary principles would suggest that altruistic motivations to provide resources to older parents would be suppressed if those resources were diverted from children and came at the expense of their grandchildren's well-being.

Altruism of adult children is typically represented the drive to care for aging parents in need. Altruistic upstream transfers are considered a virtue in most societies, particularly in less developed nations. However, from a bioevolutionary perspective unconditional altruism would be selected against because it would detract from the fitness of younger generations. This contradiction leads to questions about the boundaries of altruism; children should provide altruistically to their aging parents, but not to the point of impoverishing their own families. The condition of scarcity casts this dilemma into sharp relief. Research by Aboderin (2004) in Ghana, a society suffering under chronic abject poverty, shows that older parents are ambivalent about receiving support from their adult children who would have to divert meager resources away from their dependent children. Even in developed nations, the impulse to save adult children the time and labor costs of elder care may still be rooted in the altruistic impulse of older adults not to impair the potential of their adult children to be effective providers to their families. Older parents manifest their altruism actively by providing transfers to their children, but also passively by minimizing demands placed on their adult children. Thus, altruism of adult children is not unconditional and may be tempered by the reluctance of older parents draw on their children's resources. In addition, the active altruism of adult children may evolve into passive altruism as they age and transition into being the older generation.

In general terms, the altruism-selection model is based on the notion that life forms that act solely on the basis of individual self-interest will not achieve optimal species survival if such actions threaten the protection and sustenance of off-spring (Wilson and Sober 1994). Therefore, altruism of older organisms toward younger organisms is a positively selected trait enhancing survival of the group, a trait seen in lower life forms under experimental conditions. In yeast cultures, accelerated mortality of older organisms may be an altruistic strategy to avoid competing with younger, better-adapted organisms for scarce resources (Longo, Mitteldorf, and Skulachev 2005). Studies of mortality in yeast cells show that under conditions of scarcity 90–99 percent of the population dies and a small mutant subpopulation survives benefits by having less competition for available nutrition using the nutrients released by dead cells to grow more efficiently (Fabrizio et al. 2003). The role of similar pathways in the regulation of longevity in organisms ranging from yeast to mice raises the possibility that mammals may also undergo programmed aging as a form of altruistic self-sacrifice for the betterment of genetically related youth.

When extrapolating the altruism-selection model from simple organisms to human populations, many critical differences must be considered. How might *altruistic self-sacrifice* look in older human populations? In contemporary society, we must take altruistic suicide as a metaphor; offspring don't consume their parents as do yeast, but they consume parental resources. If devotion of emotional, financial, and time resources to older parents are sufficiently high to threaten the well-being of children and dependent grandchildren, the outcome predicted by evolutionary biology clearly favors ensuring the fitness of younger generations. Under such conditions, older individuals may resist well-intentioned upstream transfers because more resources would be conserved by their adult children.

Examining upstream intergenerational altruism as a bioevolutionary process requires creative approaches, particularly because public provisions and private markets have rendered family transfers to the elderly less relevant today than in the past, and individuals are not as frequently called upon to prioritize between dependent children and dependent older parents. Therefore, we examine the issue hypothetically by focusing on public attitudes toward the responsibility of adult children as a barometer of altruism toward aging parents.

The following section tests the *altruism-with-aging* hypothesis by examining attitudes toward a hypothetical vignette that asks how much responsibility adult children with children of their own should have for their aging parents. These attitudes denote internalized social norms or expectations regarding upstream intergenerational transfers. Of particular interest is how these expectations change as people grow older and move into the oldest position in their family's lineage (for details, see Gans and Silverstein 2006). As people age and become members of the oldest generation, strengthening expectations for upstream transfers from children would signal self-interested motivations because older parents are beneficiaries in the presented scenario; weakening expectations for upstream transfers from children would signal altruistic motivations as a reluctance to draw on children's resources.

Data for this test derived from the University of Southern California Longitudinal Study of Generations (LSOG), which began in 1971 as a mailed survey of 2,044 respondents from 328 three-generation families. The sample, ranging in age from 16 to 91, reflected a diversity of social class backgrounds but it under-represented minorities. The subsample for this analysis comprised 1,627 respondents who participated in at least one of the four waves (1985, 1994, 1997, and 2000) in which the measure of interest, filial expectations, was included in the survey. The number of observations used in the analysis totaled 4,527.

Expectations of filial responsibility for aging parents was measured with the following question: "Regardless of the sacrifices involved, how much responsibility should adult children with families of their own have (1) To provide companionship or spend time with elderly parents who are in need? (2) To help with household chores and repairs and/or to provide transportation for elderly parents who are in need? (3) To listen to the problems and concerns of elderly parents and to provide advice and guidance? (4) To provide for personal and health care needs of the elderly parent? (5) To provide financial support and/or assist in financial and legal affairs of elderly parents who are in need? (6) To provide housing for the elderly parents who are in need?" For each item the respondent assigned responsibility on a five-point Likert scale ranging from "none" to "total." Reliability coefficients were acceptably high in each year (none lower than 0.88). Item responses were summed to create additive scales with a potential range of 0 (no responsibility) to 24 (total responsibility).

Growth curves are estimated with Hierarchical Linear Modeling (Raudenbush and Bryk 2002) with time-varying covariates of age (linear and quadratic), generational succession (the first year that respondents had no parents still alive), and historical effects (1980s vs. 1990s). Estimates are adjusted for gender, education, income, martial status, and generational membership. The results are shown as a schedule of change based on model estimates for aging, parental death, and period of measurement, all of which are statistically significant (figure 6.5). This figure shows that the strength with which respondents believe that adult children with families of their own should support elderly parents weakens at an accelerating rate from mid-life to old age. In addition, generational succession—as marked by the death of both parents and promotion to the oldest generation—significantly weakens expectations for support from adult children. That is, as people grow older and reach the pinnacle of their lineage they are less likely to favor drawing on the resources of adult children for old age support. One interpretation of this growing altruism toward the younger generation is that generational succession and approaching mortality signal a reappraisal of preferences for upward transfers, with individuals now evaluating themselves as possible (or actual) recipients rather than as possible (or actual) providers.

Figure 6.5. Predicted Level of Responsibility for Elderly Parents Measured between 1971 and 2000 by Age, Generational Succession, and Historical Period ($N = 1,627$)

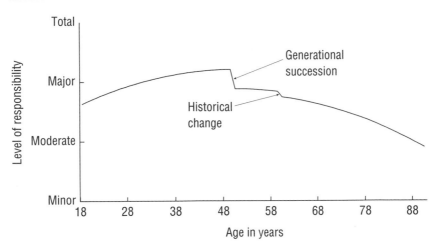

Source: Longitudinal Study of Generations, Waves 1–7 (see Gans and Silverstein [2006] for details).

Note: Generational succession occurs when both parents have died. Historical change refers to the transition from the 1980s to the 1990s. Figure shows curve for hypothetical adult child who loses second parent at age 50 and who passes from the 1980s into the 1990s at age 60.

In general, these results are consistent with research on unicellular life forms showing that older organisms conserve their consumption so as not to deprive younger organisms of resources needed to thrive and reproduce. That comparable conclusions were reached for the least developed and most developed life forms suggests that fundamental evolutionary forces may be at work.

Conclusion

The purpose of this chapter was to examine strategies by which bioevolutionary explanations of intergenerational transfers can be tested with contemporary social survey data. I have provided three empirical examples that demonstrate patterns consistent with bioevolutionary processes, but conclusions must remain tentative. The challenges of testing bioevolutionary theory with survey data are many because variables that control for competing hypotheses may not be available and corroboration of the theory is necessarily indirect. However, these challenges should not dissuade us. Empirical tests of hypotheses deduced from bioevolutionary theory—not unlike those from other grand theories in the physical and social sciences—provide the building blocks of proof even as empirical anomalies remain.

The very ambition of bioevolutionary theory and its retrospective, teleological orientation require creative approaches. I have suggested several approaches that use existing data to examine modern analogs of processes that predate modernity, and simulations that can pinpoint evolutionary factors by statistically adjusting for confounding economic and sociocultural factors. Having modest hope that universals in human behavior will be found, I offer the following empirical strategies that may hold promise for researchers in this area.

(1) *Residualist modeling:* Control for as many relevant confounds as possible, and if biological differences remain, attribute them to evolutionary selection. Good examples are studies that examine differences between biological and stepchildren in the transfers they provide to and receive from parents. In these models the choice of control variables is critical for discounting alternative social and cultural explanations.

(2) *Evolutionary-environment interactions:* Search for evidence in social ecologies, economic systems, and ethnic/national cultures where it can be predicted that the effects of bioevolution on intergenerational transfers will be particularly transparent. For example, in poor nations without public transfer programs, decisions about allocating resources to different generations rely purely on an intra-familial calculus.

(3) *Attitudes vs. behavior:* Under the most modern conditions, bioevolution may be manifest more strongly in attitudes than in behaviors. For example, nations with generous public transfer programs blunt the influence of bioevolution on transfer behaviors within the family. In those cases, responses to vignettes that present hypothetical scenarios can be used to ascertain attitudes about transfer dilemmas that may or may not be personally relevant.

(4) *Nonhuman life forms:* If social behavior in humans has an evolutionary basis, then parallels should exist across disparate species. Research identifying adaptive traits in simple life forms that are common to those found in humans provide the strongest evidence of a bioevolutionary basis for intergenerational transfers.

NOTE

This research was supported by grants from the National Institute of Aging (R01-AG07977), the National Institute of Child Health and Human Development (R01-HD042696), and the Fogarty International Center (R03-TW01060). The author would like to thank Daphna Gans, Zhen Cong, Stephen Conroy, Valter Longo, and Sarah Ruiz for their participation in this program of research.

REFERENCES

Aboderin, Isabella. 2004. "Decline in Material Family Support for Older People in Urban Ghana, Africa: Understanding Processes and Causes of Change." *Journals of Gerontology: Series-B: Psychological Sciences and Social Sciences* 59B(3): S128–S137.

Amato, Paul. R. 1994. "Father-Child Relations, Mother-Child Relations, and Offspring Psychological Well-Being in Early Adulthood." *Journal of Marriage and the Family* 56:1031–42.

Astone, Nan M., and Sara S. McLanahan. 1991. "Family Structure, Parental Practices, and High School Completion." *American Sociological Review* 56:309–20.

Attias-Donfut, Claudine. 2003. "Family Transfers and Cultural Transmissions between Three Generations in France." In *Global Aging and Challenges to Families,* edited by Vern L. Bengtson and Ariela Lowenstein (214–52). Hawthorne, NY: Aldine de Gruyter.

Cardia, Emanuela, and Serena Ng. 2003. "Intergenerational Time Transfers and Childcare." *Review of Economic Dynamics* 6(2): 431–54.

Carstensen, Laura L., Helene L. Fung, and Susan T. Charles. 2003. "Socioemotional Selectivity Theory and Emotion Regulation in the Second Half of Life." *Motivation and Emotion* 27:103–23.

Fabrizio, Paola, L. Liou, Vanessa N. Moy, Alberto Diaspro, Joan S. Valentine, Edith B. Gralla, and Valter D. Longo. 2003. "SOD2 Functions Downstream of Sch9 to Extend Longevity in Yeast." *Genetics* 163:35–46.

Gans, Daphna, and Merril Silverstein. 2006. "Norms of Filial Responsibility for Aging Parents across Time and Generations." *Journal of Marriage and the Family* 68:961–76.

Gladstone, James W. 1988. "Perceived Changes in Grandmother-Grandchild Relations Following a Child's Separation or Divorce." *Gerontologist* 28:66–72.

Hamilton, William D. 1964. "The Genetical Theory of Social Behavior." *Journal of Theoretical Biology* 7(1): 1–52.

Haurin, R. Jean. 1992. "Patterns of Childhood Residence and the Relationship to Young Adult Outcomes." *Journal of Marriage and Family* 54(4): 846–60.

Hawkes, Kristen. 2003. "Grandmothers and the Evolution of Human Longevity." *American Journal of Human Biology* 15:380–400.

Hawkes, Kristen, James F. O'Connell, Nicholas G. Blurton Jones, Helen P. Alvarez, and Eric L. Charnov. 1998. "Grandmothering, Menopause, and the Evolution of Human Life Histories." *Proceedings of the National Academy of Sciences* 95:1336–39.

Hetherington, E. Mavis, Margaret Bridges, and Glendessa M. Insabella. 1998. "What Matters? What Does Not? Five Perspectives on the Association between Marital Transitions and Children's Adjustment." *American Psychologist* 53:167–84.

Hill, Kim, and Hillard Kaplan. 1999. "Life History Traits in Humans: Theory and Empirical Studies." *Annual Review of Anthropology* 28:397–430.

Lee, Ronald D. 2000. "Intergenerational Transfers and the Economic Life Cycle: A Cross-Cultural Perspective." In *Sharing the Wealth: Demographic Change and Economic Transfers Between Generations,* edited by Andrew Mason and Georges Tapinos (17–56). Oxford, England: Oxford University Press.

Longo, Valter D., Joshua Mitteldorf, and Vladmir P. Skulachev. 2005. "Opinion: Programmed and Altruistic Ageing." *Nature Reviews Genetics* 6(11): 866–72.

Minkler, Meredith, Esme Fuller-Thomson, Doriane Miller, and Diane Driver. 2000. "Grandparent Caregiving and Depression." In *Grandparents Raising Grandchildren: Theoretical, Empirical, and Clinical Perspectives,* edited by Bert Hayslip Jr. and Robin S. Goldberg-Glen (207–20). New York: Springer.

Raudenbush, Stephen W., and Anthony S. Bryk. 2002. *Hierarchical Linear Models: Applications and Data Analysis Methods,* 2nd ed. Thousand Oaks, CA: Sage Publications.

Rosenberg, Morris. 1979. *Conceiving the Self.* New York: Basic Books.

Ruiz, Sarah, and Merril Silverstein. 2007. "Relationships with Grandparents and the Emotional Well-Being of Late Adolescent and Young Adult Grandchildren." *Journal of Social Issues* 63:793–808.

Silverstein, Merril, Zhen Cong, and Shuzhuo Li. 2006. "Intergenerational Transfers and Living Arrangements of Older People in Rural China: Consequences for Psychological Well-Being." *Journal of Gerontology: Social Sciences* 61:S256–66.

Sweet, James A., Larry L. Bumpass, and Vaughn Call. 1988. "The Design and Content of the National Survey of Families and Households." Working Paper NSFH-1. Madison: University of Wisconsin, Center for Demography and Ecology.

Tornstam, Lars. 2005. *Gerotranscendence: A Developmental Theory of Positive Aging.* New York: Springer Publishing Company.

Wilson, David S., and Elliott Sober. 1994. "Reintroducing Group Selection to the Human Behavioral Sciences." *The Behavioral and Brain Sciences* 17:585–654.

7

The Problem of Predictive Promiscuity in Deductive Applications of Evolutionary Reasoning to Intergenerational Transfers

Three Cautionary Tales

Jeremy Freese

Cox (chapter 5) proposes that evolutionary biological theory can considerably enhance the economic analyses of resource transfers within families to generate expectations specific to relevant demographic categorizations of family members. Whereas wholly abstract economic theorizing can lead to surprising, productive insights about actors characterized merely as "person 1" and "person 2,"[1] evolutionary biology offers the possibility of furthering understanding by making specific use of information that person 1 and person 2 are mother and father, son and daughter, biological child and stepchild, or even paternal grandmother and maternal grandmother. Evolutionary biological theory and economic theory have historically drawn from one another in the development of theoretical tools, as the enterprises share considerable abstract affinities because of their common preoccupation with the logic of optimization (see, e.g., Gintis 2000). Moreover, family life is one of the areas in which the potential contributions of an evolutionary perspective has seemed strongest, working from the premise that the affective bonds of kin are rooted in genetically based propensities that evolved by kin selection. In this light, one might wonder why utilization of substantive propositions from evolutionary biology in studying the economics of family life has been apparently so infrequent that Cox's essay is framed in nearly *terra incognita* terms.

In a previous essay, Cox (2003) provides some reasoning for why the relevant economic theorizing previously might have not been ready for useful incorporation of "biological basics" but is now. This contention may well be true for economics and its applications to the family. However, if one were to poll members of the Human Behavior and Evolution Society about why evolutionary theory is not more widely used in the social sciences, my wager is that most would cite the politics and politicization of academia. Many in my own field, sociology, define it less by the questions it asks and more by the content of its answers; although the boundaries of admissibly "sociological" explanations vary considerably, those that give substantial place to biology are outside sociology (Freese, Li, and Wade 2003). Sociology and biology are perceived to be engaged in an interminable zero-sum battle, in which incorporations of the latter diminish the relevance of the former, and thus many think work with "biological" explanations should proceed only with reluctance, as a matter of epistemological last resort (if even then; see Duster 2006). Worries about what those with malevolent politics might do with work that endorses the importance of "biology" has only contributed to the idea that, *almost as a matter of professional identity,* impartiality should be abandoned and alternative explanations should be given every advantage.[2] Fortunately for those who regard such sentiments as inconsistent with scientific ideals, a variety of external forces continue to erode the credibility of ignoring biology as a matter of orthodoxy, and so the intellectual environment for serious, authentic contemplation of the potential contributions of evolutionary biological reasoning in the social sciences continues to improve.

In the minds of some, turf and ideological concerns (and misunderstandings they cause) have been all that has held back a Darwinian revolution of the social sciences (Lopreato and Crippen 1999; Pinker 2002). An intellectual apparatus that combined an evolution-based theory of preferences with standard economic reasoning about behavior given those preferences—not unlike what Cox proposes—has already been one vision of what this "Darwinizing" intellectual force might look like (e.g., Kanazawa 2001a). Nonetheless, I think there is considerable reason for skepticism about the ultimate prospects of what deductive reasoning from evolutionary principles may offer students of the family. While I applaud Cox's initiative, I describe the grounds for my skepticism here.

Important to underscore at the outset, however, is that my arguments are not intended as comfort for those who would wish away the role of genetics in human affairs. There is ample reason to presume genetic commonalities and differences to be vitally important throughout much of social life—including resource transfers and other family dynamics—and my doubts are specifically with the prospect of deductive reasoning from evolutionary principles fulfilling much of its seeming promise to yield new, specific insights attributable to the historical consequences of selection for our species.

For an orienting illustration of the problems in developing predictions that prompt my concern, consider the conclusion of the draft of Cox's chapter:

> I imagine myself being well into my dotage but happy and somewhat healthy, when one day I'm diagnosed with some awful, fatal disease—albeit one that can be cured at considerable expense, affording me an extra year of gratifying geezerhood. But here's the rub: the exigencies of economics dictate that by paying for the treatment I must sacrifice one year of my granddaughter's college education. I can't vouch that I'd be thinking of Hamilton's rule (if indeed I even would remember it), but I know what it would predict.

Of course, the example is not intended to be taken too seriously, but let us consider it seriously nonetheless. Cox is sufficiently confident that a transparent prediction of behavior can be made with evolutionary principles that he leaves the prediction implicit. As Cox seems generous and loving, we might be confident that he would forgo an extra year of life for the sake of his granddaughter's education. Working *inductively* from that intuition, it is easy to imagine that an evolutionary perspective *would have predicted this result in the first place.* The scientific issue, though, is whether this is something an evolutionary perspective would have allowed us to predict for the actions of the hypothetical actor (C) in this situation.

Pretend first that we are operating with the reasoning sometimes associated with "human behavioral ecology," from which we would posit that C is basically a standard rational actor whose utility is determined by the extent to which actions prospectively maximize present inclusive fitness (Winterhalder and Alden Smith 2000). Given the current negative relationship between female education and fertility, it is not at all clear that C should be investing in his granddaughter's education in the first place, even if we imagine such education would contribute to her ability to provide for any children she does have and to the quality of her mate. Regardless, by dying, C is forgoing not just the fitness opportunities from additional children he might sire—perhaps a bleak prospect at his advanced age, although we might want to know more about C before assenting to that—but also whatever fitness gains may accrue to other family members as a result of his actions during the next year. In short, even if the granddaughter's inclusive fitness is indeed increased by the extra year of education—not at all clear in contemporary societies—it is not enough to say she would benefit from the trade-off, as the fitness price of the life of even a geezerly (but "somewhat healthy") altruist is not nothing.[3]

In any case, if we follow trends in Darwinian social science over the past twenty years, we might instead adopt an evolutionary psychological perspective, which would say the psychological mechanisms shaped under conditions of our ancestral past are relevant, and calculations of current inclusive fitness are largely irrelevant (Tooby and Cosmides 1989, 1990, 1992). I find this perspective far more plausible historically and psychologically than that of human behavioral ecology, but as behavioral ecologists are fond of pointing out, theirs is the perspective that leads more straightforwardly to precise, falsifiable predictions, at least when the quantities relevant for prediction can be specified. Evolutionary psychology posits specific psychological mechanisms that are often described as facilitating "love" and related emotional attachments that spur altruistic behavior toward kin. As a deductive matter, whether this love is strong enough to overcome preference for self-preservation is hard to imagine determining, especially because evolutionary psychologists have argued that the lack of analogy of ancestral parental investment to educational investment—particularly in daughters (Kanazawa 2001b)—would complicate predictions for behavior in this domain. To be sure, we can imagine trading off a year of life to invest in a granddaughter's education may evoke psychological mechanisms honed to the fitness consequences in ancestral contexts about one's own survival versus incremental benefits to a granddaughter's condition or future prospects. Evolutionary reasoning can help us to understand why it is not a biological puzzle that the human species might engage in kin altruism even at the expense of one's life, but the theory here is not sufficiently specific to offer a falsifiable prediction of choice.[4]

Additionally, in reflecting upon how we might see the decision dynamics making more sense in the light of evolutionary theory, one might consider how C's granddaughter would feel about the decision. We might imagine C being more willing to give up a year of his life for his granddaughter than his granddaughter is willing to accept the beneficence. No simple application of Hamilton's rule can account for this, as an altruistic act in the interest of the donor is even more in the interest of the recipient.

Obviously, expecting a theory to predict particular choices from briefly sketched details is unfairly demanding. The larger concern is the generation of predictions pertinent to *larger patterns of choices*—circumstances that would increase or decrease the probability of actors to invest in a family member at one's expense. Here again, however, making specific predictions is not as easy as it appears. (Or, more accurately, making predictions is quite easy, but figuring out the consequence of evidence consistent or inconsistent with those predictions is fraught with ambiguity.) I elaborate on my points by considering three separate examples of older relatives investing in younger relatives. The first, paternity certainty, is the subject of an exploratory case study by Cox; the second, on family structure and educational investment, is a sociological example Cox does not discuss but that further illustrates my general arguments; and the last, on differential investment in sons and daughters, concerns a literature to which I have previously contributed and which Cox reviews.

Given the self-consciously preliminary character of Cox's chapter, my pessimism might seem premature, even spoilsport. But even if economists' enthusiasm for this area is relatively new, evolutionary approaches to human behavior have an extensive track record. In the mid-1970s and the mid-1990s, there seemed to be rising enthusiasm for evolutionary thinking providing a "new science" that would serve as a flourishing (meta)theoretical foundation for considerable advances in behavioral science (Pinker 1997; Wilson 1975, 1978; Wright 1994). The new science has not come to pass, and enthusiasm for Darwinian approaches might even be waning in public intellectual interest. New efforts to bring evolutionary reasoning into economic studies of the family might profit from considering the cautionary lessons that can be drawn from past efforts.

Paternity Uncertainty

The primary case study that Cox offers in exploring the potential usefulness of an evolutionary approach to intrafamilial transfers is consideration of "how paternity certainty might affect the propensity of maternal versus paternal grandmothers to care for children." If we suppose that fathers have always confronted a kind of uncertainty over whether a child was really their offspring, then the genetic relatedness of father's side relatives are attenuated by a factor reflecting this uncertainty when compared with mother's side counterparts.[5] By this reasoning, the category of "maternal" versus "paternal" grandmother is pertinent for predicting patterns of investment because, although both can be equally assured that their children are their own, they face unequal assurance that their children's children are their own. A "paternity certainty hypothesis" about grandmothers' investment might therefore be taken as having as its first implication that we should observe at least some patterns of greater investment in children by maternal grandmothers versus paternal grandmothers. Evidence indicates that such asymmetries do exist, but, as Cox notes, there are routes other than paternity uncertainty to predicting greater investment by maternal grandmothers versus paternal grandmothers. (Cox's set of obvious alternative explanations turns on mothers more often being the primary caregiver and possibly more likely to seek and receive care from the grandparent with whom they most likely are closest, i.e., their own primary caregiver.)

When multiple hypotheses lead to the same theoretical implication, standard scientific procedure is to consider other theoretical implications, with an eye toward deriving those that would distinguish the hypotheses. Here, however, we run into an immediate and telling problem. Nowhere in his chapter does Cox explicitly articulate his paternity certainty hypothesis. Even if he did—and one can partially reconstruct his implicit hypothesis from his additional analyses—he would be merely selecting from an indefinite set of different possible "paternity uncertainty hypotheses" with different implications. Evidence contradicting one of these paternity uncertainty hypotheses does not at all adjudicate between alternative hypotheses that involve paternity uncertainty and those that do not. In other words, the clearest implication of paternity uncertainty from grandmother investment has alternative explanations, and more refined predictions come only by adding auxiliary propositions for which contrary evidence can be interpreted as a failure of either the hypothesis or particular auxiliary propositions. In the face of an indefinite but wide range of possible findings about grandmothers and investment, those inclined to believe in the importance of innate dispositions evolved in response to paternity uncertainty will be able to defend persistence in this view, whereas those disinclined to this conclusion will be able to defend remaining unpersuaded.

In this specific case, the additional kinds of implications that Cox attempts to draw on the paternity uncertainty hypothesis rest mainly on the premise that we might also expect paternal grandmothers to respond to *cues* about their daughter-in-law's fidelity (and thereby the chances that she conceived the child with a man who is not the grandmother's son). In other words, the more certain a grandmother is that her son is the father of her alleged grandchild, the more she should invest. If we adopted a behavioral ecology perspective, we might offer a simplifying assumption that grandmothers make maximally accurate use of all available cues on fidelity and discount investment accordingly. From this, if we knew or posited the probability $\Pr(father = cuckold | cues)$, we might even advance quite precise predictions about discounted investment. Such predictions, although falsifiable, seem borne more of a logical than a biological perspective, unless we really believe it plausible that, in our actual evolutionary history, the relevant environmental cues have been stable enough for long enough with enough consequences for fitness to support the development of a fitness-detecting apparatus that finely honed.[6] Otherwise, we are left with the proposition of a psychology in which paternal grandmothers have a generalized propensity to reduced attachment in their grandchildren that is moderated by some sensitivity to environmental cues.

One possible cue Cox considers involves indicators of the daughter-in-law's attitudes (her reported agreement with the proposition that "marriage is a lifetime relationship and should never be ended under extreme circumstances"); another is based on the child's physiology (degree of perceived physical resemblance to the father).[7] How sensitive a grandmother is to these cues, however, would seem to be the degree to which they invoke analogues that have indeed been reliable cues over evolutionary time.[8] In other words, lack of paternal grandmother sensitivity to hypothesized cues might reflect that they do not adequately resemble good cues to fidelity over the course of our evolutionary history, such that the expectation is a general tendency toward lower investment but not that investment will vary by the particular posited cue. For that matter, at least for the attitudinal cues, alternative explanations that paternal grandmothers will be emotionally closer to those daughters-in-law—and perhaps then more active in the grandmother role—who evince commitment to a lifelong marriage follow without recourse to paternity uncertainty or even evolved dispositions.

The point becomes plainer when we imagine, as Cox does, definitive DNA evidence on paternity. Imagine if, even in the face of indisputable evidence that their son is the baby's father, paternal grandmothers still invested less than did maternal grandmothers. Would this refute the proposition that such differences were the result of the genomic conse-quences of an evolutionary history of paternity uncertainty? No, no more than the observation that men forgo mating opportunities with an older but fertile woman for a younger woman they know cannot conceive children would refute the proposition that men have an evolved prefer-ence for youth in romantic partners (Symons 1995). Presently, abstract evolutionary hypotheses can have it either way—they offer no specific implication—on whether our evolved psychology would be expected to respond to explicit information about matters that could only be prob-abilistically inferred through indirect cues in the environments of our evolutionary past.

Indeed, if one looks over the evolutionary literature on genetic related-ness and resource transfers, different work can often be characterized as following one of two broad forks, both of which may be available writ small in particular theoretical applications. On the one hand, the mind can be posited to have been sufficiently honed by selection that investments reliably track subtle situational cues. An example would be work on the influence of child's age and sex on the amount of grief parents feel if the child dies (e.g., Crawford, Salter, and Jang 1989; Littlefield and Rushton 1986). On the other hand, the mind can be posited to have developed coarse mechanisms; indeed, so coarse that they are readily manipulated into transferring resources to others who are not even genetic relatives. The slavish devotion many pet owners display has been taken to illustrate how the neotenous features of cuddly animals can commandeer human dispositions to parental nurturance (e.g., Archer 1997; Serpell 1986; see also Wilson 1984, 126–27). Although not impossible in principle, it is a bit unsettling to think of this work cumulating in a model of mind that dispenses just the right amount of love to a 7-year-old girl vs. a 5-year-old boy, and yet which is completely snookered by the large eyes and high-pitched mewl of a kitten.

More generally, "middle-level theories" from evolutionary biology may offer only few and imprecise deductive predictions before requiring ancillary propositions about which we have little deductive guide and which do not speak to the question of whether there exist evolved genetic predispositions shaped by the theory's dynamic. The result is a consid-erably wide range of empirical states of the world that may be consistent with the theory. This range includes contradictory states; to give just one example, the theory of parent–offspring conflict (Trivers 1974) has been said to predict contradictory and potentially dubious positions on parental socialization—that children are almost completely impervious to socialization efforts (Pinker 1997, 447–48; cf. Trivers 1985, 163) and that children's interests are readily subordinated to parental manipulation (Surbey 1998). Yet, as frustrating as the capacity of a theory to accommodate ancillary propositions that yield contradictory predictions may be, it does not mean the theory is false. What it does mean is that we should not overstate the theory's deductive potential or the extent to which the theories we work with are honestly falsifiable.

Family Structure and Educational Outcomes

Further insight into the deductive problems of an evolutionary perspective is apparent if we consider one of the few papers to have appeared in the top two sociology journals yielding positive conclusions about evolutionary psychology. Cox does not discuss the paper, which is about evolutionary psychology and parental investment and uses educational attainment as a proxy for parental investment in a way similar to one of Cox's examples (see also Cox 2003). In their article, Biblarz and Raftery (1999) used four large, nationally representative datasets to examine the relationship between family structure—that is, the respondent being raised in a home with both biological parents, just one parent, or a biological parent and stepparent—and educational and occupational attainment. They found that children raised by both biological parents or by single mothers tend to do better than children raised by single fathers or in stepfamilies. They found also that these differences remained constant over the 30 years their data spanned.

Biblarz and Raftery compared these results with predictions that they derived from evolutionary psychology and various other explanatory idioms more common within sociology (socialization/learning theory, control theory, economic theory, an explanation asserting selection bias, and an explanation emphasizing exposure to marital conflict). They concluded that "among six candidate theoretical frameworks, the findings are most consistent with an evolutionary view of parental investment" (1999, 323). As such, they appear to provide an empirical victory for evolutionary psychology over more conventional social science alternatives; the victory is made more impressive by the study's use of a classic hypothesis testing framework, well-known social science datasets, and sophisticated methods of analysis.

Biblarz and Raftery's study stands as an important contribution to our understanding of the *empirical character* of family structure effects on attainment. Nevertheless, there is room for strong reservations about their theoretical conclusion. Their conclusion is based on four predictions attributed to evolutionary psychology, discussed as if it were simultaneously a perspective and yet having enough specificity to make singular predictions contrasting to other perspectives. My argument is that these predictions do not follow unambiguously from evolutionary psychology and that alternative predictions can be at least as easily generated. As a result, their results should not be taken as a real test of the evolutionary psychological perspective versus more conventional social science perspectives on attainment. Indeed, I contend the issues separating the two paradigms cannot be resolved by Biblarz and Raftery's data or analyses.

To elaborate: In characterizing the evolutionary psychological perspective, Biblarz and Raftery offer three cross-sectional (in their words, "static") predictions about the effect of family structure on outcomes, as well as one prediction about how the magnitude of family structure effects have changed over the 30 years they examine. Although Biblarz and Raftery present their predictions differently, they can be equivalently expressed as follows:

1. (Static) Children raised in two-biological-parent families will have higher educational and occupational attainment than children raised in any alternative family structure.
2. (Static) Children raised in a single-mother family will have higher attainment than children raised in a single-father family.
3. (Static) Children raised by a single parent of a given sex will do better than children raised by a parent of that sex and a stepparent. (Because of insufficient data on father-headed alternative families, Biblarz and Raftery are only able to test the prediction that children from single-mother families will outperform children from mother-and-stepfather families.)
4. (Change) The observed family structure effects on attainment will be constant over the 30-year period examined.

The other five frameworks they examine make at least some different predictions. When comparing these frameworks with their results, Biblarz and Raftery (1999, 356) conclude that "evolutionary parental investment theory was the only one where static and change predictions were both borne out by the data." Let us now look closer at each of the predictions that Biblarz and Raftery attribute to evolutionary psychology:

1. *Children raised in two-biological-parent families will have higher educational and occupational attainment than children raised in any alternative family structure.* As Biblarz and Raftery discuss, the tendency for children from two-biological-parent households to outperform those from alternative family structures (taken together) had been well documented before their study. We should perhaps not be surprised that five of their six candidate frameworks predict this known pattern, and the one that does not—their rendition of the economic perspective—fails soundly on its other predictions as well.[9] In other words, this prediction proves ultimately unimportant for differentiating among the theoretical alternatives Biblarz and Raftery present; perhaps ironically, it is also the least contestable of the predictions that they attribute to evolutionary psychology.

   Even so, their specific justification of this prediction for evolutionary psychology can be questioned. They argue that evolutionary psychology "would predict that children from two-biological-parent families will have an advantage over those from other kinds of families. The father's average resource contribution will be less than the mother's, but not by much, because humans have high male parental investment, and so children will benefit from the presence of the biological father" (Biblarz and Raftery 1999). The claim that humans have high male parental investment is a statement about humans *relative to other species.* In more than 95 percent of mammalian species, including most primates, males provide *no* (or virtually no) direct care for an offspring after it is born (Clutton-Brock 1991, 132). Thus, the inference that human fathers' parental investment in humans will differ "not by much" from mothers' simply does not follow: even if males only invested 10 percent of the effort that females did toward children after they were born, we would still be a species with relatively high levels of male parental investment.

2. *Children raised in a single-mother family will have higher socioeconomic attainment than children raised in a single-father family.* Biblarz and Raftery ascribe this position to evolutionary psychology because, they contend, "the evolutionary perspective on the family gives more weight to the role of the mother than that of the father in

determining children's fates" (1999, 325–26).[10] They then devote a paragraph to explaining the evolutionary rationale for predicting that mothers will invest more of themselves in their offspring than will fathers. Empirically, as is well known, the asymmetry in parental investment between mothers and fathers holds strongly across all human cultures (and, for that matter, among all mammals) (e.g., Rossi 1984). There have been many explanations of this asymmetry that do not give center stage to evolved sex differences in biological dispositions (e.g., Chodorow 1978). At the same time, many social scientists (myself included) would grant that there seems to be something biological about the greater investments of mothers than fathers, and that standard evolutionary psychological accounts provide a plausible explanation of why this is so.

In any event, does it actually follow from evolutionary psychological tenets that if mothers have an innate tendency to invest more in children than fathers, then children from single-mother families will attain higher average positions in societies than single-father families? Not necessarily. Evolutionary psychologists readily acknowledge that across all human societies, men control a vastly greater share of economic, political, and cultural power than women; indeed, hypothesizing about the supposed origins of patriarchy is a lively topic in the field (Hrdy 1997; Miller 1998; Smuts 1995; see also Browne 2002; Goldberg 1973, 1993). Presumably, then, an evolutionary psychologist would grant that a plausible consequence of a patriarchal social organization is that, *ceteris paribus,* a unit of paternal investment will have a greater positive effect on attainment than a unit of maternal investment. If the difference between male and female social efficacy is large, then a moderately invested single father may still be able to do more to advance his children's futures than a maximally invested single mother.

In other words, we have a trade-off between superior male societal power and superior female parental investment. Whether one predicts that children of single mothers or children of single fathers will have higher attainment does not directly follow from an evolutionary psychological perspective but instead requires ancillary assumptions about the relative weight to each side of the trade-off for determining attainment in a society. Put another way, had Biblarz and Raftery done their analyses across a range of societies and found the opposite result (that single-father families outperform single-mother families) in some, most, or all of them, *that result would in no way disconfirm an evolutionary psychological view of investment and attainment.* Instead, disconfirmation would require at least a demonstration that the unequal distribution of power between the sexes cannot explain the results.

Given that Biblarz and Raftery subtitle their article "Rethinking the 'Pathology of Matriarchy' " (that is, rethinking the idea that single mothers pose a substantial detriment to their children's attainment), it is worth noting that some well-known work of Darwinian psychology does not share their enthusiasm for single motherhood (at least in the environments of our evolutionary past). Evolutionary psychological work on neonaticide and infanticide has emphasized the contributory effects of father absence, with the argument that a new mother's having to raise the infant without a father's help may have strongly contributed to circumstances in which the infant's chances of survival and reproductive success were so low that selection favored killing it and saving resources for other opportunities (Daly and Wilson 1988, 63–64). Darwinian work on sexual development has theorized that the putatively strongly detrimental effects of father absence in our ancestral past may have led to the evolution of a tendency for children raised in fatherless homes to engage in more quantity-based mating strategies (marked by earlier age at first intercourse, greater promiscuity, and higher propensity for divorce) than those who grow up in two-parent homes (Belsky, Steinberg, and Draper 1991; Draper and Harpending 1982).

3. *Children raised by a single parent of a given sex will do better than children raised by a parent of that sex and a stepparent.* In presenting evolutionary psychology's predictions, Biblarz and Raftery write: "Children from single-mother families will also have advantages over those from stepfather/biological-mother families. The stepparent's concern with his own reproductive fitness is in competition with the stepchildren for the mother's resources, increasing the risk of abuse to children in families with a stepparent" (Biblarz and Raftery 1999, 326). They cite the well-known research of Daly and Wilson (1996; see also Daly and Wilson 1988, 1999). What Daly and Wilson (and others) have demonstrated beyond rational dispute is that children with a stepparent are several times more likely to be victims of child abuse and child homicide than are children raised by a single biological parent or both biological

parents. They also report that "step-relationships are, on average, less investing, more distant, more conflictual, and less satisfying that the corresponding genetic parent-child relationships" (Daly and Wilson 1996, 79).

Daly and Wilson can thus perhaps be read uncontroversially as predicting that children in stepfamilies will do worse than those in two-biological-parent families, but predicting that *being raised by a stepparent is worse than having no second parent at all* is an entirely different matter. This statement requires that the net contribution of the stepparent to the child's socioeconomic attainment is *negative*. But Daly and Wilson do not claim that *most* stepchildren suffer abuse at the hands of a stepparent. Moreover, they acknowledge that many stepparents provide *positive* investments in their stepchildren, and they see such investments as entirely consistent with their evolutionary psychological contentions. They argue that step-marriage should be considered partly as the mother procuring investment for the would-be stepchild as part of the terms of the marriage. Daly and Wilson write,

> Stepparents assume their obligations in the context of a web of reciprocities with the genetic parent, who is likely to recognize more or less explicitly that stepparental tolerance and investment constitute benefits bestowed on the genetic parent and child, entitling the stepparent to reciprocal considerations.
>
> In this light, *the existence of stepparental investment is not so surprising.* But the fact of such investment cannot be taken to imply that stepparents ordinarily (or indeed ever) come to feel the sort of commitment commonly felt by genetic parents. *Evolutionary thinking suggests that stepparental affection will tend to be restrained.* (1996, 80, emphases added)

The claim here is not that stepparents are, on average, bad for children, but rather that their investment will be restrained in comparison with biological parents. One could therefore use the above paragraph to argue that an evolutionary psychological perspective predicts that even though children from mother–stepfather families will attain less than children from two-biological-parent families, they will attain *more* than children from single-parent families. That Biblarz and Raftery derive the opposite prediction is based on their ancillary proposition that the average stepfather does more harm than good, a conclusion that necessarily follows neither from Daly and Wilson's work specifically nor an evolutionary psychological perspective more generally.

4. *The observed family structure effects on attainment will be constant.*
Biblarz and Raftery's data span a period in which there was a near
reversal of the ratio of alternative family structures resulting from
the death of a parent to those resulting from divorce. Comparing
the 1962 and 1992–94 samples, Biblarz and Raftery estimate that the
percentage of alternative families that were the result of parental
death declined from 68 percent to 33 percent, whereas the percentage of alternative families that were the result of divorce rose from
28 percent to 62 percent. Biblarz and Raftery assert that this transition implies different predictions for the different candidate
frameworks about how the magnitude of family structure effects
have changed over time. They claim that the evolutionary psychological perspective predicts no change, and they justify this contention as follows:

> From the evolutionary perspective, divorced and widowed single mothers
> have the same level of their own fitness tied up in the children, and so both
> types of mothers would have the same level of impetus to invest highly in
> their children. The presence of a nonbiological parent would negatively
> impact children, regardless of whether the biological father had died or the
> parents had divorced. The change in cause structure over time should not
> alter the implications for children of basic family forms. (Biblarz and
> Raftery 1999, 330)

From an evolutionary standpoint, a mother's incentives to invest
in her offspring are not affected by whether her marriage ends in
divorce or death. However, Biblarz and Raftery's argument fails
to recognize both (a) that the evolutionary incentives for the non-
cohabiting biological father to invest in his offspring are similarly
unaffected and (b) that the father's capacity to invest is certainly
affected by whether he is estranged or dead. An evolutionary view
would predict that a living, estranged father would still have concern for his child's well-being and may serve as a useful source of
investments over the child's development. Biblarz and Raftery's
failure to acknowledge this is particularly striking given their speculations about the role of families in helping their children obtain
"favoritism in hiring" or other "special favors" in translating educational achievement into socioeconomic success (1999, 357).
Tapping informal networks to help a child may be precisely the sort
of help that living non-cohabitating fathers can provide with nearly
equal facility as cohabiting ones.

As a result, we would expect that as the ratio of divorced mothers to widowed mothers increases, the negative effects of alternative family structures would not remain constant but would *decrease* over time. Biblarz and Raftery's prediction of no change requires presuming that the effect of having an estranged father is the same as the effect of having a dead one; this prediction does not obviously follow from evolutionary psychological premises, and it also sits uneasily with their earlier claims about men's high parental investment.

Taking stock, the specific predictions that Biblarz and Raftery attribute to evolutionary psychology are only one of several sets that could have been as easily derived. It just so happens that these predictions align with the observed findings, and thus the article presents their results as providing support for evolutionary theory versus alternative perspectives. The multiplicity of predictions is consistent with the skepticism about the deductive specificity of evolution-based theories, but this multiplicity does not necessarily point to some fundamental flaw or falsity in evolutionary approaches to social behavior. Indeed, the presence of competing testable predictions within a theoretical perspective may well be a sign of its vigor and health. As one evolutionary psychologist portrays the issue,

> One of the issues that is difficult to explain to people who are unfamiliar with evolutionary psychology is that it is not a monolithic set of hypotheses that yields one invariant prediction about each phenomenon. I am sometimes asked, for example, "What is the evolutionary explanation for homosexuality?" or "What is the evolutionary explanation of female orgasm?" One characteristic of a healthy science is that, on the cutting edge, there are competing hypotheses that vie for attention. (Buss 1995, 81)

In any event, evolutionary psychology is by no means unusual as a theoretical perspective in being able to generate multiple predictions, and the problems of hypothesis testing among flexible theoretical perspectives stretches well beyond both evolutionary psychology and conventional sociology. For example, Laibson and Zeckhauser (1998, 26) complain that "the promiscuous prediction problem . . . plagues mainstream economics. Both behavioral [economics] models and standard economics models are often so flexible that almost any outcome can be explained by them."

If a variety of predictions can be derived not just from psychology but from perspectives that do not posit genetically based psychological adaptations (what Cox would call nonbiological explanations), does this mean the enterprise of social science hypothesis testing is some kind of ill-reasoned illusory diversion? No, but it does suggest that trying to infer genetic causation from regressions of educational attainment on family structure may not be a very productive way of doing developmental psychology. On the relationship of evolved biology, parental investment, and socioeconomic attainment, illuminating the issues that separate evolutionary and sociological perspectives will also require both more and different data than what Biblarz and Raftery marshal. The two crucial questions may be (1) how and in what ways do different types of parental investments affect attainment and (2) how do (evolved) biological and environmental factors interact in determining how and how much parents invest in their offspring. The potential contributions of survey analysis seem much greater for the first question than for the second: my strong suspicion is that just about anything that survey data of this sort might tell us about differential parental investments could be rendered consistent with frameworks that make close reference to our evolutionary past and with frameworks that do not. Indeed, one can argue that no one seems to have a good understanding yet of either how to explicate methodologically or represent theoretically the interaction of biology and environment in the determination of social behavior, although certainly efforts are being made (more often with the idea of the interaction of genetic and environmental characteristics that each vary in populations [see Moffitt, Caspi, and Rutter 2005; Shostak 2003]).

The Trivers-Willard Hypothesis

An evolutionary hypothesis Cox discusses at some length is the Trivers-Willard hypothesis. As evolutionary theories germane to resource transfers go, the Trivers-Willard hypothesis has the virtue of being seemingly straightforward in its reasoning and leading to seemingly nonobvious, falsifiable conclusions. The Trivers-Willard hypothesis follows from the reasoning that if (1) parental "condition" is heritable and correlated with reproductive success and (2) reproductive variance is greater for males than females, then there are fitness advantages for those of better condition who produce relatively more sons and those of lower rank who produce relatively more daughters. Trivers and Willard (1973) thus develop their hypothesis in terms of expected biases in sex ratios at birth, but they also note that similar implications follow for relative investment in children.

As a final flourish of their three-page article, they also suggest that socio-economic status might be the analogue of "condition" in developed societies.

The most straightforward application of the Trivers-Willard hypothesis of parental investment to the United States would be that, as measures of socioeconomic status increase, parental investment should increasingly favor sons. In these terms, two separate studies find null results for the Trivers-Willard hypothesis for a considerable diversity of measures (Freese and Powell 1999; Keller, Nesse, and Hofferth 2001). Various means exist for continuing to assert the relevance of the Trivers-Willard hypothesis for contemporary developed societies while granting the null results of these studies. For example, one can assert that studies focused too much on an outcome too close to education, which Kanazawa (2001b) argues is an especially distant kind of investment from a Pleistocene analogue (especially for daughters). Alternatively, one can argue that direct measures of investment are flawed and instead use a distal outcome that reflects investment—that is, education (Hopcroft 2005). Depending on the strength of one's conviction that something like the Trivers-Willard hypothesis should be evinced somehow in contemporary developed societies, the hypothesis is either easily abandoned or easily preserved.

Part of what makes the Trivers-Willard hypothesis perhaps more vampirical than empirical—unable to be killed by mere evidence—is that the hypothesis seems so logically compelling that it becomes easy to presume that it must be true, and to presume that the natural science literature on the hypothesis is an unproblematic avalanche of supporting findings. In the article Cox cites, Edlund (1999, 1278) offers the brief, citation-free assessment of the literature as the following: "The Trivers and Willard hypothesis has been confirmed in a large number of studies of animal species (including humans) over the past 25 years. To my knowledge no study has found evidence against it."

In fact, the Trivers-Willard hypothesis of adaptive sex ratio variation is not at all well established in the animal kingdom. Palmer (2000), in a meta-analytic study, discusses at length adaptive sex ratio variation in birds—including hypotheses that one could characterize as extensions of the Trivers-Willard hypothesis logic (see Frank 1990 for a review)—as an example of publication bias leading to distorted conclusions. Palmer finds that "on closer inspection few, if any, compelling data exist for adaptive departure from a 50:50 sex ratio in any species" (2000, 454; see Ewen, Cassey, and Møller [2004, 1277] for another meta-analysis of birds that concludes that "facultative control of offspring sex is not a charac-teristic biological phenomenon in breeding birds").

The reason animal results are relevant is that one can easily form the opinion that the Trivers-Willard hypothesis is a well-established phe-nomenon in animals and that only through some pseudo-dualistic "human exceptionalism" might one resist its applicability to humans. Instead, we face the opposite of the famous line from "New York, New York": if the hypothesis can't make it there, should we expect it to make it anywhere? That is, if the Trivers-Willard hypothesis has fared so inconsistently in the areas of its more direct application, then how likely is it to matter in application to parental investment instead of sex ratios and to the novel investment environments of contemporary developed societies instead of the environments of our evolutionary past?

Cox reports some studies that have findings for sex ratios that seem to provide some evidence for the Trivers-Willard hypothesis for sex ratios at birth in the United States (Almond and Edlund 2006; Norberg 2004). These findings may suggest promise for the hypothesis. Still, caution is urged, especially as the Trivers-Willard hypothesis for sex ratios has pro-vided inspiration for a burst of recent studies with positive findings. Kanazawa (2007) has proposed a generalized Trivers-Willard hypothe-sis, suggesting,

> Parents who possess any heritable trait which increases male reproductive success at a greater rate (or decreases male reproductive success at a smaller rate) than female reproductive success in a given environment will have a higher-than-expected offspring sex ratio (more males). Parents who possess any heritable trait which increases female reproductive success at a greater rate (or decreases female reproductive success at a smaller rate) than male reproductive success in a given environment will have a lower-than-expected offspring sex ratio.

This generalized Trivers-Willard hypothesis has the virtue of being fecund in its testable implications, and Kanazawa and others have presented a series of findings they interpret as supporting it.[11] Kanazawa (2005) predicts that body size confers a greater adaptive advantage for men than women, and thus taller and heavier people should be more likely to have sons. Kanazawa and Vandermassen (2005) propose that persons with occu-pations suggestive of a masculine brain (e.g., engineers and mathema-ticians) will have more sons than persons with occupations suggestive of a feminine brain (e.g., nurses and teachers) because children would be more successful if they were born with a relative masculinization of their brain consistent with their gender. Kanazawa (2007) proposes that more beautiful people will be more likely to have daughters because beauty confers a greater reproductive benefit for women than men.

Nonetheless, one might question whether Kanazawa's hypothesis accurately generalizes the Trivers-Willard hypothesis. The Trivers-Willard hypothesis derives as an implication of the greater reproductive variance among males compared with that among females. In the Kanazawa (2006) application to beauty, the argument is that beauty is more pertinent for reproductive success for females than males, but a proportionally greater return for females would still not imply female-biased sex ratios unless that return was large enough to *more than offset* the greater returns to males for advantageous traits generally from their higher reproductive variance. Roughly, if reproductive variance for males is x times that of females, then a trait would have to have more than $\sqrt{x}$ times as large an effect for females relative to other females than for males relative to other males to be favored by selection. If one looks again at Kanazawa's generalized Trivers-Willard hypothesis, it might read more like a general statement about what traits one would expect selection to favor than any statement that extends the logic of the original Trivers-Willard hypothesis. Ironically, by its inattention to the animating logical detail of the Trivers-Willard hypothesis—the tendency for reproductive variance of males of many species to be greater than that of females—the generalized Trivers-Willard hypothesis might yield applications not actually consistent with Darwinian reasoning.

In any case, because evolutionary psychology often considers cues of beauty as beautiful because they are cues to health (e.g., Symons 1995), *the prediction could have just as easily gone the other way:* more beautiful parents are of better condition and so should have more sons. Again, it just so happens that the prediction Kanazawa offers matches the results presented.[12]

The merits of the reasoning or reported support for particular applications aside, an important concern about the more general viability of the generalized Trivers-Willard hypothesis—and, for that matter, the original Trivers-Willard hypothesis and the studies Cox cites—for human sex ratios bears close consideration. Namely, if the Trivers-Willard hypothesis and Kanazawa's generalized version resulted in strong influences on the probability of offspring being male or female, the hypothesis would have a plain implication for the correlation of sex within sibships. If stable traits are responsible for deviations in a parent's probability of their first offspring being a son from the population proportion of sons, then that same probability would apply to the second child as well. If a parent has an increased probability of having a daughter because he or she is smaller, less violent, has a more feminized brain, or is more beautiful, then the probability should be biased in roughly the same magnitude for subsequent children as well. Consequently, the generalized Trivers-Willard hypothesis implies a tendency toward positive correlation in the sex composition of children *within families,* even as the tendency toward relative equal numbers of males and females in the population remains.

Pretend the sex of a child is determined similarly to the flip of a coin. The generalized Trivers-Willard hypothesis is then like postulating a population in which many individuals are flipping coins where the probability of heads differs substantially from the probability of tails. This variation between couples is sometimes referred to in the sex ratio literature as Lexis variation (Edwards 1966). As long as the biases cancel out in the aggregate, a group of wildly varying and biased coins can produce the same overall count of heads and tails as a group of homogeneous, fair coins.[13] However, the same cannot be said for the distribution of *multiple* flips from those coins. Instead, Lexis variation implies greater positive correlation in sexes within sibships than would be observed in the absence of Lexis variation. The original and generalized Trivers-Willard hypothesis would seem to imply that we should be observing more imbalanced sex ratios within families than would be expected if the sex of children within a family was independently determined, and the cumulative consequence of the generalized Trivers-Willard hypothesis is limited by the total amount of Lexis variation (and even that would assume that all Lexis variation is attributable to dynamics explicable as the Trivers-Willard hypothesis or the generalized Trivers-Willard hypothesis).

Although the study of sex ratios is considerable, data quality varies. Two large studies that make use of health service data that follow births from the same mothers report similar results. In a study of 815,891 children from the Danish Fertility Database, Jacobsen, Møller, and Mouritsen (1999, 3124) write, "no significant predisposition was found of couples or individuals to have children of a particular sex ('Lexis association')." In a study of 549,048 live and stillborn children born in Scotland between 1975 and 1988, Maconochie and Roman (1997, 1051) find that "the probability of a male infant was the same regardless of the genders of all other children born to the same mother." These data sources are both almost certainly more complete and accurate than the data sources used in any of the Kanazawa or Hopcroft studies supporting the Trivers-Willard hypothesis.[14] If for no other reason than improvement in database technology and the ability to track mothers over their fertility history, these data seem superior to previous data that had been used to estimate Lexis variation (Edwards 1966; James 1975). Incidentally, Maconochie and Roman (1997) also include measures of both maternal and paternal social class, and they fail to find any evidence of a relationship between sex ratio and social class, meaning that these data should be counted among the null findings for direct studies of the original Trivers-Willard hypothesis for human sex ratios (cf. Hopcroft 2005, reporting positive findings for the hypothesis with inferior data). The hypothesis does not argue that postnatal environmental factors cannot influence sex ratios at birth—not to mention, especially in some parts of the world, selective abortion or even infanticide—but the population data do not suggest significant nondeliberate variation in the sex ratio at birth by stable parental characteristics.

For this reason, readers may wish to have a generalized skepticism toward the generalized Trivers-Willard hypothesis and may wish to be especially wary of the specter of a proliferation of findings attributing substantial differences in sex ratios to relatively indirect or unreliable measures of different phenotypic traits. The analytic techniques and data that characterize much work leave considerable room for results to reflect arbitrary or even incorrect analytic decisions difficult to evaluate on the sole basis of materials provided with publication. Moreover, given the large number of possible implications and numerous datasets or specifications by which they may be tested, the possibility of publication bias in which tests are published is large. At the very least, for the serial publication of positive (generalized or otherwise) Trivers-Willard hypothesis findings to warrant continued attention, it seems reasonable to hope that theorists will develop an account that reconciles these findings with the seeming lack of positive correlations of sex within sibships in large, high-quality data.[15]

Cox recognizes ambiguities in testing the Trivers-Willard hypothesis when he discusses educational attainment as a proxy for investment, but he concludes, "we have Trivers and Willard to thank for pointing the way toward a potentially noteworthy empirical finding." A recurrent theme in Cox's chapter is that even if evolutionary hypotheses are incorrect, they stimulate inquiry that can lead to new empirical discoveries. So long as all researchers are as reflective and contemplative of alternative explanations as Cox, I agree. The worry, however, is that enthusiasm (or, just as bad, antipathy) for evolutionary hypotheses might sometimes lead to misleading deductions of hypotheses or various kinds of publication biases that result in a cumulative literature that distorts our ultimate portrait of the underlying empirics. Additionally, enthusiasts might be more inclined to conduct tests that correspond to their intuitions rather than push for those that are less intuitive. The gambit that new hypotheses, wherever they come from, are useful if they press us to ask questions we would otherwise not is worthwhile only to the extent the questions are answered fairly and competently, and my hope is that subsequent researchers who follow Cox's call will share the genuine curiosity with which he proceeds.

Conclusion

Barring some unexpected evidentiary shift in favor of intelligent design or the creation of humanity by an alien race with a twisted sense of humor, the human species is the legacy of a long history of processes of evolution by selection. Every one of us is the product of an astonishing winning streak: our parents survived and reproduced, their parents survived and reproduced, and so on, stretching back before humans were humans and even before mammals were mammals. Evolutionary psychology, in the broadest sense, is falsifiable only by a falsification of the application of the theory of evolution itself, at least as applied to the human genome. In other words, even if you adopt an extremely environmentalist stance toward human behavior, implicit in that stance is that some history of evolution by selection is responsible for building a species about which that stance could be true. For this reason, I reject the terminology of biological versus nonbiological causes, because we are biology all the way through, and any account that makes reference to the import of human psychology—for example, the import of preferences—is biological.[16] Explanations that draw on socialization, culture, or learning are postulating changes in actors' psychology; psychological change is biological change.

The fact of evolution by selection implies that evolutionary social science has two distinct projects. The *historical* project involves taking the observable facts of human affairs, as best we can assemble and refine them, and developing an account of the history of the species that coincides with these facts. Evolutionary theorizing of this sort is regularly criticized as storytelling, and storytelling it often is—but the narrative history of our species is a story, and the stories we tell may be better or worse approximations of this real story, for which consistency with available information is our guide. The *deductive* project involves taking knowledge about our history and about the logic of selection processes and using that to develop new verifiable insights about human life. The deductive project feels more like science and avails itself to revered forms of scientific publication, but much of my argument has been that the development of substantive evolutionary reasoning–based predictions about contemporary developed societies is an enterprise fraught with ambiguity once moved past fairly simple, vague, and uncertainly contingent generalizations (e.g., mothers tending to invest more in children than fathers; parents tending to invest more in biological children than stepchildren). To be sure, the historical and deductive projects offer possibilities of productive iteration, where empirics that narrow that range of possible histories can lead to predictions that, in turn, lead to new insights that strengthen confidence in particular historical accounts. Nonetheless, my belief is that, given the complexity of human life and the specificity with which we wish to understand it, the direction of genuine knowledge production is and will continue to be vastly lopsided in the direction of observations about us now informing reconstruction of our past development as a species.

What this lopsidedness implies for Cox's project requires us to be mindful of what Cox is seeking. At least in my reading, Cox is displeased with models that treat actors as abstract entities that could just as easily be firms, robots, or simulacra, and wishes to extend knowledge to take advantage of knowledge about categorizations that can be applied to the real actors in families ("mother" and "father" instead of "person 1" and "person 2"). In this respect, Cox seems to want to posit basic category-related psychological propensities from actors and to work from these propensities toward empirical implications. Evolutionary theory provides a means of stimulating thought about what these propensities might be. I agree, but my reading of various evolutionary psychological literatures makes me worry that what is often brought out are a researcher's existing intuitions about the social world, only perhaps with the illusion added that such inferences are purely deductive rather than very much inductive. Anything that elaborates and adds coherence to our understanding of the apparent psychological propensities of actors in our population is good, so long as we do not also import misleading assessments of what we have learned.

What social scientists sometimes imagine evolutionary psychological theorizing can provide is a way of doing developmental psychology on the cheap. They want the analogue of being able to look at choices and determine not just revealed preferences but also a revealed biography of how the actor came to have those preferences. They want evolutionary psychological theory to allow researchers to use surveys of adults to settle disputes about what in our psychology reflects the genetic commonalities of a shared "human nature" and what reflects "socialization" or "culture" or "structural forces." That variants of evolutionary psychology are like other perspectives in providing many possible and sometimes contradictory predictions when applied to adults suggests we should regard this inferential errand with skepticism. More than this, individual researchers should consider to what extent they wish to be in the business of understanding the provenance of psychological traits versus trying to understand the population consequences of patterns of traits as they are. (This division is reinforced by the recognition that the extent to which traits are genetically based has no particular relationship to their malleability, which means more generally that there are no grounds for foreboding claims about genes imposing hard limits on the possibility of social interventions [Wahlsten 1990].)

If one does take the stance that it matters less for one's own purposes if particular evolutionary hypotheses are true—in the sense of providing insights into the actual evolutionary history of our species and its genomic consequences—than if they are testable and useful, then it should prompt reflection about what about the hypothesis is useful and toward what end. Much about resource transfers in families may become illuminated by working more with category-based preferences while remaining indifferent to how those preferences came about. For whatever reason, if evidence indicates that there is "something important about" certainty of genetic relatedness, we can do much to document the contours and consequences of that pattern, ideally toward useful generalizations about the circumstances that make revealed preferences for genetic relatives stronger or weaker. The extent to which analysis proves to require detailed reference to Darwinian principles, and thus specific engagement with how the behavioral tendencies originate, is a subsequent question. When analyses proceed with an indifferent or agnostic stance toward questions of provenance, this stance should be explicit.[17]

Barbara Ehrenreich (2000, 88), a writer with a Ph.D. in cell biology (who is often mistaken for a sociologist), once wrote that "there are people who reject any attempt to apply evolutionary theory to human behavior, and, as far as I'm concerned, they can go back to composing their annual letters to Santa Claus. Obviously, humans have been shaped by natural selection (though it's not always so obvious how)." Ehrenreich works as a journalist and thereby has the luxury of being able to banish the "how" to parentheses. For scientists working on human behavior, "how" is the whole thing, and intuitions of the strong relevance of our evolutionary history go nowhere without a systematic proposal about how this relevance should be incorporated into our thinking about social life. Considering the diversity of contemporary interpretations of what our evolutionary past has to say about social life in the present, Ehrenreich's statement just that it is "*not always* so obvious how" humans have been shaped by natural selection is perhaps even charitable. Given this, those interested in the implications of postulates about human psychology should be able to work forward from postulates without having to take any stance on developmental origins, much less their ultimate origins in our past. Those interested in reconstructing evolutionary history should be respected for their interest in taking on the task of trying to develop an empirically and logically consistent account of our past. Those who do wish to try working forward deductively should at least be reflective and specific about the historical and psychological assumptions required to arrive at their predictions and should scrutinize such predictions logically as well as empirically.

Economists, especially, have a proud history of being relatively unconcerned about the realism of the assumptions of their models if these models provide clear, verifiable implications (Friedman 1953). As illustrated in the preceding examples, the situation with evolutionary reasoning differs from orthodox economic practice in two important respects. First, economists' traditional tolerance for simplified models is certainly not a tolerance for *vague* models; the problem I point to above is that they often articulate evolutionary hypotheses in a way that elides the suppositions about selection implicit in that prediction, with the consequence that the capacity of the theory to follow different suppositions to a contradictory prediction is obscured. Second, the reasoning that leads most easily to "evolutionary" predictions is a model that posits that human beings act in accordance with what maximizes inclusive fitness today (i.e., a standard rational actor model with inclusive fitness serving as the lone term in the utility function). This model implies processes that are not just psychologically and historically unrealistic—which economists might otherwise be willing to tolerate—but also results in predictions, when held to any level of specificity, that are patently inconsistent with the facts of fertility and familial behavior in contemporary, developed societies. For example, one might look at declining rates of childbirth and see qualitatively some analogue to the trade-offs of quantity for quality that make sense from a fitness-maximizing standpoint, but there is no reason to think that the low levels of fertility today are optimal from the sense of a strategy for maximizing frequency of genes in future generations. For this reason, one is led to deriving predictions on the basis of the idea that we possess evolved dispositions that influence behaviors today but not in any optimizing sense, and here the content and magnitude of these dispositions is exactly the point of vagueness at which it becomes easy for people to interpret known empirics or their sense of the social world as being straightforward predictions from Darwinian theory. In the absence of explicit articulation of the psychological and historical suppositions that give rise to their predictions, putatively deductive applications should be recognized for their heuristic value, including as a way of explicating intuitions one already has about the world, but this work should not be mistaken for explanation.

NOTES

1. Indeed, such person 1/person 2 formulations are themselves inappropriately concrete, as the analysis can be carried forth without presuming that the actors are persons, as the fruitful history of applying theories articulated in individuals to organizations (e.g., firms, political parties) indicates. Indeed, rational actor theories seem often to work better for organizations than for individuals (Clark 1997; Satz and Ferejohn 1994).

2. Concerns about epistemic double standards are certainly not confined to sociology, and proponents of evolutionary approaches in psychology and anthropology have described feeling like they have had to make career sacrifices and endure the calumny and condescension of a collegiate "confederacy of dunces" to pursue their preferred theoretical perspective (see, e.g., Kenrick 1995; Segerstråle 2000; Thornhill and Palmer 2000).

3. Of course, a strict evaluation of the trade-off would also need to consider that death is irreversible, whereas a source of educational funding denied is not the same as education being denied or even postponed.

4. Or, as will be described in more detail later, we can make some simplifying assumptions and offer a prediction, but evidence consistent with or contrary to that prediction provides little or no information about the merits of the theory.

5. Paternity uncertainty also implies lower paternal versus maternal investment, but as Cox recognizes, the evolutionary logic of parental investment would predict greater maternal investment even in the absence of paternity uncertainty over time.

6. Only if we consider a highly specific kind of consequence to paternity certainty—along the lines of human behavioral ecology—might we get specific and singular predictions that would be otherwise hard to explain, but such predictions almost certainly would not withstand empirical scrutiny in their details and, upon failing, would not gainsay less precise evolutionary predictions.

7. Several studies exist on the proposition that, because it might seem in the interest of children to advertise their paternity, one might predict that babies will look more like their fathers than their mothers (compare Christenfeld and Hill 1995 with the null findings of Brédart and French 1999; Bressan and Grassi 2004). Other work has looked at whether maternal relatives point out paternal resemblance (following Daly and Wilson 1982) and whether resemblance increases paternal investment (e.g., Bressan and Dal Martello 2002; McLain et al. 2000).

8. Note that if paternal-side investment is contingent and consequential, paired females will have fitness incentives to evolve the capacity to fake cues of fidelity.

9. Biblarz and Raftery cast economic theory as predicting that children in step-families will do equally well as children in two-biological-parent families and better than children in single-parent families, on the grounds that the key distinction is whether a child has two parents providing complementary resources (citing Becker 1964, 1981). Given that children who live in stepfamilies have likely spent some time in a single-parent family (before the custodial parent re-wed) and that divorce often represents a significant initial financial setback for the custodial parents, then the economic perspective could be taken to predict that two biological parents will outperform stepfamilies. My general argument about testing predictions attributed to the evolutionary psychological perspective may perhaps also apply to predictions sometimes attributed to "economic theory," and in sociology is it common for implausible predictions to be attributed to economics and then refuted with glee. (I like to refer to this as a "economists think the darnedest things" trope in sociology.)

10. Biblarz and Raftery's reference to "determining children's fates" is slippery; in evolutionary biology, "fate" is almost always considered by reproductive success, not the idiosyncratically human fates of educational and socioeconomic attainment. As discussed earlier, in trying to generalize biological theories to humans, Darwinian social scientists sometimes try to draw theoretical parallels between an animal's health or dominance rank and human socioeconomic status.

11. The analytic strategies used in these papers have been recurrently criticized as exemplary of questionable methodological practice on the weblog of a prominent social statistician (Gelman 2006a, 2006b).

12. As an anecdotal aside, when a colleague told me of the findings of the Kanazawa study after he had read about the study in a newspaper, I presumed my colleague had it backwards and that the prediction was that beautiful people would have more sons.

13. Perhaps one wishes to believe the hypothesis predicts that the probability of the second child being a boy is much affected by the sex of the first child, so that the overall number of boys and girls produced over a parent's fertility history corresponds more precisely to some Trivers-Willard hypothesis–influenced deviation from 50:50. If so, this would have its own, opposite implications for the expectations about intrafamilial sex ratios—that pairs of same-sex offspring should be less frequent than pairs of opposite-sex offspring—which available data do not support.

14. Note that some data for testing the Trivers-Willard hypothesis seem to reveal patterns consistent with the hypothesis when the real effect is that of the child's sex upon

maternal status, given evidence that fathers may be more interested in marriage and fatherhood for sons generally versus daughters (Morgan, Lye, and Condran 1988).

15. In this regard, generalized Trivers-Willard hypothesis enthusiasts might look to James's (2000) speculation that Lexis variation exists simultaneously with so-called chaotic Poisson variation that induces *negative* correlations of sex within sibships of equivalent magnitude to the Lexis variation, so that the two cancel each other out in large datasets. A challenge for those interested in the generalized Trivers-Willard hypothesis might thus be to deploy some of the ingenuity that has thus far gone into envisioning new applications of the theory to proposing an adaptive explanation for chaotic Poisson variation that would counterbalance the correlation of sex within sibships that the generalized Trivers-Willard hypothesis would otherwise imply.

16. Turkheimer (1998) provides an interesting discussion that includes a division between a "weak" sense of a phenomenon as biological and a "strong" sense, although neither corresponds to the idea that a phenomenon is innate in the sense of a phenotype we would expect to develop similarly across a very broad range of developmental environments, which appears to be how Cox uses the term.

17. It should also be symmetric, rather than an analysis offering casual socialization or other environmental explanations but then suddenly declaring a principled agnosticism when speculations turn to genes. Indeed, to me this is one of the chief virtues of greater awareness of Darwinian theorizing: they call attention to the extent to which the concluding sections of some social science literatures are replete with casual, almost throwaway, speculations about the socialization or cultural origins of behaviors, offered without any real prospect of subsequent evaluations as a way of gesturing toward providing a developmental explanation, almost as a kind of serial secular origin mythmaking. More explicit statements that work does not and is not intended to speak to the origins of psychological traits or behaviors, when this is the case, would be more honest and ultimately more scientific.

REFERENCES

Almond, Douglas, and Lena Edlund. 2006. "Trivers-Willard at Birth and One Year: Evidence from U.S. Natality Data 1983–2001." Working paper. New York: Columbia University Department of Economics.

Archer, John. 1997. "Why Do People Love Their Pets?" *Evolution and Human Behavior* 18:237–59.

Becker, Gary S. 1964. *Human Capital.* New York: National Bureau of Economic Research.

———. 1981. *A Treatise on the Family.* Cambridge, MA: Harvard University Press.

Belsky, Jay, Laurence Steinberg, and Patricia Draper. 1991. "Childhood Experience, Interpersonal Development, and Reproductive Strategy: An Evolutionary Theory of Socialization." *Child Development* 62:647–70.

Biblarz, Timothy J., and Adrian E. Raftery. 1999. "Family Structure, Educational Attainment, and Socioeconomic Success: Rethinking the 'Pathology of Matriarchy.' " *American Journal of Sociology* 105:321–65.

Brédart, Serge, and Robert M. French. 1999. "Do Babies Resemble Their Fathers More Than Their Mothers? A Failure to Replicate Christenfeld and Hill (1995)." *Evolution and Human Behavior* 20:129–35.

Bressan, Paola, and Massimo Grassi. 2004. "Parental Resemblance in 1-Year-Olds and the Gaussian Curve." *Evolution and Human Behavior* 25:133–41.

Bressan, Paola, and Maria F. Dal Martello. 2002. "*Talis Pater, Talis Filius:* Perceived Resemblance and the Belief in Genetic Relatedness." *Psychological Science* 13:213–18.

Browne, Kingsley R. 2002. *Biology at Work: Rethinking Sexual Equality.* New Brunswick, NJ: Rutgers University Press.

Buss, David M. 1995. "The Future of Evolutionary Psychology." *Psychological Inquiry* 6:81–87.

Chodorow, Nancy. 1978. *The Reproduction of Mothering: Psychoanalysis and the Sociology of Gender.* Los Angeles: University of California Press.

Christenfeld, Nicholas J. S., and Emily A. Hill. 1995. "Whose Baby Are You?" *Nature* 378: 669.

Clark, Andy. 1997. *Being There: Putting Mind, Body, and World Together Again.* Cambridge, MA: MIT Press.

Clutton-Brock, T. H. 1991. *The Evolution of Parental Care.* Princeton, NJ: Princeton University Press.

Cox, Donald. 2003. "Private Transfers within the Family: Mothers, Fathers, Sons and Daughters." In *Death and Dollars: The Role of Gifts and Bequests in America,* edited by Alicia H. Munnell and Annika Sunden (168–97). Washington, DC: Brookings Institution Press.

Crawford, Charles B., Brenda E. Salter, and Kerry L. Jang. 1989. "Human Grief: Is Its Intensity Related to the Reproductive Value of the Deceased?" *Ethology and Sociobiology* 10:297–307.

Daly, Martin, and Margo Wilson. 1982. "Whom Are Newborn Babies Said to Resemble?" *Ethology and Sociobiology* 3:69–78.

———. 1988. *Homicide.* New York: Aldine de Gruyter.

———. 1996. "Violence Against Stepchildren." *Current Directions in Psychological Science* 5:77–81.

———. 1999. *The Truth about Cinderella: A Darwinian View of Parental Love.* New Haven, CT: Yale University Press.

Draper, Patricia, and Henry Harpending. 1982. "Father Absence and Reproductive Strategy: An Evolutionary Perspective." *Journal of Anthropological Research* 38:255–73.

Duster, Troy. 2006. "Comparative Perspectives and Competing Explanations: Taking on the Newly Configured Reductionist Challenge to Sociology." *American Sociological Review* 71:1–15.

Edlund, Lena. 1999. "Son Preference, Sex Ratios, and Marriage Patterns." *Journal of Political Economy* 107(6): 1275–1304.

Edwards, A. W. F. 1966. "Sex Ratio Data Analysed Independently of Family Limitation." *Annals of Human Genetics* 29: 337–47.

Ehrenreich, Barbara 2000. "How 'Natural' Is Rape?" *Time,* January 23.

Ewen, John G., Phillip Cassey, and Anders P. Møller. 2004. "Facultative Primary Sex Ratio Variation: A Lack of Evidence in Birds?" *Proceedings of the Royal Society of London Series B: Biological Sciences* 271:1277–82.

Frank, Steven A. 1990. "Sex Allocation Theory for Birds and Mammals." *Annual Review of Ecology and Systematics* 21:13–55.

Freese, Jeremy, and Brian Powell. 1999. "Sociobiology, Status, and Parental Investment in Sons and Daughters: Testing the Trivers-Willard Hypothesis." *American Journal of Sociology* 106:1704–43.

Freese, Jeremy, Jui-Chung Allen Li, and Lisa D. Wade. 2003. "The Potential Relevances of Biology to Social Inquiry." *Annual Review of Sociology* 29:233–56.

Friedman, Milton. 1953. *Essays in Positive Economics.* Chicago: University of Chicago Press.

Gelman, Andrew. 2006a. "Amusing Example of the Fallacy of Controlling for an Intermediate Outcome, or, the Tyranny of Statistical Methodology and How It Can Lead Even Well-Intentioned Sociobiologists Astray." http://www.stat.columbia.edu/~cook/movabletype/archives/2006/04/amusing_example.html.

———. 2006b. "Problems in a Study of Girl and Boy Births, Leading to a Point about the Virtues of Collaboration." http://www.stat.columbia.edu/~cook/movabletype/archives/2006/08/more_on_girl_an.html.

Gintis, Herbert. 2000. *Game Theory Evolving.* Princeton, NJ: Princeton University Press.

Goldberg, Steven. 1973. *The Inevitability of Patriarchy.* New York: Morrow.

———. 1993. *Why Men Rule: A Theory of Male Dominance.* Chicago: Open Court.

Hopcroft, Rosemary. 2005. "Parental Status and Differential Investment in Sons and Daughters: Trivers-Willard Revisited." *Social Forces* 83:1111–36.

Hrdy, Sarah Blaffer. 1997. "Raising Darwin's Consciousness: Female Sexuality and the Prehominid Origins of Patriarchy." *Human Nature* 8:1–49.

Jacobsen, R., H. Møller, and A. Mouritsen. 1999. "Natural Variation in the Human Sex Ratio." *Human Reproduction* 14:3120–25.

James, William H. 1975. "Sex Ratio and the Sex Composition of the Existing Sibs." *Annals of Human Genetics* 38:371–78.

———. 2000. "The Variation of the Probability of a Son Within and Across Couples." *Human Reproduction* 15:1184–88.

Kanazawa, Satoshi. 2001a. "De Gustibus Est Disputandum." *Social Forces* 79:1131–63.

———. 2001b. "Why We Love Our Children." *American Journal of Sociology* 106:1761–75.

———. 2005. "Big and Tall Parents Have More Sons: Further Generalizations of the Trivers-Willard Hypothesis." *Journal of Theoretical Biology* 235:583–90.

———. 2006. "Violent Men Have More Sons: Further Evidence for the Generalized Trivers-Willard Hypothesis." *Journal of Theoretical Biology* 239:450–59.

———. 2007. "Beautiful Parents Have More Daughters: A Further Implication of the Generalized Trivers-Willard Hypothesis." *Journal of Theoretical Biology* 244:133–40.

Kanazawa, Satoshi, and Griet Vandermassen. 2005. "Engineers Have More Sons, Nurses Have More Daughters: An Evolutionary Psychological Extension of Baron-Cohen's Extreme Male Brain Theory of Autism and Its Empirical Implications." *Journal of Theoretical Biology* 233:589–99.

Keller, Matthew C., Randolph M. Nesse, and Sandra Hofferth. 2001. "The Trivers-Willard Hypothesis of Parental Investment: No Effect in the Contemporary United States." *Evolution and Human Behavior* 22:343–60.

Kenrick, Douglas T. 1995. "Evolutionary Theory versus the Confederacy of Dunces." *Psychological Inquiry* 6(1): 56–62.

Laibson, David I., and Richard Zeckhauser. 1998. "Amos Tversky and the Ascent of Behavioral Economics." *Journal of Risk and Uncertainty* 16:7–47.

Littlefield, Christine H., and J. Phillipe Rushton. 1986. "When a Child Dies: The Sociobiology of Bereavement." *Journal of Personality and Social Psychology* 51:797–802.

Lopreato, Joseph, and Timothy Crippen. 1999. *Crisis in Sociology: The Need for Darwin.* New Brunswick, NJ: Transaction Publishers.

Maconochie, Noreen, and Eve Roman. 1997. "Sex Ratios: Are There Natural Variations within the Human Population?" *British Journal of Obstetrics and Gynaecology* 104:1050–53.

McLain, D. Kelly, Deanna Setters, Michael P. Moulton, and Ann E. Pratt. 2000. "Ascription of Resemblance of Newborns by Parents and Nonrelatives." *Evolution and Human Behavior* 21:11–23.

Miller, Geoffrey F. 1998. "How Mate Choice Shaped Human Nature: A Review of Sexual Selection and Human Evolution." In *Handbook of Evolutionary Psychology: Ideas, Issues, and Applications,* edited by Charles Crawford and Dennis L. Krebs (87–130). Mahwah, NJ: Lawrence Erlbaum Associates.

Moffitt, Terrie E., Avshalom Caspi, and Michael Rutter. 2005. "Strategy for Investigating Interactions Between Measured Genes and Measured Environments." *Archives of General Psychiatry* 62:473–81.

Morgan, S. Phillip, Diane N. Lye, and Gretchen A. Condran. 1988. "Sons, Daughters, and Risk of Marital Disruption." *Social Forces* 94(1): 110–29.

Norberg, Karen. 2004. "Partnership Status and the Human Sex Ratio at Birth." *Proceedings of the Royal Society B: Biological Sciences* 271(1555): 2403–10.

Palmer, A. Richard. 2000. "Quasireplication and the Contract of Error: Lessons from Sex Ratios, Heritabilities, and Fluctuating Asymmetry." *Annual Review of Ecology and Systematics* 31:441–80.

Pinker, Steven. 1997. *How the Mind Works.* New York: Norton.

———. 2002. *The Blank Slate: The Modern Denial of Human Nature.* New York: Viking.

Rossi, Alice S. 1984. "Gender and Parenthood." *American Sociological Review* 49:1–19.

Satz, Debra, and John Ferejohn. 1994. "Rational Choice and Social Theory." *Journal of Philosophy* 91:71–87.

Segerstråle, Ullica. 2000. *Defenders of the Truth: The Battle for Science in the Sociobiology Debate and Beyond.* New York: Oxford University Press.

Serpell, James. 1986. *In the Company of Animals: A Study of Human–Animal Relationships.* New York: Blackwell.

Shostak, Sara. 2003. "Locating Gene-Environment Interaction: At the Intersections of Genetics and Public Health." *Social Science and Medicine* 56:2327–42.

Smuts, Barbara. 1995. "The Evolutionary Origins of Patriarchy." *Human Nature* 6:1–32.

Surbey, Michelle K. 1998. "Developmental Psychology and Modern Darwinism." In *Handbook of Evolutionary Psychology: Ideas, Issues, and Applications,* edited by Charles Crawford and Dennis L. Krebs (369–404). Mahwah, NJ: Lawrence Erlbaum Associates.

Symons, Donald. 1995. "Beauty Is in the Adaptations of the Beholder: The Evolutionary Psychology of Human Female Sexual Attractiveness." In *Sexual Nature/Sexual Culture,* edited by Paul R. Abramson and Steven D. Pinkerton (80–118). Chicago: University of Chicago Press.

Thornhill, Randy, and Craig T. Palmer. 2000. *A Natural History of Rape: Biological Bases of Sexual Coercion.* Cambridge, MA: The MIT Press.

Tooby, John, and Leda Cosmides. 1989. "Evolutionary Psychology and the Generation of Culture: Part I. Theoretical Considerations." *Ethology and Sociobiology* 10:29–49.

———. 1990. "The Past Explains the Present: Emotional Adaptations and the Structure of Ancestral Environments." *Ethology and Sociobiology* 11:375–424.

———. 1992. "The Psychological Foundations of Culture." In *The Adapted Mind: Evolutionary Psychology and the Generation of Culture,* edited by Jerome H. Barkow, Leda Cosmides, and John Tooby (19–136). New York: Oxford University Press.

Trivers, Robert L. 1974. "Parent–Offspring Conflict." *American Zoologist* 14:249–64.

———. 1985. *Social Evolution.* Menlo Park, CA: Benjamin/Cummings.

Trivers, Robert L., and Dan E. Willard. 1973. "Natural Selection for the Parental Ability to Vary the Sex Ratio of Offspring." *Science* 179:90–92.

Turkheimer, Eric. 1998. "Heritability and Biological Explanation." *Psychological Review* 105:782–91.

Wahlsten, Douglas. 1990. "Insensitivity of the Analysis of Variance to Heredity-Environment Interactions." *Behavioral and Brain Sciences* 13:109–61.

Wilson, Edward O. 1975. *Sociobiology: The New Synthesis.* Cambridge, MA: Harvard University Press.

———. 1978. *On Human Nature.* Cambridge, MA: Harvard University Press.

———. 1984. *Biophilia.* Cambridge, MA: Harvard University Press.

Winterhalder, Bruce, and Eric Alden Smith. 2000. "Analyzing Adaptive Strategies: Human Behavioral Ecology at Twenty-Five." *Evolutionary Anthropology* 9:51–72.

Wright, Robert. 1994. *The Moral Animal: Evolutionary Psychology and Everyday Life.* New York: Vintage Books.

8

Beyond Theory

Individual Differences in Exchanges between Older Parents and Their Children

Steven H. Zarit

There is much to admire in Donald Cox's ambitious, engaging, and well-written chapter, "Intergenerational Caregiving and Exchange." A major thrust of the chapter is to grapple with the variability in family life and exchanges, to gain "a firm grasp of the logic of how families tick." Cox recognizes the limits of economic perspectives in accounting for these differences and engages in an attempt to bridge across disciplines and perspectives to provide a better understanding of critical issues in family life.

I applaud these goals, but unfortunately I disagree with many of Cox's points. Some of the differences between Cox's perspective and my own may be disciplinary. One of the risks of efforts to engage in dialogue with people from diverse disciplines is that they may view the same phenomena in such different ways and there may be too few points of contact for a meaningful dialogue to develop. As a psychologist who has conducted research on family care in later life for more than 25 years, I have partic-ular perspectives that lead me to make different observations and draw different conclusions than Dr. Cox does. My disciplinary training also leads me to look at theory and standards of proof in a different way. Rather than detail these disagreements, I will briefly summarize my main objections to Cox's approach and then return to his starting point—that families have considerable variability for which current theories cannot account. Instead of providing a unifying theory for these differences, however, I believe we need first to describe these individual differences in a clear and accurate way. I do this out of the belief that theory needs to begin with a solid empirical foundation, rather than reshaping the evidence to fit theoretical propositions.

Problems in Perspectives on Family Exchanges

My critique of Cox's approach can be grouped into three areas: (1) the artificial quality of the scenarios that he devises to illustrate key dilemmas; (2) problems in how assumptions are derived from evolutionary theory; and (3) the lack of direct, empirical evidence for attitudes and motivations that underlie exchanges.

Scenarios: Generalizations from Artificial Dilemmas

Moving from a research topic where we have achieved considerable expertise to a new area where our knowledge is more limited is always tricky. It is easy to gain only a superficial understanding or to miss critical features. These pitfalls characterize many of Cox's family scenarios. The scenarios had a constructed and artificial quality about them, and they seemed to be abstractions designed to make a point rather than reflect what actually takes place in family exchanges.

One example of a problematic scenario is one that introduces the concept of "crowding out." In this scenario, Cox's mother discovers that his grandmother qualifies for Medicaid benefits "that could finance *high-quality* nursing home care" (italics mine). The rest of the scenario unfolds from that basic premise.

The problem with this scenario is that it is not realistic. Unfortunately, the economics of Medicaid reimbursement mean there are few high-quality programs. Although many facilities that accept Medicaid strive to do as good a job as possible, the low reimbursement they receive means that they will rarely be able to do more than an adequate job of providing care, and many, unfortunately, cannot even do that. Although many private-pay nursing homes provide mediocre care, finding one that provides high-quality care is more likely. As an example, a private-pay nursing home near my office is clean and bright, with reasonably well-trained staff and meals served on china plates. Another facility nearby accepts Medicaid. The décor is institutional, there are few amenities or activities, and the staff are poorly trained and uninspired. Most people with the means to would choose to pay privately for their parent's nursing home care. The exception to this pattern is the well-funded charity-based nonprofit home that can subsidize out of its own resources for the amount paid by Medicaid. My point about this scenario and other examples from Cox is he often starts with a basic premise that is somewhat artificial and constructed more to make a point than to reflect key family exchange processes.

The issue that the nursing home scenario addresses, "crowding out," has been called "substitution" in gerontological policy studies and has long been a focus of research. Surprisingly, little empirical evidence has been found for substitution of publicly supported services for family help (e.g., Penning 2002; Pezzin, Kemper, and Reschovsky 1996; Shea et al. 2003; Stoller 1989; Tennstedt, Crawford, and McKinlay 1993). In part, the lack of empirical support for substitution is because of both quality and affordability of formal services. There is also some evidence that many families' commitment may be partially independent of how much paid help is available. My colleagues and I have examined differences in the amount of family help provided in the United States and Sweden (Shea et al. 2003). We expected that in Sweden—where old-age services were explicitly developed to relieve families of the burden of care—that family involvement would be lower. We found, however, that Swedish families remained as involved in care of the aged as they did in the United States. The two differences we did find were that state services were more likely to supplement the help given by families in Sweden and that people without families got help more often in Sweden than in the United States. That difference is probably because of the complex system of funding and eligibilities in the United States that makes it difficult to access services without an advocate. In the end, families in Sweden have stayed involved, and there has not been substitution of services on a large scale, even though high-quality and affordable public services are available.

Another reason there has been little evidence of substitution in the United States is that most people entering a nursing home do not qualify for Medicaid assistance, whereas Medicare pays for nursing home care only for short periods following an acute hospitalization. Instead, to qualify for Medicaid, people must "spend down" nearly all their assets; that is, they must pay out of pocket for the nursing home until they have exhausted the means to pay. Spending down is a much more common dilemma for families than the "crowding out" scenario and can be particularly distressing for a spouse caregiver. There is a mythology that rich people hide their assets so that they can qualify for Medicaid, and although that has certainly happened, state governments have put controls in place that make that strategy impossible. As for constructing a trust that protects assets, even as big a fool as King Lear would recognize that he did not want to live in a Medicaid facility if he had a choice.

Evolutionary Biology: Post Hoc and Reductionist Applications

My second, and major, disagreement with Cox is his choice of theory. Evolutionary biology has its place in social science, but its limitations are painfully apparent in Cox's application. Rather than helping us understand the variability in family functioning, evolutionary principles provide what could be called a "Gumby" theory, so flexible that it can be stretched in any direction to generate post hoc explanations that masquerade as insight. Facts such as sibling rivalry or the love of grandmothers for their grandchildren are interpreted post hoc as support for evolutionary biology, but if the opposite were found, another post hoc explanation could be used to fit the facts. In other words, facts are selectively fit to the theory, rather than formulating testable propositions from a theory. Cox notes the criticism that evolutionary biology often posits untestable and irrefutable propositions, but he does not suggest an appropriate standard of evidence nor does he provide an example in which a theoretical proposition is tested prospectively in a framework in which it could be refuted.

Again, my complaint may have to do with a disciplinary perspective. Within psychology, the role of theory is to generate testable hypotheses that can be confirmed or disconfirmed with empirical evidence and not used for weaving together a grand social perspective. There is a clear standard of proof by which theoretical propositions are evaluated. That has not always been the case. When I received my training, clinical and developmental psychology were slowly emerging from the stultifying effects of Freudian theory. Like evolutionary biology, psychoanalytic theory is reductionist and flexible—current behaviors could be explained in a post hoc manner by some prior psychodynamic event without ever testing these assumptions empirically. The primary explanatory principle is unconscious motivation, which can never be observed or measured, though it can be inferred by those steeped in psychoanalytic principles, and it can explain practically everything. Cox, in fact, notes the failure of Freudian theory but adopts an approach with similar flaws. The heart of the assumption in Cox's chapter about why people in families behave the way they do is unconscious motivation by another name. An enduring part of my own disciplinary perspective is to view these types of flexible and reductionist models with a high degree of skepticism and to ask for a standard of proof whereby testable propositions derived from evolutionary biology are evaluated systematically. Continuing to select anecdotes, no matter how clever, that can be interpreted to support evolutionary thinking is not a useful strategy for building scientific knowledge.

The model of evolutionary biology and its effects on behavior that Cox presented is also not consistent with contemporary genetic principles. Evolutionary biology assumes a mechanism by which behavioral tendencies are inherited. Everyone would agree that behavior is, in part, inherited; although that proposition is certainly true in its broadest sense, Cox assumes a relatively straightforward and direct relation between genotype and phenotype. In the various examples and anecdotes in his chapter, very specific behaviors are said to reflect evolutionary principles. Figure 8.1 illustrates this type of model, in which genotype leads directly to phenotype. The evidence of how genes affect behavior does not support that simple assumption. The causal pathway from genotype to phenotype is more complex with a more unpredictable outcome. McClearn and his colleagues (McClearn 2006; McClearn, Vogler, and Hofer 2001) have illustrated this process with just seven alleles, a small number of sites for complex behavior (figure 8.2). Genes guide the synthesis of RNA, which in turn lead to synthesis of polypeptides, which become building blocks of a variety of physiological processes. At each point, there is an interaction

Figure 8.1. A Simple Model of Genetic Effects

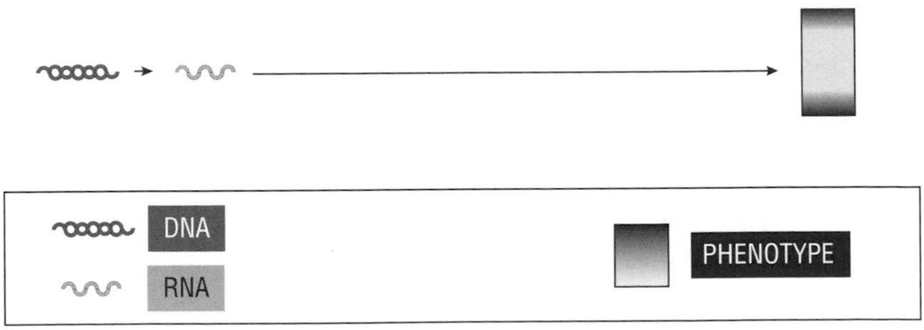

Source: Adapted from McClearn (2006).

Figure 8.2. A Schema for Genetic and Environmental Influences

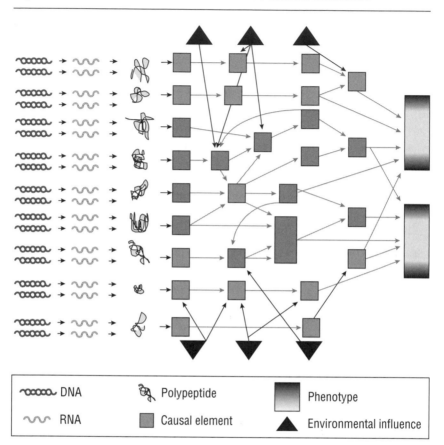

Source: Adapted from McClearn (2006).

among genetic influences and with a myriad of environmental influences, including those directly acting on physiological processes, such as availability and level of nutrients and toxins. There are also feedback loops throughout the system, which can enhance some genetic effects and suppress others. There can even be feedback from the environment, which changes physiological processes and in turn may turn off or enhance the effects of some genes or create new gene × environment and even gene × gene interactions.

McClearn (2006) argues that there is both complexity and unpredictability in this system, such that all phenomena have multiple causes, that each cause can also have multiple effects, and new properties emerge at higher levels in a hierarchical system that cannot be predicted from the simple structure of a lower level in the hierarchy. As McClearn states, "From these characterizations, we are cautioned against expecting simple all-and-only, necessary-and-sufficient, explanations when confronted by a genuinely complex system" (McClearn 2006, 314).

Genetics is an important contributing factor to behavior, but phenotypes always are the outcome of a complex causal sequence that involves gene × gene and gene × environment interactions. Any specific behavior, including exchanges between family members and their underlying motivations, will have many different origins. The strongest predictors of specific behaviors are likely to be proximal, whereas evolutionary biology could be considered a more distal cause that may make certain behaviors somewhat more probable but that could rarely be demonstrated directly. Cox's approach of selecting a specific family exchanges and then attributing the outcomes to evolutionary principles is not consistent with either genetic principles or the fact that any specific behavior is likely to have other, proximal causes that affected the course of action.

In the end, simple attributions that complex social behaviors are caused by "genetics" are not consistent with how genes influence behavior. Furthermore, just as changes at the gene level can lead to different outcomes, so can changes in the environment. The statement that Cox makes that our psychology was formed in the Pleistocene era is not correct. Even if there has been no change at the gene level since that time, so much in the environment (including such "biological" processes as prenatal and early childhood nutrition, and exposure to illness) has changed that the phenotype we observe has undoubtedly been altered in many dramatic ways.

Beliefs about Exchanges

My third main critique of Cox's chapter concerns his implicit reliance on unconscious motivation as an explanation. Much of the work he cites from economics and sociology on intergenerational exchanges, as well as other chapters in this volume, makes an inference about what the underlying reasons for allocating resources in a particular way must have been. There has been little work that has asked people for their own perspectives on these issues. Part of the undoing of Freudian approaches was the discovery that we could, in fact, understand what people were thinking and feeling if we asked them. The cognitive revolution in psychology (e.g., Beck et al. 1979) was based on the realization that the information people provided about themselves and their motivations was both reliable and predicted future behaviors. Certainly, people have different levels of awareness and some people can give more insight into their behavior than others. Nonetheless, what they believe will influence the choices they make. As we consider how people allocate resources, we need to ask them directly about their decisions, and not just assume we know or can reliably infer it.

Part of the disrepute of the use of subjective experience and beliefs in research stems from concerns about reliability. When asking people about motivation for past events, recall may indeed be faulty or shaped in a flexible way to give socially desirable responses or to make current behavior consistent with other individual characteristics. People may see themselves in control of situations where they are not in control, or as making an enlightened decision when they acted mainly out of self-interest. But as a predictor of future behavior, beliefs have an important role as one of many factors that will affect outcomes.

Family Care and Individual Differences

I now want to return to the excellent starting point Cox made about grounding our approach in an understanding of the variability of families. I will not attempt to fit families into a single, encompassing theory. That would be premature and there may not be one theory that could accomplish that goal. Rather, I will start from the other direction, describing families in one particular context: providing care to a disabled older person. In doing so, I will emphasize variability, because any larger theory has to grapple with the complexity of family structure, organization, and process.

The starting point is to look at who becomes caregiver to an elder. Cox assumes that caregiving in later life involves a parent and child, but there are many different types of care relationships. Figure 8.3 presents data from a national survey of older people with disabilities and their caregivers (Wolff and Kasper 2006). If we focus on the primary caregiver (that person who provides the most help and has the most responsibility), the most likely person to become a caregiver is a husband or wife. Children provide a lot of care, but mostly only when their parent is widowed or single, or they supplement the help one parent gives to another. A sizable proportion of caregivers fall into a category of "other," which includes

Figure 8.3. Primary Caregivers of Disabled Elders

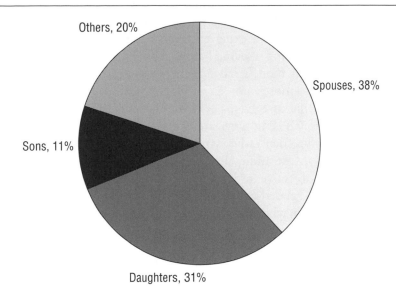

Others, 20%

Spouses, 38%

Sons, 11%

Daughters, 31%

Source: Adapted from Wolff and Kasper (2006).

some daughters-in-law, grandchildren, siblings of the person receiving care, cousins, and even people with no kin relationship to the disabled elder. Assumptions about care, then, should not be based on a single relationship (e.g., daughters caring for mothers), or even that it involves only women providing care. In fact, among spouse caregivers, 42 percent are husbands. These husbands and a growing number of sons provide extensive and high-quality care to disabled wives and mothers (Miller 1990; Wolff and Kasper 2006; Zarit, Todd, and Zarit 1986).

Building on this diversity in who becomes a caregiver is the enormous variability in family structure and organization. Families come in all shapes and sizes. There are what Burton and Bengtson (1985) call "beanpole" families, which consist of several generations, but with one or two individuals within each generation. There are also traditional extended families with large numbers of children, grandchildren, and other kin connections. Size probably matters, in that larger families will have more people who are able to help. Factors such as divorce and remarriage will complicate potential and actual help patterns, though the extent that happens remains to be determined. Beyond structure, there is considerable variability in quality of relationships, social and economic resources, and cultural expectations, all of which affect patterns of help.

The diversity of family forms and processes in caregiving play out in another way for caregivers' experience of stress or burden. The primary focus of most caregiving research has been on stress. Here again, though simple reductionist models have been proposed, the vast amount of research supports a more complex set of relationships. The simple model is that the tasks that caregivers perform, particularly in managing their relative's behavior and emotions, are stressful and lead to a set of negative outcomes, including depressive symptoms, poor health, and an increased risk of mortality. Most studies, however, have found only a modest association between objective care stressors and these outcomes. Instead, the impact that care-related activities have on caregivers depends on an unfolding process in which risk factors, resources, and the meanings that caregivers give to the events they are experiencing all play an important role (Aneshensel et al. 1995).

Figure 8.4 shows the most widely used model of caregiving stress, Leonard Pearlin's stress process model (Aneshensel et al. 1995; Pearlin et al. 1990). In this model, disease and disabilities create a context in which caregivers may experience distress, but the extent to which they do depends on other risk factors and resources in the situation. Care-related stressors, or objective stressors, as Pearlin (Pearlin et al. 1990) calls them,

Figure 8.4. The Stress Process Model of Caregiving

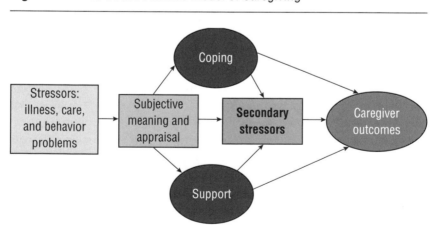

Source: Adapted from Pearlin et al. (1990).

have an immediate subjective impact. The subjective impact has to do with the meanings people give to events, the amount of perceived threat the events have, and how disruptive the events are in their lives. People look at the same stressor differently, which is why there can be such different outcomes. How people appraise stressful events in turn can lead to a spillover or proliferation into other areas of life. Caregiving activities may begin to have adverse effects on work, other family relationships, the family's economic well-being, or even the caregiver's sense of self. Pearlin refers to these processes as "secondary" stressors, not because they are less important in the stress process, but because they are not a primary component of the disease or disability that sets off this process in the first place. Even here, the presence of a role conflict is less important in affecting outcomes than the meaning a caregiver gives to these roles. As an example, some caregivers who are employed may find that the multiple demands of work and caregiving are more than they can manage, but others will report that they get a sense of accomplishment while at work that is missing when caring for a relative with dementia (Aneshensel et al. 1995). Primary and secondary stressors give rise to coping efforts to manage these events, including seeking support. The availability of coping and support resources serve to contain the impact of stressors on the caregiver's life and well-being. Finally, it is the sum of this process, not just the occurrence of stressors, that leads to critical outcomes: the impact on the health and well-being of caregivers. Just as there is no "typical" caregiver or "typical" family, the outcomes for caregivers can vary widely.

This variability in the stress process holds for the decision to place a relative in a nursing home (Aneshensel et al. 1995). Again, we find that placement does not occur at a specific point in time, or because caregivers experience a certain level of stressors. Rather, many different factors play a role. Some caregivers are quickly overwhelmed and turn to a nursing home early in the process, whereas others provide care in their own home for a relative with a degenerative illness such as Alzheimer's disease until death. Severity of stressors or even duration of caregiving are not strong predictors of the decision to place or the timing of placement. The strongest predictor is when care demands lead to what Pearlin and his colleagues (1990) call "role captivity," that is, the feeling of not having any choice in performing these activities. Caregivers with high role captivity are more likely to place a relative, and that relationship holds whether the caregiver is a spouse or daughter and outweighs other predictors of the occurrence and timing of placement. Caregivers in turn who report low role captivity are more likely to continue with care at home (Aneshensel et al. 1995; Gaugler, Zarit, and Pearlin 1999, 2003; Gaugler et al. 2000). Again, it is the subjective meaning that events have, not their objective characteristics, that have the most power in predicting a critical event such as nursing home placement.

Conclusions

I have tried to describe some of the variability in caregiving families, rather than providing a unifying, global theory of the differences. My preference for doing so is in part a function of my own training that places importance on individual differences. It also reflects a concern for how easily broad generalizations can oversimplify complex relationships, particularly as they are translated into policy and practice. In a society such as ours that has not come to grips with how to meet basic health and social needs, politicians will gladly latch onto theories that would allow them to avoid difficult decisions. I would rather see practitioners and policymakers grapple with a few empirical main points, for example, that caregiving is stressful and that we need to individualize the types of supportive programs we design for them, than to be swept up by a compelling theory that has a limited empirical foundation. That is not to say that there is no value in global theories such as evolutionary biology. Evolution and inheritance of behavioral tendencies and characteristics are an important factor in individual development, but that does not mean we can assume a simple relation between genetics and behavior or impute motivations without careful testing and observation. In the end, we may be surprised at how much can be gained by looking at individual differences.

REFERENCES

Aneshensel, Carol, Leonard I. Pearlin, Joseph T. Mullan, Steven H. Zarit, and Carol J. Whitlatch. 1995. *Profiles in Caregiving: The Unexpected Career.* New York: Academic Press.

Beck, Aaron T., A. John Rush, Brian F. Shaw, and Gary Emery. 1979. *Cognitive Therapy of Depression.* New York: Guilford.

Burton, Linda M., and Vern L. Bengtson. 1985. "Black Grandmothers: Issues of Timing and Continuity of Roles." In *Grandparenthood,* edited by Vern L. Bengtson and Joan F. Robertson (61–77). Beverley Hills, CA: Sage.

Gaugler, Joseph. E., Steven H. Zarit, and Leonard I. Pearlin. 1999. "Caregiving and Institutionalization: Perceptions of Family Conflict and Socioemotional Support." *International Journal of Aging and Human Development* 49(1): 1–25.

———. 2003. "The Onset of Dementia Caregiving and Its Longitudinal Implications." *Psychology and Aging* 18(2): 171–80.

Gaugler, Joseph. E., Adam Davey, Leonard I. Pearlin, and Steven H. Zarit. 2000. "Modeling Caregiver Adaptation Over Time: The Longitudinal Impact of Behavior Problems." *Psychology and Aging* 15(3): 437–50.

McClearn, Gerald E. 2006. "Contextual Genetics." *Trends in Genetics* 22(6): 314–19.

McClearn, Gerald E., George P. Vogler, and Scott M. Hofer. 2001. "Environment–Gene and Gene–Gene Interactions." In *Handbook of the Biology of Aging,* 5th ed., edited by Edward J. Masoro and Steven N. Austad (423–44). San Diego: Academic Press.

Miller, Baila. 1990. "Gender Differences in Spouse Caregiver Strain: Socialization and Role Expectation." *Journal of Marriage and the Family* 52(3): 311–21.

Pearlin, Leonard I., Joseph T. Mullan, Shirley J. Semple, and Marilyn M. Skaff. 1990. "Caregiving and the Stress Process: An Overview of Concepts and Their Measures." *Gerontologist* 30(5): 583–94.

Penning, Margaret J. 2002. "Hydra Revisited: Substituting Formal for Self- and Informal In-Home Care among Older Adults with Disabilities." *Gerontologist* 42(1): 4–16.

Penrod, Joan, Katherine M. Harris, and Robert L. Kane. 1994. "Informal Care Substitution: What We Don't Know Can Hurt Us." *Journal of Aging and Social Policy* 6(4): 21–31.

Pezzin, Lillian, Peter Kemper, and James Reschovsky. 1996. "Does Publicly Provided Home Care Substitute for Family Care? Experimental Evidence with Endogenous Living Arrangements." *Journal of Human Resources* 31(3): 650–76.

Shea, Dennis G., Adam Davey, Elia E. Femia, Steven H. Zarit, Gerdt Sundstrom, Stig Berg, and Michael A. Smyer. 2003. "Exploring Assistance in Sweden and the United States." *Gerontologist* 43(5): 712–21.

Stoller, Eleanor. 1989. "Formal Services and Informal Helping: The Myth of Service Substitution." *Journal of Applied Gerontology* 8(1): 37–52.

Tennstedt, Sharon L., Sibyl L. Crawford, and John B. McKinlay. 1993. "Is Family Care on the Decline? A Longitudinal Investigation of the Substitution of Formal Long-Term Care Services for Informal Care." *The Milbank Quarterly* 71(4): 601–24.

Wolff, Jennifer L., and Judith D. Kasper. 2006. "Caregivers of Frail Elders: Updating a National Profile." *Gerontologist* 46(3): 344–56.

Zarit, Steven H., Pamela A. Todd, and Judy M. Zarit. 1986. "Subjective Burden of Husbands and Wives as Caregivers: A Longitudinal Study." *Gerontologist* 26(3): 260–70.

PART III
The Nature of Negotiations within Generations

9

Intergenerational Support, Care, and Relationship Quality in Later Life

Exploring Within-Family Differences

Karl Pillemer and J. Jill Suitor

The popular children's book *I Love You the Purplest* (Joosse 1996) tells a story aimed at helping parents deal with the child's age-old question of "Who do you love the best?" On a fishing outing with their mother, two boys ask her who is the best at digging worms, rowing, fishing, and, at the end of the day, which son she loves most. The mother carefully and creatively follows an equity principle, answering the questions in a way that highlights each boy's special qualities without stating a preference. As a final symbol of equality, as she tucks them into bed at night she tells one child she loves him "the bluest," and the other "the reddest." In the book's final page, this is symbolized in an equal blending of emotions: simultaneously loving both boys "the purplest."

Reflected in this story are themes that resonate with parents of young children and scholars alike. Popular books counsel parents about how to eliminate rivalry and avoid favoritism (Sonna 2006). Social scientists have widely examined the notion of within-family differences in families with young children and adolescents. Research in developmental psychology in particular suggests that there are differences in parent–child relationships within families that develop in the earlier years.

Studies of younger families have shown that parents of young and adolescent children differentiate between their children in terms of both affection and disapproval (Brody and Stoneman 1994; Brody, Stoneman, and McCoy 1992; McHale et al. 1995). The role of birth order has also been of substantial interest to scholars across a wide range of disciplines, from evolutionary biology (Daly and Wilson 1988) to psychology (Sulloway 1996; Whiteman, McHale, and Crouter 2003), sociology (Conley 2004; Downey 1995; Steelman et al. 2002), and economics (Becker 1991; Becker and Tomes 1986). This line of research has focused primarily on the ways in which birth order differentially affects the experiences and opportunities of children within the family.

Further, there is preliminary evidence that such patterns continue into adulthood. Studies by Bedford (1992) and Baker and Daniels (1990) showed that a substantial proportion of adult children felt that their parents favored some children in the family over others, whereas Aldous, Klaus, and Klein (1985) and Brackbill, Kitch, and Noffsinger (1988) found that most parents reported that they differentiated among their children in adulthood in affection, pride, and disappointment. Although these studies were small and did not use representative samples, they do indicate the possibility that within-family differences in parent–child relationships will be encountered in later life.

Despite this evidence that within-family differences, such as parental preference and differential treatment of siblings, exist across the life course, within sociology the designs of most studies of older parent–adult child relationships do not permit an examination of these issues. The majority of these studies asked parents about their adult children in the aggregate, rather than about each child separately, or focused on only one target child. Even the work on within-family differences in adulthood cited above did not collect data from both generations within the same family. Thus it is difficult to develop a picture of the extent of, explanations for, and consequences of within-family differences in parent–adult child relationships.

Our goal is to shed light on this critically important but underresearched topic. The important role of kin and nonkin relationships in well-being has been demonstrated convincingly across the past two decades (Allen, Blieszner, and Roberto 2000; House, Landis, and Umberson 1988; Kawachi and Berkman 2001; Uchino 2004). Because of the salience of the parent–child relationship in the lives of most people, patterns of interaction and support in these relationships hold particularly high potential for affecting well-being (Friedman et al. 1995). Despite a long history of research on the effects of parents and children on one another, little is known about the extent to which older parent–adult child relationships vary within the family and the ways in which such variations affect both parents and children. Thus it is critical to address a research need that has been frequently identified in the gerontological literature but that has not yet been examined empirically (Davey, Janke, and Salva 2005; Lye 1996; Troll and Fingerman 1996): expanding scientific knowledge about the relationship formed by each parent and child by conceptualizing each parent–child dyad in the family as an independent unit, different from other family dyads.

We begin by presenting the conceptual framework we have developed for understanding the quality of parent–child relationships in later life. We then summarize the findings of four separate but related analyses we have conducted over the past several years on differentiation for interpersonal support and care. First, we explore the extent of mothers' differentiation among children within the family in several domains. Second, we present data on the extent to which there is agreement among parents and children about such differentiation. Third, we examine the degree to which parents differentiate among their children in allocating assistance to them and the factors associated with these patterns. Finally, we address the question of how a particular child is selected as the likely caregiver from all children.

These analyses use data we collected in the first large-scale study dedicated to exploring within-family differences in parent–adult child relationships, the Within-Family Differences Study (WFDS). We collected data from mothers who reported about all of their adult children; whenever possible, we also conducted interviews with the children themselves. The aims of the WFDS were to explore the extent to which parents differentiate among their adult children, to identify factors that explain why parents hold preferences toward specific children across a range of relational contexts, and to understand why individual parent–child dyads in the same family differ in such areas as intergenerational assistance and relationship quality.

Conceptual Framework

Over the past two decades, scholars have spent substantial effort on describing the demographic structure of parent–child relationships in later life and the amount and type of contact, interaction, and exchanges between the generations. Indeed, the sociological literature contains an abundance of empirical insights, based on prominent large-scale surveys and panel studies and hundreds of small-scale interview and case studies. Some observers, however, have expressed concern that the development of innovative conceptual approaches to intergenerational relationships has been slow. In particular, social scientists have begun to search for models that better capture the complexity of relationships between older parents and adult children as they are played out in contemporary society (Blieszner, Usita, and Mancini 1996; Connidis 2001; Fingerman 2001; Lye 1996; Pillemer and Luescher 2004). This chapter attempts to contribute to that effort by translating important insights from the developmental psychological literature on younger families—specifically a focus on within-family differences and parental preference—to intergenerational relations in later life.

This effort is guided by a conceptual framework we have developed to predict the quality of older parent–adult child relationships, derived from sociological and social psychological perspectives on interpersonal relations. We believe that it is important to hypothesize potential factors that may lead parents to treat children differentially. It is likely that factors on the level of the individual child may lead to preference (or the lack of it), such as temperament or ability. Further, characteristics of the relationship (such as similarity of social statuses or values) affect various outcomes. Our framework takes these dimensions into consideration, focusing on three general sets of explanatory factors for which there is strong evidence of effects on parent–child relationship quality in later life and that can be expected to be sensitive to within-family differences. These factors are similarity between parents and children; developmental history, including children's problems and attainment of normative adult statuses; and patterns of exchange and equity.

Similarity between Parents and Children

Similarity has been shown to be important in understanding the development and maintenance of relationships throughout the life course (Feld 1982; Lazarsfeld and Merton 1954; McPherson, Smith-Lovin, and Cook 2001; Suitor, Pillemer, and Keeton 1995; Wellman and Wortley 1990). Theories of role structure and reference groups suggest that such patterns of homophily exist because individuals who are similar on important social dimensions—such as marital status, parental status, educational attainment, age, and gender—tend to hold similar values and are more knowledgeable about one another's circumstances, resulting in greater empathy and understanding (Coser 1991; Homans 1950; Lazarsfeld and Merton 1954; Merton 1968; Suitor, Pillemer, Keeton, and Robison 1995; Wellman and Wortley 1990). It is also possible that this relationship may operate in the reverse direction; that is, that value similarity affects the adult statuses that adult children eventually select. Regardless of the causal direction, similarity of both statuses and values are important determinants of social relations.

We suggest that this line of theory and research is applicable to family relationships as well. Indeed, the literature on intergenerational relations reveals the same general pattern found in the broader study of interpersonal relations. In particular, parents tend to have closer, less conflictual and ambivalent, and more supportive relationships with adult children who share their social structural positions (Kaufman and Uhlenberg 1998; Pillemer and Suitor 2002; Umberson 1992) and values (Pillemer and Suitor 2002; Suitor and Pillemer 2006; Welsh and Stewart 1995). Further, studies have shown that relationship quality is very responsive to increases and decreases in status and value similarity (Suitor and Keeton 1997).

Developmental Factors

A key orientation of our work in this area is a life course perspective. This approach highlights the importance of linked lives among family members as well as processes of developmental change over the life span (Elder 1998; Elder and Johnson 2003; Elder, Robertson, and Conger 1996; Moen 1995; Settersten 2003). There is a large set of developmental and life course issues that may affect interpersonal relations; two are particularly relevant in explaining relationship quality between parents and adult children: (a) children's achievement and maintenance of normative adult statuses and (b) adult children's problems.

A powerful social norm holds that children should attain adult statuses in a timely fashion, establish independent lives, and ultimately become potential sources of support for parents. To the extent that adult children experience these normative transitions, relationship quality tends to improve. This pattern occurs because such transitions confirm that the adult child is conforming to societal norms for maturational development. As Ryff and colleagues (1996) make clear, parents wish their children to attain and maintain adult statuses and to become and remain independent. Nevertheless, when this does not occur, they feel obligated to assist them (Hagestad 1986), and such children serve as a reminder that parents have not achieved their task of socialization (Aldous 1978; Cohler and Grunebaum 1981; Pillemer and Suitor 2002). Thus, normative transitions, such as marrying, becoming a parent, and being employed are expected to improve intergenerational relationships, whereas problematic transitions (e.g., divorcing or losing one's job) are expected to affect parent–adult child relations negatively.

Adult children's problems also have the potential to create stress in parent–child relationships not only because they often reduce similarity between the generations but also because they increase children's demands and violate parents' expectations for normative adult status attainment. For example, parent–child relations tend to become strained when adult children develop problems such as substance abuse (Pillemer and Suitor 1991) or experience nonnormative transitions such as job loss (Newman 1999) and divorce (Kaufman and Uhlenberg 1998; Umberson 1992). Children with serious life problems are also less likely to be able to be reliable sources of support for their parents.

Exchange and Equity

Exchange theory has been used for several decades to explain the quality of family relationships, including those between parents and adult children (cf. Nye 1979; Reis and Shaver 1988; Suitor, Pillemer, and Sechrist 2006). Exchange theorists propose that individuals attempt to minimize their costs and maximize their rewards in interactions. This theory also holds that individuals expect the rewards they provide to other persons to be reciprocated, although not necessarily immediately or in kind. In nonfamily relationships, when reciprocity is no longer achieved, the relationship is very likely to end (Roberto and Scott 1986). However, it has been pointed out that families provide special instances of exchange in which it may not be feasible to end a relationship, even when reciprocity is absent. In such a situation, relationship quality may suffer (B. Schwarz 2006; Troll and Fingerman 1996). Conversely, as equity theory suggests, if individuals' inputs to and outcomes from a relationship are balanced, relationship quality is likely to be high (Hatfield et al. 1985). The literature on exchange in later-life families suggests that such issues are important in explaining parent–child relationships. In particular, it appears that relationships suffer when parents continue to provide their adult children with high and unreciprocated levels of care and support (Cohler and Grunebaum 1981; Lee 1988; Mutran and Reitzes 1984; Pillemer and Suitor 2002; Teo et al. 2003).

Application to the Study of Within-Family Differences in Intergenerational Relations

The three sets of explanatory factors discussed above are highly applicable to the study of within-family differences. Specifically, a within-family perspective necessitates viewing each parent–child relationship as embedded in a network of other intrafamilial relationships. Classic work on social interaction from both sociology (Simmel 1964) and psychology (Heider 1958) proposes that the relationship between two members of a dyad is affected by their relations with others outside that relationship. Consistent with this argument, a key conceptual underpinning of our approach is that a parent's relationships with other adult children in the family will likely affect the relationship between that parent and any one of his or her adult children. The conceptual framework lends itself to studying these issues, because each of these sets of factors can vary within the family, producing differential relations between parents and children.

It is useful to provide a concrete example of the way in which these processes may function. Whether an adult child's transition to parenthood affects the quality of the relationship between that adult child and his or her mother may depend, in part, on the parental status of other adult children in the family. If the adult child is the first to become a parent, this transition may have a greater effect on parent–adult child closeness and contact than if that child is the second or third in the family to enter parenthood. Other social statuses that parents and children share may also have "conditional" effects. Thus, it is not only the degree of social structural similarity between that child and his or her parent that affects their relationship, it is also the degree of similarity between the parents and each of their other children.

To provide another example, let us take the case of predictors of a child becoming a family caregiver. It has been suggested that children's competing roles (such as parent, worker, or spouse) may deter their assumption of caregiving responsibility. Studies to date of this issue have used between-family designs, comparing a single child from one family with individual children from other families. In this case, the variation may result from confounding between-family differences such as socioeconomic status, family structure, or religion (Dick et al. 2002). In contrast, within-family approaches allow exploration of whether different levels of competing roles among adult children in the same family affect which particular child the parent views as the most likely caregiver (an issue we will examine empirically). Similarly, achieving a higher educational status may encourage a child's selection as a caregiver; a within-family design allows us to determine the importance of a child's education (e.g., being a college graduate) relative to his or her siblings.

Fundamental to the within-family approach is the view that the characteristics of individual children and of parent–child dyads will, relative to those of other children and dyads in the family, help explain patterns of parents' relationships with a particular adult child. Our data set has provided us with the opportunity to explore some of the issues raised here. Following a description of the methods of the WFDS, we provide several illustrations of the analyses we have conducted with this data set. Our goal in presenting data on these issues is to illustrate possible strengths of within-family approaches to studying assistance and care in later life and to point toward new avenues for investigators.

Methods of the Within-Family Differences Study

Our design involved selecting a sample of mothers 65–75 years of age with at least two living adult children and collecting data from mothers regarding each of their children. Further, we included only community-dwelling mothers in the sample to reduce the likelihood that the women would be in need of extensive caregiving, thus allowing us to study relationships prior to the onset of care.

The Greater Boston area was chosen as the research site. Boston is a diverse metropolitan area with a mixture of ethnic, religious, and socioeconomic groups. To be eligible for the study, a woman had to meet the following criteria: (a) be between the ages of 65 and 75; (b) have at least two living children related to her by birth or adoption; and (c) be able to be interviewed in English. Interviewers were able to complete screening in 97.5 percent of the sampled households. Forty-five percent of screened households had an eligible respondent. We attempted to interview all eligible women and completed interviews with 61 percent of the eligible households.

Our design called for interviewing 550 mothers; we were able to slightly exceed this number, collecting data on 566 mothers. The interviewers began contacting potential respondents and continued until they had reached the target number of cases. The interviews were conducted between August 2001 and January 2003. Each of the mothers was interviewed for between one and two hours. More than 90 percent of the interviews were taped and fully transcribed. Field notes were prepared for each interview that was not fully taped.

At the end of each interview, the mothers were told about the study component involving adult children and were asked if they would provide contact information for their children. Approximately 70 percent of the mothers agreed to provide information, and approximately 70 percent of those children agreed to participate, resulting in a total child sample of 773 cases. In 300 families, data were collected from mothers and at least one child; in 246 families, data were collected from mothers and at least half of their adult children, and in 120 families, mothers and all of the adult children in the family participated.

We also informed the mothers of the father component of the study and asked for permission to contact her husband. Of the 260 married mothers, 68 percent gave permission for the interviewers to contact their husbands; 73 percent of the husbands agreed to participate, resulting in a final sample of 130 husbands. We interviewed the husbands only if they were the biological or adoptive parents of the wife's children or if they were stepfathers who had raised the offspring since early childhood.

Sample Characteristics

Mothers' Characteristics

The mothers were between the ages of 65 and 75 (mean = 70.9; SD = 3.1) at the time of the interviews. Forty-six percent of the mothers were currently married, 36 percent were widowed, 17 percent were divorced or separated, and 1 percent had never been married. On education level, 24 percent of the mothers had completed less than high school, 43 percent had completed high school, and 33 percent had completed at least some college. Most mothers (82 percent) were not employed. On total family income, 34 percent had a total family income of less than $20,000 in the previous year, 26 percent had an income between $20,000 and $29,999, 12 percent had an income between $30,000 and $39,999, 8 percent had an income between $40,000 and $49,999, and 20 percent had an income of $50,000 or more. The religious affiliations of the mothers were Catholic (46 percent), Protestant (45 percent), and Jewish (5 percent), with 4 percent reporting another religion or no religious affiliation. Sixty-nine percent of the mothers were white, 28 percent were African American, and 3 percent were evenly divided among Asian, Hispanic, and American Indian/Native American.

The number of living children the women in the sample had ranged from two to thirteen (mean = 4.4; SD = 1.7). Although the mean number of living children is higher than would be found in a nationally representative sample of women ages 65 to 75, it is important to remember that this mean is primarily caused by the criterion that all participants have at least two living adult children. The mean number of children of women is similar to that found in national samples, such as the National Survey of Families and Households (Sweet and Bumpass 1996) when compared specifically to mothers in the same age group who have two or more children.

Fathers' Characteristics

One hundred-thirty fathers participated in the study. The fathers were between the ages of 60 and 83 (mean = 70.6; SD = 4.5) at the time of the interviews. Only fathers who were married to the mothers participated. On education level, 12 percent of the fathers had completed less than high school, 27 percent had completed high school, and 61 percent had completed at least some college. Most fathers (62 percent) were not employed. The religious affiliations of the fathers were Catholic (45 percent), Protestant (32 percent), and Jewish (14 percent), with 9 percent reporting another religion or no religious affiliation. Ninety-three percent of the fathers were white; 5 percent were African American, 1 percent were Asian, and 1 percent were Hispanic.

Adult Children's Characteristics

Mothers provided reports on 2,160 children. The children were between the ages of 20 and 61 (mean = 42.8; SD = 5.9). Forty-nine percent were daughters. Fifty-seven percent of the adult children were currently married, 6 percent were cohabiting, 15 percent were divorced or separated, 21 percent were never married, and 1 percent were widowed. On education level, 44 percent of the adult children had completed high school,

13 percent had completed some college, 28 percent were college graduates, and 15 percent had completed some graduate work. Most of the children (81 percent) were employed. Of the adult children, 70 percent were themselves parents (mean number of children = 2.3; SD = 1.2). The subsample of 773 children who were directly interviewed in the study did not differ systematically from the full sample of children on whom the mothers reported, with one exception: African-American sons were underrepresented in the subsample of children who participated.

Measurement Approach

One of the major goals of the WFDS was to examine the degree to which parents in fact differentiate among their adult children in closeness, preference for support, and other dimensions of the relationship. An innovation of the WFDS is the methodological approach used to overcome limitations in the way in which parents generally are asked about the nature and quality of their relationships with their adult children. Traditional methods for studying relationship quality, for example, typically ask parents to respond to identical questions about each individual child, without asking respondents to make specific comparisons among them.

The National Survey of Families and Households provides an example of the most broadly used approach to measuring parent–adult child closeness (Sweet and Bumpass 1996). This survey asks parents to describe the quality of their relationships with each of their children, ranging from "very poor" (1) to "excellent" (7) in wave 1 (1988) and from "really bad" (0) to "absolutely perfect" (10) in wave 2 (1993). Most mothers report very high closeness to all of their children, making it difficult to detect favoritism that may exist, especially in families in which the mothers have relatively close relationships with all of the children.

We propose that measures that ask mothers specifically to differentiate among their children will reveal variations in relationship quality that are likely to be masked when using measures of quality that allow parents to rate all of their children in the same way. Traditional measures of parent–adult child closeness are able to differentiate adequately among children in families in which there are marked differences in relationship quality; however, these measures may not be able to tap subtle differences. Measures focused on choice can reveal distinctions in families in which parents feel closeness with all of their children but may nevertheless feel closer to one child. In several of our analyses of the WFDS, we have found greater ability to detect differences in mothers' relationships with their adult children by asking mothers to choose among their children rather than by asking mothers to report ratings of closeness to all of their children (Suitor and Pillemer 2006). For example, we found that we were able to explain more variance using within-family comparison questions than traditional closeness measures; further, the pattern of predictors using the comparison measures more closely mirrored theoretical models of parent–adult child relationship quality than did the traditional measures.

In the WFDS, in addition to traditional measures, we asked the parents a series of questions about their relationships with their children. Included in this series of items were questions about which of his or her children the parent (a) would be most likely to talk to about a personal problem; (b) would prefer help from if he or she became ill or disabled; (c) would turn to first in a crisis; and (d) felt the most emotional closeness to. Each child was coded as 0 for each item for which he or she was not chosen and 1 for each item for which she or he was chosen. Several of our analyses rely on these dichotomous measures of parental preference for individual children

Exploring Within-Family Differentiation in Later Life

We have raised a number of issues that merit further study regarding the role of within-family differences in later life. In this section, we provide several illustrative analyses of the way in which a within-family perspective can shed new light on intergenerational relations. As noted earlier, we focus on four questions that a within-family design can address: (1) How extensive is differentiation within families? (2) To what extent is there agreement among parents and children on such differentiation? (3) Do parents differentiate among their children in allocating assistance to them, and why do such patterns occur? (4) How is a particular child selected as the likely caregiver among all children?

Analysis I: How Extensive Is Differentiation within Families?

The results of a series of related analyses confirmed that in addition to the distribution of economic resources, most older parents differentiate among their adult children across a range of areas, including instrumental and emotional support and closeness (Pillemer and Suitor 2006; Suitor, Pillemer, and Sechrist 2006; Suitor, Sechrist, et al. 2006). More than 90 percent of both mothers and fathers differentiated among their adult children on at least one relational dimension. Among mothers, 72 percent named a child who they would prefer care for them in times of illness or disability, 79 percent named a child to whom they would turn first in a crisis, 78 percent named a child whom they would approach when faced with a personal problem, and 64 percent were willing to name a child to whom they were most emotionally close. Further, more than three-quarters of the mothers differentiated among their children in providing them emotional and instrumental support.

Among fathers, 70 percent named a child who they would prefer care for them in times of illness or disability, 79 percent named a child to whom they would turn in a crisis, 67 percent named a child to whom they would turn when faced with a personal problem, and 68 percent were willing to name a child to whom they were most emotionally close (Suitor, Sechrist, et al. 2006). In sum, these sets of analyses demonstrated that the majority of mothers and fathers differentiate among their children in emotional closeness, preferences for support, and the provision of support to children. Despite powerful norms that promote equal preference for and treatment of children, most parents perceive clear differences among their offspring and are easily able to articulate them.

Analysis II: To What Extent Is There Agreement among Parents and Children about Parents' Differentiation?

One of our aims in the WFDS was to determine the extent to which children's and parents' accounts of various aspects of the relationship agree. One of the most intriguing questions, in our view, is the degree to which parents and adult children agree on the topic of within-family differences. We approached this question in two ways. First, are children aware of whether mothers express preferences for specific children or not? That is, do parents and offspring agree that the mother is able to express a preference (rather than saying she views all children as equal)? To assess agreement between parents' and adult children's reports we focused on two aspects of relationships: the child the mother stated she was most emotionally close to and the child she would turn to as a source of support. The analysis used data from interviews with the 300 mothers whose children participated in the study and the 769 adult children on whom we have data. That is, we used data from 769 mother–child dyads nested within 300 families to explore the accuracy of adult children's perceptions of mothers' patterns of favoritism. (Suitor, Sechrist, et al. 2006 reports the full results.) All mother–child dyads were included in the analysis regardless of whether all of the children or only some of the children in each family participated in the study.

We used the combination of the mothers' and children's reports to create two sets of measures of reporting congruence. We began by designing a measure of congruence for each of the two relational contexts—emotional closeness and confiding. First, we created a variable to measure mother–child agreement about whether the mother had named a child she was emotionally closest to or the mother had said that she could not choose among her children. This variable was coded 1 (mother's and child's reports agreed that she either had or had not chosen a child) or 0 (mother's and child's reports differed on whether the mother named a child). A second consistency variable was created that measured whether, among those dyads in which mothers did select a child, the child accurately reported which offspring the mother named. This variable was also coded 1 (mother and child named the same offspring as mother's favorite) or 0 (mother and child named different offspring). The same two variables were created for confiding.

We created a second set of variables designed to measure the extent to which adult children's reports accurately reflected their mothers' reports. For these variables, we summed the number of instances in which the adult child accurately reported the preferences his or her mother stated. The first measure summed the number of times the adult child was correct in his or her reports on whether the mother had reported favoring a child for either emotional closeness or confiding. Thus, the range of scores could vary from 0 (child was never accurate) to 2 (child was accurate for both emotional closeness and confiding). The second measure summed the number of times the child was correct about which specific child the mother had named; the range of scores for this measure was also 0–2. Finally, we computed a measure of child's accuracy across both differentiation and specific child named. This measure ranged from 0 (child was never accurate) to 4 (child was correct about whether the mother had differentiated and which child she had chosen for both relational contexts).

In this set of analyses, the child, rather than the parent, was the unit of analysis; thus the observations were not independent. To address this concern, we used ordinary least squares regression with robust standard errors to correct for dependence among children in the same family. This approach allowed us to take into consideration family-level as well as child- and dyad-level factors.

There was substantial agreement between mothers and children on whether mothers were able to differentiate at all on the two characteristics (i.e., whether the mother expressed any preference for a child, regardless of which one was chosen). Thus 60 percent of the children correctly reported that their mothers were more emotionally close to one child than others, and 78 percent correctly reported that their mothers confided in a particular child when facing personal problems (Suitor et al. 2006).

However, among those families in which mothers had named specific children in these contexts, only 39 percent of the children correctly identified the *specific* child to whom mothers were most emotionally close, and only 55 percent correctly identified in which child their mothers would confide. Interestingly, agreement was much greater in most other domains. For example, comparisons between reports of mothers and adult children indicated that more than 80 percent of the dyads agreed in their reports of the children's developmental history in childhood and adulthood, including whether the child had physical and mental health problems, difficulty in school, problems with peers, problems with drugs or alcohol, and trouble with the law (Suitor and Pillemer 2000). Unlike these other areas, children are perhaps surprisingly unaware of their mother's preferred children.

What leads to greater within-dyad congruence about parental preference? As shown in table 9.1, multivariate analyses revealed that congruence in reporting was predicted by similarity of religious participation, whether the children were themselves parents, and family size (Suitor et al. 2006). Specifically, adult children who were similar to their mothers in religious participation were more likely to accurately report their mothers' preferences, whereas children who were also parents were less likely to provide accurate reports. Family size predicted children's accuracy of reporting, although the direction of effects varied by relational context; children from larger families more accurately reported whether their mothers favored particular children at all in the family but less accurately identified the particular favored children.

Taken together, these findings suggest that patterns of actual parental preference and perceived preference by children are very widespread.

Table 9.1. Regression Analysis of Adult Children's Reporting Accuracy Regarding Mothers' Favoritism

	Model 1 Accuracy regarding whether mother favored any child		Model 2 Accuracy regarding which child mother favored among dyads in which mothers and children identified a favorite child		Model 3 Accuracy regarding whether mother favored any child and which child mother favored	
	B	SE B	B	SE B	B	SE B
Similarity						
Gender	0.02	0.05	0.08	0.07	0.11	0.10
Outlook (mother's perception)	0.02	0.03	0.02	0.04	0.02	0.05
Outlook (child's perception)	0.03	0.03	0.03	0.05	0.03	0.06
Religious participation	0.05	0.05	0.13+	0.07	0.17*	0.09
Education	0.08	0.06	0.01	0.07	0.02	0.10
Child's maturation						
Age	−0.00	0.00	0.01	0.07	0.00	0.01
Parental status	−0.12**	0.05	−0.20***	0.07	−0.34***	0.09
Employment	0.03	0.06	0.03	0.11	0.05	0.14
Contact with mother	0.02	0.02	0.03	0.03	0.05	0.03
Favoritism in childhood	0.01	0.02	−0.02	0.03	0.01	0.04
Mother's characteristics						
Race	−0.08	0.08	0.10	0.13	0.13	0.15
Number of children	0.06***	0.01	−0.07***	0.02	−0.07***	0.03
Model R^2	0.05		0.08		0.07	
Degrees of freedom	12		12		12	
F	2.44***		2.60***		2.41**	
N[a]	676		411		408	

Source: Suitor, Sechrist, Steinhour, and Pillemer (2006), © The Gerontological Society of America, reproduced by permission of the publisher.

Notes. This analysis was conducted using ordinary least squares with robust standard errors (SE).

a. The number of cases in models 2 and 3 differ from that in model 1 because models 2 and 3 include only cases in which mothers did choose a particular child, whereas model 1 also includes cases in which mothers did not choose among their children. The number of cases differs from model 2 to model 3 because in three dyads, data were not available on all four items used to create the measure.

*p < .10, **p < .05, ***p < .01

However, although adult children are often correctly aware that their mothers have a preferred child, they are frequently inaccurate about which child is preferred. The most obvious implication of the findings is the need to obtain data from both members of parent–child dyads in studies of quality of older parent–adult child relationships. This insight is of course well-known to clinicians and caseworkers involved with aging families, but it has not extensively permeated research on parent–child relations. Indeed, it has been argued that the study of the aging family should embrace the concept of multi-perspectivity as a tenet of research (Luescher and Pillemer 1998; Pillemer and Suitor 2005). Given that discrepancies exist on closeness and confidence—features central to relationships—it is likely that each family member's perspective is to some degree unique due to his or her niche in the family (Pillemer and McCartney 1991).

Analysis III: Do Parents Differentiate among Their Children in Allocating Assistance to Them, and Why Do Such Patterns Occur?

We now turn our attention to a substantive issue regarding within-family differences: the ways in which mothers provide support differentially to their adult children, and the factors that explain such differentiation. Specifically, we ask To what extent do patterns of support from mothers to adult children vary within the family? and Can the factors derived from the conceptual framework described earlier explain patterns of within-family differences? To understand the ways in which mothers differentiate among their adult children in how they allocate support, we focused on three factors derived from the conceptual framework: similarity between parents and children; reciprocity; and children's need (Suitor, Pillemer, and Sechrist 2006).

Similarity and Intergenerational Support

As noted, studies of kinship have shown that gender and attitudes are two of the most salient dimensions of similarity explaining relations between mothers and adult children (Silverstein and Bengtson 1997; Suitor 1987; Suitor and Pillemer 2000). We anticipated that these factors would play an important role in explaining within-family variations in support.

Reciprocity

The literature has shown that reciprocity helps to explain children's provision of support to parents. Specifically, parents who provided high levels of support to their children in earlier stages of the life course are more likely to receive support in their later years (Eggebeen and Davey 1998; Hogan, Eggebeen, and Clogg 1993; Silverstein, Parrott, and Bengtson 1995). However, less is known about the effect of reciprocity on parents' provision of support to their children in the parents' later years. The findings of the few studies that have examined this issue are mixed but in some cases suggest that parents are more likely to provide support to children who have themselves been a source of support (Hogan et al. 1993). Although the empirical literature on this issue is not consistent, we believe that the strong theoretical arguments about exchange, combined with the importance of reciprocity in explaining child-to-parent support, provide a basis for hypothesizing that mothers would be more likely to provide support to those children who provided them with support.

Adult Children's Need

Finally, we anticipated that mothers would differentiate among their children for support on the basis of need. There are two conditions of need that we believe are the most likely to explain mothers' differentiation. The first of these comprises situations that impose limitations on children's ability to manage independently, such as illness, injury, substance abuse, or trouble with the law. The second condition of need that we anticipated would affect a mother's differentiation among her children was the availability of alternate sources of support. The literature has shown that individuals who are married are more likely to receive high levels of support from members of their networks; further, married people report greater satisfaction with their levels of support than do unmarried people (Kim and McKenry 2002; Waite and Lehrer 2003). Thus we hypothesized that mothers would be most likely to provide support to those children who were unmarried and therefore at greater risk of receiving inadequate support.

In summary, we hypothesized that mothers would be the most likely to provide support to their adult children who were female, were unmarried, had provided their mothers with support during the previous year, were perceived by the mother as sharing similar values, and had experienced serious health problems but had not engaged in deviant behaviors.

We asked mothers a series of questions about the support they had provided to each of their adult children. The interview was structured such that mothers would discuss each child at length, beginning with the eldest and moving on to answer the same set of questions about each next oldest child. We asked the mothers the following questions: In the past year, have you given [child's name] (a) help during an illness; (b) comfort during a personal crisis; (c) help with regular chores, such as shopping, yard work, or cleaning; or (d) financial help, such as money or a loan. Each form of support was coded as 0 (no support provided) or 1 (support provided).

Extent of Within-Family Differences in Support

The findings revealed a substantial degree of within-family variation in mothers' support to adult children. More than six in ten mothers gave comfort to some but not all of their adult children, approximately half reported giving financial assistance to some of their children, and nearly half gave help with chores and assistance during illness to some but not all of their children (table 9.2). Thus, it is clear that there are sizeable differences in mothers' patterns of support to children, with differentiation most likely for comfort in a personal crisis and least likely for help during illnesses.

Explaining Within-Family Differences in Support

To test our hypotheses, we conducted a series of conditional logistic regression analyses. Conditional logistic regression is preferable to standard logistic regression in this case because the procedure controls on mothers' characteristics, much as would be the case if a dummy variable were created for each of the 566 mothers and included in the regression equations in which the mother–child pair was the unit of analysis (see (Menard 2002; Pendergast et al. 1996). This procedure is appropriate for these analyses because we do not have specific hypotheses for individual mothers' characteristics. Rather, in keeping with the within-family analysis, we are interested in factors that can vary among the children (either child or relationship characteristics). Conditional logistic regression allows us to focus on our primary question of interest—within each family, which child does the mother choose?—while controlling on mothers' characteristics.

Table 9.2. Within-Family Differences in Support Provided by Mothers to Children during the Previous Year

Type of support[1]	Percentage who gave support
Help to child when ill	
Gave to no children	54.0
Gave to some children	44.4
Gave to all children	1.6
Financial help	
Gave to no children	40.3
Gave to some children	51.3
Gave to all children	8.4
Comfort to children with personal crisis	
Gave to no children	16.0
Gave to some children	61.8
Gave to all children	22.3
Help with chores	
Gave to no children	49.4
Gave to some children	46.3
Gave to all children	4.3

Source: Suitor, Pillemer, and Sechrist (2006), © The Gerontological Society of America, reproduced by permission of the publisher.

The findings provided support for many but not all of our hypotheses, as shown in table 9.3. The most consistent findings were the effects of child's health, gender, and reciprocity. Mothers were more likely to have provided all four types of support to children with health problems than to their other children. Mothers were also more likely to have provided support to daughters than sons across all dimensions but financial assistance. Contrary to expectation, the child's gender had no greater effect on mothers' provision of emotional support during a crisis than on their provision of help during illness or help with household chores.

Although reciprocity has received little attention in studies of parent-to-child support, this factor appears to be important in explaining these patterns. Across three of the four dimensions—help during illness, comfort

Table 9.3. Conditional Logistic Regression Analysis of Mother-to-Child Support during the Previous Year

	Help during Illness		Comfort during Crisis		Help with Chores		Financial Help	
	B (SE)	Odds ratio	B (SE)	Odds ratio	B (SE)	Odds ratio	B (SE)	Odds ratio
Similarity								
Daughter	.511**	1.67	.231**	1.26	.696**	2.01	.079	1.08
	(.136)		(.075)		(.128)		(.101)	
Similar outlook	.095	1.10	.005	1.01	−.088	0.92	.078	1.08
	(.081)		(.046)		(.079)		(.062)	
Support from child	.394*	1.48	.331**	1.39	.437**	1.55	−.229	0.80
	(.168)		(.105)		(.149)		(.185)	
Children's neediness								
Child married	−.267	0.77	−.180*	0.84	.035	1.04	−.319**	0.73
	(.147)		(.082)		(.135)		(.115)	
Deviant behavior as adult	.357	1.43	.121	1.13	−.049	0.95	.406**	1.50
	(.206)		(.120)		(.217)		(.156)	
Health problems as adult	.748**	2.11	.253**	1.29	.337*	1.40	.287*	1.33
	(.151)		(.091)		(.156)		(.125)	

(continued)

Table 9.3. *(Continued)*

	Help during Illness		Comfort during Crisis		Help with Chores		Financial Help	
	B (SE)	Odds ratio	B (SE)	Odds ratio	B (SE)	Odds ratio	B (SE)	Odds ratio
Controls								
Distance from mother	-.083*	0.92	-.008	0.99	-.165**	0.85	-.042	0.96
	(.041)		(.021)		(.037)		(.028)	
Child's age	-.008	0.99	-.006	0.99	-.028*	0.97	-.036**	0.97
	(.013)		(.007)		(.012)		(.010)	
Child's education	-.099	0.91	-.018	0.98	-.042	0.96	-.081	0.92
	(.061)		(.033)		(.058)		(.045)	
Model χ^2	80.535**		40.234**		92.658**		57.004**	
Degrees of freedom	9		9		9		9	
n[a]	998		1748		1060		1247	

Source: Suitor, Pillemer, and Sechrist (2006), © The Gerontological Society of America, reproduced by permission of the publisher.

Note: SE = standard error.

a. The number of cases differs across support dimensions because the cases included in the analyses are only those in which mothers provided support to any of their children.

*$p < .05$, **$p < .01$

during a crisis, and help with chores—mothers were more likely to provide support to children who had served as sources of support for them during the previous year. Mothers were less likely to provide emotional or financial support to children who were married and less likely to provide instrumental assistance to children who lived farther away than other children. Finally, mothers provided help with chores and financial assistance to their younger children more often.

In sum, it appears that similarity, children's needs, and reciprocity affected mothers' differentiation of support among their children. However, contrary to expectation, not all dimensions of these domains affected mothers' patterns of support. First, in the case of similarity, gender but not attitude similarity affected mothers' choices. Second, regarding children's needs, health problems explained mothers' differentiation across all four support contexts, whereas child's marital status affected only comfort and financial assistance. This may be due to normative expectations that married couples will rely on one another for immediate tasks such as household chores and care if ill, whereas emotional comfort and financial assistance remain a continuing feature of the parental role. Third, reciprocity of support helped to explain mothers' differential provision of care during illness, comfort, and help with chores but not financial assistance. In fact, mothers were somewhat less likely to provide financial assistance to adult children who had helped them financially during the past year, suggesting that mothers' financial support is affected more by children's needs than reciprocity; children who could afford to provide assistance to their mothers probably had fewer needs for financial assistance.

The one hypothesis for which there was no support was the effect of children's deviant behaviors. Mothers were no less likely to provide children with support if they had problems with drugs or alcohol or had been in trouble with the law. In fact, the odds of mothers providing financial assistance to these children rather than their siblings were 50 percent greater. It is possible that parents respond to a norm that they should provide some form of assistance to children in trouble, even when problems result from the child's deviance or antisocial behavior (Cohler and Grunebaum 1981; Pillemer and Suitor 1991).

Support for a within-family differences approach comes from our findings on differential support by mothers. The study revealed that the majority of mothers differentiated among their adult children on one or more dimensions of support. These findings suggest that within-family variations in parents' provision of interpersonal resources do not end when children enter adulthood. A methodological implication of this finding is the need to collect data about multiple offspring in the same family to obtain a complete picture of support exchange. It is likely that the "target child" approach masks variation among dyads within the family in these domains.

Analysis IV: How Is a Particular Child Selected as the Likely Caregiver among All Children?

Thus far, we have used the WFDS to describe patterns of within-family differentiation in later life and to examine predictors of mothers' differential allocation of support to adult children. In this section, we turn to the issue of mothers' reliance on adult children for support, exploring factors that predict the expectation that an adult child will become her caregiver (for detailed results, see Pillemer and Suitor 2006).

Assuming the role of family caregiver for an impaired older person represents a major life course transition that typically has far-reaching consequences for the caregiver's physical, mental, and social well-being (Aneshensel et al. 1995; Pillemer and Suitor 1996; Schulz and Martire 2004). Despite the extensive literature on family caregiving, the question has been virtually unexplored: how do particular children among all offspring within a family assume greater caregiving responsibility? The preponderance of the literature has focused on the consequences of caregiving, with virtually no attention to the factors that propel one child into greater role responsibilities and deter or exempt others. Although studies have been conducted on predictors of routine assistance by adult children, researchers generally have not examined factors related to assuming the role of primary caregiver.

The within-family design of the WFDS permits a detailed examination of this issue. We continue to rely on the conceptual framework described above in this analysis, focusing on the roles of similarity, exchange, and developmental factors as predictors of caregiving patterns.

Similarity

Given the prominent role that similarity plays in other dimensions of kin relations, we anticipate that it will also help determine which child assumes greater caregiving responsibilities. First, we expect that value similarity will be related to which adult children mothers name as the likely care-giver. Sickness or disability can require a long-term caregiving relation-ship and can compromise one's autonomy. In such a situation, parents are likely to perceive a more similar child as willing to follow their wishes if they are unable to carry them out themselves. Gender similarity is also likely to predict which child mothers select. Daughters are heavily over-represented as helpers with personal and health-related care, and both mothers and fathers have stronger affectional ties with daughters than with sons (Fingerman 2001; Rossi and Rossi 1990; Silverstein and Bengtson 1997; Suitor and Pillemer 2006). In the case of mothers, daughters' greater likelihood of assuming caregiving responsibilities is a reflection of both gender similarity and daughters' greater empathy.

Exchange

We anticipate that the history of help from adult children will predict which offspring become caregivers to parents. As Eggebeen and Davey (1998) note, caregiving tends to evolve from earlier role relationships in the family. Parents frequently expect to receive care from a child who is already helping them in various ways, and the selection of a potential caregiver may depend on past success in receiving such support. Devel-oping hypotheses based on past help from parent to child is more com-plex. Some studies of the helping behaviors of adult children indicate that past provision of support from the parent predicts assistance from offspring, fueled by a desire to reciprocate assistance received (Dellmann-Jenkins and Brittain 2003; Henretta et al. 1997; Silverstein et al. 2002). However, several studies have suggested that other features of situations in which parents provide help to adult children confound this pattern. Specifically, the provision of help to adult children often occurs as the result of a troubling failure on the part of the child to achieve indepen-dence (Pillemer and Suitor 1991). Thus, children receiving high levels of recent support from parents may not be a position to provide parents with greater care.

Developmental Factors

Finally, we anticipate that within-family differences in both children's prob-lems and children's normative adult status attainment will help to explain which offspring are likely to assume greater caregiving responsibilities.

First, children's personal problems are expected to reduce the likelihood that they will assume caregiving responsibilities, primarily because such problems will diminish children's ability to invest the interpersonal resources necessary to provide such care. Second, we anticipate that children's attainment of normative adult statuses will also reduce the likelihood of assuming heavy caregiving responsibilities. Although such status attainment increases positive affect between the generations (Pillemer and Suitor 2002; Ryff et al. 1996), competing roles, such as marriage, parenthood, and employment, generally detract from the ability to provide care (Dautzenberg et al. 2000; Laditka and Laditka 2001; Moen 2003; Wolf, Freedman, and Soldo 1997). Thus, we hypothesized that both children who have problems and those who have competing roles will be less likely to assume caregiving responsibilities.

The findings of our analyses revealed substantial support for several of these hypotheses regarding which children mothers named as likely caregivers (for a complete report, see Pillemer and Suitor 2006). First, as shown in table 9.4, the analysis provided consistent evidence of the importance of similarity: both gender similarity and similarity of attitudes predicted which children in the family mothers named. In fact, the odds of mothers naming daughters as caregivers were more than three and a half times the odds of naming sons, clearly the strongest predictor in the analysis. Emotional closeness was also an important predictor of mothers' expectations about caregiving; the odds of mothers naming a child to whom they were closer increased by more than 50 percent for each unit increase in closeness.

The analysis revealed only limited support for our hypotheses about the effects of availability and exchange. As anticipated, mothers were unlikely to name adult children who lived at a greater distance as caregivers. Further, children who were employed were somewhat less likely to be named. However, no other dimension of availability—including children's competing marital or parental roles and responsibilities, education, or problems—were related to which child the mother viewed as the likely caregiver.

Children who had provided more support to their mothers in the previous year were substantially more likely to be named as potential caregivers, as predicted; however, children who had received support from their mothers were no more or less likely to be named than were other children in the family. It is worth noting that mothers were also asked an open-ended question about why they selected the particular child. Strikingly, although gender and proximity were frequently mentioned, not a

Table 9.4. Conditional Logistic Regression Analysis of Mother's Selection of Child as Likely Caregiver

Independent variable	B (SE)	Standard error	Odds ratio
Similarity			
Gender	1.27**	0.15	3.55
Attitudes	0.26**	0.09	1.30
Emotional closeness	0.44**	0.10	1.55
Exchange			
Past help to parent	0.60**	0.08	1.82
Past help to child	0.01	0.07	1.01
Availability			
Competing roles and responsibilities			
Marital status	0.11	0.17	1.11
Employment	−0.38*	0.19	0.68
Parent	0.08	0.18	0.92
Child's problems			
Health	0.05	0.18	0.96
Deviant behaviors	0.12	0.27	1.11
Education	−0.02	0.07	0.98
Distance from mother	−0.40**	0.06	0.67
Child's age	0.02	0.02	1.02
Model χ^2		322.05**	
Degrees of freedom		13	
n[a]		1542	

Source: Pillemer and Suitor (2006), © The Gerontological Society of America, reproduced by permission of the publisher.

*$p < .05$, **$p < .01$

single mother explained her choice of caregiver based on help the mother had provided to the child in the past (Pillemer and Suitor 2006).

Taken together, the results suggest a general pattern for identification of the likely caregiver by mothers. Mothers appear to be heavily influenced by factors that represent comfort, trust, and reliability in interpersonal relations, such as gender and attitudinal similarity, emotional closeness, availability of the child by residing nearby, and a history of the child providing support. Less important are instrumental and contextual factors that might appear objectively to make a child a less appropriate caregiver, including competing family roles or serious life problems.

Particularly surprising is the lack of importance of a factor that the intergenerational assistance literature has highlighted: reciprocity. A sentiment that mothers are owed care by children they have helped does not appear to influence mothers, despite the evidence that it is precisely such children who are most likely to provide help when needed (Silverstein et al. 2002).

Discussion

In this chapter, we have made a case for expanding the study of intergenerational relations to include attention to within-family differences. Taking as a starting point insights from developmental psychology that show as much within-family as between-family differences on the part of children, we argue that gerontology may be missing a substantial part of the picture of family relationships. With a few notable exceptions (Cohler and Altergott 1995; Pillemer and McCartney 1991; Rossi and Rossi 1990; Ryff et al. 1994), the study of parent–child relations has employed models specific to later life while paying only limited attention to the broader issues that have interested social scientists studying families of young children and adolescents. Although scholars have called for bridging the gap between models for the study of families in earlier and later life course stages (Hagestad 1986; Rossi and Rossi 1990), such efforts remain rare.

In contrast, the present study extended an important insight from the developmental psychological literature to the study of later-life families: the importance of within-family differences. Highlighting in particular the issue of parental preference for children in various domains, we have provided data to support the assertion that individual parent–child dyads within a single family constitute to some degree separate microenvironments and differ among themselves. We believe that understanding the causes and consequences of within-family differences in parent–adult child relations has important substantive, methodological, and practical implications. We note several of these implications here.

Directions for Future Research

One goal of the approach we described was to determine what leads to parental preference for specific children. Broadly speaking, the conceptual framework we proposed, although derived from sociological and psychological sources, finds a parallel in the field of economics, where an extensive literature has examined motives that can explain financial transfers between the generations. As discussed in chapter 1, the exchange perspective posits that individuals engage in intergenerational transfers to maximize benefits to themselves, in the same way that individuals attempt to benefit in other economic transactions. Altruistic motives, in contrast, are based on promoting the best interests of other family members. In that case, the motivation for parental support to children lies in concern for the well-being of the child, and parents would be expected to provide more support to needier offspring.

A consensus has not been reached regarding support for either of these two models within economics (Light and McGarry 2003). Further, as Kohli and Künemund (2003) have noted, there is as much unresolved complexity in the sociology of intergenerational relations, in which fewer attempts have been made to test alternative hypotheses of altruism, exchange, and reciprocity. It has been suggested that an integrative approach is preferable to the either/or dichotomy of altruism versus exchange (chapter 1, this volume; Charness and Haruvy 2002; M. Schwarz 2006). Although not expressly engaging with the economic literature, what we have termed "developmental factors"—for example, experiencing problems as an adult or failing to attain adult statuses—are indicative off the neediness of children. Similarly, our inclusion of reciprocity is consistent with the notion of exchange as a motivation for support. The findings described support the notion that a critical task is to integrate the altruism and exchange perspectives, leading to a more complex view of intergenerational relationships.

The findings from analysis III paint a relatively complex picture of the way in which mothers may allocate support differentially among their adult children. The patterns our results reveal may seem contradictory: Mothers appear to provide support to children who are more vulnerable or needy (younger, unmarried individuals who have had health problems) but also appear to be motivated by social exchange principles, whereby they provide more help to children from whom they have received assistance (domains that appear to correspond to the competing altruism and reciprocity explanations for inter vivos transfers in the economic literature). There is mounting evidence, however, that this type of contradiction is by no means uncommon and may in fact be characteristic of older parent–adult child relations.

Specifically, several scholars have pointed to the fact that when older parents are called upon to help children, they tend to experience conflict between two powerful norms: the norm of reciprocity and the norm of solidarity (George 1986). Parents are motivated by both the norm of reciprocity, which suggests that profit and loss should be equitable between relationship partners, and the norm of solidarity, which implies that individuals should give close family members whatever help they need, without concern for a "return on investment." Indeed, there is evidence that these competing norms produce ambivalence in older parents related to helping offspring (Cohler and Grunebaum 1981; Farber 1989; Pillemer and Suitor 2002, 2004). Future research using within-family designs should take into account the potential existence and empirical importance of conflicting motivations in intergenerational support.

Methodologically, the most pressing need is for longitudinal studies of the causes and consequences of within-family differences in later life. For example, prior research suggests that the quality of relationships with adult children affects older parents' well-being over time. However, it is likely that the methodological approaches in this line of research have masked the differential effects of relationships with various children. Because previous work has focused on only one target child or children in the aggregate, it has not been possible to explore the degree to which variations in relationship quality within the same family affect well-being. In contrast, a longitudinal design would allow one to determine the effects of within-family differences on such outcomes as parent and child well-being, the provision of routine support, and both the pathways to caregiving and the consequences of various pathways for caregiver and care recipient well-being.

Further, the findings of the WFDS provide strong evidence that it is necessary to collect data from both generations and from multiple members of each generation to fully understand family relations in later life. Previous work has shown that there are systematic discrepancies in the reports of older mothers and their adult children (Aquilino 1999; Bengtson and Kuypers 1971; Giarrusso, Stallings, and Bengtson 1995; Pruchno, Burant, and Peters 1994). However, analyses of the WFDS data (including those presented in analysis II) have shown is that there are also substantial within-family differences in parents' and children's reporting congruence (Suitor et al. 2006). Studies that collect longitudinal data from parents' and children's perspectives will increase understanding of the extent and types of discrepancies between parents' and adult children's reports as well as discrepancies among siblings, and whether such discrepancies change over time. This understanding can be the basis for developing research designs that provide the most complete and accurate picture of family relations.

Practical Implications

Finally, we would note that increased attention to the issue of within-family differences in later-life families may have practical value as well. Our data touch on a phenomenon that family practitioners are very familiar with among their clients: parental preference for specific adult children along key socioemotional dimensions and the consequences of such differentiation for caregiving and for well-being. There are several implications of these findings for practitioners working with older persons and their families.

First, further study of the issue will increase understanding of the nature and importance of preferences and expectations for care from children, which may be of use to family therapists and counselors. Second, the insights are likely to be useful for community agencies that sponsor educational programs on the topic of the aging family (such as county offices for the aging and cooperative extension associations). Because of the powerful norm of equal treatment of offspring in families, the issue of real or perceived parental preference is rarely dealt with (and may even be seen as a taboo topic). Family life education that involves older persons can use the knowledge generated about patterns of within-family preference over time on the part of parents and how adult children perceive such patterns. Third, there are potential implications of the study for a better understanding of planning for eventual care and assistance. Illuminating patterns of parents' preference and discrepancies with children's perceptions may help prevent family conflict over caregiving from arising. Caregiver education programs increasingly include a component on the parent's preferences for care and on the expectations of offspring; such training may benefit from the study findings.

NOTE

This project was supported by Grant RO1 AG18869-01 from the National Institute on Aging (J. Jill Suitor and Karl Pillemer, coprincipal investigators). Karl Pillemer also acknowledges support from Grant 1 P30 AG022845, an Edward R. Roybal Center grant from the National Institute on Aging (Karl Pillemer, principal investigator). We thank Michael Bisciglia, Rachel Brown, Ilana S. Feld, Alison Green, Kimberly Gusman, Jennifer Jones, Dorothy Mecom, Michael Patterson, and Monisa Shackelford for their assistance in preparing the data for analysis and for participating in the analysis of the qualitative data. We also thank Mary Ellen Colten and her colleagues at the University of Massachusetts, Boston, for collecting the data for the project.

REFERENCES

Aldous, Joan. 1978. *Family Careers: Developmental Changes in Families.* New York: Wiley.

Aldous, Joan, Elisabeth Klaus, and David M. Klein. 1985. "The Understanding Heart: Aging Parents and Their Favorite Children." *Child Development* 56(2): 303–16.

Allen, Katherine R., Rosemary Blieszner, and Karen A. Roberto. 2000. "Families in the Middle and Later Years: A Review and Critique of Research in the 1990s." *Journal of Marriage and Family* 62(4): 911–26.

Aneshensel, Carol S., Leonard I. Pearlin, Joseph T. Mullan, Steven H. Zarit, and Carol J. Whitlatch. 1995. *Profiles in Caregiving: The Unexpected Career.* San Diego: Academic Press, Inc.

Aquilino, William S. 1999. "Two Views of One Relationship: Comparing Parents' and Young Adult Children's Reports of the Quality of Intergenerational Relations." *Journal of Marriage and Family* 61(4): 858–70.

Baker, Laura A., and Denise Daniels. 1990. "Nonshared Environmental Influences and Personality Differences in Adult Twins." *Journal of Personality and Social Psychology* 58:103–110.

Becker, Gary S. 1991. *A Treatise on the Family.* Cambridge, MA: Harvard University Press.

Becker, Gary S., and Nigel Tomes. 1986. "Human Capital and the Rise and Fall of Families." *Journal of Labor Economics* 4(3 pt. 2): S1–S39.

Bedford, Victoria H. 1992. "Memories of Parental Favoritism and the Quality of Parent-Child Ties in Adulthood." *Journal of Gerontology: Social Sciences* 47: S149–S155.

Bengtson, Vern L., and Jim A. Kuypers. 1971. "Generational Difference and the Developmental Stake." *Aging and Human Development* 2:249–60.

Blieszner, Rosemary, Paula M. Usita, and Jay A. Mancini. 1996. "Diversity and Dynamics in Late-Life Mother-Daughter Relationships." *Journal of Women and Aging* 8(3–4): 5–24.

Brackbill, Yvonne, Donna Kitch, and William B. Noffsinger. 1988. "The Perfect Child (from an Elderly Parent's Point of View)." *Journal of Aging Studies* 2(3): 243–54.

Brody, Gene H., and Zolinda Stoneman. 1994. "Sibling Relationships and Their Association with Parental Differential Treatment." In *Separate Social Worlds of Siblings: The Impact of Nonshared Environment on Development,* edited by Eileen Mavis Hetherington, David Reiss and Robert Plomin (129–42). Hillsdale, NJ: Lawrence Erlbaum Associates, Inc.

Brody, Gene H., Zolinda Stoneman, and J. Kelly McCoy. 1992. "Parental Differential Treatment of Siblings and Sibling Differences in Negative Emotionality." *Journal of Marriage and Family* 54:643–51.

Charness, Gary, and Ernan Haruvy. 2002. "Altruism, Equity, and Reciprocity in a Gift-Exchange Experiment: An Encompassing Approach." *Games and Economic Behavior* 4(2):203–31.

Cohler, Bertram J., and Karen Altergott. 1995. "The Family of the Second Half of Life: Connecting Theories and Findings." In *Handbook of Aging and the Family,* edited by Rosemary Blieszner and Victoria Hilkevitch Bedford (59–94). Westport, CT: Greenwood Press.

Cohler, Bertram J., and Henry Grunebaum. 1981. *Mothers, Grandmothers, and Daughters: Personality and Childcare in Three-Generation Families.* New York: Wiley.

Conley, Dalton. 2004. *The Pecking Order: Which Siblings Succeed and Why.* New York: Pantheon Books.

Connidis, Ingrid Arnet. 2001. *Family Ties and Aging.* Thousand Oaks, CA: Sage.

Coser, Rose L. 1991. *In Defense of Modernity: Role Complexity and Individual Autonomy.* Stanford, CA: Stanford University Press.

Daly, Martin, and Margo I. Wilson. 1988. "The Darwinian Psychology of Discriminative Parental Solicitude." In *Nebraska Symposium on Motivation: Vol. 35 Comparative Perspectives in Modern Psychology,* edited by Daniel W. Leger. Lincoln: University of Nebraska Press.

Dautzenberg, Maaike G. H., Jos P. M. Diederiks, Hans Philipsen, Fred C. J. Stevens, Frans E. S. Tan., and Myrra J. F. J. Vernooij-Dassen. 2000. "The Competing Demands of Paid Work and Parent Care: Middle-Aged Daughter Providing Assistance to Elderly Parents." *Research on Aging* 22(2): 165–87.

Davey, Adam, Megan Janke, and J. Salva. 2005. "Antecedents of Intergenerational Support: Families in Context and Families as Context." In *Annual Review of Gerontology and Geriatrics, Volume 2: Intergenerational Relations Across Time and Place,* edited by Merril Silverstein, R. Giarrusso, and V. L. Bengtson (29–54). New York: Springer.

Dellmann-Jenkins, Mary, and Lisa Brittain. 2003. "Young Adults' Attitudes Toward Filial Responsibility and Actual Assistance to Elderly Family Members." *Journal of Applied Gerontology* 22(2): 214–29.

Dick, Danielle M., Jennifer K. Johnson, Richard J. Viken, and Richard J. Rose. 2002. "Testing Between In-Family Associations in Within-Family Comparisons." *Psychological Science* 11(5): 409–513.

Downey, Douglas B. 1995. "When Bigger Is Not Better: Family Size, Parental Resources, and Children's Educational Performance." *American Sociological Review* 60:746–61.

Eggebeen, David J., and Adam Davey. 1998. "Do Safety Nets Work? The Role of Anticipated Help in Times of Need." *Journal of Marriage and Family* 60(4): 939–50.

Elder, Glen H. 1998. "The Life Course and Human Development." In *Handbook of Child Psychology, Vol. 1: Theoretical Models of Human Development,* edited by Richard M. Lerner (939–91). New York: Wiley.

Elder, Glen H., and Monica Kirkpatrick Johnson. 2003. "The Life Course and Aging: Challenges, Lessons, and New Directions." In *Invitation to the Life Course: Toward New Understandings of Later Life,* edited by Richard A. Settersten (49–81). Amityville, NY: Baywood Publishing Company, Inc.

Elder, Glen H., Elizabeth B. Robertson, and Rand D. Conger. 1996. "Fathers and Sons in Rural America: Occupational Choice and Intergenerational Ties across the Life Course." In *Aging and Generational Relations: Life-Course and Cross-Cultural Perspectives,* edited by Tamara K. Hareven (31–59). New York: Aldine De Gruyter.

Farber, Bernard. 1989. "Limiting Reciprocity Among Relatives: Theoretical Implications of a Serendipitous Finding." *Sociological Perspectives* 32:307–30.

Feld, Sheila L. 1982. "Social Structural Determinants of Similarity among Associates." *American Sociological Review* 47:797–801.

Fingerman, Karen L. 2001. *Aging Mothers and Their Adult Daughters: A Study in Mixed Emotions.* New York: Springer Publishing Co.

Friedman, Howard S., Joan S. Tucker, Joseph E. Schwartz, Carol Tomlinson-Keasey, Leslie R. Martin, Deborah L. Wingard, and Michael H. Criqui. 1995. "Psychosocial and Behavioral Predictors of Longevity: The Aging and Death of the 'Termites.' " *American Psychologist* 50(2): 69–78.

George, Linda K. 1986. "Caregiver Burden: Conflict Between Norms of Reciprocity and Solidarity." In *Elder Abuse: Conflict in the Family,* edited by Karl Pillemer and Rosalie S. Wolf (67–92). New York: Auburn House.

Giarrusso, Rosann, Michael Stallings, and Vern L. Bengtson. 1995. "The Intergenerational Stake Hypothesis Revisited: Parent-Child Differences in Perceptions of Relationships 20 Years Later." In *Adult Intergenerational Relations: Effects of Societal Change,* edited by Vern L. Bengtson, K. Warner Schaie, and Linda M. Burton (227–96). New York: Springer Publishing Co.

Hagestad, Gunhild O. 1986. "Dimensions of Time and the Family." *American Behavioral Scientist* 29:679–94.

Hatfield, Elaine, Jane Traupmann, Susan Sprecher, Mary Utne, and Joel Hay. 1985. "Equity and Intimate Relations: Resent Research." In *Compatible and Incompatible Relationships,* edited by William Ickes (309–322). New York: Springer-Verlag.

Heider, Fritz. 1958. *The Psychology of Interpersonal Relations.* Mahwah, NJ: Lawrence Erlbaum Associates, Publishers.

Henretta, John C., Martha S. Hill, Wei Li, Beth J. Soldo, and Douglas A. Wolf. 1997. "Selection of Children to Provide Care: The Effect of Earlier Parental Transfers." *Journal of Gerontology: Social Science* 52:110–19.

Hogan, Dennis P., David J Eggebeen, and Clifford C. Clogg. 1993. "The Structure of Intergenerational Exchanges in American Families." *The American Journal of Sociology* 98:1428–58.

Homans, George C. 1950. *The Human Group.* New York: Harcourt, Brace.

House, James S., Karl R. Landis, and Debra Umberson. 1988. "Social Relationships and Health." *Science* 241:540–45.

Joosse, Barbara M. 1996. *I Love You the Purplest.* San Francisco: Chronicle Books.

Kaufman, Gayle, and Peter Uhlenberg. 1998. "Effects of Life Course Transitions on the Quality of Relationships Between Adult Children and Their Parents." *Journal of Marriage and Family* 60(4): 924–38.

Kawachi, Ichiro, and Lisa F. Berkman. 2001. "Social Ties and Mental Health." *Journal of Urban Health* 78(3): 458–67.

Kim, Hyoun K., and Patrick C. McKenry. 2002. "The Relationship Between Marriage and Psychological Well-Being: A Longitudinal Analysis." *Journal of Family Issues* 23:885–911.

Kohli, Martin, and Harald Künemund. 2003. "Intergenerational Transfers in the Family: What Motivates Giving?" In *Global Aging and Challenges to Families,* edited by Vern L. Bengtson and Ariela Lowenstein (123–42). New York. Aldine de Gruyter.

Laditka, James N., and Sarah B. Laditka. 2001. "Adult Children Helping Older Parents: Variations in Likelihood and Hours by Gender, Race, and Family Role." *Research on Aging* 23(4): 429–56.

Lazarsfeld, Paul F., and Robert K. Merton. 1954. "Friendship as Social Process: A Sub-stantive and Methodological Analysis." In *Freedom and Control in Modern Society*, edited by Monroe Berger, Theodore Abel, and Charles H. Page (18–66). New York: Litton.

Lee, Gary R. 1988. "Marital Satisfaction in Later Life: The Effects of Nonmarital Roles." *Journal of Marriage and Family* 50:775–83.

Luescher, Kurt, and Karl Pillemer. 1998. "Intergenerational Ambivalence: A New Approach to the Study of Parent-Child Relations in Later Life." *Journal of Marriage and Family* 60(2): 413–45.

Lye, Diane N. 1996. "Adult Child-Parent Relationships." *Annual Review of Sociology* 22:79–102.

Light, Audrey, and Kathleen McGarry. 2003. "Why Parents Play Favorites: Explanations for Unequal Bequests." *The American Economic Review* 94:1669–81.

McHale, Susan M., Ann C. Crouter, Shirley A. McGuire, and Kimberly A. Updegraff. 1995. "Congruence Between Mothers' and Fathers' Differential Treatment of Sib-lings: Links with Family Relations and Children's Well-Being." *Child Development* 66(1): 116–28.

McPherson, Miller, Lynn Smith-Lovin, and James M. Cook. 2001. "Birds of a Feather: Homophily in Social Networks." *Annual Review of Sociology* 27:415–44.

Menard, Scott W. 2002. *Applied Logistic Regression Analysis.* Thousand Oaks, CA: Sage.

Merton, Robert King. 1968. *Social Theory and Social Structure* New York: Free Press.

Moen, Phyllis. 1995. "Introduction." In *Examining Lives in Context: Perspectives on the Ecology of Human Development*, edited by Phyllis Moen, Glen Elder and Kurt Luscher (1–11). Washington, DC: American Psychological Association.

Moen, Phyllis. 2003. "Linked Lives: Dual Careers, Gender and the Contingent Life Course." In *Social Dynamics of the Life Course: Transitions Institutions and Interrelations*, edited by Walter R. Heinz and Victor W. Marshall (237–58). New York: Aldine de Gruyter.

Mutran, Elizabeth, and Donald C. Reitzes. 1984. "Intergenerational Support Activities and Well-Being among the Elderly: A Convergence of Exchange and Symbolic-Interaction Perspectives." *American Sociological Review* 49(1): 117–30.

Newman, Katherine S. 1999. *No Shame in My Game: The Working Poor in the Inner City.* New York: Alfred A. Knopf, Inc.

Nye, F. Ivan. 1979. "Choice, Exchange, and the Family." In *Contemporary Theories about the Family*, edited by Wesley R. Burr, Ruben Hill, F. Ivan Nye, and Ira L. Reiss (1–41). New York: Free Press.

Pendergast, Jane F., Stephen J. Gange, Michael A. Newton, Mary J. Lindstrom, Mari Palta, and Marian R. Fisher. 1996. "A Survey of Methods for Analyzing Clustered Binary Response Data." *International Statistical Review* 64:89–118.

Pillemer, Karl, and Kurt Luescher, eds. 2004. *Intergenerational Ambivalences: New Per-spectives on Parent-Child Relations in Later Life.* Stamford, CT: Elsevier/JAI Press.

Pillemer, Karl, and Kathleen McCartney, eds. 1991. *Parent-Child Relations Throughout Life.* New York: Erlbaum.

Pillemer, Karl, and J. Jill Suitor. 1991. " 'Will I Ever Escape My Child's Problems?': Effects of Adult Children's Problems on Elderly Parents." *Journal of Marriage and Family* 53(3): 585–94.

————. 1996. " 'It Takes One to Help One': Effects of Similar Others on the Well-Being of Caregivers." *Journals of Gerontology: Psychological Sciences and Social Sciences* 51(5): S250–S257.

————. 2002. "Explaining Mothers' Ambivalence toward Their Adult Children." *Journal of Marriage and Family* 64(3): 602–13.

————. 2005. "Ambivalence in Intergenerational Relations over the Life-Course." In *Intergenerational Relations across Time and Place*, edited by Merril Silverstein, Rosann Giarrusso, and Vern L. Bengtson (1–28). New York: Springer.

————. 2006. "Making Choices: A Within-Family Study of Caregiver Selection." *The Gerontologist* 46: 439–48.

Pruchno, Rachel A., Christopher J. Burant, and Norah D. Peters. 1994. "Family Mental-Health-Marital and Parent-Child Consensus as Predictors." *Journal of Marriage and Family* 56(3): 747–58.

Reis, Harry T., and Phillip Shaver. 1988. "Intimacy as an Interpersonal Process." In *Handbook of Personal Relationships: Theory, Research and Interventions* edited by Steve Duck (367–389). New York: John Wiley & Sons.

Roberto, Karen A., and Jean Pearson Scott. 1986. "Equity Considerations in the Friendships of Older Adults." *Journal of Gerontology* 41(2): 241–47.

Rossi, Alice S., and Peter H. Rossi. 1990. *Of Human Bonding: Parent-Child Relations across the Life Course.* Hawthorne, NY: Aldine de Gruyter.

Ryff, Carol D., Pamela S. Schmutte, and Young Hyun Lee. 1996. "How Children Turn Out: Implications for Parental Self-Evaluation." In *The Parental Experience in Midlife*, edited by Carol D. Ryff and Marsha Mailick Seltzer (383–422). Chicago: University of Chicago Press.

Ryff, Carol D., Young Hyun Lee, Marilyn J. Essex, and Pamela S. Schmutte. 1994. "My Children and Me: Midlife Evaluations of Grown Children and of Self." *Psychology and Aging* 9(2): 195–205.

Schulz, Richard, and Lynn M. Martire. 2004. "Family Caregiving of Persons with Dementia: Prevalence, Health Effects, and Support Strategies." *American Journal of Geriatric Psychiatry* 12(3): 240–49.

Schwarz, Beate. 2006. "Adult Daughters' Family Structure and the Association between Reciprocity and Relationship Quality." *Journal of Family Issues* 27(2): 208–28.

Schwarz, Mordechai. 2006. "Intergenerational Transfers: An Integrative Approach." *Journal of Public Economic Theory* 8(1): 61–95.

Settersten, Richard A. 2003. "Propositions and Controversies in Life-Course Scholarship." In *Invitation to the Life Course: Toward New Understandings of Later Life*, edited by Richard A. Settersten (15–45). Amityville, NY: Baywood Publishing Company, Inc.

Silverstein, Merril, and Vern L. Bengtson. 1997. "Intergenerational Solidarity and the Structure of Adult Child-Parent Relationships in American Families." *American Journal of Sociology* 103(2): 429–60.

Silverstein, Merril, Tonya M. Parrott, and Vern L. Bengtson. 1995. "Factors That Predispose Middle-Aged Sons and Daughters to Provide Social Support to Older Parents." *Journal of Marriage and Family* 57:465–75.

Silverstein, Merril, Stephen J. Conroy, Haitao Wang, Rosann Giarrusso, and Vern L. Bengtson. 2002. "Reciprocity in Parent-Child Relations Over the Adult Life Course." *Journals of Gerontology: Psychological Sciences and Social Sciences* 57(1): S3.

Simmel, Georg. 1964. *Conflict and the Web of Group-Affiliations.* New York: Free Press.

Sonna, Linda. 2006. *The Everything Parent's Guide to Raising Siblings: Tips to Eliminate Rivalry, Avoid Favoritism, and Keep the Peace.* Boston: Adams Publishing Group.

Steelman, Lala Carr, Brain Powell, Regina Werum, and Scott Carter. 2002. "Reconsidering the Effects of Sibling Configuration: Recent Advances and Challenges." *Annual Review of Sociology* 28:243–69.

Suitor, J. Jill 1987. "Mother-Daughter Relations When Married Daughters Return to School: Effects of Status Similarity." *Journal of Marriage and Family* 49(2): 435–44.

Suitor, J. Jill, and Shirley Keeton. 1997. "Once a Friend, Always a Friend? Effects of Homophily on Women's Support Networks Across a Decade." *Social Networks* 19(1): 51–62.

Suitor, J. Jill, and Karl Pillemer 2000. "Did Mom Really Love You Best? Exploring the Role of Within-Family Differences in Developmental Histories on Parental Favoritism." *Motivation and Emotion* 24:104–19.

———. 2006. "Choosing Daughters: Exploring Why Mothers Favor Adult Daughters Over Sons." *Sociological Perspectives* 49:139–60.

Suitor, J. Jill, Karl Pillemer, and Shirley Keeton. 1995. "When Experience Counts: The Effects of Experiential and Structural Similarity on Patterns of Support and Interpersonal Stress." *Social Forces* 73(4): 1573–88.

Suitor, J. Jill, Karl Pillemer, and Jori Sechrist. 2006. "Within-Family Differences in Mothers' Support to Adult Children." *Journal of Gerontology: Social Science* 16: S10–S17.

Suitor, J. Jill, Karl Pillemer, Shirley Keeton, and Julie Robison. 1995. "Aged Parents and Aging Children: Determinants of Relationship Quality." In *Aging and the Family: Theory and Research,* edited by Rosemary H. Blieszner and Victoria H. Bedford (223–242). Westport, CT: Greenwood Press.

Suitor, J. Jill, Jori Sechrist, Michael Steinhour, and Karl Pillemer. 2006. " 'I'm Sure She Chose Me!' Consistency in Intergenerational Reports of Mothers' Favoritism in Later-Life Families." *Family Relations* 55:526–38.

Sulloway, Frank J. 1996. *Born to Rebel.* New York: Pantheon Books.

Sweet, James A., and Larry L. Bumpass. 1996. *The National Survey of Families and Households—Waves 1 and 2: Data Description and Documentation.* Madison: Center for Demography and Ecology, University of Wisconsin.

Teo, Peggy, Elspeth Graham, Brenda S. A. Yeoh, and Susan Levy. 2003. "Values, Change and Intergenerational Ties Between Two Generations of Women in Singapore." *Ageing and Society* 23(3): 327–47.

Troll, Lillian E., and Karen L. Fingerman. 1996. *Connections Between Parents and Their Adult Children.* San Diego: Academic Press, Inc.

Uchino, Bert N. 2004. *Social Support and Physical Health: Understanding the Health Consequences of Relationships.* New Haven, CT: Yale University Press.

Umberson, Debra. 1992. "Relationships Between Adult Children and Their Parents: Psychological Consequences for Both Generations." *Journal of Marriage and Family* 54:664–74.

Waite, Linda J., and Evelyn L. Lehrer. 2003. "The Benefits from Marriage and Religion in the United States: A Comparative Analysis." *Population and Development Review* 29:255–75.

Wellman, Barry, and Scot Wortley. 1990. "Different Strokes from Different Folks: Community Ties and Social Support." *American Journal of Sociology* 96:558–88.

Welsh, Wendy M., and Abigail J. Stewart. 1995. "Relationships Between Women and Their Parents: Implications for Midlife Well-Being." *Psychology and Aging* 10:181–90.

Whiteman, Shawn D., Susan M. McHale, and Ann C. Crouter. 2003. "What Parents Learn from Experience: The First Child as a First Draft." *Journal of Marriage and Family* 65:608–21.

Wolf, Douglas A., Vicki Freedman, and Beth J. Soldo. 1997. "The Division of Family Labor: Care for Elderly Parents." *Journal of Gerontology: Social Science* 52:102–9.

10

Unanticipated Lives

Inter- and Intragenerational Relationships in Families with Children with Disabilities

Marsha Mailick Seltzer, Jan S. Greenberg, Gael I. Orsmond,
Julie Lounds Taylor, and Matthew J. Smith

Pillemer and Suitor's chapter, "Intergenerational Support, Care, and Relationship Quality in Later Life: Exploring Within-Family Differences," contains a rich analysis of within-family differences of aging mother–adult child relationships, with a special focus on which adult child is emotionally closest to the mother and which child she expects will take care of her when she no longer is able to be independent. This question has significant policy implications, especially in the era of longer life spans, smaller families, and greater geographic mobility of adult children. An additional factor that may be important is how these dynamics are altered when one of the adult children has a lifelong or long-term disability that might add to or compete with the mother's need for care. This type of family is the focus of the commentary in this chapter.

Pillemer and Suitor point out that each parent–adult child dyad should be conceptualized as an independent unit. One parent–child dyad should not be seen as a proxy for the others in the family, as has been the practice in many surveys of the family life course, which often focus on a randomly selected adult child. This is a particularly important point when one adult child has a disability. Such atypical parent–adult child dyads tend to be invisible in surveys that have a selected child design, as such children tend not to be selected to report on intergenerational relations. To reveal how having a child with a disability might alter the exchange relationships between aging mothers and their other adult children, we focus on factors that Pillemer and Suiter hypothesized would affect these relationships in typical families and then examine data from families that include an adult child with a disability.

Among the questions Pillemer and Suitor address are "To which adult children do mothers provide more support?" and "Which adult child is the mother likely to name as a future caregiver?" In answering these questions, Pillemer and Suitor hypothesized three sets of factors to predict outcomes: similarity, developmental history of achieving adult status, and history of exchange and equity. Similarity in gender, for example, was predicted to lead to greater closeness and the expectation of future caregiving. Achieving adult status and freedom from problems was another factor that was predicted to lead to greater closeness and a higher probability of the caregiver-designate role. Finally, a history of exchange and equity was predicted to set the stage for a close relationship and future expectation of care.

On the first question, Pillemer and Suitor report that mothers provide more support to their adult daughters than to their adult sons, confirming the gender similarity prediction. The picture is not as clear for achievement of adult status. Mothers provide more support to those who have greater health problems and are no less likely to provide support if the child had manifested deviant behavior. Thus, achievement of adult status does not appear to predict maternal provision of support. Rather, need for support is the driving factor that overrides achievement of adult status in determining the willingness of mothers to provide support to the adult child. Finally, with respect to a history of exchange in the mother–adult child relationship, Pillemer and Suitor found that mothers were closer to those adult children who have provided more support to the mother in the past, confirming the exchange prediction.

For the second question, Pillemer and Suitor report that daughters were more likely to be identified as future caregivers than sons, again supporting the gender similarity hypothesis. On the exchange hypothesis, adult children who provided more support for the mother in the previous year were more likely to be identified by their mothers as future caregivers, but those who received support from their mothers were no more likely to be named than other siblings in the family. Thus, it is provision of support rather than exchange of support that leads to the expectation by mothers that a particular child will care for them in the future. Overall, these findings provide support for the framework that Pillemer and Suitor hypothesized.

Inter- and Intragenerational Relations in Families with Children with Disabilities

Our 15-year program of research on mothers and adult siblings in families in which child has a disability provides data that can extend the Pillemer and Suitor framework to families facing additional challenges (for reviews, see Lounds and Seltzer 2007; Seltzer, Greenberg, et al. 2005). Demographically, having a sibling with a disability is not a rare event. It is estimated that nearly 4 million families (5.5 percent of all families) in the United States have at least one child with a disability (LaPlante et al. 1996). Given the prevalence of this type of family constellation, there are significant policy implications of detecting divergent patterns of within-family closeness and capacity for providing care to parents as they age.

In a series of parallel prospective longitudinal studies with common measures, we studied aging families of adults with mental retardation over a 12-year period (Krauss and Seltzer 1999), aging families of adults with schizophrenia over a 5-year period (Smith, Greenberg, and Seltzer 2007), and midlife families with a son or daughter with autism over a 5-year period (Seltzer, Shattuck, et al. 2004). Across all studies, we collected data about the relationship between the mother and the child with the disability, about the sibling relationships in the family, and about the consequences of family transitions including the decline of health in the mother and maternal death.

Mother–Child Relationship Quality

Our program of research begins with the observation made by Pillemer and Suitor that each parent–child dyad has a unique relationship, past, and future. Questions about closeness in the mother–child dyad have been the focus of much of our research. For example, in our study of families who have adolescent or adult children with autism, we have investigated which factors may lead to a closer relationship between the mother and the son or daughter with autism (Orsmond et al. 2006). Because of the similarity in measures in Pillemer and Suitor's study and in our various studies, we are able to examine the factors Pillemer and Suitor reported to affect the closeness in the mother–child relationship: gender similarity, attainment of adult status, and exchange in the relationship.

Our measure of relationship quality in this and all other studies we describe was the positive affect index (Bengtson and Schrader 1982), which assesses the mother's perception of affective solidarity with her son or daughter. Ten self-report items were used from this scale, five questions addressing the mother's feelings of positive affect toward her son or daughter (e.g., "How much affection do you have toward your son/daughter?") and five questions representing the mother's perception of positive affect from her son or daughter (e.g., "How much affection do you feel that your son/daughter has for you?"), each rated on a six-point scale. Each set of five questions addresses the dimensions of understanding, trust, fairness, respect, and affection in the relationship. Two summary scores represent positive affect from the mother toward the son or daughter and positive affect perceived by the mother as coming from the son or daughter.

Counter to the patterns Pillemer and Suitor report, we found that neither child gender nor attainment of adult status by the child with the disability (as measured by finishing high school) were related to the closeness of the mother–child relationship. Rather, we found that the health of the adolescent or adult child with autism and the degree to which the child manifested behavior problems were predictive of variability in the quality of the mother–child relationship. When the adolescent or adult with autism was in better health, the mother perceived more positive affect coming from the son or daughter to her. Similarly, when the son or daughter manifested fewer behavior problems, the mother gave higher ratings of her feelings of closeness toward her son or daughter and also perceived more positive affect coming from the son or daughter to her (Orsmond et al. 2006).

It is possible that disability characteristics such as health and behavior problems are proxies for the child's ability to exchange emotional support with the mother, and in this sense, perhaps the normative patterns for exchange that Pillemer and Suitor report are borne out also in the context of disability in the family. Indeed, when we compare mother–child relationship quality across diagnoses, we find support for this possibility. In one analysis with the positive affect index (Greenberg et al. 2004), we compared mothers of adults with Down syndrome, autism, and schizophrenia, and reported that mother–child relationship quality was closest when the adult child's diagnosis was Down syndrome, least close when the adult child had schizophrenia, and in the middle of the two extremes for autism. A prominent symptom in both autism and schizophrenia but not Down syndrome is difficulty with social relationships, including a qualitative impairment in reciprocal social interactions (American Psychiatric Association 2000; Rosner et al. 2004; Travis and Sigman 1998). Such interpersonal impairments may make it less likely for the son or daughter with schizophrenia or autism, compared with those who had Down syndrome, to be able exchange support with the mother and build a close relationship.

Relationship Quality between Siblings when One Has a Disability

Our studies also make it possible to examine how disability in one sibling affects intragenerational sibling relationships. Overall, we have found a pattern of continuity of contact between the nondisabled sibling and the brother or sister with the disability, but the frequency of contact varies by diagnostic group. For those who have mental retardation, we found that 30 percent of the nondisabled siblings reported weekly or more frequent phone contacts with the brother or sister with the disability, 41 percent reported in-person visits at least once a week, and 58 percent lived within a 30-minute drive of the sibling's home (Krauss et al. 1996). By contrast, the comparable data for adult siblings of individuals with autism show sharply less contact, with 8 percent of the siblings reporting weekly or more frequent phone contacts, 18 percent reporting in-person visits at least once a week, and 35 percent living within a 30-minute drive of the sibling's home (Orsmond and Seltzer 2007). Similar to the siblings of individuals with mental retardation, 24 percent of siblings of adults with schizophrenia reported talking on the phone at least weekly with their brother or sister, and 51 percent lived within 30 minutes of him or her. However, only 19 percent of siblings of adults with schizophrenia reported weekly or more visits, comparable to the siblings of adolescents or adults with autism (Smith et al. 2007).

These patterns of contact are also reflected in the closeness of the sibling relationship. We compared siblings whose brother or sister had Down syndrome or autism (Orsmond and Seltzer 2007). Consistent with the findings on frequency of sibling contact and also mother–child relationship quality, the sibling relationship was closer when the child's diagnosis was Down syndrome than when the sibling with the disability had autism. Thus, the interpersonal impairments associated with autism may make it less likely for the sibling with the disability to be able to exchange support with the nondisabled sibling and build a close relationship than the impairments associated with Down syndrome.

In the context of these patterns of sibling contact, we have found gender to be an interesting and important factor that conditions the sibling relationship. Gender similarity in the sibling–sibling dyad is a function of the gender of each sibling, and therefore there are four possible dyads. In our studies of siblings of adults with mental retardation (Orsmond and Seltzer 2000), we found that nondisabled brothers who have a brother with mental retardation are very close to that sibling. Of the four possible types of dyads, this group has the highest scores on positive affect, lowest scores on negative affect, and the least worries about the future well-being of his brother with mental retardation. In sharp contrast, brothers who have a sister with mental retardation showed the opposite profile—they had lowest scores on positive affect, highest on negative affect, and were most worried about the future. The gender of the sibling with mental retardation did not matter for the sisters, who tended to have high scores on positive affect, low scores on negative affect, and moderate levels of worry, but not as extreme on any of these dimensions as the brothers, regardless of the gender of her sibling with the disability. Thus, gender similarity is an important factor for nondisabled brothers but not for nondisabled sisters in conditioning their feelings about the sibling with mental retardation.

We also found other evidence that similarity matters in the sibling relationship, even when one sibling has a disability. For example, among siblings with a brother or sister with autism, we found that the sibling relationship is closer when the nondisabled sibling has lower levels of education, reflecting less educational disparity with the brother or sister with the disability. Among siblings of adults with Down syndrome, we found that siblings share more activities when the sibling with the disability is more functionally independent, again suggesting that less disparity leads to greater sibling involvement (Orsmond and Seltzer 2007). Thus, in general, similarity may loom as a larger force conditioning intragenerational relationships than intergenerational relationships in families with members with disabilities.

Finally, on reciprocity in the sibling relationship, in an analysis of siblings who had a brother or sister with schizophrenia (Smith et al. 2007), we found that nondisabled siblings who perceived greater reciprocity in the relationship expected to be more involved in the future care of and more emotionally involved with the brother or sister with schizophrenia after the mother relinquishes the caregiving role.

Linked Lives Across and Within Generations

Studies of families with members who have disabilities also reveal the extent to which the lives of individual family members are linked across as well as within generations. In our research on siblings who have a brother or sister with schizophrenia, we obtained independent data from each sibling (Smith and Greenberg 2007). We found that a closer sibling relationship, as rated by the nondisabled sibling, was predictive of a more favorable quality of life, as rated by the sibling with schizophrenia. These data provide evidence about the salience of intragenerational relationships for individuals with disabilities.

Whether such relationships remain as close after the parent generation begins to require care from the nondisabled sibling has not been examined in this study of aging families who have a member with schizophrenia, but that was the focus of an analysis of aging families who have a member with mental retardation (Seltzer et al. 2001). In that analysis, we found that, on average, over a three-year period, siblings increased in the number of activities they shared with their brother or sister with mental retardation. Such activities included going out for a meal in a restaurant, shopping, going to movies, visiting a friend or a relative, going on vacation together, etc. The increase was most gradual when the mother was in stable health during the three-year period, more accelerated when the mother was in declining health, and steepest when the mother died during the three-year period between the two points of data collection. This set of findings suggests that the increase in siblings' level of shared activities is a function of decline in maternal caregiving capacity. These siblings become more involved with each other after maternal death, as the nondisabled sibling inherits the responsibility for caregiving for the brother or sister with the disability.

Conclusions

The sibling relationship is the longest-lasting family tie, beginning with the birth of the younger sibling and ending with the death of either sibling. Normatively, patterns of equity and reciprocity characterize the sibling relationship, but when one sibling has a disability, the exchange of support is less balanced. As the family ages, the nondisabled siblings are positioned to assume responsibility for the care of the aging parents as well as the oversight and care of the brother or sister with the disability. These families constitute an exceptional example of the sandwich generation, whereby nondisabled siblings have simultaneous responsibilities for family members in the older generation (their parents), their own generation (their sibling with the disability), and the younger generation (their children). As such, these families offer a unique opportunity for the study of intergenerational exchanges and transfers.

NOTE

Prepared for the 2006 National Symposium on Family Issues, "Caring and Exchange within and across Generations," The Pennsylvania State University. Support for the preparation of this chapter was provided by the National Institutes of Health grants R01 AG08768, R01 MH55928, R03 HD039185, P30 HD03352, T32 HD07489, and T32 MH065185.

REFERENCES

American Psychiatric Association. 2000. *Diagnostic and Statistical Manual Of Mental Disorders*, 4th ed. Washington, DC: American Psychiatric Association.

Bengtson, Vern L., and Sandi S. Schrader. 1982. "Parent-Child Relationships." In *Research Instruments in Social Gerontology, Vol. 2: Social Roles and Social Participation*, edited by David J. Mangen and Warren A. Peterson, 115–55. Minneapolis: University of Minnesota Press.

Greenberg, Jan S., Marsha M. Seltzer, Marty W. Krauss, Rita Chou, and Jinkuk Hong. 2004. "The Effect of Quality of the Relationship Between Mothers and Adult Children with Schizophrenia, Autism, or Down Syndrome on Maternal Well-Being: The Mediating Role of Optimism." *American Journal of Orthopsychiatry*, 74:14–25.

Krauss, Marty W., and Marsha M. Seltzer. 1999. "An Unanticipated Life: The Impact of Lifelong Caregiving." In *Responding to the Challenge: International Trends and Current Issues in Developmental Disabilities*, edited by Hank Bersani. Brookline, MA: Brookline Books.

Krauss, Marty W., Marsha M. Seltzer, Rachel Gordon, and Donna H. Friedman. 1996. "Binding Ties: The Roles of Adult Siblings of Persons with Mental Retardation." *Mental Retardation* 34:83–93.

LaPlante, Mitchell P., Dawn Carlson, H. Stephen Kaye, and Julia E. Bradshar. 1996. *Families with Disabilities in the U.S.* Washington, DC: U.S. Department of Education, National Institute on Disability and Rehabilitation Research.

Lounds, Julie, and Marsha M. Seltzer. 2007. "Family Impact across the Lifespan." In *Handbook on Developmental Disabilities*, edited by Samuel L. Odom, Robert H. Horner, Marty Snell, and Jan Blacher. New York: Guilford Press.

Orsmond, Gael I., and Marsha M. Seltzer. 2000. "Brothers and Sisters of Adults with Mental Retardation: The Gendered Nature of the Sibling Relationship." *American Journal on Mental Retardation* 105:486–508.

————. 2007. "Siblings of Individuals with Autism or Down Syndrome: Effects on Adult Lives." *Journal of Intellectual Disability Research* 51:682–96.

Orsmond, Gael I., Marsha M. Seltzer, Jan S. Greenberg, and Marty W. Krauss. 2006. "Mother-Child Relationship Quality Among Adolescents and Adults with Autism." *American Journal of Mental Retardation* 111:121–37.

Rosner, Beth A., Robert M. Hodapp, Deborah J. Fidler, Jacklyn N. Sagun, and Elisabeth M. Dykens. 2004. "Social Competence in Persons with Prader-Willi, Williams, and Down's Syndromes." *Journal of Applied Research in Intellectual Disabilities* 17:209–17.

Seltzer, Marsha M., Jan S. Greenberg, Gael I. Orsmond, and Julie Lounds. 2005. "Life Course Studies of Siblings of Individuals with Developmental Disabilities." *Mental Retardation* 43:354–59.

Seltzer, Marsha M., Marty W. Krauss, Jinkuk Hong, and Gael I. Orsmond. 2001. "Continuity or Discontinuity of Family Involvement Following Residential Transitions of Adults with Mental Retardation." *Mental Retardation* 39:181–94.

Seltzer, Marsha, M. Paul Shattuck, Leonard Abbeduto, and Jan S. Greenberg. 2004. "The Trajectory of Development in Adolescents and Adults with Autism." *Mental Retardation Developmental Disabilities Research Reviews* 10:234–47.

Smith, Matthew J., and Jan S. Greenberg. 2007. "The Effect of the Quality of Sibling Relationships on the Life Satisfaction of Adults with Schizophrenia." *Psychiatric Services* 58:1222–24.

Smith, Matthew J., Jan S. Greenberg, and Marsha M. Seltzer. 2007. "Siblings of Adults with Schizophrenia: Expectations About Future Caregiving Roles." *American Journal of Orthopsychiatry* 77: 29–37.

Travis, Lisa L., and Marian M. Sigman. 1998. "Social Deficits and Interpersonal Relationships in Autism." *Mental Retardation Developmental Disabilities Research Reviews* 4:65–72.

11

Families as Nonshared Environments for Siblings

Susan M. McHale and Ann C. Crouter

Most children grow up with siblings—indeed, in the United States today, more children live with a sibling than with a father (Hernandez 1997). In turn, sibling relationships are the longest lasting relationships in most people's lives. In the face of their ubiquity, however, siblings' role in family life and individual development has been neglected by family and developmental researchers, and this is especially true in the literature on adult development and family relationships (Walker, Allen, and Connidis 2005). Pillemer and Suitor's analysis of differences between siblings' relationships with parents breaks new ground by extending study of siblings' family roles and experiences well into adulthood. As Pillemer and Suitor suggest, their work also highlights the methodological advantages and novel research questions that arise when siblings are incorporated into family and developmental research.

Our discussion focuses on both the substantive and research design issues Pillemer and Suitor highlight. Specifically, we describe examples of phenomena surrounding siblings' nonshared family experiences in childhood and adolescence from our own research; our findings corroborate, and in some cases extend, Pillemer and Suitor's analyses. We conclude by considering some of the implications of within-family designs for understanding how families work.

In discussing siblings' differential experiences in childhood, we draw on data from the Penn State Family Relationships Project, a set of longitudinal family studies, and a companion study, the Juntos Project, directed by Kim Updegraff at Arizona State University, all funded by the National Institute of Child Health and Human Development. In these projects, we have built on research and theory that highlight parents' differential treatment of siblings as a key family dynamic and influence on youth development. By way of background, in 1995, we launched a first set of longitudinal studies of two-parent, primarily dual earner, European American families from central Pennsylvania. These studies, one focused on middle childhood and one on adolescence, were designed to allow us to examine siblings' family experiences at the same point in time as well as when siblings were at about the same chronological age. We later extended our work to study samples of African American and Mexican American families and extended our middle childhood study across the adolescent years, concluding a year after the firstborn's graduation from high school. In each study, we conducted annual home interviews with mothers, fathers, and two siblings that focused on individuals' personal qualities and experiences and on family relationship qualities. In about half of the study years, we also conducted a series of seven telephone interviews to collect data on family members' activities and experiences and parents' knowledge of their children's daily experiences during the day of each call with a modified daily diary procedure. (See Crouter et al. 1999; McHale, Crouter, and Tucker 1999; McHale et al. 2005; and McHale et al. 2006 for details about these studies' design and procedures.) The empirical examples we describe come from these studies.

Theoretical and Empirical Roots for a Within-Family Approach

The earliest empirical study of children's differential treatment by parents was conducted by Joan Lasko with data from the Fels Longitudinal Study and was published in 1954. Lasko grounded her research in the birth order literature and compared siblings' experiences with their mothers when siblings were about the same age, a design decision that has important strengths but that has been used rarely since then. Her findings revealed small but predictable differences in mothers' treatment of their children. Writing at roughly the same time, Talcott Parsons (1974/1942) suggested that equal treatment of offspring by parents was normative in our democratic society. In the face of proscriptions about equality, however, Lasko's results forecast the findings of every other published study of parents' differential treatment in childhood. Now, with Pillemer and Suitor weighing in on adult experiences, it seems quite clear that parents' differential treatment of their offspring is a dynamic in families across the life span.

For almost 30 years after Lasko's work, there was a hiatus in research on parents' differential treatment. Beginning slowly in the 1980s, motivated by an emerging interest in sibling relationships (e.g., Bryant and Crockenberg 1980), and increasing rapidly in the 1990s, motivated by behavioral geneticists' interest in the nonshared family environment (e.g., Daniels and Plomin 1985), child development researchers have produced an exciting body of research on parents' differential treatment. Most of this work has been directed at three kinds of questions, the first two of which Pillemer and Suitor addressed: (1) What is the nature of mothers' and fathers' differential treatment? (2) Under what conditions is differential treatment more likely? (3) What are the implications of differential treatment for individual development and well-being and for dyadic family relationships? We will consider each of these questions, reviewing the conceptual/theoretical frameworks on which empirical research has been grounded and highlighting some of the complexities that have emerged in our analyses.

What Is the Nature of Mothers' and Fathers' Differential Treatment?

One reason Pillemer and Suitor's chapter is especially interesting to a child developmentalist is because they assessed dimensions of differential treatment—such as which offspring parents go to for help and support—that have not yet been studied in research on younger populations. Instead, reflecting relationship dimensions that have been the focus of research on child and adolescent parent–offspring relationships, most work on younger families has examined parental warmth/affection and control/discipline. Like Pillemer and Suitor, we in the Penn State Family Relationships Project used a rating scale approach (adapted from Daniels and Plomin 1985) to ask parents and youth directly about whether differential treatment occurs; unlike Pillemer and Suitor, we assessed parents' differential treatment of two target children. Our findings show that family members do report differential treatment. Patterns vary, however, depending on whom we ask and what dimensions of differential treatment we ask about. Patterns also vary by cultural context (McHale et al. 2005; Tucker, Crouter, and McHale 2003).

In European American families, mothers and fathers report fairly similar patterns of differential treatment (figure 11.1). Whereas youth report more differential treatment in domains having to do with privileges and responsibilities, parents report more differential treatment in domains that describe parent–child interactions (i.e., warmth, discipline). Rates of differential treatment in the domains of responsibility and warmth are low in comparison to the rates Pillemer and Suitor report in the domains of help giving and emotional closeness (both closer to 70 percent). Pillemer and Suitor, however, asked about differential treatment toward *any* offspring, a strategy that likely increases the possibility of differential treatment relative to the rates when only two offspring are targeted. It also may be that the norm of equal treatment is stronger for families during the child-rearing years. As far as we know, no one has asked parents or children to reflect on their attitudes about whether and when siblings should be treated differently. A question for life span researchers

Figure 11.1. Proportions of Youth (Mean Age, 14.9), Mothers, and Fathers Reporting Differential Treatment of First- vs. Second-Born Siblings by Domain (*N* = 394 families)

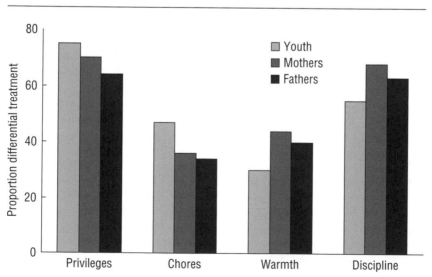

is whether the norm of equal treatment holds across time and place, a topic to which we will return.

A consistent pattern across both our and Pillemer and Suitor's studies pertains to the multidimensionality of differential treatment. As we suggested, some differential treatment dimensions seem to reflect relational processes, such as affection and emotional closeness, whereas other dimensions may pertain more to family roles and circumstances (e.g., responsibilities, privileges, instrumental support). Importantly, the adjustment and family relationships correlates of differential treatment vary across domain (McHale, Updegraff, Jackson-Newsom, Tucker, and Crouter 2000). A direction for life span study is to develop a topography of differential treatment so that we can see when and where particular dimensions of differential treatment are salient in family life and how particular kinds of differential treatment—such as having fewer family responsibilities or receiving privileged treatment—are maintained or transformed across time.

The Family Contexts of Differential Treatment

Like Pillemer and Suitor, most child development researchers have found that the extent of differential treatment varies across families and have raised questions about what factors account for this variability. Two conceptual frameworks provide insights into the family conditions of differential treatment. First, as we suggested, findings from the behavioral genetics literature have been an important impetus for research on differential treatment: Research on sibling similarity as a function of genetic relatedness shows that, compared with shared environment effects, nonshared environment effects often account for more of the variance in sibling differences across a range of domains, including personality, interests, and adjustment (Dunn and Plomin 1990). Although shared and nonshared environment effects are not actually measured directly in most behavior genetics studies, conceptualizations of the nonshared environment direct attention to (a) siblings' effects on one another, (b) extra-familial experiences such as peer and school influences; (c) idiosyncratic experiences, including the timing of children's experiences of family events such as parental divorce or residential moves; and (d) parents' differential treatment (Dunn and Plomin 1990). From this perspective, however, individuals, by virtue of their genetic heritage, create their unique environments (Scarr 1992). By evoking reactions from the social world (because of their genetically grounded temperament or personality characteristics) and by the increasingly active role individuals play in selecting environmental niches as they mature, differences in siblings' family experiences may become more pronounced with age. Some of Pillemer and Suitor's findings on the role of individuals' personal qualities in patterns of differential treatment are consistent with behavior geneticists' ideas.

To learn more about why parents treat their children differently, we collected data on parents' reasons for differential treatment by asking them to rate specific reasons on a five-point scale. As figure 11.2 shows, from parents' perspectives, some reasons are more important than others. Within-person analyses revealed that, for both mothers and fathers, differences in siblings' personalities and age/maturity levels were more often endorsed than reasons having to do with opportunity, one child's particular needs, and parent–offspring similarity. We only asked whether sex differences were important when the family included a mixed-sex sibling dyad, but a sex difference between siblings was rarely endorsed as a reason for differential treatment. Sex constellation effects indicated, however, that both mothers and fathers endorsed personality and interest differences

Figure 11.2. Mothers' and Fathers' Ratings of Reasons for Differential Treatment of First-Born (Mean Age, 12.8) and Second-Born (Mean Age, 10.2) Offspring ($N = 201$ families)

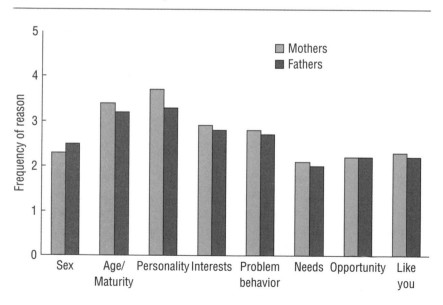

between their offspring, and fathers endorsed opportunity issues as more important reasons for differential treatment when they had firstborn sons and younger daughters. Fathers also were more likely to say the sex difference between their children was a reason for differential treatment when they had firstborn sons and second-born daughters. We also found that mothers were more likely to say that they treated their offspring differently because one of their children was more like them when they had two daughters.

Our analysis of how parents' differential treatment unfolds over time also highlighted the role of the sex constellation of the sibling dyad in parents' patterns. For example, we found that mothers of firstborn girls and second-born boys showed an increasing preference for their daughters in the domain of warmth from childhood through adolescence. By contrast, for other dyads, mothers' preference for firstborns declined in firstborns' early and middle adolescence but began to recover when firstborns reached late adolescence and second-borns were in middle adolescence (Shanahan et al. 2007). In these analyses, we measured differential treatment by asking siblings about their dyadic relationship experiences and calculating the difference score between older and younger siblings' reports. In our experience, this strategy has some methodological advantages. First, it minimizes social desirability pressures that may elicit reports of equal treatment. It also measures differential treatment along a continuum, allowing for a statistical test of whether the experiences of siblings differ significantly, and, by increasing variability, allows one to readily identify family and individual correlates of differential treatment and its patterns of change over time, a topic to which we will return. Finally, because we collect measures of each sibling's dyadic experiences with a parent, these measures can be treated as control variables to determine whether differential family experiences account for variance—for example, in youth adjustment—beyond what is accounted for by *dyadic* parent–offspring relationship quality.

More generally, our findings on the significance of sibling gender constellation are congruent with the tenets of a second conceptual framework on which our research has been based: a feminist family sociological perspective (Ferree 1990). In contrast to traditional models of the family that highlight family cohesiveness and solidarity and imply that an understanding of the family requires the report of only one family member, a feminist perspective directs attention to the different and often competing goals of family members and to questions about who wins and who loses in the allocation of family resources. In this way, like a behavior genetics perspective, a feminist perspective focuses on the family as a nonshared environment. Unlike a behavior genetics approach, however, this perspective highlights gender as a primary basis for the structuring of family roles, relationships, and activities. Child development researchers interested in gender development and socialization have most often used between-family designs, comparing the socialization experiences of girls and boys in different families and concluded that parents do not treat their children in sex-typed ways (Lytton and Romney 1991). As we have argued, however, using within-family designs to compare the experiences of sisters versus brothers better illuminates the nature of sex-typed differential treatment in families (figure 11.3). In these analyses, for example, the nonsibling boy versus girl comparison of children's time spent on chores at about age 10 was not statistically significant. By contrast, the within-family comparison of older sisters versus younger brothers showed that girls spent significantly more time on chores than their brothers when both siblings were approximately 10 years old (i.e., the data were collected at different times).

Figure 11.3. Time in Household Tasks by Girls vs. Boys and Sisters vs. Brothers at About Age 10 (*N* = 201 families)

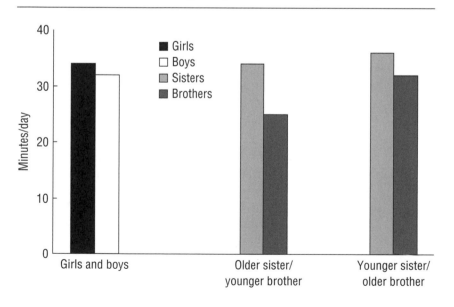

Implications of Differential Treatment for Individual Adjustment and Dyadic Relationships

Lasko grounded her 1954 study in a theoretical frame, the individual psychology theory of Alfred Adler, which highlighted children's position in their families *relative to their siblings* as a key influence on psychosocial development. Specifically, Adler proposed that, in an effort to limit sibling rivalry for parental love and other family resources, sisters and brothers would, through both conscious and unconscious processes, differentiate or *de-identify* with one another, such as by developing different interests and skills or by picking different family roles (Ansbacher and Ansbacher 1956). Adler placed children's experiences with their siblings at the center of family influences on development and, in contrast to most developmental and family theories, proposed that family influences would often operate to make siblings different. Adler's theory also highlighted parents' differential treatment of siblings and children's resulting feelings of jealousy and rivalry as key forces in individuals' life choices, personality development, and psychological adjustment.

Most child development research has focused on the potential implications of parents' differential treatment for youth adjustment and dyadic family relationships. Findings in the child development literature are generally consistent with Adler's theory in showing that parents' differential treatment, particularly in the domains of affection and discipline, is linked to less positive and more conflictual sibling relationships and, especially for the less preferred child, poorer individual adjustment. Systematic study of the links between parents' differential treatment and adult siblings' well-being and sibling relationship qualities is an important direction for research. Given that siblings tend to have long-lasting relationships and in light of contemporary changes in family size (making for fewer siblings) and structure (making for variability in siblings' genetic relatedness), understanding how parenting patterns are linked to siblings' close and supportive relationships across the life span may be a fruitful topic for adult mental health research.

Recent studies reveal that the story of how differential treatment affects individual well-being and sibling relationships may not be quite as straightforward as Adler envisioned. Specifically, some work suggests that differential treatment may have different meanings—and thereby different psychosocial implications—in different family contexts. In a study of the family experiences of children with younger disabled versus nondisabled siblings, for example, we found the expected associations between less preferred treatment and adjustment problems in families with only nondisabled youth (McHale and Pawletko 1992). In contrast, preferential treatment through greater attention and warmth toward a younger, disabled sibling was not linked to adjustment problems in older, nondisabled siblings. These findings lead us to suggest that children's understanding of parents' differential treatment might moderate its effects; in other words, equitable treatment of siblings does not always mean being treated the same. Following these results, we and others began to study factors such as children's evaluations of how fair their parents are in their treatment of themselves versus their siblings and parents' reasons for treating their children differently as part of the differential treatment–adjustment process. Relevant to Pillemer and Suitor's findings on need-based reasons for differential treatment, Kowal and Kramer (1997) found that, when children reported that their siblings were treated differently because they needed special treatment, differential treatment did not have negative adjustment correlates. Our work shows that children's perceptions of parental fairness are consistent correlates of youth adjustment and sibling relationship evaluations (McHale et al. 2000). Nonetheless, our longitudinal analyses indicate that differential treatment continues to account for differences in youth adjustment and sibling relationship evaluations, even after children's fairness ratings and their evaluations of their dyadic relationships with parents are controlled (Shanahan et al. 2008).

We have begun to look at differential treatment in different cultural groups in an effort to understand how cultural values may moderate the links between differential treatment and youth well-being. Cultural anthropologists who study sibling experiences have argued that Western views of sibling relationships are culturally biased (e.g., Nicholls 1993). These researchers contend that, in societies in which communal values prevail and parents' differential treatment and sibling roles are proscribed on the basis of birth order and gender, rivalry and competition are not the central theme in sibling relationship dynamics, as Adler had suggested. Consistent with this argument, we have shown that when Mexican American youth report high familism values—values that emphasize the importance of the needs of the family group over those of the individual—the links between parents' differential treatment and youth adjustment and parent–child relationship evaluations were not as strong or consistent as they were for youth with weaker familism values (McHale et al. 2005).

Findings such as these suggest that examining the role of cultural values and practices in siblings' family roles and relationships is a worthy direction for life span research.

Implications of Within-Family Analyses for Understanding Families

As these data examples imply, looking within the family to understand potential differences among family members' experiences, the conditions under which those differences arise, and the implications of differential experiences for family members' well-being and development provides new insights about how families work. The impetus for such an approach comes from a diverse range of perspectives, including feminist, behavior genetic, and psychoanalytic, perspectives one would not ordinarily expect to coalesce around a common idea!

Findings from research that conceptualizes families as nonshared environments challenge an assumption implicit in most child development research: that we can understand how families work by studying the experiences of a single individual or dyadic relationship. Not only do individuals have different perceptions of and experiences in their families, but the social comparisons individuals make of their own and others' places in the family are an important dynamic in families, with implications for the well-being of family members and the quality of family relationships. More generally, we have argued that to understand how families work as systems—a goal that family researchers often articulate but less often act upon—we need to target constructs that take us beyond individuals and dyads. Studying within-family differences in dyadic relationships is one way to move beyond the dyadic level, and doing so places siblings' experiences at the center of our analyses of family relationships.

NOTE

We thank Matt Bumpus, Kelly Davis, Aryn Dotterer, Melissa Fortner, Heather Helms, Julia Jackson-Newsom, Marni Kan, Ji-Yeon Kim, Mary Klute, Lilly Shanahan, Cindy Shearer, Corinna Tucker, Kimberly Updegraff, Shawn Whiteman, Megan Winchell, and Laura Wray and a large staff of graduate and undergraduate interviewers for their help in conducting this research, and the participating families for their cooperation. This work was funded by grants from the National Institute of Child Health and Human Development (R01-HD29409 and R01-HD32336, Ann C. Crouter and Susan M. McHale, co-principal investigators, and R0l-HD39666, Kimberly Updegraff, principal investigator).

REFERENCES

Ansbacher, Heinz L., and Rowena R. Ansbacher. 1956. *The Individual Psychology of Alfred Adler.* New York: Basic Books.

Bryant, Brenda, and Susan Crockenberg. 1980. "Correlates and Dimensions of Prosocial Behavior: A Study of Female Siblings with Their Mothers." *Child Development* 51:529–44.

Crouter, Ann C., Heather Helms-Erikson, Kimberly Updegraff, and Susan M. McHale. 1999. "Conditions Underlying Parents' Knowledge about Children's Daily Lives in Middle Childhood: Between- and Within-Family Comparisons." *Child Development* 70:246–59.

Daniels, Denise, and Robert Plomin. 1985. "Differential Experience of Siblings in the Same Family." *Developmental Psychology* 21:747–60.

Dunn, Judy, and Robert Plomin. 1990. *Separate Lives: Why Siblings Are So Different.* New York: Basic Books.

Ferree, Myra M. 1990. "Beyond Separate Spheres: Feminism and Family Research." *Journal of Marriage and the Family* 52:866–84.

Hernandez, Donald J. 1997. "Child Development and Social Demography of Childhood." *Child Development* 68:149–69.

Kowal, Amanda, and Laurie Kramer. 1997. "Children's Understanding of Parental Differential Treatment." *Child Development* 68:113–26.

Lasko, Joan. 1954. "Parent Behavior toward First and Second Children." *Genetic Psychology Monographs* 49:97–137.

Lytton, Hugh, and David M. Romney. 1991. "Parents' Differential Socialization of Boys and Girls: A Meta-Analysis." *Psychological Bulletin* 109:267–97.

McHale, Susan M., and Terese M. Pawletko. 1992. "Differential Treatment of Siblings in Two Family Contexts." *Child Development* 63:68–81.

McHale, Susan M., Ann C. Crouter, and Corinna J. Tucker. 1999. "Family Context and Gender Role Socialization in Middle Childhood: Comparing Girls to Boys and Sisters to Brothers." *Child Development* 70:990–1004.

McHale, Susan M., Kimberly A. Updegraff, Lilly Shanahan, and Sarah A. Killoren. 2005. "Siblings' Differential Treatment in Mexican American Families." *Journal of Marriage and Family* 67:1259–74.

McHale, Susan M., Kimberly A. Updegraff, Julia Jackson-Newsom, Corinna J. Tucker, and Ann C. Crouter. 2000. "When Does Parents' Differential Treatment Have Negative Implications for Siblings?" *Social Development* 9:149–72.

McHale, Susan M., Ann C. Crouter, Ji-Yeon Y. Kim, Linda M. Burton, Kelly A. Davis, Aryn Dotterer, and Dena P. Swanson. 2006. "Mothers' and Fathers' Racial Socialization in African American Families: Implications for Youth." *Child Development* 77:1387–1402.

Nuckolls, C. W. 1993. "An Introduction to the Cross-Cultural Study of Sibling Relations." In *Siblings in South Asia,* edited by C. W. Nuckolls (19–44). New York: Guilford Press.

Parsons, Talcott. 1974/1942. "Age and Sex in Social Structure." In *The Family: Its Structures and Functions,* edited by R. L. Coser (243–55). New York: St. Martins.

Scarr, Sandra. 1992. "Developmental Theories for the 1990s: Development and Individual Differences." *Child Development* 63:1–19.

Shanahan, Lilly, Susan M. McHale, Ann C. Crouter, and D. Wayne Osgood. 2008. "Parental Differential Treatment of Siblings: Links with Depressive Symptoms and Sibling Relationships from Middle Childhood through Adolescence." *Journal of Marriage and Family* 70: 480–94.

————. 2007. "Warmth with Mothers and Fathers from Middle Childhood Through Adolescence: Within and Between Family Comparisons." *Developmental Psychology* 43: 551–63.

Tucker, C. J., Susan M. McHale, and Ann C. Crouter. 2003. "Dimensions of Mothers' and Fathers' Differential Treatment of Siblings: Links with Adolescents' Sex-Typed Personal Qualities." *Family Relations* 52:82–89.

Walker, Alexis J., Katherine R. Allen, and Ingrid A. Connidis. 2005. "Theorizing and Studying Sibling Ties in Adulthood." In *Sourcebook of Family Theory and Research*, edited by V. Bengtson, A. Accock, K. Allen, P Dilworth Anderson, and D. Klein (167–81). Thousand Oaks, CA: Sage.

12

Family Bargaining and Long-Term Care of the Disabled Elderly

Liliana E. Pezzin, Robert A. Pollak, and Barbara S. Schone

Economists bring powerful analytical tools to the study of long-term care of the disabled elderly. The two fundamental theoretical assumptions of economics are maximizing behavior and equilibrium. Maximizing behavior is the fundamental premise of the rational actor model, which plays a central role in economics and an influential one in sociology, psychology, and political science. Maximizing behavior, however, is an empty vessel into which we must pour substantive assumptions about individuals' preferences—that is, about what individuals seek to maximize. (Economists interpret "preferences" expansively. As Pollak and Watkins point out, "Noneconomists, and even economists in mufti, distinguish among 'preferences,' 'tastes,' 'desires,' 'wants,' 'needs,' 'attitudes,' 'aspirations,' 'goals,' 'values,' 'interests,' and 'ideology.' Economists typically treat all of these terms as synonymous with 'preferences' " [1993, 481].)

At its best, the assumption of maximizing behavior is a powerful analytical tool that provides insight into the behavior of individuals. At its worst, it is a circular assertion that individuals do what they do because they want to do it. Gary Becker, a Nobel Prize–winning economist whose *Treatise on the Family* (1981, 1991) is the foundational text of the economics of the family, has rightly insisted that family members are not narrowly self-interested but are concerned about each other's well-being. Pollak (2003) provides a summary and critical analysis of Becker's contributions to the economics of the family.

Equilibrium ensures the compatibility of the decisions made by individuals. Every undergraduate who studies economics learns about supply and demand: consumers and firms respond to market prices over which they have no control, but market price adjusts to an equilibrium level that equates supply and demand. For many issues involving long-term care of the disabled elderly, such as the market for home health care workers and the market for long-term care insurance, supply and demand are the appropriate tools. They are, however, the wrong tools for analyzing the role of the family in providing long-term care for the disabled elderly and, more generally, they are the wrong tools for analyzing interactions in which the number of actors is small.

Game theoretic bargaining models provide a framework for analyzing strategic interactions among a small number of actors and have been applied to studies of countries, firms, and, increasingly, the family. To introduce the long-term care problem, consider a traditional nuclear family: father, mother, and their joint children. Suppose that in their 70s the parents' health begins to fail. The first long-term care problem is "Who's going to take care of the first parent to become disabled?" Because Dad is typically older than Mom, and because men have a shorter life expectancy than women, the first parent to become disabled is likely to be Dad. Hence, the problem becomes "Who's going to take care of Dad?" For expositional purposes, for the balance of this chapter, we assume that Dad is the first parent to become disabled, although the gender of the disabled parent plays no role in our analysis. The second problem—"Who's going to take care of the second parent to become disabled?"—then becomes "Who's going to take care of Mom?"

Once we have posed the questions, the answers are obvious. Everyone knows that Mom will take care of Dad. And everyone knows that the children will take care of Mom. In a series of papers we have argued that economic analysis and, more specifically, a game theoretic bargaining analysis, sheds some light on the care that family members provide for one another and helps explain why family caregiving has become more tenuous as family structure has changed as the result of divorce, remarriage, and nonmarital fertility.

The assistance provided to disabled elderly family members is often the product of numerous individual and joint decisions by family members with different preferences facing different resource constraints. Family members not only make caregiving decisions on behalf of disabled family members but often provide hands-on care themselves and share the financial consequences of caregiving decisions. Moreover, the preferences of the disabled elderly may differ from those of their spouses and their adult children, and the preferences of one child may differ from those of another. Differences may arise about the type of care desired for the disabled elderly and the setting in which they receive it. For example, children may want a parent to enter a nursing home, while the parent prefers to live independently; or, a brother may want his sister to care for their mother while the sister wants her brother or the brother's wife to be the primary caregiver. The possibility of conflict over caregiving and the roles of different family members in providing care suggest that family members may have incentives to behave strategically.

In this chapter we review the economics literature on family caregiving, discuss the concepts of distribution and efficiency, and sketch a model of family caregiving for the disabled elderly. The model captures important features of the complex interactions between elderly parents and adult children and among the children. The partnered (e.g., married) disabled elderly are likely to receive care from their partners (e.g., spouses) rather than from children (Dwyer and Coward 1991) and are less likely than the unpartnered to enter an institution (Freedman 1996). Hence, because of the costs the unpartnered disabled elderly impose on government budgets, they are a group of particular policy interest. For this reason, we focus on care of the unpartnered disabled elderly.

Long-term care for the disabled elderly has sparked a growing literature within economics. This literature, surveyed in Norton (2000), focuses on the supply and demand for nursing home care and on long-term care insurance but pays little attention to the family. Early studies that discuss the role of the family concentrate primarily on support from children to parents in the form of shared housing, analyzing the determinants of living arrangements (Börsch-Supan 1989; Börsch-Supan, Kotlikoff, and Morris 1991; Börsch-Supan et al. 1992; Börsch-Supan, McFadden, and Schnabel 1996; Ellwood and Kane 1990; Kotlikoff and Morris 1990).

To analyze interactions among adult children, we build on research that has modeled intrafamily allocation within a game theoretic framework (Lundberg and Pollak 1993, 1994, 2003; Manser and Brown 1980; McElroy and Horney 1981). Game theoretic models are especially suitable for analyzing intergenerational living arrangements and transfers of time and money because such models recognize the divergent and often conflicting interests of family members. Game theoretic models specify a process for translating these divergent interests into equilibrium outcomes. In models of supply and demand, which assume many actors, all of the actors are insignificant relative to the total market so that they can reasonably ignore the responses of others to their own actions. In contrast, game theoretic models are appropriate in situations involving few actors where the reactions of others cannot be neglected.

Game theoretic models stand in contrast to Becker's model of allocation within the family. Becker (1974, 1981) proposed the first model of intrafamily allocation, the "altruist model." Becker's model assumes that one family member, the altruist or "head," cares about the well-being of other family members and has a privileged position in the family bargaining game. Pollak characterizes the altruist as "husband-father-dictator-patriarch" (1988, 242) or as a "quasi-dictator" (2003, 128). Becker argued that, under certain assumptions, family members would automatically adjust their behavior so as to maximize the altruist's utility subject to the family's resource constraints.

Models that imply family behavior consistent with utility maximization by a single actor are called unitary models. Utility maximization is essentially equivalent to the rational actor model. A utility function represents preferences in the sense that it assigns higher numbers to preferred alternatives. The terminology correctly suggests its connection with the utilitarian tradition of Jeremy Bentham, James Mill, and John Stuart Mill. Thus, Becker's altruist model provides a rationale for treating the family as a single rational actor.

The first generation of research on families' care arrangements relied on Becker's model of the family (Ettner 1995, 1996; Kemper and Pezzin 1996; Wolf and Soldo 1994). More recent work has used game-theoretic bargaining models to examine family care arrangements. Examples include Pezzin and Schone (1999a, 2002b), Heidemann and Stern (1999), and Engers and Stern (2002).

Much of the research examining family caregiving has focused on the parent–child dyad. Although most studies have included variables summarizing the characteristics of the remaining family network (Kotlikoff and Morris 1990; Pezzin and Schone 1999b, 2002a; Pezzin, Pollak, and Schone 2006a; Stern 1994, 1995), little work has analyzed interactions among the adult children. Papers that analyze caregiving and allow for interactions of two or more children include Engers and Stern (2002), Checkovich and Stern (2002), Pezzin and Schone (2001), and Pezzin, Pollak, and Schone (2005a, 2005b, 2006b).

Distribution and Efficiency

Government long-term care policies have both distributional and efficiency effects. By distribution, economists mean winners and losers—who benefits and who pays. The distributional implications of government long-term care policies are widely recognized and are analogous to the distributional implications of social security, Medicare, and other programs that benefit the elderly. That is, government policies redistribute the burden of caring for the elderly between generations, within generations, between families, and within families. For example, under Medicare the burden of providing medical care to the elderly is shared by Medicare recipients, who pay some portion of the cost with their Medicare premiums, and working-age adults, who pay the remainder of the cost with their taxes. More specifically, Part A of Medicare (hospital insurance) is funded through earmarked payroll taxes; for supplemental Part B coverage, beneficiaries pay approximately 25 percent of the cost of the program through premiums, with the rest being funded through general tax revenue.

Economists' definition of *efficiency*—formally, Pareto efficiency—is best approached by defining *inefficiency*. A situation is inefficient if it is possible to rearrange things in such a way as to make everyone better off. For example, if a pie is to be divided between two people, a division that gives half to one person and one-third to the other is inefficient. An efficient allocation is one that is not inefficient. For example, a division that gives two-thirds to one person and one-third to the other is efficient, as is a division that gives nine-tenths to one person and one-tenth to the other. The definition of efficiency implies that a situation is efficient if it is impossible to make one person better off without making someone else worse off. (This is the standard definition of Pareto efficiency, but noneconomists often find it unintuitive.)

The efficiency of social arrangements, institutions, and practices is a central concern of economics. In the mid-20th century, economists reinterpreted and formalized the claim that Adam Smith advanced in 1776 in the *Wealth of Nations*—the claim that each individual pursuing his own interest is led as if by an "invisible hand" to promote the interest of society—as a claim about the efficiency of equilibrium in competitive markets. Economists recognize that as a guide to policy, efficiency by itself is an incomplete and potentially misleading criterion. It is incomplete precisely because it neglects distribution—a division of the pie in which one person gets 99/100 and the other 1/100 is efficient; a division in which each gets 49/100 is inefficient. Thus an observer, even an economist, might prefer a particular inefficient allocation (such as 49/100 and 49/100) to a particular efficient allocation (such as 99/100 and 1/100) because the distribution is more equitable.

Discussions of the efficiency implications of government long-term care policies often treat the disabled elderly as individuals rather than as members of families. When families are recognized, the long-term care literature has typically assumed that families respond efficiently to the incentives created by government policy. The work by Stern and his collaborators is an important exception. Unitary models such as Becker's altruist model imply or assume families allocate resources efficiently. Some models that permit strategic interactions among family members are compatible with inefficient decisions within families. Pollak (2003) discusses the source of Becker's efficiency conclusion, a discussion likely to interest economists who study the family but perhaps few other readers.

A Game Theoretic Model of Caregiving

Before describing a particular long-term care game, a few remarks about economic analysis are in order. Economists specify models and analyze them. Analysis is the rigorous, scientific part of economics. Specification of models is more art than science. A specification must isolate the critical features of reality and yet be sufficiently simple that the model is tractable. Any economic model overemphasizes certain features of the reality and neglects others. The trick is to choose the right features to overemphasize and the right features to neglect.

We begin by describing a two-stage game with three players: a disabled parent and two adult children. The first stage determines the living arrangements and the second stage determines intrafamily transfers of time and money. The stages are related because the first-stage decision about living arrangements affects second-stage bargaining power; the stages are distinct, however, because we assume that family members cannot or will not make binding commitments that restrict their future behavior. We show that, even if the second stage is conditionally efficient (i.e., efficient given the living arrangements determined in the first stage), the equilibrium of the two-stage game may be inefficient.

To avoid analytical complications and to gain insight into the type of strategic behavior likely to arise, we focus on the case of a widowed parent with unmarried adult children who are childless. This narrow focus provides a useful starting point because it brackets the complications associated with in-laws who may also require care, and with the adult children's spouses who may have little or no interest in providing care for the adult child's parent and who may have caregiving responsibilities for their own parents.

We ignore the possibility that transfers from children to their disabled elderly parents are motivated by the expectation of bequests, as suggested by the strategic bequest model of Bernheim, Shleifer, and Summers (1985). Pollak (1988) argues that, if the parents would prefer to divide their wealth equally among their children, then the threat to disinherit a child who fails to provide sufficient attention is not credible. Perozek (1998) discusses empirical problems in Bernheim et al. (1985). McGarry (2008) surveys the literature on bequests and inheritances, and Laferrère and Wolff (2006) survey the literature on family transfers.

We now turn to the specification of our two-stage caregiving game involving a disabled elderly parent and two adult children. We first describe the overall structure of the game, then describe in more detail the second-stage game and finally the first-stage game. We proceed in this order because beginning at the end of the game—a procedure game theorists call "backwards induction"—is the logical way to analyze a sequential game.

We consider four possible living arrangements for the parent: living in a nursing home, living alone in the community, living with child 1, and living with child 2. The parent's utility in each of these living arrangements depends on the living arrangement itself and on her consumption. We assume that children care about their own consumption and about the parent's consumption. We also assume that the children care about the parent's living arrangement, which affects the parent's well-being and the child's privacy.

We model family interactions as a two-stage game. The first stage determines the living arrangement and second stage determines consumption. We assume that family members cannot or will not make binding agreements at the first stage about caregiving at the second stage. Hence, the assistance that a child provides at the second stage, although it may be predictable at the first stage, is determined at the second stage.

Although we cannot directly observe the impact of not having binding agreements on decisions made at the second stage, the lack of binding agreements may partially explain some empirical regularities associated with caregiving. For example, the concentration of caregiving by coresident caregivers and the relatively small amount of assistance from the non-coresident children may reflect the fact that, once the parent begins to live with one child, the other children reduce the care they provide, confident that the coresident child will make up the difference.

An example will clarify our model. Suppose that the first stage begins with the children deciding, separately and simultaneously, whether or not to invite the parent to coreside. It ends with the parent choosing among the feasible living arrangements: the parent can move into a nursing home, live alone, or accept the invitation of any child who has offered coresidence. At the second stage, taking as given the living arrangement determined at the first stage, the children and the parent make decisions that determine resource allocation under that living arrangement.

The fundamental distinction in game theory is between cooperative and noncooperative games. Noncooperative games are specified by the moves or strategies available to the players. An example of a noncooperative game is the familiar "prisoners' dilemma." Kreps describes the setting:

> The police have apprehended two individuals whom they strongly suspect of a crime (and who in fact committed the crime together). But the police lack the evidence necessary to convict and must release the two prisoners unless one provides evidence against the other. They hold the two in separate cells and make the following offer to each: Implicate your colleague. If neither of you implicates the other, each of you will be held for the maximum amount of time permitted without charges being made. If one of you implicates the other and is not implicated, we will release the first and prevail upon the judge to give the recalcitrant second party the maximum sentence permitted by law. If both of you implicate the other, then both will go to jail, but the judge will be lenient in view of your co-operation with the authorities. (Kreps 1990, 37–38)

The prisoners' dilemma is a game in which the two players decide, separately and simultaneously, on their strategies (i.e., whether or not to confess). It is a game in which each prisoner's best strategy is to confess regardless of the strategy the other prisoner chooses. Yet when both prisoners confess, the outcome is worse for both of them than the outcome if neither had confessed. The prisoners' dilemma is a standard example of a noncooperative game whose equilibrium is Pareto inefficient. Some noncooperative games have unique equilibria that are Pareto inefficient; others have unique equilibria that are Pareto efficient or have multiple equilibria, some of which may be inefficient. Our living arrangement game in which the children decide, separately and simultaneously, whether or not to invite the parent to coreside and the parent then chooses among the feasible living arrangements may fall into any one of these three categories.

Cooperative games are usually described as games in which the players can make binding, costlessly enforceable commitments. Cooperative games are described not by strategies or moves but by the payoffs that the players can obtain by forming coalitions. The "solution" to a cooperative game is a set of payoffs satisfying a set of axioms or assumptions, one of which is Pareto efficiency.

Economists debate whether family decisionmaking is better modeled as a noncooperative game or a cooperative game. Shubik asserts that non-cooperative game theory "is generally not so useful to describe complex, loosely structured social interaction" (1989, 103). Family bargaining—whether between spouses within marriage, between an adult child and a disabled parent, or among adult children—exemplifies such interactions. But the usefulness of cooperative game theory is also problematic. First, although cooperative game theory allows us to proceed without specifying the rules of the game—the strategies available to each player or the sequence of moves and the information available to each player at each move—noncooperative game theory teaches that the rules of the game are often crucial determinants of the outcome. Thus, by modeling interactions as a cooperative game we necessarily disregard the strategic factors that may determine the outcome. Second, as we have argued, the efficiency of social arrangements and practices is a central concern of economics and of public policy, yet cooperative bargaining models assume that outcomes are Pareto efficient. Hence, cooperative bargaining models are incapable of investigating the conditions that make it possible to achieve and sustain efficient outcomes because cooperative models refuse to recognize the possibility of inefficiency. Because complex, loosely structured social interactions are very difficult to model, we regard the choice between modeling family interactions as a noncooperative or a cooperative game not a matter of principle but of research strategy. We now consider the consequences of alternative specifications of the second stage game.

The Second-Stage Game

For each of the four possible living arrangements, we consider several specifications of the second-stage game, which determines transfers from children to the parent. We assume that each child's utility is increasing in the parent's consumption and in her own consumption, but that it is independent of her sibling's consumption. Hence, a child's utility increases if the sibling's contribution to the parent increases.

There are a number of ways to model the second-stage game, some of which imply Pareto efficient solutions and others do not. (For a detailed analysis, see Pezzin, Pollak, and Schone 2007.) We can pass over the modeling of the second-stage game by supposing, as Shubik would have us assume in analyzing a "complex, loosely structured social interaction," that the second-stage game is cooperative. Under this assumption, conditional on the living arrangement, the second-stage equilibrium is Pareto efficient. Alternatively, if the second-stage game is noncooperative, then the second-stage equilibrium may or may not be Pareto efficient.

We do gain some insight into the likelihood that the solution to the second stage is efficient by considering separately the games corresponding to each of the four possible living arrangements. In Pezzin, Pollak, and Schone (2007) we argue that when the parent lives on her own in the community or in a nursing home, Pareto efficiency in the second-stage game is plausible but not necessary. When the parent coresides with one of her adult children, however, Pareto efficiency is not as plausible.

Coresidence increases the strategic asymmetry between the children and weakens the bargaining power of the coresident child. Of course strategic asymmetry is always present. Even when the parent lives independently in the community or in a nursing home, the children may differ in gender, family responsibilities, labor force attachment, and attachment or proximity to the parent. Like coresidence, many of these differences are endogenous. For definiteness, and without loss of generality, for the remainder of the discussion in this case in which the parent coresides with a child, we suppose that the parent coresides with child 1. (Formally, we are simply designating as child 1 the child with whom the parent lives.)

We emphasize the strategic asymmetry between the coresident and the noncoresident child because it has implications for the choice of living arrangements in the first-stage game. Using the model proposed by Weiss and Willis (1985) in the context of child support following divorce, we examine the implications of coresidence for the noncoresident child's ability to monitor the way transfers (e.g., of money) are used by the coresident child. We then consider the way in which coresidence and the frequency of contact it implies is likely to affect the coresident child's awareness of the parent's needs or her attachment to the parent.

Weiss and Willis provide a framework for analyzing the effect of coresidence on bargaining power. Their concern is child support following divorce, but the strategic position of the noncoresident child contemplating contributing to the coresident household is analogous to that of the noncustodial parent contemplating child support. In Weiss and Willis, both parents value the child's well-being. Each parent, however, is also concerned with his or her private consumption and unconcerned with the private consumption of the ex-spouse. The noncustodial parent, for definiteness, the divorced father, because he does not coreside with the child, is poorly positioned to monitor his ex-wife's allocation of child support between herself and the child. Weiss and Willis view the inability of the father to monitor the mother's allocation of resources between herself and the child as the crucial feature of the strategic situation. The inability to monitor precludes binding, enforceable agreements between the parents: the father is rationally concerned that if he increases his contribution, his ex-wife will spend some of his additional contribution on herself. As Weiss and Willis show, the equilibrium allocation in this game is Pareto inefficient: both parents would prefer an allocation in which they both reduced their private consumption and increased their transfers to the child.

The analogy between long-term care of a disabled elderly parent and the Weiss and Willis model of child support is closest when the parent has a cognitive disability such as severe Alzheimer's that precludes her active participation in the allocation process. Under these circumstances, the coresident child allocates resources between herself and the parent, just as in Weiss and Willis the mother allocates resources between herself and a child.

Once coresidence is established, the coresident child may have incentives to maintain it because termination would impose high psychic costs or adversely affect instrumental or affective relationships with other family members. That is, once coresidence becomes the status quo, the coresident child may find termination difficult and costly. We can interpret the coresident child's incentives to continue coresidence in terms of rewards offered for continuing or, equivalently, in terms of punishments threatened for terminating. The noncoresident child, knowing that her sister cannot easily terminate coresidence, realizes that if she reduces her contribution, the coresident child will respond by increasing hers. England and Folbre (2003, 73), describing the predicament of paid care workers, write, "these emotional bonds [to those receiving care] put care workers in a vulnerable position. We might call the workers 'prisoners of love'; a kind of emotional 'hostage effect' comes into play." The logic of their argument applies with even greater force to care provided by family members.

We conclude that Pareto efficiency is less plausible when the parent coresides with one of the children. In Pezzin, Pollak, and Schone (2007), we explore the case in which the parent is an active player and bargains with the coresident child. Of course Pareto efficiency in the coresident household is guaranteed if the parent and the coresident child play a cooperative game. The difficulty, however, is not only within the coresident household but also in interactions between the coresident household and the noncoresident child. Analogous to the noncustodial parent in Weiss and Willis, the noncoresident child might be willing to contribute more to the disabled elderly parent but refrains from doing so because she is concerned that the coresident child will "tax" the increased contribution and spend some portion of it on herself. To summarize: the solution to the second-stage game need not be Pareto efficient; it is more likely to be Pareto efficient when the parent lives on her own in the community or in a nursing home than when the parent coresides with one of her adult children.

The First-Stage Game

Having analyzed the second-stage game, we now turn to the first-stage game. We first show that the equilibrium of our two-stage game can be Pareto inefficient even when the second stage game is Pareto efficient conditional on the living arrangement. We then show that the equilibrium may depend on the precise specification of the first-stage game (e.g., when the game is sequential, the equilibrium may depend on which child moves first). We also consider a model in which the parent is an active player.

We can simplify the analysis if we treat family members as if they have direct preferences over living arrangements. The legitimacy of this simplification rests on two assumptions: (1) the parent and children can predict the transfers of time and money that each child would make to the parents in each possible living arrangement, and (2) each living arrangement is associated with unique levels of private consumption, care for the parent, and privacy for each child and for the parent.

As an initial example, we model the first stage as consisting of simultaneous moves by the siblings, followed by a decision by the parent, who chooses among the living arrangements available to her. Each child has two moves: inviting coresidence or not inviting coresidence. For each profile of moves (e.g., both children invite coresidence; child 1 invites coresidence and child 2 does not, etc.), we assume that the resulting levels of utility are known to each child (e.g., if both invite coresidence, they know that the parent will choose to live with child 1).

In the first-stage example described above, the parent will choose her preferred living arrangement from the available options determined by the children's invitations. This choice is based on the parent's calculation of the utility levels attainable in each living arrangement. The parent faces at most four alternatives, depending on whether both children invite coresidence, neither child invites coresidence, or one child invites coresidence and the other does not.

Pareto Inefficient Equilibria

To construct an example of a game with an inefficient equilibrium, we begin by specifying the preferences of each family member. Suppose the parent prefers to live with child 1 but would rather live with child 2 than live independently. Suppose each child prefers that the parent coreside with the other child, and each child would prefer that the parent live independently rather than coreside with the parent. Suppose that the nursing home is the lowest ranked alternative for both children and for the parent. The unique equilibrium of any game in which the children have these preferences has the parent living independently.

Suppose, however, that each child would invite coresidence if she knew her sister would contribute "enough" and that the sister would rather contribute enough than have the parent live independently. An omniscient and omnipotent social planner could impose a solution on the family that would make everyone—the parent and both children—better off by requiring that the parent live with child 1 and requiring child 2 to contribute enough. But the family cannot achieve this or any other Pareto-efficient solution and is misguided, as if by an invisible hand, to a Pareto inefficient equilibrium. The demonstration of inefficiency depends on comparing a living arrangement and transfer pattern that a social planner might impose with the living arrangement and transfer pattern that would emerge as the equilibrium of a two-stage game. Our argument does not establish nor do we claim that for all configurations of preferences the equilibrium of the two-stage game is inefficient. We have established that for *some* configurations of preferences the equilibrium is inefficient.

Lundberg and Pollak (2003) describe and analyze a related two-stage game in the context of bargaining within marriages: the "two-earner couple location problem." In Lundberg and Pollak, spouses play a two-stage game in which the first stage determines the location (e.g., whether the couple moves to the husband's preferred location or the wife's preferred location), and the second stage determines allocation within marriage. When the spouses prefer different locations, inefficient outcomes (e.g., inefficient divorces) are possible even when the second-stage game is efficient conditional on the location determined in the first stage. An analogous result holds in our long-term care game—the equilibrium of the two-stage long-term care game may be an inefficient living arrangement, even when second-stage transfers are efficient conditional on the living arrangement. The crucial features of both the two-earner couple location game and our long-term care game are that first-stage decisions affect future bargaining power and that family members cannot or will not make binding agreements. A promise by the noncoresident sibling to provide assistance if the parent lives with the other sibling may not be enforceable.

Outcomes Depend on the Structure of the First-Stage Game

To construct an example in which the equilibrium living arrangement depends on the precise specification of the first-stage game, we again begin by specifying each family member's preferences. Suppose the parent prefers to live with child 1 but would rather live with child 2 than live independently. Each child prefers that the parent coreside with the other child, but each child prefers coresidence with the parent to having the parent live independently. Both children and the parent prefer having the parent live independently rather than in a nursing home.

Using these preferences, we consider alternative specifications of the first-stage game. We first consider two specifications of the noncooperative first-stage game in which the children move before the parent, then two specifications in which the parent moves before the children.

Children Move Before the Parent

We consider two sequential games that differ in which child moves first. When child 1 moves first, she does not invite the parent to coreside; the best response of child 2 is to invite the parent to coreside, and the parent accepts the invitation. When child 2 moves first, she does not invite the parent to coreside; the best response of child 1 is to invite the parent to coreside, and the parent accepts the invitation. These examples demonstrate that the equilibrium of our two-stage game can depend on the precise specification of the game (i.e., which child moves first in the sequential game).

Parent Moves before the Children

When the parent moves first, she can be a strategic player. Suppose that the parent can commit herself to reject particular invitations, if she should receive them. (Shelly Lundberg suggests that the parent might achieve this result by insulting a child's spouse.) More specifically, the game begins with the parent choosing among three moves:

(1) Preemptively reject an invitation from child 1.
(2) Preemptively reject an invitation from child 2.
(3) Make no preemptive rejection of any invitation.

The children then move sequentially, as described above. Finally, the parent chooses a living arrangement: she can live independently or in a nursing home or accept any invitation she has received except those she has preemptively rejected.

The analysis of these games is straightforward. The parent begins by committing to reject an invitation from child 2. The equilibrium of both sequential games is an invitation from child 1, which the parent accepts. This example shows that the ability of a family member (in this case, the parent) to commit can alter the equilibrium outcome and, in this case, commitment enables the parent to achieve the outcome she prefers.

Conclusion

We have used a two-stage bargaining model to analyze the living arrangement of a disabled elderly parent and transfers of time and money to the parent from her adult children. The first stage determines the living arrangement, the second, child-to-parent transfers. Working by backward induction, we first calculate the level of transfers that each child would provide to the parent in each living arrangement. We then analyze the living arrangement(s) that emerge as equilibria of the first-stage game. Because the living arrangement affects bargaining power in the second-stage game, and because family members at the first stage are unwilling or unable to make binding agreements regarding transfers at the second stage, the equilibria of the two-stage game may be Pareto inefficient even if the equilibrium of the second-stage subgame is conditionally efficient. The model also shows how strategic interactions among family members can affect their behavior and alter the ultimate outcome.

A better understanding of the process by which families come to assume the responsibility and share the burden of caring for the disabled elderly is essential for designing and evaluating long-term care policies. Governments have long recognized that their long-term care policies have distributional implications. That is, long-term care policies affect how the burden of long-term care is shared between generations, within generations, between families, and within families. As governments increasingly explore policies to address the needs of their growing disabled elderly populations, the possibility that families' long-term care decisions may result in inefficient outcomes suggests an additional role for public policy: promoting efficiency. Initiatives may be tailored to family living arrangements—for example, by taxing noncoresiding adult children or subsidizing coresiding adult children for both their informal care services and their relative loss of bargaining power—to promote more efficient outcomes.

While government transfer schedules that are independent of family living arrangements are analytically simpler than schedules that are not, contingent transfer schedules may avoid some of the inefficiency associated with government efforts to ensure the availability of long-term care. Public long-term care policy will be enhanced by recognizing that the caregiving behavior of family members responds to the incentives created by public programs.

NOTE

Much of the material in this paper is drawn from Pezzin, Pollak, and Schone (2007). We are grateful to National Institutes of Health grant R01 AG24049-01 for financial support. Robert A. Pollak is grateful to the John D. and Catherine T. MacArthur Foundation for their support. The views in this chapter are the authors'. No official endorsement by the

Agency for Healthcare Research and Quality of the Department of Health and Human Services is intended or should be inferred.

REFERENCES

Becker, Gary S. 1974. "A Theory of Social Interactions." *Journal of Political Economy* 82(6): 1063–93.

———. 1981. *Treatise on the Family.* Cambridge, MA: Harvard University Press.

———. 1991. *Treatise on the Family,* enlarged edition. Cambridge, MA: Harvard University Press.

Bernheim, B. Douglas, Andrei Shleifer, and Lawrence H. Summers. 1985. "The Strategic Bequest Motive." *Journal of Political Economy* 93(6): 1045–76.

Börsch-Supan, Axel 1989. "Household Dissolution and the Choice of Alternative Living Arrangements Among Elderly Americans." In *The Economics of Aging,* edited by David Wise (119–50). Chicago: University of Chicago Press.

Börsch-Supan, Axel, Lawrence Kotlikoff, and John Morris. 1991. "The Dynamics of Living Arrangements of the Elderly: Health and Family Support." In *The Economics of Care of the Elderly,* edited by Jozef Pacolet and Celeste Wilderom (114–35). London: Avebury.

Börsch-Supan, Axel, Daniel McFadden, and Reinhold Schnabel. 1996. "Living Arrangements: Health and Wealth Effects." In *Advances in the Economics of Aging,* edited by David Wise (193–212). Chicago: University of Chicago Press.

Börsch-Supan, Axel, Vassilis Hajivassiliou, Lawrence Kotlikoff, and John Morris. 1992. "Health, Children and Elderly Living Arrangements." In *Topics in the Economics of Aging,* edited by David Wise (79–103). Chicago: University of Chicago Press.

Checkovich, Tennille J., and Steven Stern. 2002. "Shared Caregiving Responsibilities of Adult Children with Elderly Parents." *Journal of Human Resources* 37:441–78.

Dwyer, J. W., and R. T. Coward. 1991. "A Multivariate Comparison of the Involvement of Adult Sons Versus Adult Daughters in the Care of Impaired Adults." *Journal of Gerontology: Social Sciences* 46:S259–S269.

Ellwood, David, and Thomas Kane. 1990. "The American Way of Aging: An Event History Analysis." In *Issues in the Economics of Aging,* edited by David Wise (121–47). Chicago: University of Chicago Press.

Engers, Maxim, and Steven Stern. 2002. "Long-Term Care and Family Bargaining." *International Economic Review* 43:1–44.

England, Paula, and Nancy Folbre. 2003. "Contracting for Care." In *Ten Years Beyond Economic Man,* edited by Marianne Ferber and Julie Nelson (61–79). Chicago: University of Chicago Press.

Ettner, Susan L. 1995. "The Impact of Parent Care on Female Labor Supply Decisions." *Demography* 32:63–80.

———. 1996. "The Opportunity Costs of Elder Care." *Journal of Human Resources* 31:189–205.

Freedman, Vicki A. 1996. "Family Structure and the Risk of Nursing Home Admission." *Journal of Gerontology: Social Sciences* 51B:S61–S69.

Heidemann, Bridget, and Steven Stern. 1999. "Strategic Play Among Family Members When Making Long-Term Care Decisions." *Journal of Economic Behavior and Organization* 40:29–57.

Kemper, Peter, and Liliana E. Pezzin. 1996. "The Effect of Public Provision of Home Care on Living and Care Arrangements: Evidence from the Channeling Experiment." In *Alternatives for Ensuring Long-Term Care,* edited by Roland Eisen and Frank Sloan (125–46). Amsterdam: Kluwer Press.

Kotlikoff, Lawrence, and John Morris. 1990. "Why Don't the Elderly Live with Their Children? A New Look." In *Issues in the Economics of Aging,* edited by David Wise (149–69). Chicago: University of Chicago Press.

Kreps, David M. 1990. *A Course in Microeconomic Theory.* Princeton, NJ: Princeton University Press.

Laferrère, Anne, and Francois-Charles Wolff. 2006. "Microeconomic Models of Family Transfers." In *Handbook of Giving, Altruism, and Reciprocity,* edited by Serge-Christophe Kolm and Jean Mercier Ythier (889–969). Amsterdam: North-Holland.

Lundberg, Shelly, and Robert A. Pollak. 1993. "Separate Spheres Bargaining and the Marriage Market." *Journal of Political Economy* 101:988–1010.

———. 1994. "Noncooperative Bargaining Models of Marriage." *American Economic Review* 84:132–37.

———. 2003. "Efficiency in Marriage." *Review of Economics of the Household* 1:153–68.

Manser, Marilyn E., and Murray Brown. 1980. "Marriage and Household Decision Making." *International Economic Review* 21:31–44.

McElroy, Marjorie B., and Mary Jean Horney. 1981. "Nash-Bargained Household Decisions: Toward a Generalization of the Theory of Demand." *International Economic Review* 22:333–49.

McGarry, Kathleen. 2008. "Inheritances and Bequests." In *The New Palgrave Dictionary of Economics,* 2nd ed., vol. 4, edited by Steven N. Durlauf and Lawrence E. Blume (349–54). New York: Palgrave MacMillan.

Norton, Edward C. 2000. "Long-Term Care." In *Handbook of Health Economics,* vol. 1B, edited by Anthony J. Culyer and Joseph P. Newhouse (955–94). Amsterdam: North-Holland.

Perozek, Maria G. 1998. "A Reexamination of the Strategic Bequest Motive." *Journal of Political Economy* 106:423–45.

Pezzin, Liliana E., and Barbara S. Schone. 1999a. "Intergenerational Household Formation, Female Labor Supply, and Informal Caregiving: A Bargaining Approach." *Journal of Human Resources* 34:475–503.

———. 1999b. "Parental Marital Disruption and Intergenerational Transfers: An Analysis of Lone Elderly Parents and Their Adult Children." *Demography* 36:287–98.

———. 2001. "Examining the Motives for Intergenerational Transfers: A New Test Based on Siblings' Behavior." Working paper. Rockville, MD: Agency for Healthcare Research and Quality.

———. 2002a. "Exploring the Theoretical Foundations of Altruism: An Analysis of the Effects of Divorce and Remarriage on Intergenerational Living and Care Arrangements." In *Gender and Development,* edited by Parvesh K. Chopra and B. N. Ghosh, (93–118). Leeds: Wisdom House Press.

———. 2002b. "Intergenerational Transfers of Time and Elderly Living Arrangements: A Bargaining Model of Family Resource Allocation Decisions." Working paper. Rockville, MD: Agency for Healthcare Research and Quality.

Pezzin, Liliana E., Robert A. Pollak, and Barbara S. Schone. 2005a. "Bargaining Power and Intergenerational Coresidence: Adult Children and Their Disabled Elderly Parents." Working paper. St. Louis: Washington University in St. Louis.

———. 2005b. "Long-Term Care of the Disabled Elderly: Do Children Increase Caregiving by Spouses?" Working paper. St. Louis: Washington University in St. Louis.

———. 2006a. "Marital Disruption, Step Children, and Transfers to the Elderly." *Swiss Journal of Economics and Statistics* S-16:103–6.

———. 2006b. "Marital History, Family Structure, and Transfers to the Elderly." Working paper. St. Louis: Washington University in St. Louis.

———. 2007. "Efficiency in Family Bargaining: Living Arrangements and Caregiving Decisions of Adult Children and Disabled Elderly Parents." *CESifo Economic Studies* 53:69–96.

Pollak, Robert A. 1988. "Tied Transfers and Paternalistic Preferences." *American Economic Review* 78:240–44.

———. 2003. "Gary Becker's Contributions to Family and Household Economics." *Review of Economics of the Household* 1:111–41.

Pollak, Robert A., and Susan Cotts Watkins. 1993. "Cultural and Economic Approaches to Fertility: Proper Marriage or Mésalliance?" *Population and Development Review* 19:467–96.

Shubik, Martin. 1989. "Cooperative Games." In *The New Palgrave, Game Theory,* edited by John Eatwell, Murray Milgate, and Pater Newman (103–7). New York: W. W. Norton.

Stern, Steven. 1994. "Two Dynamic Discrete Choice Estimation Problems and Simulation Method Solutions." *Review of Economics and Statistics* 96:695–702.

———. 1995. "Estimating Family Long-Term Care Decisions in the Presence of Endogenous Child Characteristics." *Journal of Human Resources* 30:551–80.

Weiss, Yoram, and Robert J. Willis. 1985. "Children as Collective Goods in Divorce Settlements." *Journal of Labor Economics* 3:268–92.

Wolf, Douglas, and Beth Soldo. 1994. "Married Women's Allocation of Time to Employment and Care of Elderly Parents." *Journal of Human Resources* 29:1259–76.

PART IV
Private and Public Provision in Care of Kin: Who Feels an Obligation for Whom?

13

The Distribution of Obligations

Steven L. Nock, Paul W. Kingston, and Laura M. Holian

Our goal is to show how norms of caring and obligations can be studied. Our larger goal is to explain how Americans see their own obligations to others and how those obligations are understood as part of a collective responsibility. We believe there are strong social patterns of obligations—norms that call for us to help others. Such norms inhere in social relationships. When two people are united by their membership in a social group (e.g., family, kin group, congregation), norms of obligation define how they should respond to one another's needs. These norms are the subject of this chapter and our larger research project.

Individual obligations, however, are only part of such norms. As the chapter indicates, we believe that obligations are distributed among various agents. This is a unique feature of our work. When confronted with a situation involving a need (a sister's, a friend's), we think individuals will evaluate that situation in the context of their beliefs about what others owe. What someone believes to be a personal obligation, in other words, depends on the perceived obligation of others. Our work attempts to map this normative distribution of obligations. Such an understanding of what others should do, we think, is a preliminary step in attempting to understand personal behaviors or beliefs. We have found, for example, that patterns of norms correlate in understandable ways with individuals' political positions. Those who are conservative see a smaller role for government than those who are liberal, for example. And those who believe the state should play a smaller role in helping thus assume a proportionately greater personal role.

We ask the following questions: When and why do individuals believe they should assume responsibility for others' needs—their kin's, their friends,' and strangers'? When and why are others' needs deemed the responsibility of the state or churches and charities? To what extent is responsibility for such needs shared?

Our findings indicate that personal obligations are clearly and systematically related to beliefs about the obligations of the government, other relatives, churches, and charities. We also show that these patterns of norms are related to a number of individual characteristics such as age, gender, and income. We offer a strategy for investigating rival theories about intergenerational obligations (e.g., are personal obligations connected to childhood events?). We hope that our focus on the individual as but only one consideration in the exchange of help will stimulate others to consider the simultaneous and complementary roles other agents (e.g., the government) play in influencing individual behaviors.

Our research on obligations is the first about the distributional dimension of obligations for helping. Rossi and Rossi (1990) established a foundation for studying obligations. Their research investigated the dimension of personal obligations to help (mainly to help kin). They showed how relationship distance influences feelings of personal obligation. As individual relatedness declines, so does personal obligation. Our work expands this perspective by considering norms of obligations to be part of a package that also includes other relatives, churches and charities, and the government.

We conclude with some public policy suggestions drawn from our findings about how the prevailing understanding of obligations appears to differ from prevailing practices in some obvious ways. Our findings are generally consistent with earlier work in showing greater personal obligations for immediate kin (e.g., Rossi and Rossi 1990), but there are apparent inconsistencies with how people envision the responsibility of the government and the role it actually plays. Our results suggest that most people believe the state should play a much smaller role than it typically does.

Understanding Obligations

The research investigated both intragenerational and intergenerational obligations for matters traditionally presumed to be the responsibility of families: basic heath, housing, and training or education. Many of the related needs have become shared obligations. For example, children look after infirm parents at the same time as government assistance supports them. Caring for others is often shared among individuals and the state. Our work tries to explore the extent to which particular troubles are considered private, family-based matters, a legitimate concern for government, or some mixture of the two. This question may become increasingly acute. Any public discussion of what government should now do must be guided by an understanding of what individuals believe they owe different family members, in both preceding and succeeding generations.

Whatever the typical view, the extent to which Americans agree about obligations is also at issue. Perhaps a general consensus does prevail so that, for example, adult children are deemed responsible for their elderly parents except in instances of catastrophic medical needs, when they become a collective responsibility. Or perhaps Americans tend to agree that their own obligations to help the infirm extend only to their close kin (Rossi and Rossi 1990). On such matters we can draw on some research or intuitions to reasonably suggest that some consensus exists. But on a host of other matters (e.g., responsibility for the homeless) it is difficult to say if Americans agree and whether these views divide along the often-significant fault lines of gender, class, and race.

We did not examine the correspondence between what people say should be done and what they actually do when confronted with a situation. We believe, as do most sociologists, that social norms influence collective behaviors. To the extent that there is broad agreement about the role of government in solving personal problems, this agreement will probably be reflected in how people deal with their relatives' need for help. We cannot specify the nature of that relationship here.

Measuring Obligations

The first challenging design decision we made was about measuring obligations. Although we recognize that personal obligations might be demonstrated in many ways (offering personal services, giving time, etc.), we believe that this first study of the distribution of obligations should identify a common metric that could be used for not only personal obligations but also public ones. If an individual offers an hour of assistance every day to help her frail aunt, that is clearly a manifestation of helping. If this individual told us that she felt that she *should* offer this much help, that is, presumably, a manifestation of helping norms. In either case, it is unclear how such help might be compared with what this person thinks should come from the government. We explored the possibility of establishing some equivalence translation (an hour of help is worth $25, etc.). Ultimately, however, we concluded that measuring beliefs about how much each agent should do to help should begin with a common metric. For this reason, we limit the meaning of the concept and consider only obligations that involve some financial cost. The needs of people are often indexed by their dollar costs. We reasoned, therefore, that obligations can also be measured that way. Individuals who differ in how many dollars they are willing to give someone in need likewise differ in their sense of obligation to that person. (Of course the resources one has may condition the financial obligation. We account for this effect.) Finally, by measuring obligations in dollars, we also make it possible to express the need for help and the response to that need in the same metric. That is, we could describe the need for help in a metric (dollars) that could be directly compared with the amount individuals said they should contribute.

The decision to rely on dollars as our measure of need and obligation has obvious implications for our results. Some people may feel obligated to help another person but unable to contribute much financially. We acknowledge such possibilities. But we still believe that the advantages of having a common metric of both need and obligation outweigh such potential problems.

Design and Methods

Our analysis involves assessing respondents' understanding of how much financial help they believe they should provide and how much should come from others to help a hypothetical needy person. We asked respondents to indicate how much they would be willing to contribute to solving the problem and the amount they think other relatives, churches and charities, and the government should contribute.

Short descriptions of people in need (vignettes) were created by randomly rotating key dimensions of the situation that might affect senses of obligation (e.g., the relationship of the needy person to the respondent and the culpability of the needy person in creating the problem). These factors were developed over the course of a year in which we scrutinized the available research and theory on interpersonal obligations. We believe we identified most primary dimensions. Past research has focused on the central role played by kinship, which we felt was required. We also felt it critical to include some indication of costs and benefits involved in helping. We also included the seriousness of the problem, the culpability of the needy person, and the cost to solve the problem.

We describe the dimensions of the hypothetical situations and analyze the influence of the situation (items 1–6) and the personal traits of the respondent (the "rater," item 7) in reacting to it.

1. **Type of Need.** We have identified four realms of life in which people have needs that might invoke a sense of obligation from others. In every case, we explained to respondents that the person in need had exhausted all of their own personal resources. Our intent was to convey the impression that the needy individual had no personal resources left. The question, therefore, is about the responsibility of others in such circumstances. The vignettes included a statement about the needy person's lack of resources. All vignettes began by describing an individual with a type of need. We used vernacular expression in a few places (e.g., "they" instead of "he" or "she") because pretest results suggested such usage would be easier to understand.

   "Imagine that you have a [person of a specific relationship to you]:

   "a. who is unemployed and lacks the training to get a decent job. They need job training.

   "b. who is unable to take care of themselves and requires nursing care, but doesn't have insurance coverage for this problem.

   "c. who has been diagnosed with a health problem that requires medical treatment but doesn't have insurance coverage for this problem.

   "d. who has been evicted from their home and can't afford another place to live."

   We attempted to create hypothetical situations of need that were plausible. For example, although all Americans age 65 and older have access to Medicare, this federal program does not cover all health problems. Therefore, it is entirely plausible that an elderly relative would need medical treatment that insurance would not cover.

2. **Relationship.** Relationship distance is related to senses of moral obligation (Rossi and Rossi 1990), but what remains unspecified is how far the special consideration of family ties extends. The vignettes listed the people in need as parent, child, brother or sister, grandparent, grandchild, aunt or uncle, niece or nephew,

cousin, son- or daughter-in-law, mother- or father-in-law, close friend, coworker, close neighbor, or a person in Richmond unknown to you.

3. **Degree.** We reasoned that the greater the potential harm to the person in need, the more individuals will feel that some agent should provide help, though greater need does not necessarily imply greater personal obligation. The third element was an indication of the seriousness of the problem. Each phrase began with "Without help, your [person of a specific relationship] will have . . ." and then described five degrees of hardship (very small, small, fairly large, large, and very large). For medical or nursing problems, we included "may possibly die" and "will almost certainly die."

4. **Culpability.** To what extent is the need a product of the person's own making, the result of the needy person's failure to have taken reasonable past action or precautions? We might expect that the blameless person in need may invoke greater sympathy. Degree of culpability ranged over seven levels, from "[person] couldn't have done anything to prevent this problem" to "if [person] had acted more responsibly in the past, this problem would not exist."

5. **Benefits.** Next was an indication of the possible benefits of helping the hypothetical person. Benefits included the possibility of thanks (from the person, from your family and friends, and from your community) and repayment of any money given. The benefit of thanks ranged from "if you help out, you may never be thanked by anyone" (coded 0) to "your family, friends, and many people in the community will praise you for your generosity" (coded 4). The benefit of repayment ranged from "you are unlikely to get repaid for any of the financial help you give" (coded 0) to "you are likely to get repaid for all the financial help you give" (coded 3).

6. **Costs.** The final element on the vignettes was the cost of solving the problem. The statement read "Solving this problem will cost about . . . ," and values ranged from $100 to $10,000 in $100 increments. For nursing and health problems, we made the minimum cost $1,500. For training, we limited the cost to a maximum of $3,500. We imposed these limits after pretesting revealed that without them, certain combinations appeared implausible to respondents (e.g., solving a need for nursing care for $100).

7. **The Rater.** In this analysis we focus primarily on whether age, gender, income, parenthood, and race affect the distribution of obligations and whether the impact of the dimensions incorporated

in the vignettes differs by these sociodemographic characteristics. For illustrative purposes, we also consider a range of circumstances and experiences that adults reported about their childhoods.

A Note on Factorial Surveys

Factorial surveys (vignettes) are distinctly useful for investigating the multiple considerations underlying norms, including those about moral obligation. Peter Rossi (Rossi and Nock 1982) first developed this research technique; it has been used to model social judgments in such areas as distributive justice, social status, criminal sentencing, sexual harassment, and crime seriousness. The method has been used to assess specific family obligations as well (Ganong et al. 1998; Rossi and Rossi 1990).

The factorial survey method creates hypothetical descriptions that vary on all dimensions. Vignettes for this study were created by randomly (subject to necessary restrictions) selecting values for each of six dimensions just described. The result is a simple random sample from the universe of all hypothetical vignettes. For the analysis we report here, each respondent read a random sample ($n = 19$) of all possible vignettes. Thus, participants are as likely to read a description of a grandparent who needs nursing care as a daughter who needs such assistance. Similarly, a high degree of culpability for a housing problem is no more or less likely than low culpability for a deficit in job training. In effect, these factors are independent variables with multiple values that are randomly combined.

This sample of vignettes from a factorial survey has several notable design features. First, it provides much better coverage of all possible combinations of values than would be possible in a conventional survey. Second, because the correlations among all independent variables are approximately zero, there is virtually no correlation among the independent variables incorporated within the vignettes. Third, the distribution for each vignette variable is essentially rectangular because almost every possible value of each variable has an equal probability of being selected (some restrictions are required to eliminate illogical or impossible combinations). Rectangular distributions have maximum variance, a desirable feature of independent variables in multivariate analysis. Finally, the hypothetical world represented by the vignette sample differs from the real world in exactly the ways one would wish; that is, unlikely and unusual combinations are found as frequently as more typical ones. This feature permits the researcher to estimate effects for all variables and combinations of them.

Given that six factors are to be included on each vignette, and given the range of values for each, a total of 878,080 combinations are possible without the restraints noted above (about 6,000 fewer due to minimal restraints we place on illogical combinations). With 507 respondents, each asked to evaluate 19 vignettes, we generated a random sample of 9,633. The sample for each respondent is (probabilistically) representative of the universe of all vignettes (it is strictly a simple random sample). Therefore, it is possible to study whether different types of individuals respond in particular ways.

It is reasonable to question the meaning of responses to these hypothetical dilemmas. Admittedly, we asked the respondents to undertake a fairly complex intellectual task involving abstract reasoning and the ability to think in hypothetical terms (not everyone has a cousin, much less one with medical needs). In many "real world" instances, however, decisions about obligations require that we step into a hypothetical world. Our orientations toward poor mothers on Medicaid, homeless strangers, or even elderly dependent relatives are real, even if they are based on incomplete perceptions or no firsthand experience.

We readily acknowledge that a computer click indicating a sense of obligation to cover $1,000 of a cousin's medical bill may not translate into a $1,000 check to cover costs in the real world. But this is not our concern. Instead, we consider the aggregated responses to these hypothetical questions as a good indicator of the collective sense of what should occur—that is, of norms. People's understanding of what the government and other relatives should do when one of their family members is in need establishes a context in which their decisions about helping are formed. Likewise, people's understandings of their own personal obligations help establish a framework for thinking about the role of the government and others.

Finally, we acknowledge that the ability to help another person may strongly condition the sense of how much one should help. This, however, is an empirical analytical question we address. We can determine the extent to which income (and other indicators of ability to help) conditions the pattern of responses.

Methods of Data Collection

The analysis relies on original data collected in face-to-face interviews with 507 adults conducted between June and September 2003. The sample was drawn from the metropolitan statistical area of Richmond, Virginia. SIR Inc., a professional research firm, managed the sampling, recruiting, and administration of interviews. The questionnaire and vignette-rating task were pretested and revised before the final administration.

We used a random digit-dialing process on all days of the week between 10:00 AM and 8:30 PM to sample the population. We first administered a series of screening questions to assess basic eligibility of household members for participation (at least 18 years old, resident of the Richmond metropolitan statistical area, able to understand basic English), to randomly select one adult from those eligible, and to offer a $50 incentive. We then interviewed the selected respondents for approximately one hour in the downtown Richmond office of SIR Inc. We interviewed at a central location because of the complexity of the task, the need for supervision, and the need for a central computerized system. This was an essential but difficult sampling decision for the project. We anticipated that requiring respondents to travel to the central office for an interview (a distance of up to 10 miles) would significantly limit our sample.

After deleting ineligible phone numbers, we contacted adults in 1,076 households. A little more than one-third of these (409, 38 percent) were unable or unwilling to schedule an on-site interview. We scheduled 667 interviews and mailed the individuals a formal letter of invitation. We completed interviews with 504 (46.8 percent) of the adults we had contacted. Obviously, this response rate means that our results may generalize only to a population of Richmond metropolitan statistical area residents willing and able to travel downtown for an interview.

In an effort to estimate the type of self-section that may have occurred, we compared the sample of 504 with Richmond metropolitan statistical area data from the 2000 census (table 13.1). To the extent that these limited and basic comparisons reflect self-selection, our sample is somewhat more affluent, has fewer men, and is older than the general Richmond adult population.

The Interview

After arriving for an interview and signing the appropriate informed consent agreement, respondents were introduced to an interviewer. The interviewer then gave each respondent an overview of the study and ascertained his or her level of comfort with a computer. For the self-administered portion of the study, interviewers instructed respondents on the use of the

Table 13.1. Characteristics of Participants in Richmond Financial Obligation Interviews and Residents of Richmond MSA

	Richmond MSA[a]	Our sample ($N = 507$)	Difference	X^2
Race/ethnicity				7.57
White	64.0	68.6	4.6	
Black	29.5	25.7	−3.8	
Hispanic	2.3	1.4	−0.9	
Asian	2.0	1.0	−1.0	
Other/multiple races	4.0	4.7	0.7	
Education				2.27
Less than high school	17.4	19.7	2.3	
High school	26.2	26.6	0.4	
At least some college	56.4	53.8	−2.6	
Annual household income				14.35*
Less than $9,999	7.6	6.6	−1.0	
$10,000–$19,999	10.4	6.6	−3.8	
$20,000–$49,999	33.8	33.7	0.0	
$50,000–$99,999	33.5	40.0	6.5	
$100,000 or more	13.3	13.1	−0.2	
Male gender[b]	48.0	41.2	−6.8	**
Age				48.7**
18–29 years	21.1	13.2	−7.9	
30–39 years	21.6	18.6	−3.0	
40–49 years	21.8	21.0	−0.8	
50–59 years	15.6	24.8	9.2	
60–69 years	9.0	11.8	2.8	
70 years and older	10.9	10.2	−0.7	

Notes: MSA = metropolitan statistical area. Chi-square goodness of fit and binomial goodness of fit (Z approximation) statistics are two tailed.

a. Richmond MSA data come from U.S. Census Bureau, "Profile of General Demographic Characteristics, 2000."

b. Male gender numbers are binomial test Z approximation.

*$p < .01$, **$p < .001$.

survey's computer program and guided them through three sample questions to introduce the basic format. The interviewer and the respondent sat in front of identical computer terminals facing each other. The interviewer could not see the respondent's answers but could see the questions. Whenever respondents expressed concern or discomfort about using a computer, the interviewer read the questions and keyed in their answers. The interview covered many background matters: family of origin; parental traits; recollections of home environment; marital, cohabitation, and fertility history; receipt of assistance; social and political attitudes; scales of trust and empathy; questions about giving and receiving help; and demographic and household composition.

Half of the interview consisted of reading and responding to the hypothetical vignettes. The vignettes were midway through the interview and were preceded by an instructional session. In this section of the interview, the interviewer gave each respondent an overview of the vignettes and their purpose and instructed the respondent on the use of a computer program designed for the presentation of the vignettes. A centralized computer generated vignettes as the interview progressed. As each vignette appeared, both respondent and interviewer saw the same screen. The interviewer then read each vignette aloud to the respondent and entered responses to the four questions if the respondent requested it. Otherwise, the respondent entered the answers. Figure 13.1 shows the basic starting screen.

Dependent Variables

The respondents saw each of the 19 vignettes on the computer as shown in figure 13.1 along with an empty pie chart representing the cost of solving the problem. Beneath the vignette were the following four questions:

1. How much should you contribute?
2. How much should relatives of this person contribute?
3. How much should churches and/or charities contribute?
4. How much should the government contribute?

When the respondent first saw a vignette (figure 13.1), only the first question appeared. The pie chart was entirely red (representing 100 percent unmet needs). Each source of help had its own color for use in the pie chart. After the respondent entered a value for each contribution ($0 to any dollar amount, even beyond what is needed), the pie chart would auto-

Figure 13.1. Initial Computer Screen in the Richmond Financial Assistance Interviews

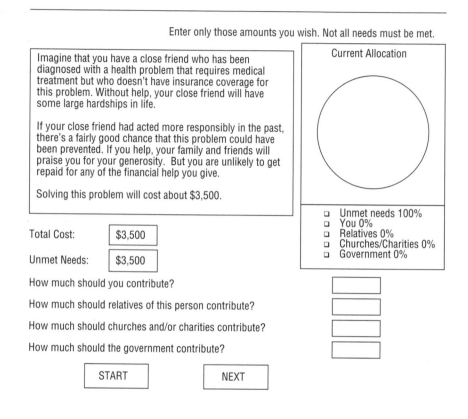

Enter only those amounts you wish. Not all needs must be met.

Imagine that you have a close friend who has been diagnosed with a health problem that requires medical treatment but who doesn't have insurance coverage for this problem. Without help, your close friend will have some large hardships in life.

If your close friend had acted more responsibly in the past, there's a fairly good chance that this problem could have been prevented. If you help, your family and friends will praise you for your generosity. But you are unlikely to get repaid for any of the financial help you give.

Solving this problem will cost about $3,500.

Current Allocation

☐ Unmet needs 100%
☐ You 0%
☐ Relatives 0%
☐ Churches/Charities 0%
☐ Government 0%

Total Cost: $3,500

Unmet Needs: $3,500

How much should you contribute?

How much should relatives of this person contribute?

How much should churches and/or charities contribute?

How much should the government contribute?

START   NEXT

matically update to show the color-coded proportions. If the respondent contributed $1,000, 29 percent (1,000/3,500) of the pie would be "you" (green), and the unmet need percentage would change accordingly. At this point, the second question would appear, and so on. Before going to the next vignette, the respondent would see all distributions, color coded and indexed with amounts and percentages, and would have an opportunity to increase or decrease values. The respondent would click "next" to move to the next vignette.

Statistical Methods

Each respondent made four judgments about each of 19 vignettes. This means that the responses about what the government should do in a particular case are related to what the respondent says about personal obligation and that of churches or charities. In short, the four judgments about any one vignette are correlated. Moreover, because each respondent made judgments about 19 different vignettes, the vignettes themselves are not independent (i.e., decisions about one vignette correlate with those about another evaluated by the same respondent). The complex error structure produced by within-vignette and within-respondent correlations meant that statistical adjustments had to be made accordingly. We employed multivariate hierarchical linear modeling in which we considered the four judgments as nested within each vignette (level 1), and the 19 vignettes as nested within each respondent (level 2). We simultaneously estimated the four judgments for each vignette and then estimated equations for each of the four resulting coefficients with vignette characteristics (e.g., culpability, cost). In other words, each vignette characteristic was evaluated to see how it influenced each judgment about the help to be given by each source. Then we asked whether these vignette characteristics had more or less influence depending on the characteristics of the respondent. This three-step technique allowed us to answer the question of whether the relationship between the vignette-level dimensions and the amounts to come from each source differed among respondents and, if so, what particular respondent characteristics explained the difference.

Beyond the obvious statistical rationale for relying on nested models, we should insert a word here about the substantive rationale for simultaneously estimating the four judgments—that is, the amount of obligation attributed to self, other relatives, charities and churches, and the government. We believe that it is only sensible to view personal obligations as inherently conditioned by the amount of obligation one attributes to other possible sources of assistance, just as the amount of obligation attributed to these sources is inherently conditioned by one's sense of personal obligation. In effect, people see their own obligations as part of a possible "package deal." To estimate personal obligations statistically, we can't simply control for the other three judgments because all of the judgments are almost linear functions of one another (not entirely because some small amount of need is typically left unmet). Instead, by simultaneously estimating personal obligations in the context of the other judgments, we consider the determinants of personal generosity within each person's overall package of obligations.

Our first step was to create as many records as there were judgments. Each vignette produced four responses. Accordingly, we created four records, one for each source of help including the amount of dollars the respondent allocated from that source. For example, suppose a vignette evoked responses of $1,500 from the respondent, $3,000 from relatives, $300 from churches, and $1,000 from the government. We created one record for each amount and source and estimated the following equation.

Level 1

$$\text{dollars allocated} = \pi_1[\text{respondent}] + \pi_2[\text{relatives}] + \pi_3[\text{churches/charities}] + \pi_4[\text{government}] + e,$$

where respondent, relatives, churches/charities, and government are binary indicators of the source of help. There is no intercept. This equation is estimated for every vignette, requiring the creation of 38,532 records (507 respondents × 19 vignettes × 4 judgments). The four records for each vignette included four binary (dummy) indicators to identify the source of the amount. This entire exercise simply creates an equation for every vignette that includes one coefficient for each source of help. Those coefficients are the amounts allocated from each source for that particular vignette. For the one vignette illustrated above, this exercise results in four coefficients: $\pi_1 = \$1,500$, $\pi_2 = \$3,000$, $\pi_3 = \$300$, and $\pi_4 = \$1,000$. Variation in these coefficients (among vignettes) becomes the outcome for the next level of analysis. At that level (level 2), the question is the role of various vignette characteristics (cost of solving the problem, relationship of the person in need, etc.) in explaining variation in the various π_i. There is now one equation for each π_i as follows:

Level 2 (one equation for every π in level 1)

$$\pi_1 = \beta_{1i}(\text{vignette characteristics}_i) + r_1$$
$$\pi_2 = \beta_{2i}(\text{vignette characteristics}_i) + r_2$$
$$\pi_3 = \beta_{3i}(\text{vignette characteristics}_i) + r_3$$
$$\pi_4 = \beta_{4i}(\text{vignette characteristics}_i) + r_4$$

These equations are estimated for every vignette ($n = 9,633$).

Now we are asking about the substantive significance of each vignette characteristic for influencing the amount the respondent allocates from each source. Suppose, for example, that the first vignette characteristic is culpability. The four equations (above) would provide separate estimates of the influence of culpability on personal obligations (π_1), obligation of other kin (π_2), obligations of churches and charities(π_3), and obligation of the government (π_4).

Finally, we investigate systematic differences among respondents in the role of vignette characteristics. For example, we might ask whether men and women respond differently to culpability in their understanding of the distribution of obligations. At this next level (level 3), variation in the coefficients for each vignette characteristic (β_{1i}) is explained as a function of respondent traits. Therefore, there are as many equations as there are respondents (507).

Level 3 (one equation for every β above)

$$\beta_{1j,\,2j,\,3j,\,\text{and}\,4j\,\text{for all}\,j} = \lambda_{1i}, \lambda_{2i}, \lambda_{3i}, \text{and } \lambda_{4i} \text{ (respondent traits)}$$

These equations are estimated for every rater ($n = 507$).

Basically, we are asking two sorts of questions. First, how do various aspects of the hypothetical situation affect personal obligations (and the perceived role of government, relatives, and churches or charities). This involves, for example, how a person's relationship to the one in need influences the amount he or she feels should be contributed to help solve the problem. The second question is whether the respondents' personal traits, such as age or family background, affect the influence of the first set of results. For example, do older respondents react to culpability differently than younger respondents?

All continuous variables are centered around the means for each respondent (intercepts of equations, therefore, represent predicted averages when all variables are at their mean). Dummy variables represent each relationship, with "unknown person in Richmond" deleted. Likewise, the problems (realms) are represented as dummy variables with "needs somewhere to live" deleted. As a result, each of the coefficients for relationships and type of problem are relative to a homeless stranger.

Results

In relating our findings, we first focus on the amount individuals feel personally responsible for compared with how much they think should come from other potential sources of assistance. After presenting these findings, we move to a more detailed examination of personal responsibility. We are interested in how relationship distance and social locations (e.g., race) are associated with understandings of personal obligation. After investigating this issue, we turn finally to the role of childhood experiences in affecting in adults' senses of personal obligations.

Summary measures for all statistics used in the following analyses are presented in table 13.2. The first (top) panel shows averages, ranges, and standard deviations for the dependent variables. The vignette variables follow in the second panel. Their distributions are determined by design and reflect the random assignment used to create the vignettes. The final panel includes summary measures for the 507 respondents in the study.

The Basic Distribution

The coefficients in the first row of table 13.3 (intercepts) indicate the average amount individuals say was their own personal responsibility and the amounts they allocate to the other sources. The first entry (166.23) is the average personal obligation when all variables are at their average, the problem is a need for housing, and the relationship is an unknown stranger. In short, respondents felt that their obligation to a homeless stranger with average needs is about $166. Moving across the first row, the second value ($1,730.30) is the average amount respondents felt the homeless stranger should receive from his or her relatives. Another $633 is seen as the responsibility of local churches and charities. And finally, the government is expected to contribute $624. In all, $3,154 was typically allocated to help the hypothetical homeless stranger. As the table of descriptive statistics (table 13.2) shows, the average cost of solving a problem was $4,136.94. Therefore, the allocated amount ($3,154) is about 76 percent of the cost of solving the problem, leaving the rest unmet from these four sources. Presumably, respondents felt that this unmet portion was the legitimate responsibility of other sources not mentioned in our project or of the homeless individual.

Personal Responsibility

We now turn briefly to how situational (vignette) factors affect personal senses of responsibility (see column 1 in table 13.3). The circumstances surrounding the need for help matter in predictable ways. However, they are much less important than the relationship implied between the needy person and the respondent. Kinship and friendship distances dominate in matters of personal obligations. Social roles, in other words, are more predictive of personal obligations than are the circumstances surrounding the need.

Degree of Need

Over the entire range of seven values that this factor could assume, severity of need is associated with a difference in personal obligations of only

Table 13.2. Descriptive Statistics for All Variables

Variable	N	Mean ($)	SD	Minimum ($)	Maximum ($)
Dependent variables					
Amount from respondent	9,633	1,102.86	1,570.50	0	10,000
Amount from relatives	9,633	1,552.04	1,828.77	0	10,000
Amount from church/charity	9,633	304.94	650.27	0	9,000
Amount from government	9,633	642.84	1,305.61	0	10,000
Level 1 (vignette) variables					
Degree (seriousness)	9,633	3.54	1.81	1	7
Culpability	9,633	4.01	2.00	1	7
Thanks (will you be thanked?)	9,633	302	1.42	1	5
Repaid (will you be repaid?)	9,633	249	1.12	1	4
Cost (cost of solving problem)	9,633	4,136.94	2,721.64	100	10,000
Training: type of need	9,633	0.25	0.43	0	1
Housing: type of need	9,633	0.25	0.43	0	1
Health: type of need	9,633	0.25	0.43	0	1
Nursing: type of need	9,633	0.25	0.43	0	1
Person in need					
Parent	9,633	0.00	0.26	0	1
Child	9,633	0.00	0.26	0	1
Sibling	9,633	0.00	0.25	0	1
Grandparent	9,633	0.00	0.25	0	1
Grandchild	9,633	0.00	0.26	0	1
Aunt or uncle	9,633	0.00	0.26	0	1
Niece or nephew	9,633	0.00	0.25	0	1
Cousin	9,633	0.00	0.26	0	1
Child-in-law	9,633	0.00	0.26	0	1
Parent-in-law	9,633	0.00	0.25	0	1
Close friend	9,633	0.00	0.26	0	1
Coworker	9,633	0.00	0.26	0	1
Close neighbor	9,633	0.01	0.27	0	1
Stranger	9,633	0.00	0.26	0	1
Level 2 (respondent) variables					
Age (years)	507	48.06	15.30	18	103
Years of education	507	14.30	2.49	10	20
Household income ($1,000s)	507	59.77	36.18	0	150

(continued)

Table 13.2. *(Continued)*

Variable	N	Mean ($)	SD	Minimum ($)	Maximum ($)
Male (1 = male, 0 = female)	507	0.41	0.49	0	1
White (1 = white)	507	0.70	0.46	0	1
Black (1 = black)	507	0.26	0.44	0	1
Other (1 = other)	507	0.04	0.20	0	1
Has had a child	507	0.771	0.416	0	1

Note: SD = standard deviation.

about $387 ($7 \times 55.31$, about 0.25 of one standard deviation). This small effect is a result of the much stronger influence of other features of need, especially the relationship between the individual and the needy person.

Culpability of the Needy Person

When problems are of the individual's own making, people feel less responsible for helping, but only by a small amount. At most, over the range of seven values, culpability reduces the level of personal obligation by only $187 ($7 \times -26.67$).

Likelihood of Thanks

The consequence of helping included various levels of thanks and praise. But respondents seemed notably unmoved by the prospect of thanks. Even if the norm of reciprocity is commonly invoked and seems to guide much social behavior, respondents profess little concern for thanks. Perhaps the norm is to appear unconcerned with getting such a return on kindness.

Likelihood of Repayment

The possibility that personal help might be repaid in part or in total does condition obligations. The certainty of repayment has the potential to increase personal obligations very minimally by about $267 ($4 \times 66.86$).

Table 13.3. Effects of Vignette Factors on Amount Expected from Each Source (in dollars)

Amount expected	From me	From relatives	From church or charity	From government
Intercept	166.23*	1,730.30*	632.99*	624.38*
Severity of problem[a]	55.31*	−14.04*	0.19	1.72
Culpability of needy person[a]	−26.67*	4.46	−4.97	0.679
Likelihood of thanks[a]	10.34	−0.82	5.67	−13.99
Likelihood of repayment[a]	66.86*	−14.59	−10.79	−24.62*
Needs nursing	162.56*	−0.8	19.04	442.46*
Needs training	−139.64*	−200.36*	−16.6	375.39*
Needs medical care	137.31*	47.71	20.65	343.95*
Needs housing	ref	ref	ref	ref
Cost[a]	0.1713*	0.3619*	0.0831*	0.1892*
Relationship				
Parent	1,777.91*	−490.35*	−452.27*	−416.71*
Child	2,536.38*	−1,288.37*	−464.98*	−481.48*
Brother/sister	1,234.08*	−261.74*	−388.29*	−315.44*
Grandparent	1,084.48*	−120.75*	−412.46*	−143.56*
Grandchild	1530.6*	−438.28*	−441.46*	−480.44*
Aunt or uncle	520.33*	12.41	−323.49*	−150.38*
Niece or nephew	613.6*	94.65	−353.36*	−276.94*
Cousin	317.27*	120.55*	−306.12*	−174.06*
Child-in-law	1,140.61*	−129.37	−392.67*	−497.11*
Parent-in-law	1,140.45*	−197.13*	−394.32*	−320.81*
Close friend	532.39*	128.71*	−297.87*	−251.89*
Coworker	58.46*	222.88*	−197.63*	−135.83*
Neighbor	122.54	331.92*	−242.49*	−163.35*
Stranger	ref	ref	ref	ref
N at level 1	38,532			
N at level 2	9,663		% var. exp.	51.9%
N at level 3	507		ICC	16.1%

Notes: Level 1 refers to the total number of judgments (4 per vignette), level 2 refers to the number of vignettes, and level 3 refers to the number of respondents.

a. Centered at mean.

*$p < .01$

Type of Need

Our design specified four types of need (nursing, training, medical care, and housing) to assess whether different sorts of need evoked different responses. It is certainly imaginable that some needs pull on the heartstrings more than others. However, there were only small differences in personal obligations associated with the type of problem faced. The need for education (or training) evoked the lowest level of personal obligation. Somewhat more compelling was the need for housing (the reference category), followed by medical care, and then nursing. Substantively, however, all such differences are very small, suggesting that allocation of obligations reflects a few basic principles that cut across types of problems.

Cost of Solving the Problem

How much it would cost to solve the problem had a pronounced average effect on personal feelings of obligation as expected since our dependent variables were evoked in response to this amount. Recall that in the vignettes the cost of solving a problem ranged from $100 to $10,000. Differences in personal obligations predictably follow; a $100 need would be met with about $17 on average, whereas a $10,000 cost would produce about $1,713 in personal obligations. This average effect, however, is very strongly moderated by the relationship to the needy person. That is, the proportion of the cost of solving the need that individuals assume (or allocate to other sources) differs quite a bit depending on the relationship involved. We will return to this factor to consider the relative amounts expected from each of the four potential sources of help.

Relationship

As we noted, the largest difference in personal obligations is associated with the hypothetical relationship implied in the vignettes. Compared with an unknown stranger, a coworker evinces only $58 more personal obligation. On the other hand, a child or parent produces vastly greater obligations—$2,536 and $1,778, respectively. We focus much of our subsequent discussion on the role of relationship distance.

Six Levels of Kinship Obligation

The pattern of obligations at different relationship degrees is a story of some complexity. By relying on a series of simultaneous tests of these coefficients, it was possible to identify those that tend to cluster, or that do not significantly differ. First is a child for whom obligations to are distinct and greater than for any other. Then come parents and grandchildren. A fourth level includes grandparents, children-in-law, parents-in-law, and siblings. Next are tertiary relations, including cousins, aunts and uncles, nieces and nephews, and close friends. Least compelling are unrelated individuals, including an unknown stranger, a coworker, and a close neighbor.

In other words, norms of personal obligations distinguish sharply among close relations (child, parent, grandchild) but less so as relationship distance increases. In-laws, grandparents, and siblings occupy a similar position in the relationship dimension of personal obligations. All other relatives and close friends also constitute a cluster. Finally, tangential figures in most people's lives (coworkers, neighbors, and strangers) represent the least compelling object of personal responsibility.

Distributing Obligations

We turn now to a discussion of how obligations are distributed among possible agents of assistance for 14 different types of relationships. Here we are asking what percentage of the cost of solving the need should come from each source for each relationship. Table 13.4 provides the average proportionate amounts of the cost to solve the problem that respondents indicated for each source and relationship combination in addition to the cost that was not allocated to any source. Figure 13.2 gives an image of the relative responsibility of each agent for each of these relationships. These results were obtained by multiplying the cost of solving the need by each relationship dummy and then adding these interaction terms to the basic model shown in table 13.3.

Several basic patterns are evident for relationship distance. First, the amount of unmet cost (presumably, that for which the needy person is responsible) generally increases with relationship distance. Only for grandparents is there no unmet need. Second, beginning with grandparents and moving outward, other relatives are responsible for a fairly constant fraction of the costs of solving the problem, about 40 percent. Third, the government is expected to contribute a fairly sizable fraction for problems affecting grandparents (28 percent) and other relationships that are not children, roughly one-fifth. The large government role for grandparents probably reflects prevailing patterns of government assistance that are most generous for seniors (i.e., Social Security and Medicare). Finally,

Table 13.4. Percentage of Problem Expected to Be Solved by Each Source

Source of money	Me	Relatives	Church charity	Government	Unmet costs
Relationship					
Parent	35.8	32.7	5.6	14.4	11.5
Child	60.8	11.1	4.6	11.8	11.8
Brother or sister	22.1	38.1	8.4	19.6	11.8
Grandparent	26.1	40.2	5.5	2.8	0.4
Grandchild	33.8	30.5	7.0	9.7	19.0
Aunt or uncle	11.4	41.7	13.1	21.4	12.4
Niece or nephew	13.3	42.3	8.9	20.0	15.5
Cousin	5.0	42.4	8.1	23.5	21.1
Child-in-law	22.7	39.4	8.0	11.6	18.3
Parent-in-law	20.0	38.7	6.9	18.5	17.8
Close friend	11.1	40.3	9.8	19.3	19.5
Coworker	2.2	42.7	10.7	20.6	23.8
Close neighbor	3.1	45.1	9.5	20.0	22.3
Stranger	0.2	40.2	14.3	23.4	21.9

respondents think churches and charities should play only a modest role in solving problems, contributing between 5 percent and 14 percent depending on the relationship. In all cases, churches and charities have a lesser role than the government, usually substantially so.

Differences among Respondents in the Distribution of Obligations

Individuals differed significantly in the amounts they allocated for each source of potential assistance, including for themselves. We now consider factors that may explain such differences. To make the task manageable, we focus solely on how individuals differ in their personal obligations. Complementary results were found for the other sources of assistance (when personal obligations are higher, other sources of potential obligation are lower).

Each slope (effect) for each relationship in table 13.3 is now treated as a dependent variable. We investigate how respondent characteristics influence the variation in those slopes. For example, in responding to the

Figure 13.2. Proportion Expected from Each Source

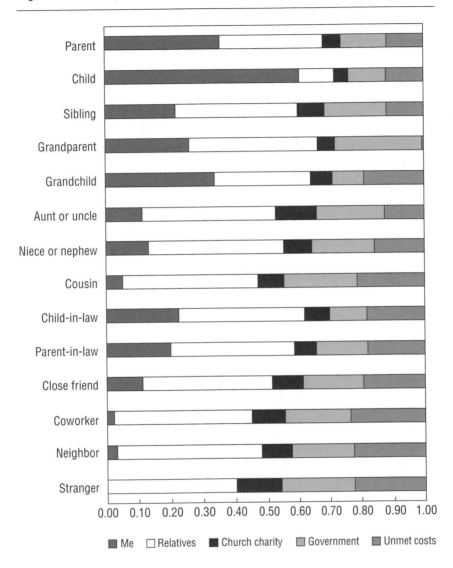

needs of parents, higher-income respondents assumed greater personal responsibilities than did lower-income ones. This type of difference occurs in a model where the individual slopes for personal responsibility for parents are regressed on personal income. Accordingly, table 13.5 has as many dependent variables as relationship categories.

The next two sets of analyses illustrate how the vignette technique may be applied to investigate competing ideas about factors responsible for the distribution of obligations. Here we consider social locations (sociodemographic characteristics) and childhood experiences.

Sociodemographic Characteristics

We first consider major social positions that are consequential for a wide range of behaviors and attitudes. We proceed with the common-sense presumption that personal income had to be controlled in assessing the assumption of personal responsibility. Our initial foray into this issue considered these other basic social factors: age, education, sex, race, and parenthood. We measured age and education attained in years. Income was measured in dollars (thousands). Race was treated as a dummy variable. Parenthood was also a dummy variable, distinguishing only between those with and without children (of any age).

Preliminary analysis revealed that obligations for a relation varied significantly among respondents (i.e., respondents varied in how they responded to the needs of the same relation). That same analysis showed that the other vignette characteristics (e.g., culpability and likelihood of repayment) did not vary the responses. Therefore, only the slopes for relationships are treated as dependent variables.

The top panel of table 13.5 displays the results of treating the relationship slopes as dependent variables. The first column pertains to variation in the amounts assumed for parents. The first entry (intercept = $1,798.52), for example, implies that when age, education, and income are at their averages and the respondent is white and has no children, the average personal obligation for parents was $1,798.52 (plus or minus any fixed values from the vignettes). The entry below this ($18.11) means that for every additional year of age beyond the average, respondents assume about $18 more personal responsibility.

When individual (respondent) traits are considered, several patterns appear. First, respondents with higher incomes routinely assumed more personal responsibility for others' needs. That is hardly surprising. What is remarkable is the fact that other social factors are consequential net of the ability to absorb the cost of solving a problem. Older respondents felt they should assume more responsibility than did younger respondents for several types of relatives: parents, siblings, grandparents, and in-laws. Males generally expressed more financial obligation than females for many close and distant relationships. Black respondents felt more obligation for par-

Table 13.5. Effects of Sociodemographics on Personal Obligations (in dollars)

Respondent traits	Parent	Child	Sibling	Grand-parent	Grand-child	Aunt, uncle	Niece, nephew	Cousin	Child-in-law	Parent-in-law	Close friend	Coworker	Close neighbor
Intercept	1,798.52**	2,261.28**	1,527.48**	1,054.84**	2,261.28**	480.18**	437.22**	280.21*	981.79**	1,140.97**	691.21**	-84.5	134.26
Age (years)	18.11**	5.89	13.13**	12.96**	5.89	8.34	0.28	3.84	9.95**	10.23**	4.14	0.57	1.6
Education (years)	49.27**	23.67	100.84	38.82*	23.67	-16.01	9.28	26.33	-12.65	41.97*	5.48	7.98	-3.87
Income ($1,000s)	4.12**	11.56**	1.41	4.17**	11.56**	3.16*	1.68	2.66*	4.71**	5.97**	2.42	-1.38	0.67
Male	270.14**	560.87**	129.33	99.6	560.87**	259.28**	311.64**	152.42	379.67**	339.38**	84.44	182.39*	205.27*
Black	220.26*	-194.01	41.93	220.73*	-194.01	6.32	266.33*	202.64*	-25.17	-246.74*	198.75*	13.37	105.82
Other races	251.69	49.73	-238.65	-385.02	49.73	-53.74	-325.03	261.26	-120.65	-537.51**	-76.67	265.67	-135.75
White	ref												
Any children?	-242.01*	173.74	-430.07**	-61.1	173.74	-79.48	-0.59	126.09	16.6	-74.19	-216.71*	68.61	-161.83

Fixed for all outcomes

Intercept	163.64**
Severity of problem	56.65**
Culpability of person	-27.05**
Likelihood of thanks	9.58
Likelihood of repayment	64.76**
Needs nursing	156.43**
Needs training	-132.82**
Needs medical care	147.68**
Needs housing (ref)	Ref
Cost to solve problem ($)	0.1743**

Notes: This equation also included fixed coefficients for relative's obligation, churches and charities, and government responsibility. Reference relationship is unknown stranger.

** *p* < .01, * *p* < .05.

ents, grandparents, nieces and nephews, cousins, and close friends than did their white counterparts, but less for parents-in-law. Finally, whether a respondent was a parent or not had very little effect (assuming less responsibility for parents, siblings, and close friends). Personal responsibility, in sum, varies according to basic social locations (sex, age, income, etc.)

As just detailed, this analysis indicates that a number of sociodemographic characteristics are substantially related to the assumption of personal responsibility. However, obligations for all relationship categories except coworker and close neighbor are significantly different from those for a stranger, even after controlling for all of these respondent traits. In short, the assumption of responsibility for different categories of relationships is not solely due to the personal and sociodemographic factors we have considered in this table.

Childhood Experiences

If we are attempting to explain variations in personal responsibility, it is clear that we must move beyond the type of factors considered above. Although these are relevant and often statistically significant, they do not explain (reduce to insignificance) the differences found for relationship categories. Our second analysis, therefore, focuses on a range of childhood experiences reported by respondents. Our initial research plan proposed that obligations would be a result of (among other things) relationships in childhood. We reasoned that an adult's account of his childhood would help explain how he sees needs. Adults who recall their parents (or primary caretakers) as warm and trusting, for example, would feel more obligated toward them than those who recall their parents as distant. Without strong theoretical guidance, we cast our net widely by including the following questions to tap various prosocial experiences and specific circumstances that may affect senses of need:

Below is a list of experiences some people have had when they were growing up. For each one, please indicate whether or not you personally have experienced this while you were growing up (each was answered yes = 1 or no = 0)

Prosocial experiences

a. *You belonged to a youth group or something similar.*
b. *You did some kind of volunteer work.*

c. *You went door to door to raise money for a cause or organization.*
d. *You were active in a religious organization.*

Experiences with Acute Needs

e. *You were seriously ill.*
f. *You grew up in poverty.*
g. *You saw people living in extreme poverty firsthand.*

Experienced Help

h. *You were helped in a significant way by someone other than a relative.*

Intact Family at Age 12? On the basis of a retrospective family history battery, we determined whether the respondent was living with both biological parents at various ages. Preliminary analysis indicated that age 12 was the most relevant age to consider because older ages were redundant (if a child was in a disrupted household at age 12, he probably still was when he became older). We also included questions designed to tap reflections of warmth and trust in the adult's childhood family.

Parent–Child Trust. We asked respondents two two-part questions to gauge reflections of parent–child trust. *As best as you can remember, how often was the following statement true when you were about 16 years old? "My mother trusted me." "My father trusted me?"* (1 = never true to 5 = always true). Respondents who grew up with alternative primary caregivers were asked about those individuals. *As best as you can remember, how often was the following statement true when you were about 16? "I trusted my mother" and "I trusted my father."* We computed two measures based on available information. The first is a measure of how much the respondent trusted his or her parents. The second is a measure of how much the respondent felt trusted by his or her parents.

Family Closeness. Now, think about your relationship with just your parents at the time you were 16 years of age. Some people remember having a very close relationship with their parents. Others remember having a fairly distant relationship with their parents. Using a 10-point scale, where 1 is very distant and 10 is very close, how close were you to your mother at the time you were 16? The same was asked about the father.

The results presented in table 13.6 mirror those presented in table 13.5 with the exception that all the childhood variables (above) have been added as predictors. Several simple results are immediately obvious. First, for all relationships beyond grandchildren, the intercepts are not statistically significant. This indicates that whatever variation there was in how respondents met the needs of these relations was eliminated by controlling the childhood characteristics. Childhood experiences or memories appear to play a significant role in how people respond to the needs of people who are not close relatives.

Second, the influence of social demographic factors (shown in table 13.4) are essentially unchanged (with a few exceptions) when childhood factors are included. This suggests that such demographic traits are largely unrelated to the memories people have of childhood.

Third, to the extent that childhood experiences matter, they do so selectively. For example, adults who remember that a nonrelative gave them significant help respond more generously to a wide range of others in need but are less generous with their own parents.

The prosocial experiences we included (volunteered, raised money for charity, active in a religious organization) are generally shown to have small or negative effects on generosity. For example, a youth group membership is associated with greater generosity toward one's child but less toward a parent-in-law. On the other hand, having worked as a volunteer is associated with lower obligations to parents and grandchildren.

Having witnessed severe poverty or having grown up in poverty both influence responses to others' needs. Those who saw severe poverty first-hand allocated less to children and in-laws than did those who did not recall seeing destitution. But those who recall growing up in poverty appeared more generous in a couple of cases (grandparents and children-in-law). In other analyses (not shown), we further investigated this issue by adding a variable that indicated whether the respondent recalled ever living in a family (before age 16) that received some form of public assistance. We did not find any effect of this variable, but few respondents (fewer than 5 percent) recalled receiving public assistance as a child. Witnessing poverty and growing up poor were still statistically significant predictors.

Those adults who were helped in a significant way as children by non-relatives are notably distinct in their distribution of obligations. In particular, they respond less to the needs of parents and more to those of children, grandchildren, nieces, and nephews. They are even more responsive to the problems of coworkers. Presumably, the circumstances that led someone outside their family to provide significant help left a mark that makes such individuals particularly sensitive to the problems of children.

Neither having been religiously active as a youth nor living in a non-intact biological home as a child has much measurable consequence once all the other items in these equations are controlled.

The last three items in table 13.6 refer to memories of intergenerational trust and closeness. All three are uniformly positive in their effects, even

Table 13.6. Effects of Childhood Experiences on Personal Obligations (in dollars)

Respondent traits	Parent	Child	Sibling	Grand-parent	Grand-child	Aunt, uncle	Niece, nephew	Cousin	Child-in-law	Parent-in-law	Close friend	Coworker	Close neighbor
Intercept	1,256.99**	1,812.27**	405.21	782.63*	2,042.47**	162.59	−41.81	71.68	162.61	549.98	325.08	1.69	99.47
Age (years)	13.85**	3.41	9.62*	12.23**	9.57**	8.99*	1.08	3.33	8.44*	8.71*	2.52	1.31	2.21
Education (years)	45.89*	12.91	7.47	50.87*	9.62	−9.32	−2.1	25.96	−9.95	45.64*	4.82	6.94	−4.59
Income ($1,000s)	3.97**	11.71**	0.98	4.398**	4.33*	3.38*	1.51	2.54	4.49**	5.67**	2.25	−1.30	0.75
Male	245.97**	560.99**	137.94	109.73	244.70*	226.55*	284.61**	143.42	434.97**	372.46**	167.33	182.78*	179.24*
Black	210.73*	−232.44*	−5.56	138.82	−246.16*	−31.51	232.42*	207.81	−125.48	−325.63**	151.70*	−2.14	77.58
Other races	339.39	296.01	−132.34	−394.65	−639.78**	−40.16	−371.02	260.89	−176.89	−523.37*	−8.82	204.70	−152.58
White	ref												
Any children?	−264.99**	212.64	−437.69**	−60.14	−241.04*	−102.78	−12.82	−117.78	53.23	−82.65	−204.22	83.72	−150.72
					Childhood								
Prosocial experiences													
Youth group	215.98	448.39**	51.29	75.99	−154.59	104.71	−59.53	−14.75	126.48	−288.60*	159.46	−53.21	−91.57
Volunteer	−231.68*	−220.55	−61.05	173.37	−237.09*	179.96	72.92	84.48	9.07	182.49	68.61	44.28	44.99
Raised money	−83.12	−221.96*	18.76	−153.55	100.33	−135.33	−75.48	−127.26	26.19	−118.94	−33.59	−7.08	−47.54
Active religiously	37.61	−136.07	287.71*	97.27	43.51	−74.99	31.15	43.35	92.24	90.54	75.35	−11.22	8.09
Experience with acute need													
Seriously ill	162.93	226.95	−128.50	95.28	−100.86	30.39	−126.61	96.29	−34.58	−11.79	11.30	−53.11	−58.16
Grew up poor	68.27	−180.07	−90.36	464.92**	−176.89	194.62	−205.14	−60.05	422.36**	236.98	256.79	25.84	−17.97
Saw poverty	−168.69	−261.42*	57.78	−177.55	−222.86*	88.32	−4.09	6.35	−267.27*	−258.19*	−193.51	−37.42	131.38

(continued)

Table 13.6. (Continued)

Respondent traits	Parent	Child	Sibling	Grand-parent	Grand-child	Aunt, uncle	Niece, nephew	Cousin	Child-in-law	Parent-in-law	Close friend	Coworker	Close neighbor
Experienced help													
Nonrelative helped	-302.77**	308.99**	-95.05	-39.50	229.80*	-120.17	264.75**	12.65	153.65	51.41	-28.92	158.69*	28.92
Biological parents	170.29	-175.03	-25.78	-250.24*	-24.05	-187.25	61.62	13.78	-101.02	84.65	-133.91	29.78	-23.01
Trusted by parents	-5.55	132.89*	166.55*	81.04	-15.07	30.47	-78.77	13.59	87.74	75.53	146.77*	-4.19	78.10
Trusted parents	4.21	64.54	105.95	-70.47	-117.45	50.4	168.73*	59.5	85.48	74.91	-66.98	-32.53	-58.19
Family close	85.49*	-34.70	-26.94	42.15	66.65*	7.59	-2.16	-19.19	-10.05	10.97	-11.16	3.11	-1.96
Fixed for all outcomes													
Intercept	160.14**												
Degree	57.02**												
Culpability of person	-27.59**												
Likelihood of thanks	7.71												
Likelihood of repayment	65.12**												
Needs nursing	151.92**												
Needs training	-120.71**												
Needs medical care	154.62**												
Needs housing (ref)	Ref												
Cost to solve problem ($)	0.1744**												

Notes: This equation also included fixed coefficients for relative's obligation, churches and charities, and government responsibility. Reference relationship is unknown stranger. $n = 38,532$ outcomes, 9,663 vignettes, and 507 respondents.

** $p < .01$, * $p < .05$.

if weak and inconsistent. Adults who recall their parents as having trusted them respond more generously to the problems of children, siblings, and friends. There is only one significant effect for having trusted parents: more generosity to nieces and nephews. Finally, those who reported their family as having been close assume more personal obligations for parents and grandchildren.

Conclusions

Our underlying goal is to describe how people understand the distribution of obligations among potential sources of help. We found that there is a clear and graded degree of personal obligation that corresponds to relationship distance. There is also a corresponding and complementary distribution of obligations to other sources of help as relationship distance increases. Not surprisingly, people appear to expect more from the government when the needy person is a stranger than when it is a parent or child. But even in matters of parents and children, there is a significant perceived role of government (and of other relatives). For no relationship we studied did people assume complete personal responsibility. They always thought that others should also provide help. One rationale for our project was that this package view of helping is central to how individuals understand their responsibilities. If we wish to explain when and why individuals believe they should help others, we should begin by understanding their mental map of obligations—the role they play in the context of others' roles.

Our results consistently show that norms of obligation are patterned more by relationship than by circumstances. In all analyses, circumstances of need (e.g., degree of culpability, severity of the problem) were significant and consistent in their direction of effects. However, they were relatively small compared with the role that relationship plays in evoking obligations.

For example, personal obligations do not have their origins in particular childhood experiences. Although childhood experiences were shown to condition personal obligations, and in a significant fashion, they did not do so in a patterned or predictable fashion. For example, having witnessed severe poverty as a child and having grown up poor both mattered, but they did not matter in the same direction (i.e., sometimes increasing obligations, sometimes decreasing them) and not consistently.

On the other hand, higher incomes and age consistently influenced personal obligations in the same direction. The effect of income, we believe, is a capacity issue. Those with more to give may respond to the circumstances we described by saying they should give more. The age and sex effects, however, are more suggestive.

Relationships, age, and sex play a significant role in the pattern of obligations. These findings are provocative because they speak directly to social roles (the target of social norms). As the "oughts" of social life, norms represent collective agreements that certain people (i.e., those who occupy certain social roles) should do certain things (or refrain from doing certain things). For example, parents should treat children differently than they treat their siblings. Retired people, likewise, appear to respond to well-known age norms (e.g., volunteering at high rates, etc.). This response should not suggest that norms fully explain such behaviors. However, they are a part of the story. Older (retired) people are asked to volunteer more than younger generations. Culturally, the norm of volunteering as an older person appears to exist. It seems that older people have different norms of obligation to others.

In work not shown here, we investigated another adult role. We analyzed the distribution of obligations by marital status. Many believe in social norms about marriage (typically expressed as vows). It has been shown that when men get married, their pattern of giving and helping shifts to focus more on relatives and less on friends, neighbors, and coworkers (Nock 1998). Our findings in this matter must be tempered by our inability to control for race in the models (race and marital status are too highly correlated in our sample to permit the derivation of separate estimates). With that proviso, however, our findings show very little difference in personal obligations associated with marital status for parents and children. There were minimal differences for siblings. For grandparents, grandchildren, parents-in-law, and children-in-law, married adults felt a greater personal obligation to help. As relationship distance increased beyond immediate kin (to friends, neighbors, coworkers) the never-married saw greater personal obligations than did the currently or formerly married. The norms of marriage appear to focus obligations on more immediate relatives (albeit beyond parents, children, and siblings) and less on more distant kin, friends, coworkers, and neighbors.

It is likely that norms of helping differ for the sexes. We consistently found higher personal obligations among males. Do men understand their obligation as providing money (consistent with most masculine adult roles) and women with providing care (also consistent with dominant feminine adult roles)? Is it possible that marital status operates independently of race? We believe our work suggests that social roles (e.g., relationship, marriage, sex, age) are all involved in the distribution of obligations. We also believe that we have demonstrated how such issues may be investigated.

Limitations and Future Directions

As we have noted, our project required many design decisions that previous research could not inform. Although theories of philanthropy and generosity exist, and we spent considerable time developing measures of the requisite constructs, we did not find strong and consistent effects of such things as empathy or trust. Future work should investigate the relationship between the distribution of obligations and generosity.

Our specification of the circumstances of need (for the needy person) was also unsatisfying. We did not include any negative sanctions for failing to help someone. Although incorporating sanctions would be challenging, it could be important because possible personal disapproval and rejection may be powerful threats that induce people to greater generosity.

More generally, our interviews did not focus enough on the situational factors that might influence obligations. We included obvious experiences (e.g., having been the recipient of public assistance) but failed to include questions about the type of relationship individuals may have had with other relatives (beyond parents). Our results do not suggest that these or other situational factors would have profound effects on obligations. Social roles appear to be consistently more important than any situational or background issue we investigated. Still, a better theoretical model of situational/background determinants of personal obligations would be helpful.

A more important line of work to incorporate into studies of obligations, we believe, is the distributive justice literature. In a long line of work spanning philosophy (e.g., Rawls 1971, 1999) and sociology (Jasso 1980, 1999) the distributive justice field has attempted to answer the questions "What do I deserve?" and "What are the consequences of receiving less than I deserve?" This literature inspired our work as we sought to answer "What do I owe?" Indeed, we included four vignettes in our study that asked people to imagine that they had a need they could not solve with their resources. We asked them how much they felt entitled to receive from relatives, from churches and charities, and from the government. In the end, we were unable to successfully model the relationship between entitlement and obligations because we had too few vignettes per respondent. Our expectation was that there would be a very strong positive correlation for personal obligations and senses of entitlement. What we referred to as the "golden rule hypothesis" predicated that those who expect to be treated well by others will treat others well and vice versa. Our limited results (simple bivariate correlations) did reveal strong positive correlations between the amounts respondents felt entitled to receive from others and the amounts they assumed as personal obligations to others. We could not investigate this further by distinguishing among entitlement from the government, other relatives, and private sources. Because a well-developed distributive justice literature exists, we feel it is important to reconcile that theory and findings from the type of study we conducted. An integrated theory of obligations and entitlements would undoubtedly be a major advance in our understanding of when and why people help others.

Implications for Social Policy

We can only speculate whether norms of obligations and actual helping behaviors are related. However, we believe that the vignette task we set before our respondents captures or at least points to underlying beliefs about hypothetical others in need of help. And these are of significant policy importance.

Norms of caring and obligations are central elements of social welfare policies. Those without others to offer and provide assistance in times of need are the primary focus of means-tested assistance such as Temporary Assistance for Needy Families or Medicaid. They are the ones who, we hope, the social safety net catches. Relatives continue to provide the overwhelming majority of care, especially for dependent youths and the elderly. Our work confirms that norms of personal obligations are greatest for children, parents, and grandchildren but decline with relationship distance. Nonkin evoke only a weak sense of personal obligation but have relatively large expectations from relatives.

The role of the state, we found, was significant though modest across the entire range of relationships. There is little evidence of a strong sense of collective (government) obligation for those who are not close. Others' needs deserve to be met (there is little unmet need in our findings), but the role of government, churches, and charities is relatively limited in accomplishing this objective.

To the extent that American welfare policies on health, housing, or training are financed through federal tax policy, they are collective (socialized). But our results suggest that most people see only a modest role for such collective assistance. The government is, of course, an important source of help for people we are not that close to. Its role for parents is about 14 percent, whereas for distant relatives and strangers it is closer to 20–25 percent. So there is clear evidence of a collective (socialized) norm of helping, but it is not that large. And as we noted earlier, this sentiment does not differ appreciably from one type of need to another.

It should be remembered that the task we set before our respondents was to indicate how much assistance should come from the various sources. We did not ask about how much assistance does in fact come from the government. And though we have no hard evidence on this, it is possible that our respondents have little real knowledge of the state's role. On the other hand, they may be answering our questions truthfully by saying that the state should play a modest role. We favor the latter interpretation because is it consistent with decades of opinion research on the perceived role of the government (always viewed as too large in a long series of questions about federal spending priorities in the General Social Surveys conducted since 1972) (National Opinion Research Center 1972–2006).

Assessments of "modest" or "large" in matters of normative obligations for personal or government help are extremely difficult to benchmark. But to help put matters in perspective, the Medicare program for the general elderly (not needy) population pays between 50 percent and 60 percent of enrollees' personal health care costs. Although Medicare does not cover significant medical costs, it does cover the majority of medical costs (Caplan 2002). The average needy person who qualified for Medicare spent $210 out of pocket for medical costs in 2002 (Ku and Broaddus 2005). This amount represents the sum of uncovered services and "nominal" copayments or cost sharing that cannot typically exceed $3 per service, visit, or prescription. Assuming that an average medical charge (visits, prescriptions, or procedures) is $100, the government share is 97 percent in Medicaid cases. Those who receive housing assistance (in the form of subsidized public or private units) pay 30 percent of their income in rent. Based on an average fair-market rent ($579/month) and average low-income-earner monthly wages of $1,120, the individual pays $336 rent and the government pays $243 (Zedlewski 2002). A student seeking higher education who qualified for maximum federal educational aid could finance the majority of the costs (instructional costs, fees, living expenses, etc.) at the average public four-year college using only a Pell grant and discounted tuition ("general subsidy") from state institutions that regularly charge tuition below the costs of education (Congressional Budget Office 2004, figure 3). Whether these three examples are overestimates or underestimates of the government role is unimportant. Unless they are vastly out of range, all are much higher than the portion allocated to government responsibility by our respondents. Respondents did not see the government as a major source of help to those in need. Alternatively, and to the extent we are tapping normative beliefs, our respondents are saying that the government *should not be* a major source of help. For those who receive government assistance, however, it is in fact a major source of help.

Respondents allocated twice the responsibility to relatives beyond immediate family members as they did to the government. In sum, Americans expect close relatives to help for the types of need in our project.

The modest collective sentiment is also reflected in the relatively small amounts respondents attributed to churches and charities. Although such agents of philanthropy are routinely seen as providing help, the magnitude of their expected assistance is always less than 10 percent except in the case of total strangers (where it rises to 14 percent), even less than the role of government. There seems little doubt, then, that private help is normatively dominant, with the state, churches, and charities playing a smaller role.

Some of our findings may reflect political divides in addition to norms. For example, our measure of liberalism and conservatism correlated predictably with personal obligations and expectations from the state (i.e., liberals thought the state should play a larger role in helping than conservatives did). We may be tapping some part of the liberal/conservative dimensions of American politics with our findings of the effects of sex, income, and other personal traits on obligation to help.

Overall, what are the policy implications of such a privatized view of need and helping? Recall that our work concerns situations and circumstances where needy people are unable to help themselves. So the question is what happens beyond that point. We take our results to suggest that individuals will resist universal collective solutions more than individual private and semiprivate ones. With baby boomers retiring and aging, it may be easier to enact health and housing solutions that focus on some form of supported home care rather than sweeping reformulations of the entire health care financing or public housing system. In supported home care, elderly and ill individuals receive care at home. Relatives are indirectly compensated (by the services offered to their needy relative) for providing the care. Though this approach would typically rely on licensed providers for specialized care, there is good reason to consider whether relatives (or friends) who wished to could share the care with such individuals and also be compensated through existing policy mechanisms (e.g., Medicare or Medicaid, with suitable revision).

Such a policy would resemble the existing "kinship care" provisions of current U.S. welfare law. Kinship care is an alternative to foster care or adoption that relies on relatives to provide a minor with needed care. Under this arrangement, a child lives with relatives (typically a grandmother or aunt) in situations that range from completely informal sharing of care to permanent and minimally supervised arrangements. Ties to the birth family are not severed, and some birth parents continue to visit and have close relationships with the children in question. Kin caregivers receive the same subsidies paid to foster parents (Brinig and Nock 2003).

Enhancing individuals' ability to help their relatives through existing programs, or with federal tax policy that would grant credits for caring for sick parents, would probably fare better in public opinion, and be more resonant with norms and beliefs, than expanding services and programs through centralized governmental (i.e., public) organizations. This outcome seems especially likely given that the government would otherwise be forced to ask Americans to help collectively solve the needs of hypothetical strangers, whom respondents in our study helped the least.

We believe that our work affirms the central place of relationships and social roles for how people envision the package of help that should be provided. Social roles, and the norms attached to them, have received too little attention from social scientists. But because norms are beliefs, they are elements of culture. How are norms embedded in a culture? How are they sustained or changed? Religion is an obvious candidate here, as are media, music, folklore, and rituals. As we continue to investigate the intergenerational exchange of help, we must consider such elements of culture. This will be challenging for researchers because we cannot yet specify where culture resides (other than in the mind). But our work has shown that one can systematically investigate beliefs and their correlates. We are hopeful that future work will expand by rigorously investigating and theorizing about the cultural bases of social norms.

NOTE

This research was supported by a grant from the National Science Foundation (SES-0136339, S. Nock, principal investigator, P. Kingston, coprincipal investigator).

REFERENCES

Brinig, Margaret F., and Steven L. Nock. 2003. "How Much Does Legal Status Matter: Adoptions by Kin Caregivers." *Family Law Quarterly* 36:449–74.

Caplan, Craig. 2002. "What Share of Beneficiaries' Total Health Care Costs Does Medicare Pay?" http://www.aarp.org/research/medicare/outofpocket/aresearch-import-657-DD78.html.

Congressional Budget Office. 2004. "Private and Public Contributions to Financing College Education." http://www.cbo.gov/showdoc.cfm?index=4984&sequence=0.

Ganong, Lawrence, Marilyn Coleman, Annette Kusgen McDaniel, Tim Killian. 1998. "Attitudes Regarding Obligations to Assist an Older Parent or Stepparent Following Later-Life Remarriage." *Journal of Marriage and Family* 60:595–610.

Jasso, Guilermina. 1980. "A New Theory of Distributive Justice." *American Sociological Review* 45:3–32.

———. 1999. "How Much Injustice Is There in the World? Two New Justice Indexes." *American Sociological Review* 64:133–168.

Ku, Leighton, and Matthew Broaddus. 2005. "Out-of-Pocket Medical Expenses for Medicaid Beneficiaries Are Substantial and Growing." http://www.cbpp.org/5-31-05health.htm.

National Opinion Research Center. n.d. "General Social Survey 1972–2000." http://webapp.icpsr.umich.edu/GSS.

Nock, Steven L. 1998. "The Consequences of Premarital Fatherhood." *American Sociological Review* 63(2): 250–63.

Rawls, John. 1971. *A Theory of Justice.* Cambridge, MA: Harvard University Press.

———. 1999. *A Theory of Justice.* Rev ed. Cambridge, MA: Harvard University Press.

Rossi, Alice, and Peter H. Rossi. 1990. *On Human Bonding: Parent-Child Relations over the Life Course.* Hawthorne, NY: Aldine de Gruyter.

Rossi, Peter H., and Steven L. Nock. 1982. *Measuring Social Judgments: The Factorial Survey Approach.* Beverly Hills, CA: Sage Publications.

Zedlewski, Sheila Rafferty. 2002. "The Importance of Housing Benefits to Welfare Success." Washington, DC: The Urban Institute. http://www.urban.org/publications/410458.html.

14

Race and Ethnic Influences on Normative Beliefs and Attitudes toward Provision of Family Care

James S. Jackson, Toni C. Antonucci, Edna E. Brown,
Svein Olav Daatland, and Besangie Sellars

N ock, Kingston, and Holian, in chapter 13, present a compelling argument for how normative obligations, measured in willingness to give dollars in hypothetical vignettes, differ as a function of race and ethnicity of the informant and structural relationships among family members. Although the vignette approach to social phenomena has been around since research on social stereotyping in the 1930s and 1940s, its use in the public policy arena of private and public support for vulnerable populations is unique. The authors note the multitude of potential methodological and conceptual questions in this approach and make several limiting assumptions and restrictions. Notable among these are the sole use of dollars as the medium of exchange, a possibly large number of potential domains, relationships hampered by respondents' experience and age, an admittedly small number of potential contributors (including a lack of presentation rotation among the four selected), and lack of attention to other normative beliefs that significantly affect exchange behaviors among family and nonfamily members (e.g., reciprocity and generalized reciprocity). On the other hand, they raise interesting issues for understanding the role of normative beliefs in need-based contributions. The central results indicating the influence of kin closeness and race as important factors in the size of obligation (in dollars) match a long history of research findings on support exchanges.

We focus on the implications of these findings for a broadened view of how these important factors may condition family perspectives on obligations in a larger set of exchanges and caregiving. We consider the implications of age and ethnic changes in the demography of the world's populations and the implications of these changes for the private and public care of the elderly. We begin with a brief review of generational structure, relations, and population aging to set the context for understanding ethnic diversity in aging, multicultural societies. Finally, we briefly discuss data from a recently completed study of five European nations, Israel, and the United States, identifying generational differences in attitudes and orientations toward care of the elderly.

Over the next 40 years an increasingly larger proportion of the total population will be older than 65 years (Anderson, Bulatao, and Cohen 2004; Angel and Hogan 2004; Jackson and Sellers 2001; Jackson, Brown, and Antonucci 2004; National Research Council 2001; Siegel 1999). This increase is largely because of a decline in mortality rates and the large birth cohorts from immediately after World War II. Changes in demographic composition (Angel and Hogan 2004) have resulted in more extensive physical health and mental health needs among these increased numbers of older individuals (Allery et al. 2004; Skinner et al. 2001). Population aging in ethnic and racial minority groups is occurring at a faster rate than in the general population (Angel and Hogan 2004; Antonucci and Jackson 2003; Brown, Jackson, and Faison 2006). Demographic trends and projections indicate a significant rise in the mean age of minority populations and increased proportions in all age ranges above 45 years old. Growth in both black and white populations older than age 65 is substantially greater than the increase in the total population (Angel and Hogan 2004). From 1970 to 1990, the growth rate of Hispanic elderly exceeded that of both black and white non-Hispanic populations. Projections indicate this increase in the proportions and numbers of elderly will continue through 2050. Even conservative projections show that the white elderly population should increase by about 20 percent by 2030, and the black elderly population should increase by 50 percent. The largest proportionate increase of older adults is predicted to occur in the over-75 age group, at least through 2030, with a gradual tapering off through 2050. This trend will be slightly more accelerated for racial and ethnic minorities than for whites. These increases are due to changes in population fertility and to the greater material and social advantages (especially among black and some Hispanic groups) of these racial/ethnic minority cohorts in comparison to past birth cohorts. Thus, overall declining fertility in non-Hispanic white groups, increased immigration, and absolute population growth among domestic older age groups of color, will lead to large proportionate and absolute increases in all the respective populations of ethnic elders. The greatest proportionate growth over the next several decades will be among the groups over the age of 70 (Whitfield 2004a). Many of these oldest-old possess only native-language or poor English skills, educational deficiencies, few socioeconomic and social resources, and varying culturally determined behaviors, beliefs, and preferences. Older ethnic groups of color (with the exception of some Asian American groups) are poorer than their white counterparts. In addition to greater poverty and less formal educational attainment, they manifest a lower proportion of marriage for both men and women and a more unbalanced sex ratio in all age groups above the age of 65 (with the unusual exception of those over the age of 80, where black Americans have a more balanced sex ratio than whites).

The lack of material and social resources will have significant implications for how older racial and ethnic minorities seek and secure needed services and how communities and families cope with the burdens of increasingly larger proportions of older individuals. Because acculturation of these populations will not occur to the same extent or in the same manner as it has occurred among white ethnic immigrants, cultural distinctiveness in language, food selection and preparation customs, self-medication, and strong family bonds will continue to challenge health delivery systems to provide adequate geriatric care in the short and long terms. Thus, it is imperative that we understand and address how these culturally distinctive patterns of beliefs and behavior influence health status, functioning, and the quality of informal and formal care delivery and services (Antonucci, Akiyama, and Birditt 2004).

Structural Lag, Opportunities, and Family Obligation Norms

M. Riley and her colleagues (Riley 1994a, b; Riley and Loscocco 1994; Riley and Riley 1993) have for a number of years proposed that cohort succession and structural lag must be considered in models of aging and human development. Their main argument has been that as people age they encounter changing role opportunities and circumstances in society. At the intersections of lives and structures there are reciprocal influences. This interplay between individual lives and role opportunities for individuals can never be in synchrony; there must always be asynchronies. Thus, there must always be structural lags, that is, "changes in social structures that provide role opportunities and norms do not keep pace with the 20th century metamorphoses in people's lives" (Riley and Riley 1994, 17).

One of the issues only briefly touched upon in the Rileys' work on structural lag and age integration is the role of the family as an important mediator in the relationship between individual and social structure. For many ethnic and racial minorities in this country and, in fact, many countries around the world, age integration is accomplished not so much by individuals directly in their relationship to complex social structures, but instead through family systems that provide productive relationships and connections across the age span. Some of these functions have been formal, such as the assumption with age of leadership positions in complex tribal and family economic systems. Many of these role functions have been informal, involving important work within the family as counselors, helpers for the youngest and most dependent, or sources of informal work for the economic and social well-being of the family (Daatland 1990); this has certainly been true among race and ethnic minorities in the United States (Jackson et al. 2005).

Now, because of some of the structural changes that Riley and her colleagues have discussed, this formal and informal familial set of arrangements is in danger. These changes threaten to remove one important buffer and facilitator in the lives of older Americans, an insulator that has shielded them from the structural changes Riley discusses and buffered the continuing, pernicious effects of unfair, institutional treatment, especially among ethnic minorities (e.g., Jim Crow laws), that transcend the types of structural changes in employment, Social Security systems, and growth in urban areas. In fact, the continuing oppression of discrimination interacts with structural changes to make it even more difficult to cope with these changes. For example, systematic barriers to education exist for racial and ethnic and racial minorities—barriers that affect not only the aging cohort members but also their offspring (Crimmins, Hayward, and Seeman 2004). That is exactly the situation in the United States. And it is much more widespread than just education. Riley notes the following:

However, other segments of older people in future cohorts may be less advantaged than their predecessors, as, for example their lives will reflect their earlier experience with the deteriorating economic conditions of today, the rise of disadvantaged minorities, the loosening family structure, the spreading use of drugs, and the increasing proportions of younger people who are failing to meet acceptable standards of academic achievement. (Riley 1994b, 1216)

What is notable about this quote is that in every example—deteriorating economic conditions, loosening family structures, spreading use of drugs, increasing poor educational and technical training—racial and ethnic minorities are disadvantaged.

Significant improvements in the life situations of blacks (Farley 2000), particularly in health, have occurred over the past forty years (Jackson 2000). On the other hand, recent literature (Jackson 2005) documents the disproportionate negative life events and structural barriers, particularly for poor blacks, that still exist. These problems include the difficulties of single parenting, high infant mortality and morbidity, childhood diseases, poor diets, lack of preventive health care, deteriorating neighborhoods, poverty, adolescent violence, unemployment and underemployment, teen pregnancy, drug and alcohol abuse, and broken marriages (FIFAS 2004; Hayward and Heron 1999; Hummer, Benjamins, and Rogers 2004).

Health Care Delivery and Health Service Utilization

Disproportionate growth of the older segment of the population, particularly in the very old ages, will create severe cost and support burdens in the care of frail individuals. An increasingly elderly society is already placing strains on public sources of health care financing for the health needs of older people. Black and other minority older adults are more dependent than whites on government-provided health care resources because their lower earnings and job instability have made many of them ineligible for private pension plans, made it impossible for them to accumulate personal savings, and made them only eligible for reduced levels of government support. New cohorts of older racial minorities may find it increasingly difficult to meet the rising health care costs that result from greater restrictions on public programs and the increased privatization of health care delivery systems. In addition, lifestyle and cultural reasons may make institutional care less desirable.

In 1985, 5 percent of Americans older than 65 years were in nursing homes (Siegel 1999). By 2040, persons older than 85 years will constitute more than 50 percent of the demand for long-term services. By 2040, there will be 13.3 million Americans older than 85, 4 million of whom will require some type of personal assistance in daily living. These numbers could translate into a total need of 2.7 million nursing home beds. Rates of nursing home use, however, differ greatly by race and ethnic group, age, and sex (Angel and Hogan 2004). Rates are 11 times higher for men older than age 85 than for men ages 65 to 69. For women, rates are 16 times higher for those older than 85 than for women ages 65 to 69. The use of nursing homes by both sexes has increased since 1963 (Whitfield 2004a). Although blacks have used nursing homes significantly less than other race groups, they have increased their use of them over time, perhaps because of a change in the availability or quality of community services (Daatland 1990).

Researchers have proposed several reasons for elderly minorities using nursing homes less than whites, including cultural aversion, strong family and community networks, and discrimination. It seems clear, however, that minority, especially black and Hispanic, use of nursing homes is increasing (Whitfield 2004a). This increase may reflect a weakening in cultural norms, the long-term effects of economic adversity on the family, a decrease in discrimination, or a change in the availability of community supports.

Generational Structure and Obligation Norms

Research on family life and relationships indicates that the lives of family members are interdependent and that individuals continually interact with close family members (Antonucci et al. 2004; Riley and Riley 1993). At the same time, the structure of contemporary American families is clearly changing as a result of divorce, single-parent families, and increased life spans. These changes have made multigenerational family units an important factor in the lives of family members of all generations (Bengtson 2001). The traditional family, consisting of two parents and two children, with only the father employed outside the home, was once the norm but now represents only 6 percent of U.S. families (Jackson et al. 2005). On the other hand, two-earner families and single-parent households are much more common, and with increased life expectancies, grandparents can and often do play a more active role in the lives of their grandchildren (Caldwell, Antonucci, and Jackson 1998). Although older people are spending many more years as active, healthy adults, the oldest-old are the fastest growing portion of the aging population (Myers 1990). With greater age, the probability of health problems and of needing care is significantly increased.

In most cases families are accepting the increased burden of caring for their oldest-old relatives and the children of working parents. The nature and quality of these relationships have important implications for the well-being of all generations. Most close relationships are with the spouse, children, and parents; thus, maintaining positive intergenerational relationships are critical in ensuring needed help. Changing demographics, including both increased life expectancy and decreased fertility, have changed the very structure of intergenerational relationships. At the beginning of the 20th century, family structure in most societies resembled that of a pyramid, with a large base consisting of children younger than 5 years old and many fewer individuals older than 65. Treas (1995) and others (e.g., Farkas and Hogan 1995) have argued that by 2030, this pyramid will lose its base and will even out to look like a beanpole, with fairly equal numbers of individuals in each generation and with more family generations alive than there were a century ago. This scenario translates into fewer younger people available to take care of the increasing number of older people. In these circumstances the nature of intergeneration intrafamily relations will have important implications for the well-being of all family members.

Another important consideration is the average distance in age between generations. When people are marrying early and having children at relatively young ages, the average age distance between generations will be short, about 15 to 20 years, but when marriage and childbearing is delayed, the distance between generations can be much longer, about 30 to 40 years. Ethnic groups vary considerably in the average age distance between generations and in the number of children born, with some ethnic groups and immigrants having less distance between generations and more children than other ethnic groups or nonimmigrants.

These differences change the nature of the family structure can potentially change the relationship between generations. A 35-year-old grandparent has very different expectations and abilities than an 80-year-old one. Studies of intergenerational family relations indicate that families are involved in shared kinship activities, have frequent contact with each other, and are engaged in networks of mutual assistance, both within and between generations (Bengtson and Cutler 1976; Daatland 1990; Hill et al. 1970; Markides, Boldt, and Ray 1986). Rossi and Rossi (1990) report a high degree of familial proximity, interaction, and kinship exchanges among three-generation families. Both parents and grandparents reported being involved in giving and receiving aid and having a high degree of satisfaction with the amount of contact they had with kin. Roberts and Bengtson (1996) suggest that intergenerational relations remain stable over several decades and that positive relations are beneficial to family members. Specifically, levels of affection remain high for members of each generation over the years, providing positive long-term psychological benefits for both sons and daughters into adulthood. Moreover, when improvements in parent–child relationships occur, self-esteem increases (Giarrusso et al. 2001).

Changing family demographics and family structure have implications for socialization, parenting, and social support. For example, with people living longer children are more likely to have interactions with grandparents as they grow older (Uhlenberg 1996), and both aging parents and grandparents have the opportunity to provide family continuity, stability, and support (Giarrusso, Silverstein, and Bengtson 1996). Negative consequences of this phenomenon could also potentially emerge. Antonucci (1985) has suggested that people conceptualize their long-term support exchanges as a support bank, an accounting system something like a savings bank. Deposits made early (e.g., through the provision of support to others) have direct implications for withdrawals that will be available later (e.g., when support is needed). Thus, grandparents who provide child care may expect, and be more likely, to receive care from their children when they become dependent. Similarly, a lifetime of conflict-laden relationships is likely to have opposite implications when affection and care are needed by the elder.

Norms and Expectations for Family Care

The recently completed OASIS (Old Age and Autonomy: The Role of Service Systems and Intergenerational Family Solidarity) study provides data from over 1,000 respondents from several countries ($N = 6,106$ from England, Germany, Norway, Israel, and Spain) (Lowenstein and Ogg 2003) on a variety of questions about norms and expectations for care of the elderly. The 2003 National Survey of American Life provides complementary data with its 3,511 respondents, including representative samples of three major subgroups in the United States, non-Hispanic whites, African American blacks, and Caribbean blacks (Jackson et al. 2004). In this section we summarize the similarities and differences across countries and U.S. subgroups.

When respondents ages 25 and older in the OASIS countries and 18 and older in the United States were asked "should elders depend on their children for help when they need it?" more than half the respondents in all countries (with the exception of England) agreed that they should (Daatland and Herlofson 2003; Jackson et al. 2005). What is impressive is the range of responses. More than 90 percent of the American respondents agreed with this statement whereas only 41 percent of the English respondents did. People from Spain (60 percent), Norway (58 percent), Germany (55 percent), and Israel (51 percent) were about equally likely to agree with this statement.

Younger people (ages 25–49) in England and Israel reported stronger filial norms than those nations' older people (ages 75 and older). Older people in Spain and Germany, however, reported slightly stronger filial norms, whereas in Norway no age differences emerged. In the United States, younger people were consistently more likely than older people to agree that elders should depend on their children for help. Although the differences across most of the adult age groups in the European countries were not large, it is impressive because it is against self-interests that older people were much less likely to agree with this statement (Daatland and Herlofson 2003).

Contrary to expectations, men in Norway and England were more likely to agree to the filial norms than were women. There were no gender differences in Germany, Spain, Israel, or the United States.

In the United States African American blacks are more likely than Caribbean blacks and whites to endorse the concept of filial obligation (Antonucci and Jackson 2003; Jackson et al. 2005). These results reveal that there are overall differences between whites and blacks but that the differences can be further broken down for Caribbean and African American blacks. It is not clear whether history, current geographical mobility patterns, cultural variations, or socioeconomic status accounts for these differences, although it should be noted that the differences are relatively small.

Public and Private Provision of Care

Another set of issues involves who should pay for the increased need for elder care in the coming years (Lingsom 1997). Government policies appear to have the largest effects on individual attitudes and beliefs. When asked if they felt the state was either totally or mainly responsible for the care of the elderly, country differences emerged that directly paralleled the current welfare policies of that state. In the United States, which has the poorest public health care coverage of the surveyed countries, only 23 percent of the population felt that providing financial support to needy elders was the responsibility of the state. By contrast, fully 79 percent of the respondents from Norway, which provides considerable welfare benefits, agreed with this statement. Israel (50 percent) and Spain (40 percent) were in relative agreement, whereas England (35 percent) and Germany (34 percent) were the least likely to agree. In the United States, an examination of age differences indicated that younger people (ages 18–34) were least likely to agree with this statement, whereas older age groups were more likely to agree with this statement (range: 26–31 percent). Older people in all of the European countries except Spain generally agreed that the state should be responsible for the needs of their elders. In the United States, 22 percent of whites agreed that the state should provide for the financial needs of the elderly, whereas African Americans and Caribbean blacks were slightly more likely to agree with this statement (29 and 30 percent, respectively). There were hardly any gender differences in response to this question in the United States. Across the European countries there were few gender differences; women were more likely than men to endorse the responsibility of the government in Norway, while the reverse was true in Spain.

When asked who should pay for the increased costs in the years ahead for the care of the elderly, Americans were most likely to say the private sector or volunteers should pay (66 percent) but were also likely to endorse the need for higher taxes (50 percent). They were somewhat less likely to feel that adult children should pay (35 percent) and least likely to feel that elderly users should pay (12 percent). Germans were less likely to feel that the private sector or volunteers should pay for the increased cost (29 percent), and the Spaniards (19 percent), Norwegians and Israelis (both 16 percent), and English (15 percent) were least likely to agree. On raising taxes as the best way to pay for increased needs and costs of the elderly, the British were even more likely than Americans to agree with this statement (75 percent vs. 50 percent); respondents from the other four countries were in considerably less agreement (Norway, 29 percent; Israel, 22 percent; Spain, 20 percent; and Germany, 15 percent). A great many British respondents (43 percent) felt that it was the adult children's financial responsibility, although this was much less true in Germany (16 percent), Spain (14 percent), Israel (13 percent), and Norway (9 percent). Americans were intermediate in their beliefs that the elder user should be responsible for his or her care, with Germans (21 percent), Norwegians (17 percent), and English (16 percent) agreeing with this policy, but Israelis (8 percent) and Spaniards (7 percent) somewhat less likely to agree.

Finally, age differences were not as great as one might have predicted. Younger people in the United States agreed (73 percent) that the private sector and volunteers should be responsible, but older people were much less likely to feel this way (58 percent). The middle-aged groups were less likely than younger people but more likely than older people to agree with this statement (ages 35–49, 68 percent agree; ages 50–64, 61 percent agree). Older and younger people were about equally likely (47 percent) to agree that collecting higher taxes was the way to pay for this expense, with middle-aged people slightly more likely to agree with this point of view. Approximately one-third of the people in each age group felt that the adult children should pay for the care of their elders, while very few people felt that older people should be required to pay—people over 65 were considerably more likely to feel they should (19 percent) than middle-aged and younger people (10 to 14 percent). In the United States there were relatively few race or gender differences (Jackson, Brown, and Antonucci 2004).

Summary and Conclusions

Based upon the well-documented changes in population aging, the focus of this chapter was to consider how well the needs of an increasingly older population will be met and to consider the degree to which there are national differences (Antonucci et al. 2004) and, in the United States, how opinions on elder care might be affected by race, ethnicity, and cultural differences (Mendes de Leon and Glass 2004; Whitfield and Hayward 2003). As we consider population data, it is critical to recognize the role that race, ethnicity, and culture will play in the aging experience of older people. Long-standing ethnic diversity and recent immigration patterns indicate that special attention needs to be paid to these differences (Anderson et al. 2004). Data from long-running surveys of European Publics (the Euro-barometer) trend studies suggest that Europeans have some serious concerns about the immigration patterns they have been experiencing (Jackson and Antonucci 2006). On the other hand, OASIS data from Europe indicate that most young people expect and plan to provide care to their aging relatives, which is above and beyond the expectations of older people themselves (Lowenstein and Ogg 2003).

We suggest that these two bodies of data (Eurobarometer and OASIS) provide an appropriate backdrop for approaching formal and informal provision of assistance in the future. Although there are and will continue to be important ethnic and cultural differences, there appear to be some universal beliefs and norms about older age care (Antonucci et al. 2004). However, these beliefs are clearly affected to some degree by the policies and the immigration experiences of the countries concerned. At the same time, although people worry about their own resources, they are almost unanimous in their belief that all people should have the same rights and privileges. Clearly, as the findings in chapter 13 by Nock, Kingston, and Holian suggest, this is an area of paradox and contradiction.

There are some universal similarities (e.g., younger people having higher expectations of care for their elders than the elders themselves), and it is clear that government policies fundamentally influence these attitudes (Daatland and Herlofson 2003; Jackson et al. 2005; Lowenstein and Ogg 2003). We should take advantage of the potential to influence attitudes and behaviors, recognizing that we must not only attend to the needs of our elders but also shape the views of all of age groups to create societies for all ages that care for all of its current and future citizens (Jackson 2000).

REFERENCES

Allery, Alan J., Maria P. Aranda, Peggye Dilworth-Anderson, Martin Guerrero, Mary N. Haan, Hugh Hendrie, Ladson Hinton, et al. 2004. "Alzheimer's Disease and Communities of Color." In *Closing the Gap: Improving the Health of Minority Elders in the New Millennium,* edited by Keith E. Whitfield (81–86). Washington, DC: The Gerontological Society of America.

Anderson, Norman B., Randy A. Bulatao, and Barney Cohen, eds. 2004. *Critical Perspectives on Racial and Ethnic Differences in Health in Late Life.* Washington, DC: The National Academies Press.

Angel, Jacqueline L., and Dennis P. Hogan. 2004. "Population Aging and Diversity in a New Era." In *Closing the Gap: Improving the Health of Minority Elders in the New Millennium,* edited by Keith E. Whitfield (1–12). Washington, DC: The Gerontological Society of America.

Antonucci, Toni C. 1985. "Personal Characteristics, Social Support, and Social Behavior." In *Handbook of Aging and the Social Sciences,* 2nd ed., edited by R. H. Binstock and E. Shanas (94–128). New York: Van Nostrand Reinhold.

Antonucci, Toni C., and James S. Jackson. 2003. "Ethnic and Cultural Differences in Intergenerational Social Support." In *Global Aging and Challenges to Families, Aging, and Social Support,* edited by Vern L. Bengtson and Ariela Lowenstein (355–70). New York: Aldine de Gruyter Publishing Co.

Antonucci, Toni C., Hiroko Akiyama, and Kira Birditt. 2004. "Intergenerational Exchange in the United States and Japan." *Annual Review of Gerontology and Geriatrics* 24:224–48.

Bengtson, Vern L. 2001. "Beyond the Nuclear Family: The Increasing Importance of Multigenerational Bonds (The Burgess Award Lecture)." *Journal of Marriage and the Family* 63:1–16.

Bengtson, Vern L., and Neal E. Cutler. 1976. "Generations and Inter-Generational Relations: Perspectives on Age-Groups and Social Change." In *The Handbook of Aging and the Social Sciences,* edited by Robert H. Binstock and Ethel Shanas (130–59). New York: Van Nostrand Reinhold.

Brown, Edna, James S. Jackson, and Nakesha Faison. 2006. "The Work and Retirement Experiences of Aging Black Americans." In *The Crown of Life: Dynamics of the Early Postretirement Period,* edited by Jacquelyn B. James and Paul Wink (39–60). New York: Springer Publishing Company.

Caldwell, Cleopatra H., Toni C. Antonucci, and James S. Jackson. 1998. "Supportive/Conflictual Family Relations and Depressive Symptomatology: Teenage Mother and Grandmother Perspectives." *Family Relations: Interdisciplinary Journal of Applied Family Studies* 47(4): 395–402.

Crimmins, Elaine M., Mark D. Hayward, and Teresa E. Seeman. 2004. "Race/Ethnicity, Socioeconomic Status, and Health." In *Critical Perspectives on Racial and Ethnic Differences in Health in Late Life,* edited by Norman B. Anderson, Randy A. Bulatao, and Barney Cohen (310–52). Washington, DC: The National Academies Press.

Daatland, Svein O. 1990. "What Are Families For? On Family Solidarity and Preferences for Help." *Ageing and Society* 1:1–15.

Daatland, Svein O., and Katharina Herlofson. 2003. "Norms and Ideals about Elder Care." In *OASIS—Old Age and Autonomy: The Role of Service Systems and Intergenerational Family Solidarity. Final Report,* edited by Ariela Lowenstein and James Ogg (127–64). Haifa, Israel: The University of Haifa, Center for Research and Study of Aging.

Farkas, James, and Dennis Hogan. 1995. "The Demography of Changing Intergenerational Relationships." In *Adult Intergenerational Relations: Effects of Societal Change,* edited by James Farkas and Dennis Hogan (1–29). New York: Springer Publishing Co.

Farley, Reynolds. 2000. "Demographic, Economic, and Social Trends in a Multicultural America." In *New Directions: African Americans in a Diversifying Nation,* edited by James S. Jackson (11–44). Washington, DC: National Policy Association.

Federal Interagency Forum on Aging-Related Statistics. 2004. *Older Americans 2004: Key Indicators on Well-Being.* Washington, DC: U.S. Government Printing Office.

FIFAS. See Federal Interagency Forum on Aging-Related Statistics.

Giarrusso, Roseann, Merril Silverstein, and Vern L. Bengtson. 1996. "Family Complexity and the Grandparent Role." *Generations* 22(1): 17–23.

Giarrusso, Roseann, Du Feng, Merril Silverstein, and Vern L. Bengtson. 2001. "Grandparent–Adult Grandchild Affection and Consensus: Cross-Generational and Cross-Ethnic Comparisons." *Journal of Family Issues* 22(4): 456–77.

Hayward, Mark D., and Melonie Heron. 1999. "Racial Inequality in Active Life among Adult Americans." *Demography* 36(1): 77–91.

Hill, Robert, Neal Foote, James Aldous, Robert Carlson, and Robert MacDonald. 1970. *Family Development in Three Generations.* Cambridge, MA: Schenkman.

Hummer, Robert A., Maureen R. Benjamins, and Richard G. Rogers. 2004. "Racial and Ethnic Disparities in Health and Mortality among the U.S. Elderly Population." In *Critical Perspectives on Racial and Ethnic Differences in Health in Late Life,* edited by Norman B. Anderson, Randy A. Bulatao, and Barney Cohen (53–94). Washington, DC: The National Academies Press.

Jackson, James S., ed. 2000. *New Directions: African Americans in a Diversifying Nation.* Washington, DC: National Policy Association.

Jackson, James S., and Toni C. Antonucci. 2006. "Physical and Mental Health Consequences of Aging in Place and Aging out of Place among Black Caribbean Immigrants." *Research in Human Development* 2(4): 229–44.

Jackson, James S., and Sherrill L. Sellers. 2001. "Health and the Elderly." In *Health Issues in the Black Community,* 2nd ed., edited by Ronald L. Braithwaite and Sandra E. Taylor (81–96). San Francisco: Jossey-Bass.

Jackson, James S., Edna Brown, and Toni C. Antonucci. 2004. "A Cultural Lens on Biopsychosocial Models of Aging." In *Recent Advances in Psychology and Aging,* edited by Paul T. Costa and Ilene C. Siegler (221–41). Amsterdam: Elsevier B. V.

Jackson, James S., Edna Brown, Toni C. Antonucci, and S. O. Daatland. 2005. "Ethnic Diversity in Aging, Multi-Cultural Societies." In *The Cambridge Handbook of Age and Ageing,* edited by Malcolm Johnson, Vern L. Bengston, Peter G. Coleman, and Thomas B. L. Kirkwood (476–81). Cambridge: Cambridge University Press.

Jackson, James S., Myriam Torres, Cleopatra H. Caldwell, Harold W. Neighbors, Randy M. Nesse, Robert J. Taylor, Steven J. Trierweiler, and David R. Williams. 2004. "The National Survey of American Life: A Study of Racial, Ethnic, and Cultural Influences on Mental Disorders and Mental Health." *International Journal of Methods in Psychiatric Research* 13(4): 196–207.

Jackson, Pamela B. 2005. "Health Inequalities among Minority Populations." *Journal of Gerontology: Social Sciences* 60B(S2): 63–67.

Lingsom, Susan. 1997. *The Substitution Issue. Care Policies and Their Consequences for Family Care.* NOVA rapport 6/97. Oslo, Norway: NOVA, Norwegian Social Research.

Lowenstein, Ariela, and James Ogg, eds. 2003. *OASIS—Old Age and Autonomy: The Role of Service Systems and Intergenerational Family Solidarity. Final Report.* Haifa, Israel: The University of Haifa, Center for Research and Study of Aging.

Markides, Kyriakos S., Joanne S. Boldt, and Laura A. Ray. 1986. "Sources of Helping and Intergenerational Solidarity: A Three Generations Study of Mexican Americans." *Journal of Gerontology* 41:506–11.

Mendes de Leon, Carlos F., and Thomas A. Glass. 2004. "The Role of Social and Personal Resources in Ethnic Disparities in Late-Life Health." In *Critical Perspectives on Racial and Ethnic Differences in Health in Late Life,* edited by Norman B. Anderson, Randy A. Bulatao, and Barney Cohen (353–405). Washington, DC: The National Academies Press.

Myers, George C. 1990. "Demography of Aging." In *Handbook of Aging and the Social Sciences,* 3rd ed., edited by Robert H. Binstock and Linda K. George (19–44). San Diego: Academic Press.

National Research Council. 2001. *Preparing for an Aging World: The Case for Cross-National Research.* Washington, DC: National Academy Press.

Riley, Matilda W. 1994a. "Aging and Society: Past, Present, and Future." *The Gerontologist* 34:436–46.

———. 1994b. "Changing Lives and Changing Social Structures: Common Concerns of Social Science and Public Health." *American Journal of Public Health* 84:1214–17.

Riley, Matilda W., and Karen A. Loscocco. 1994. "The Changing Structure of Work Opportunities: Toward an Age Integrated Society." In *Aging and the Quality of Life,* edited by Ronald P. Abeles, Helen C. Gift, and Marcia G. Orey (235–52). New York: Springer Publishing.

Riley, Matilda W., and John W. Riley. 1993. "Connections: Kin and Cohort." In *The Changing Contract across Nations,* edited by Vern L. Bengtson and William A. Achenbaum (169–89). New York: Aldine de Gruyter.

Riley, Matilda W., and John W. Riley Jr. 1994. "Age Integration and the Lives of Older People." *The Gerontologist* 34:110–15.

Roberts, Robert E. L., and Vern L. Bengtson. 1996. "Affective Ties to Parents in Early Adulthood and Self-Esteem across 20 Years." *Social Psychology Quarterly* 59(1): 96–106.

Rossi, Alice S., and Peter H. Rossi. 1990. *Of Human Bonding: Parent–Child Relations across the Life Course.* New York: Aldine de Gruyter.

Siegel, Jay S. 1999. "Demographic Introduction to Racial/Hispanic Elderly Populations." In *Full-Color Aging: Facts, Goals, and Recommendations for America's Diverse Elders,* edited by Toni P. Miles (1–20). Washington, DC: The Gerontological Society of America.

Skinner, John H., Jeanne A. Teresi, Dennis Holmes, Sidney M. Stahl, and Anita L. Stewart, eds. 2001. *Measurement in Older Populations.* New York: Springer Publishing.

Treas, Judith. 1995. "Older Americans in the 1990s and Beyond." *Population Bulletin* 50:2–46.

Uhlenberg, Peter. 1996. "Mortality Decline in the Twentieth Century and Supply of Kin over the Life Course." *The Gerontologist* 38:681–85.

Whitfield, Keith E. 2004a. *Closing the Gap: Improving the Health of Minority Elders in the New Millennium.* Washington, DC: The Gerontological Society of America.

———. 2004b. "Sources of Individual Differences in Indices of Health Disparities among Older African Americans." *Phylon* 50(1–2): 145–59.

Whitfield, Keith E., and Mark Hayward. 2003. "The Landscape of Health Disparities among Older Adults." *Public Policy and Aging Report* 13(3): 1–7.

15

Between the Motion and the Act

Psychological Perspectives on the Distribution of Obligations

Adam Davey

W hat can you say about the study that sets out to do nearly everything? At a minimum, this is an extremely ambitious piece of research. In chapter 13 on the distribution of obligations, Nock, Kingston, and Holian consider a randomly selected subset of conditions from a factorial study with six factors representing a grand total of more than 878,000 different conditions. It is certainly possible that the authors are capable of understanding all of these conditions in their nuanced glory. I confess, however, that I am not. As such, I wish that the authors had considered a smaller number of potential conditions in fuller detail. Partly as a result, I have been yearning for some synthesis that can help with the process of data reduction. For me, one of the strategies to better understand a phenomenon begins with the process of focusing on what it is not.

In the sections that follow, I present some considerations derived primarily from a psychological perspective on caring and exchange within and across generations as they apply to the chapter by Nock, Kingston, and Holian. In the opening section, I present some considerations from a theoretical standpoint. The second section considers the study and its methodology. Subsequent sections address issues of policy and applications of this work, as they can enhance our knowledge base and point out some key limitations.

Between the Idea and the Reality

Organization of Support Networks

The idea that obligations are graded on the basis of relationship distance is not a new one. Nor does it derive primarily from Rossi and Rossi's (1990) seminal work, which in turn drew heavily from the earlier concepts and measures developed by Bengtson and colleagues (e.g., Mangen, Bengtson, and Landry 1988). Although we can certainly trace the origins back considerably earlier, Cantor's (1975) work strongly established relationship differences in preferred sources of assistance.

Cantor's hierarchical compensatory model suggested that social relationships formed the basis of preferences for receipt of care; elderly individuals would prefer to be cared for first by their spouse, then children, other family members, friends, and lastly, formal caregivers. Each group successively provides assistance when a preferred source of care is either not available or unable to meet the needs of the care recipient. This model assumes the substitutability of one service for another, but with a preferred ordering. Although the literature is consistent about individuals' preferences for caregivers, there is little evidence to support the compensatory nature of the informal care network (Denton 1997; Penning 1990).

I raise this issue primarily for two reasons. First, Cantor's work emphasized the hierarchical nature of these obligations. From her theoretical vantage point, it was the availability or absence of a particular relationship that colors and contextualizes the nature of an obligation. In this way, the obligation may make little sense without knowing what other sources of assistance may be available to an individual. This issue is important for a second reason as well. For more than thirty years, we have known that these attitudes and preferences are insufficient to explain actual involvement in a care network. It would be very helpful if Nock, Kingston, and Holian had focused on this context for each of the needs that they investigate, although it is not clear whether their data are sufficient to permit them to explore this avenue more fully. An excellent pair of studies by Lawrence et al. (2002) use a scenario approach to consider many of these aspects of care for parents.

Theory of Planned Behavior

No work can or should attempt to tackle every aspect of a problem. As noted, Nock, Kingston, and Holian attempt to tackle more aspects than most. However, the authors recognize early one very important component on the distribution of obligations that they cannot address. Specifically, they note that "We did not examine the correspondence between what people say should be done and what they actually do when confronted with a situation. We believe, as do most sociologists, that social norms influence collective behaviors" (281). Before letting the authors off of the hook with their well-placed qualifier, and with sincere apologies to T. S. Eliot, I would like to step for a moment into (out of?) the shadow between the idea and the reality.

Ajzen and Fishbein (1977) observed that individuals very often behave in a manner that is inconsistent with their attitudes. This is often true even for attitudes that an individual holds very strongly. Many people who smoke believe (know) that it is causes health problems; many people who are very religious do not attend religious services regularly; many people who believe that family has the primary responsibility to provide aid in the face of health problems, job loss, or homelessness simply do not do so. There are a variety of reasons for this discrepancy, and it turns out that a variety of factors can interrupt the association between beliefs and behaviors. Over their years of inquiry, Ajzen and Fishbein (2005) have elaborated upon their model of planned behavior to include a variety of concepts. In the process, they have made some progress toward increasing the power to predict actual behaviors.

Focusing only on the portion of their theory of planned behavior that pertains to norms highlights some of the extensions that are necessary before the results of a study can be useful for predicting actual behaviors. Most fundamentally, *normative beliefs* represent perceived behavioral expectations. What do we think is expected of us (and others) in a particular context or situation? In turn, *subjective norms* derive from the perceived pressure to comply with such norms. They represent the sum of all of our normative beliefs, weighted by their salience. Norms, together with *attitudes* and *perceived behavioral control* jointly contribute to our intentions, our readiness to actually engage in a *behavior*. Finally, tempering the indirect association between perceived control and behavior is our *actual level of control,* which is a complex amalgam of our actual skills, resources, and abilities. Although I tend to agree with Nock, Kingston, and Holian that social norms influence collective behaviors, the theory of planned behavior still leaves plenty of room for future work to consider what that influence ultimately looks like.

Diffusion of Responsibility

In situations where responsibility for a particular activity is not clearly assigned, there exists the possibility of diffusion of responsibility. From a social psychological perspective, for this to occur, a group has to have a critical mass, and it is not at all clear what the critical mass of potential sources of support are in the context of this study. However, the introduction of both government and charities suggests that the network can be quite large indeed.

One very important potential consequence of obligations being distributed is that individuals may be more likely to fall through the cracks with no single entity feeling responsibility. In situations where social norms are very clear about these obligations, it would seem likely that relatively few individuals would have their needs unmet. If society makes it clear that the eldest son (or more accurately, his wife) bears this responsibility then there will be the possibility of sanctions for going against this established pattern of behavior. Although family is almost always the most common source of help for older adults, many Scandinavian countries have established services for when family is not available (or for tasks for which family is not primarily responsible). On the other hand, when obligations are diffuse or distributed, we might expect that many more individuals would be at risk for having no one providing assistance. In other words, I would like to raise the possibility that the more parties are somewhat responsible, the less any one party is ultimately responsible.

Social Structural Considerations

The model includes social location variables but could integrate them more fully into the analysis. The authors placed certain constraints on the factorial nature of their design by eliminating some conditions that seemed unlikely or improbable. However, social structural considerations constrain the likelihood of some opportunities to provide assistance in other ways as well. Parent care, for example, is most often associated with women, both daughters and daughters-in-law. This association may be true for a number of reasons.

Whereas most research on caregiving has focused on a primary caregiver, we sought to elaborate on the nature of care networks with our recent research. Some of our recent work has used data from the University of

Michigan Health and Retirement Study to examine patterns of parent care by siblings. We have also used the same data source to consider the situation where spouses share providing household help (Davey and Szinovacz 2008) or assistance with activities of daily living (Szinovacz and Davey 2008) for a parent or parent-in-law.

On the one hand, there are social norms to provide assistance to one's own parents. On the other hand, there are also norms for same-sex assistance. Because women tend to outlive men and because women tend to marry men who are older than they are, social structural considerations play out such that married women are more likely than married men to have living parents. If women have living parents-in-law, they are likely to be older than their husbands' parents-in-law. In our research, we find that the effects of lineage norms are much stronger than the gender norms. Wives do provide more assistance overall. However, husbands actually provide the majority of assistance to their own parents (as reported by their wives). The authors made some strong first steps toward unraveling the importance of social demographic variables in their models, and I encourage them to pursue this thinking further in subsequent work.

Between the Motion and the Act

Several aspects of Nock, Kingston, and Holian's methodology caught my attention. They include consideration of how the outcome variable was treated, decisions about parameterization of the statistical models, presentation of the results, and some potential considerations for the design they used.

As illustrated in figure 13.1, the authors have designed a study with a complex set of outcomes. The entire responsibility for assistance in a particular scenario can be divided up and attributed to oneself, family, charities, government, or unmet need, which the authors define as an individual's rightful responsibility. They have chosen to handle the non-independence of norms for each form of assistance by omitting one category (unmet need) and modeling the remainder as a level-1 outcome within a multilevel framework. As long as there is at least some attribution to unmet need, the remaining four outcomes need not be completely collinear. This is certainly one way to account for the nonindependence of their results, but I am not convinced that it is the most informative way for them to treat their data.

Alternative operationalizations that seem to hold considerable potential might include the following. First, with their emphasis on diversity across relationships, it seems as though focusing on the proportion of needs that are unmet or attributable to the individuals themselves might be of interest. Simplification of the outcome to this level of analysis, while still providing censored data at the high and low extremes, might bring the opportunity to consider variability across two dimensions simultaneously (e.g., relationship and type of need). Alternatively, emphasis on the most central consideration, proportion of responsibility attributable to the respondent, provides a similar initial opportunity to see how these norms play out across the range of their complex design. Finally, construction of a theoretically relevant mutually exclusive set of patterns can serve to capture some of the relevant influences between the outcome categories themselves.

Aside from the fact that they necessarily sum to 100 percent, what are the implications of one's own responsibility for other likely sources of support? Would individuals rather provide assistance in concert with government or charitable sources? Likewise, in situations where individuals are largely removed from responsibility, does responsibility reside with a single institution or multiple institutions? Some information is certainly lost through each of the decisions but may be justified by the opportunity to simplify the results and their presentation.

The authors also make several decisions about the parameterization of their models that may benefit from a more detailed presentation. Fuller explanation of which levels of analysis include or exclude an intercept term, for example (and why), can help guide the reader through the authors' decisionmaking process. Similarly, fuller explanation of which of the model effects are treated as fixed and which are treated as random can help us to see what is being estimated and how.

In the presentation of their findings, the authors emphasize the dimension of relationship distance. Although this is certainly an appropriate decision for a symposium on family issues, the type of need being considered is equally interesting. We turn to different individuals for different things. If our spouse is about to become homeless (not a situation considered in this study), then we are likely about to become homeless as well. Providing money to bail them out is probably not an option. Presentation of the findings as a function of both need and relationship has the potential to be fairly illuminating, because not all needs are created equal.

It seems almost unfair to regard them as "limitations," but the implications of several aspects of the design are worthy of discussion. First, the authors make the very sensible decision to focus on money as the outcome. Given this, however, the implications for time (and thus gender, income, etc.) may not be done full justice. Fuller consideration of the aspects of these scenarios for which money does not substitute may be useful. Second, out of necessity each participant completed 19 different scenarios, suggesting that each participant provided norms for the same need under an average of five different conditions. Exposure to so many different experimental conditions suggests that participants would be able to extract at least some notion of the relevant dimensions of this study. For this reason, the authors should address the potential threats to validity introduced by this within-subjects design.

Between the Conception and the Creation

There are several potential implications and practical extensions of this work. In this study, the authors focus primarily on a set of fairly acute needs. As a result, their findings are likely to capture aspects of obligations that surround the onset and activation of assistance. At the same time, however, many family needs may be becoming increasingly chronic in nature. What are one's obligations to *continue* providing assistance? To what extent do one's past behaviors commit an individual to continue providing assistance, and to what extent do they relieve an individual of further responsibility?

Another important consideration is that, as evidenced by figure 13.2, the chapter adopts a relatively monolithic and normative approach to obligations. Social norms are likely to be more nuanced and are likely to require a more pluralistic treatment than the authors detail. There is unlikely to be a single set of norms on obligations to children or parents-in-law. And it is likely to vary as a function of a number of social demographic characteristics. If there is some way for the authors to develop this perspective more fully in this or future research, it is likely to have greater applicability to the scenarios families actually face.

Between the Emotion and the Response

To me, one of the most interesting aspects of the chapter was the apparent comfort with relatively large levels of unmet need. Interpreted as the extent of an individual's own legitimate responsibility, the idea of unmet need makes sense. In practical terms, however, it translates into help an individual needs but will not receive. Further, the scenarios make it clear that the individual has no resources of his or her own to meet these needs. Unpacking the aspect of this model that is labeled as unmet need seems to warrant further consideration to understand how individuals make sense of this component. There may also be room for substantial cohort differences in this aspect of the distribution of obligations. Baby boomers, for example, may be more comfortable with their parents' "legitimate responsibilities" as unmet need than with their own future responsibilities.

NOTE

This work was partially supported by a grant (R01AG024045) from the National Institute on Aging to Maximiliane E. Szinovacz and Adam Davey.

REFERENCES

Ajzen, Icek, and Morris Fishbein. 1977. "Attitude-Behavior Relations: A Theoretical Analysis and Review of Empirical Research." *Psychological Bulletin* 84:888–918.

———. 2005. "The Influence of Attitudes on Behavior." In *The Handbook of Attitudes*, edited by David Albarracín, Bruce T. Johnson, and Mark P. Zanna (173–221). Mahwah, NJ: Lawrence Erlbaum Associates.

Cantor, Marjorie H. 1975. "Life Space and the Social Support System of the Inner City Elderly of New York." *Gerontologist* 15(1): 23–27.

Davey, Adam, and Maximiliane E. Szinovacz. 2008. "Division of Care among Adult Children." In *Caregiving Contexts: Cultural, Familial, and Societal Implications*, edited by Adam Davey and Maximiliane E. Szinovacz (133–59). New York: Springer.

Denton, Margaret. 1997. "The Linkages between Informal and Formal Care of the Elderly." *Canadian Journal on Aging* 16(1): 30–50.

Lawrence, Jeanette A., Jacqueline J. Goodnow, Kerry Woods, and Gery Karantzas. 2002. "Distributions of Caregiving Tasks Among Family Members: The Place of Gender and Availability." *Journal of Family Psychology* 16(4): 493–509.

Mangen, David J., Vern L. Bengtson, and Pierre H. Landry. 1988. *Measurement of Intergenerational Relations*. Thousand Oaks, CA: Sage.

Penning, Margaret. 1990. "Receipt of Assistance by Elderly People: Hierarchical Selection and Task Specificity." *Gerontologist* 30: 220–27.

Rossi, Alice S., and Peter H. Rossi. 1990. *On Human Bonding: Parent-Child Relations across the Life Course*. New York: Aldine de Gruyter.

Szinovacz, Maximiliane E., and Adam Davey. 2008. "Division of Parent Care between Spouses: Variations by Kin Relationship." *Ageing and Society*.

16

Interpreting Norms of Obligation as Planners' Preferences for Distributional Justice

A Formal Economic Model

Robert J. Willis

Chapter 13, by Steven L. Nock, Paul W. Kingston, and Laura M. Holian, is extremely interesting. It presents evidence on the distribution of economic obligations that Americans (or at least citizens of Richmond, Virginia) feel that they, together with other individuals and institutions, have in helping to solve personal problems of people who have exhausted their resources. The data are from a survey about hypothetical individuals facing various problems. The survey listed the cost to fix each problem. Each respondent was asked to specify how much money he or she *should* contribute to solve the problem and how much relatives of the individual, churches and charities, and the government *should* contribute. These amounts came from respondents filling in pie charts that initially showed 100 percent unmet needs for the hypothetical person in need. The respondent could leave some residual unmet need, which the authors would interpret as the respondent's view of how much the needy person should cover himself. A factorial design of the type pioneered by Peter Rossi and Steven Nock generated survey responses from each respondent to 19 vignettes with randomly varied covariates, permitting a rich statistical analysis using hierarchical linear models of the distribution and determinants of obligations in the population.

Nock et al. interpret the responses as measures of an individual's views of his or her personal obligations toward others and how these obligations should be shared among individuals and institutions in society. When averaged across individuals, they interpret the results as reflecting or mapping social norms about how people or institutions should behave. Although they stress their belief that there is a distribution of norms of obligation across society, they also note that when a sufficient number of individuals within a group deviates from a norm, it ceases to be a norm. In addition, they are ambivalent about the connection between these social norms and actual behavior. They explicitly deny any claims that what people say they should do is a good predictor of what they will do. However, this denial is immediately followed by an expression of their belief—in solidarity with other sociologists—that "social norms influence collective behaviors."

The methods, data, and empirical analysis in chapter 13 are both innovative and well executed. My comments are primarily directed toward fitting the authors' approach into a theoretical framework that is familiar to economists in hopes of suggesting some interesting extensions of their approach in future work. One focus is on the relationship between norms and behavior. I develop a simple model from economics in which an individual's behavior depends on the interaction of his preferences and the constraints he faces. Following the literature on altruism introduced by Becker (1974, 1981), an individual's total utility depends not only on the utility he derives from his own consumption, but also on the welfare of those he cares about. In a simple case, this altruistic utility function is simply the weighted sum of the utilities of everyone the individual cares about, where the weights are "altruism parameters" that measure the rate at which an individual is willing to give up utility from his own consumption to raise the welfare of another. I hypothesize that these altruism parameters might be the underlying source of obligations. Depending on the institutional setting, actual behavior may or may not be directly related to these parameters. After presenting the model, I suggest that it would be interesting to extend the vignette methodology to confront survey respondents with variations in the institutional setting in which they make contributions. Data from this extension could be used both to identify the altruism parameters and to explore how these parameters relate to behavior.

Altruistic Preferences and Obligations

Assume that person A is the survey respondent (or "reporter"). Person B is the vignette's hypothetical individual with characteristics (e.g., relationship to R, the likelihood of repaying) and a problem. To avoid notational clutter, I will not subscript any variables with indicators of the characteristics of a specific vignette but will bring up differences across vignettes when relevant.

Assume that A may be altruistic toward B in the sense introduced by Becker (1974, 1981). Specifically, assume that A's total utility, denoted by V_A, is the sum of the utility he obtains from his own consumption, $U_A(C_A)$, and B's utility, U_B, weighted by an altruism parameter, α, which measures the degree of A's altruism toward B, where $\alpha = 0$ if there is no altruistic connection between A and B and $0 < \alpha < 1$ measures the strength of the connection if A is altruistic. Thus, A's utility function is

(1) $V_A = U_A(C_A) + \alpha U_B$

Note that α is likely to vary according to the biological relationship between A and B and could vary for other reasons, too. For example, altruism might depend on proximity, on B's personal qualities, and so on. However, for simplicity and parsimony, I will assume that α only varies with biological relationship.

In chapter 13, an individual respondent has an equal chance of being asked about helping a person who has any one of 14 different degrees of relationship to him, ranging from a child or parent to other kin and unrelated persons such as friends, coworkers, or strangers. Taken together, people in these categories would include the entire population of the United States.[1] The total utility of person A, taking into account all of these people may be written as

(2) $V_A = U_A(C_A) + \sum_{j=1}^{14} \alpha_j N_j U_j$

where α_j is the altruism parameter for a person in the jth relationship category and N_j is the number of such people. Intuitively, the α_j are likely to decline rapidly as the relationship distance increases and people in that category become more numerous.[2] On the hypothesis that the altruism parameters are indicators of obligation, such a pattern would be consistent with the empirical findings of Nock et al.

A Two-Person Model

Before returning to a preference function covering all relationships such as equation (2), I will consider a two-person model involving an altruistic person A and a needy person B to explore the relationship between norms of obligation and behavior.

A two-person model provides a convenient point of departure in thinking about how vignettes about obligations might be interpreted within the economists' model of altruism. Following chapter 13, let us assume that B suffers from a particular problem that can be solved for a given price or expenditure, P.

First, suppose B must confront the problem using only his own resources, given by income, Y_B. If no resources are expended to deal with his problem, B spends all of his income on consumption, that is, $C_B = Y_B$, so that his utility is

$$(3) \quad U^B\left(Y_B, problem\right) = U^B(Y_B) - \phi,$$

where ϕ measures the psychic cost or disutility caused by the problem. In the vignettes, variation in the type of problem and its severity are meant to induce variation in ϕ, and P is varied independently. If B chooses pay the cost to solve the problem, his consumption would be $C_B = Y_B - P$ and his utility would be

$$(4) \quad U^B\left(Y_B - P, \text{ no problem}\right) = U^B(Y_B - P).$$

B will decide to solve the problem or live with it (in some vignettes, risking death) depending on which choice yields the highest utility. Clearly, it would be infeasible for B to solve the problem if his income is lower than the cost of solving the problem. But even if it is feasible, B may choose to not to solve the problem on his own because to do so would reduce his consumption to an unacceptably low level. Conversely, as his income increases, the marginal utility of consumption falls and, at some level of income, B will choose to solve the problem on his own.

Let $C_B^* = Y_B^* - P$ denote the level of consumption at which B would be indifferent between solving the problem or leaving it unsolved, where Y_B^* is the minimum level of income B requires to solve the problem on his own. These threshold values for consumption and income are defined implicitly by the indifference relation given by $U^B(Y_B^* - P) = U^B(Y_B^*) - \phi$. This threshold occurs when $\phi = U^B(Y_B^*) - U^B(Y_B^* - P)$, which is when the disutility caused by the problem is equal to the disutility of the reduction in consumption caused by paying the costs of solving the problem.

Person A has an income of Y_A, which he may divide between his own consumption, C_A, and a transfer to B, denoted by T_{AB}. I will assume that B takes as given whatever transfer he receives from A and then decides, given his total resources of $Y_B + T_{AB}$, whether or not to spend P dollars to solve the problem. A's decision is to choose whether and how much to transfer to B. He chooses the value of T_{AB} that maximizes his utility:

(5) $V_A = U_A(Y_A - T_{AB}) + \alpha\max\left[U_B(Y_B + T_{ab} - P), U_B(Y_B + T_{ab}) - \phi\right].$

For analyzing the vignettes, the focus is on the conditions under which A's transfer is both needed to solve the problem and will be sufficient to do so. As discussed above, A's transfer is needed if B is potentially willing to solve the problem (i.e., $\phi \leq U^B(Y_B^*) - U^B(Y_B^* - P)$) but does not have sufficient resources to do so on his own (i.e., $Y_B < Y_B^*$). Assuming this to be the case, A's transfer will be sufficient if its magnitude is at least $T_{AB}^* = Y_B^* - Y_B$. A will choose to make a transfer at least this large if the marginal value of a dollar spent on transfers, evaluated at $T_{AB} = T_{AB}^*$, is positive; that is, if

(6) $\dfrac{dV_A}{dT_A} = -U_A'(Y_A - T_{AB}) + \alpha U_B'(Y_B + T_{ab} - P) \geq 0,$

where the primes denote derivatives or marginal utilities of consumption of A and B.

Assuming diminishing marginal utility of consumption (i.e., $U'' < 0$), it is straightforward to show from equation (6) that A is more likely to be willing to transfer enough to B to solve the problem the higher his own income, the more altruistic he is toward B, the lower B's income, and the higher the cost of solving the problem that B faces. These implications are unsurprising, except perhaps the final one. The reason is that, other things equal, B's net income, $Y_B - P$, is lower; hence, his marginal utility of consumption is higher, the higher is P, leading A to increase his transfer. Note, however, that a higher value of P makes it less likely that B would choose to solve the problem. Note that it is quite possible that $T_{AB}^* < P$. With the language from the vignettes, this means that "unmet needs" will remain after A's optimal transfer, which will be met from B's own resources. Finally, the likelihood that A will help B and the magnitude of his optimal transfer are positively related to the size of the altruism parameter, α. Assuming that α diminishes as the relationship distance between A and B increases, so too will the size of transfers.

These implications of the two-person altruism model are all consistent with the empirical findings for personal transfers in chapter 13. These findings therefore provide support for the hypothesis that altruistic preferences may determine norms of obligation and, additionally, that these norms would be predictive of actual behavior. Yet, as I argue in the next section, there are many reasons that patterns of actual transfers may diverge from patterns of altruistic preferences. It is an important strength of Nock and colleagues' vignette approach and factorial design that it may be able to retrieve the patterns of altruistic preferences from hypothetical choices that are obscured in data on actual transfer relations. In the final section, I suggest that direct data on altruistic preferences obtained through vignettes might be fruitfully combined with data on actual behavior in ways that could help provide empirical tests of a variety of models on economic, political, and social behavior.

Divergences between Norms of Obligations and Actual Behavior

In equation (2) above, A's altruistic utility function is equal to a branch measuring his utility from his own consumption plus a weighted sum of the utilities of all the rest of the people in the United States, where the weights are altruism coefficients with magnitudes varying inversely with the relationship distance between A and the person in question. Imagine for a moment that A is a (somewhat) benevolent dictator who controls all resources in the country and allocates these resources by maximizing equation (2) subject to a resource constraint given by U.S. national income. Also assume that there is some subsistence level of consumption such that the marginal utility of consumption approaches infinity as an individual's level of consumption approaches the subsistence level. Given these assumptions, it might seem that A would allocate resources to himself and others as a monotonic but nonlinear function of the altruism coefficients. In particular, he would give himself the most consumption, next most to each of his children, and so on, with declining amounts to more distant relatives and the least to strangers. However, as long as α_j is positive for people in the jth relationship class, he will give them at least a subsistence level of consumption. Although the population is better off with A as dictator than it would be with a purely selfish ruler, the distribution of income appears to be quite unequal.

As a matter of logic, the analysis in the preceding paragraph is misleading because it fails to take account of the fact that the utility of people A cares about themselves care about others to whom they are related, thus increasing the effective degree of altruism between A and other people. The most famous application of this aspect of altruistic preferences is the dynastic model of the family employed by Barro (1974), who argued that the effect of increased public transfers through a social security system would be neutralized by equal and opposite private transfers through the family. Whereas Barro used a single representative dynastic family to establish his neutrality result, Bernheim and Bagwell (1988) showed that, if the model is taken literally, in a cross-sectional population everyone would be linked altruistically to everyone else such that the effects of variations in income and price on individual consumption would be eliminated by offsetting transfers—leading to the absurd implication that "everything is neutral"! Altonji, Kotlikof, and Hayashi (1992, 1997) empirically test and soundly reject the implications of the altruism model for intra- and interfamily transfers in response to income shocks. On the other hand, the literature—including Altonji, Kotlikof, and Hayashi (1992)—has shown that family transfers may be altruistically motivated to some extent. For example, in my own work with Lillard (Lillard and Willis 1997), we found evidence in Malaysian data that was consistent with a model of altruistically motivated parental investment in children's education, coupled with partial repayment by adult children, and argued that such transfers played a significant role in the growth of education in that country.

The neutrality implications of the altruism model depend on the existence of "operational linkages"—jargon for positive transfers—between households, but these implications lose force if households are at a "corner solution"—jargon for an optimal transfer equal to zero. Because the overwhelming majority of households in the United States do not engage in a transfer relationship with any given household, it is obvious that operational linkages are the exception and that observed transfer behavior may provide little guidance about patterns of obligations.

One possible reason that transfer relationships are so rare is, of course, that the altruism model itself is wrong. But even if altruism is important, there are a number of reasons for the prevalence of corner solutions. For example, Weiss and Willis (1985) show that a divorced father who has altruistic feelings for a child in the custody of the mother may choose to be a "deadbeat dad," providing no child support if he cannot monitor how the mother allocates her income between her own consumption and the child's. More generally, if I make a transfer to a needy person, I may worry that I will simply displace the transfers of others. In effect, the welfare of the needy person is a "collective good" from the point of view of all those who care about him, and individuals have an incentive to free ride on the contributions of others, thereby gaining the benefits of the collective good without paying the cost.

In practice, free rider problems and other transaction costs involved in making transfers may outweigh the gain to the donor of making transfers to those he or she cares about, especially if the altruistic linkage is weak and the potential donor and recipient are not close to one another in time or space. For the most part, people get by using their own resources.

Nonetheless, altruistic feeling may be of real importance in particular situations (like those in the vignettes), where the respondent learns of a specific needy person and his or her problem, along with knowledge of the problem's remedy. A key feature of Nock and colleagues' design is to present an individual's obligation as part of a package deal in which the respondent is able to control all the actions (including other individuals and institutions required to solve the problem) by himself. Nock, Kingston, and Holian provide a rationale for this approach: "We believe that it is only sensible to view personal obligations as inherently conditioned by the amount of obligation one attributes to other possible sources of assistance, just as the amount of obligation attributed to these sources is inherently conditioned by one's sense of personal obligation" (291).

The authors' intuition conforms to the public goods problem's classic "solution" proposed by the Swedish economist Lindahl (1958), in which each individual faces a price per unit of the public good equal to his marginal willingness to pay, evaluated at the optimal scale of the public good. In the Lindahl equilibrium, the sum of the marginal contributions from all parties is equal to the marginal cost of the good. In effect, each beneficiary of the public good shares in its costs in proportion to the marginal value he receives from the cost of public good. The Lindahl mechanism has the fatal flaw of not being incentive compatible, meaning that each individual has an incentive to understate his valuation of the public good in an attempt to free ride by shifting the cost of provision to others. However, it is possible to express the optimal solution to a public goods problem that a beneficent social planner would choose in Lindahl prices that measure the optimal percentage distribution of how the costs are shared.

The design of the vignettes invites the respondent to play this social planning role. In the vignettes, each potential object of an altruistic connection for the survey respondent is an identified person with a specific problem which can be remediated at a known cost, and this person is known to have insufficient resources to solve the problem without outside help. In short, the vignettes are designed to induce an operational linkage between the survey respondent and the hypothetical person, thus rendering the distribution of obligations across members of society measurable.

The empirical results of the study are broadly consistent with what one would expect about the distribution of Lindahl prices, given the declining values of the altruism parameter α, as relationship distance increases. In table 13.4, 60 percent of the cost of a problem faced by the respondent's child is borne by the respondent, and only 11 percent by other relatives of the child. In contrast, the costs are borne about equally between the respondent and other relatives in the case of a parent. This result is predicted by Lindahl pricing if there are two siblings with similar tastes and incomes. The proportion of help from the government for siblings or beyond is relatively constant, at about 20–25 percent. This proportion is also consistent with Lindahl pricing, where there are, from the respondent's point of view, a large number of people not related to the hypothetical person who have a low-level altruistic connection to him. Each of these people is expected to make a very small tax payment to solve that individual's problem; summed over all such people, these contributions amount to not more than a quarter of the cost.

To the extent that the vignettes measure Lindahl prices, they yield data that may help predict not only how a given individual will behave in his private helping decisions, but also how he would vote on public policies that compel cost sharing through taxation.

Extensions of the Vignette Approach

I have hypothesized that the sociological concept of the distribution of norms of obligations is related to the economic concept of altruistic preferences. I have tried to show that the empirical results in chapter 13 are consistent with this hypothesis. This consistency suggests that it might be interesting to extend the vignette technique to further test the correspondence between the sociological and economic concepts. For instance, it would be useful to set up vignettes in which economic theory predicts that individuals will understate their preferences. This hypothesis could be tested by seeing whether individuals would reduce their own contributions when the contribution of others is exogenously increased. Or, one could test the deadbeat dad theory of Weiss and Willis (1985) with vignettes about child support. Indeed, the experimental economics literature is full of experiments on public goods, fairness, and other concepts that might be modified to be feasible within a factorial vignette framework.

It would be most interesting to connect the measures of norms of obligation or altruistic preferences to actual transfer and voting behavior. This connection could be made by embedding vignettes in a survey that contains measures of actual behavior. If this direction is taken, there will be a premium on designing vignettes as efficiently as possible to avoid imposing too much survey burden. It would also be interesting to extend these techniques to other countries to see how much variations in the importance of the welfare state coincide with variations in these norms.

NOTES

1. Presumably, with suitable vignettes involving specified strangers from foreign countries, one could include the entire world population.

2. Indeed, in an intergenerational context, Barro and Becker (1989) point out that a utility function of the form in equation (2) is not properly behaved unless the product $\alpha_j N_j$ is a decreasing function of N_j.

REFERENCES

Altonji, Joseph G., Fumio Hayashi, and Laurence J. Kotlikof. 1997. "Parental Altruism and Inter Vivos Transfers: Theory and Evidence." *The Journal of Political Economy* 105(6): 1121–66.

Altonji, Joseph G., Laurence J. Kotlikof, and Fumio Hayashi. 1992. "Is the Extended Family Altruistically Linked? Direct Tests Using Micro Data." *The American Economic Review* 82(5): 1177–98.

Barro, Robert J. 1974. "Are Government Bonds Net Wealth?" *Journal of Political Economy* 82(6): 1095–1117.

Barro, Robert, and Gary S. Becker. 1989. "Fertility Choice in a Model of Economic Growth." *Econometrica* 57(2): 481–501.

Becker, Gary S. 1974. "A Theory of Social Interactions." *Journal of Political Economy* 82(6): 1063–93.

———. 1981. *A Treatise on the Family.* Cambridge, MA: Harvard University Press.

Bernheim, B. Douglas, and Kyle Bagwell. 1988. "Is Everything Neutral?" *Journal of Political Economy* 96(2): 308–38.

Lillard, Lee A., and Robert J. Willis. 1997. "Motives for Intergenerational Transfers: Evidence from Malaysia." *Demography* 34(1): 115–34.

Lindahl, Erik. 1958. "Just Taxation—A Positive Solution." In *Classics in the Theory of Public Finance,* edited by Richard Musgrave and Alan Peacock (98–123). London: Macmillan.

Weiss, Yoram, and Robert J. Willis. 1985. "Children as Collective Goods and Divorce Settlements." *Journal of Labor Economics* 3(3): 268–92.

17

Expanding the Horizon
New Directions for the Study of Intergenerational Care and Exchange

Cassandra Rasmussen Dorius and Laura Wray-Lake

Jean, a widow, told a story about having surgery performed last year: "If there has ever been a doubt, I certainly found out, [my children] were right there for me when I had my artery surgery, because both of them live a busy life. And yet they arranged it between the two, my daughter and son, that they would both, well they both came down every day (two hour drive) . . . when I got home from the hospital one would be here all day and all night, and the next day the other one would come. So I knew that I was very well, you know, they cared." (Peters, Hooker, and Zvonkovic 2006, 547)

Jean's description of her surgery and her children's subsequent caregiving behavior reflects many of the themes found in this book and highlights the interconnectedness of family life. Although intergenerational care and exchange are often described as occurring between individuals (usually a parent and child), neither the behavior nor the emotional tie are strictly personal matters. Rather, they are family issues that extend beyond the giver and the receiver to affect, and be affected by, other familial relationships. As in the opening vignette, siblings often negotiate among themselves to create caregiving strategies that meet their elderly parents' needs. These strategies may be equitable or asymmetric and are often motivated by social norms, personal preferences, and feelings of obligation toward a particular family member. Like the children in the story, many people have busy lives that influence the type, quality, or amount of caregiving they can perform, especially when the need for resources is chronic. Further, many people connect caregiving with the emotional tie of care (i.e., because the children helped her, Jean knew they cared about her), although the two concepts are distinct and can exist independently of one another. Previous research has shown that several intrafamilial relationships—including siblings, in-laws, grandparents, and spouses—may affect caregiving. Care and exchange within families are also contextualized by extrafamilial factors such as population processes, government policies, community resources, and workplace characteristics, and by other institutional and structural determinants such as gender, race, and class.

This concluding chapter builds on the theories, methods, and findings found in this book and puts forth three recommendations to extend these approaches in future research. First, future work should contextualize studies by considering relevant population processes such as the aging population, changing family size and structure, and increases in ethnic diversity that may influence intergenerational care and caregiving. Second, researchers can better test ideas by integrating cross-disciplinary theories with methodological improvements such as broadening the unit of analysis, collecting longitudinal data, and utilizing innovative techniques of data collection. Third, the substantive foci of intergenerational care and caregiving should be enlarged to include the range of family members involved in the family system (e.g., grandparents, fathers, siblings, and in-laws), to consider more fully how caregiving impacts the well-being of the receiver and donor, and to be more explicit about policy. Before discussing these new directions, however, we first provide a brief overview of the basics of intergenerational care and exchange as described by the authors of this volume.

The Basics of Intergenerational Care and Exchange

Because an interest in intergenerational relationships and caregiving unites all of the research presented in this volume, a variety of empirical findings can be woven together to answer a core set of questions about care and exchange. Who is involved in intergenerational care and caregiving? What resources are given? When and where do these relationships and exchanges occur? Why do people choose to participate?

Who Is Involved in Intergenerational Care and Caregiving?

Intergenerational caregiving includes at least two people, the person giving care and the person receiving assistance. Currently most of the intergenerational transfers in the United States go downstream, from parent to child, with a much smaller portion going upstream from child to parent (chapter 1). According to Pillemer and Suitor (chapter 9), parental preferences influence decisions about who should provide assistance when more than one caregiver is available. Partiality for a caregiver may stem from a gender preference among children and children-in-law, with parents choosing daughters and daughters-in-law more frequently than sons and sons-in-law (see also chapters 9 and 15). Gender also influences the type and amount of assistance provided, with men consistently demonstrating higher personal obligations to provide money than women (chapter 13) and women providing more time-intensive caregiving than men (Gerstel and Sarkisian 2006). Gender also predicts whether people will require inter- or intragenerational caregiving during their lifetimes; Pezzin, Pollak, and Schone (chapter 12) point out that because fathers tend to be older than mothers, they are more likely to receive help from their wives, whereas women often outlive their husbands and thus receive help from their children.

Though less of a focus in the volume, intergenerational care is also affected by other relationships in the family system and is often tied to gendered explanations of behavior. Personal characteristics and relationship history are important in determining the emotional bond between a parent and child, and research suggests that other family members, such as the other parent, other offspring, and the spouse of the child, influence these affective ties. In addition, "kinkeepers," who manage family relationships and act as "the bridge between generations," may influence ties between generations (Turner, Young, and Black 2006, 588). Most frequently, women are the kinkeepers of their families and are responsible for overseeing nuclear and extended family ties. Married women in particular seem to take on the role of kinkeeper and are "expected to create bonds and maintain the ties and traditions of both sides of the family," although they usually focus on maintaining connections with those from the matrilineal line (Turner et al. 2006, 589). Ascertaining the kinkeepers' preferences is critical to understanding the development and maintenance of family relationships as well as feelings of obligation to provide caregiving for parents, siblings, and other less-integrated family members such as in-laws.

What Resources Are Given?

A variety of resources can be transferred within and across generations; the most common are money, time, and goods or services (Bianchi et al.). Pillemer and Suitor expand this notion of transfers to include emotional support (e.g., comfort during a crisis) along with the more frequently used concepts of instrumental support (e.g., help when a child is ill) and financial support. Seltzer et al. (chapter 10) emphasize emotional support as a resource in intergenerational care and demonstrate how it can be used to reciprocate other types of transfers, as in the case of parents who provide for children with disabilities by giving money, time, and goods and services through adulthood while the child reciprocates by providing emotional support. Although there are numerous types of transfers within and across generations, much of the current literature focuses on financial transfers that can be more easily compared across studies and units of analysis (e.g., individuals, government, civic groups, and religious organizations). Nock, Kingston, and Holian, for instance, rely solely on financial assistance to measure the distribution of obligation among a host of kin and non-kin relationships to assess the importance of degree of closeness on feelings of obligation. Thus it appears that although numerous resources can be given, the methodological and theoretical constraints of a particular study play a large role in determining the type of transfer examined.

When Does Caregiving Occur?

The general pattern of caregiving over the life course indicates that most parents are involved in providing downstream transfers to their children from birth through adulthood. If parents live long enough, however, they will likely experience a "transfer switch" wherein the parent becomes a recipient more often than a donor, and the transfer of resources changes direction from downstream to upstream (see figure 2.1). During this transition, unique emotional, financial, and cognitive changes may affect the amount and type of resources provided. For example, Silverstein (chapter 6) suggests that as parents move from providing for their elderly parents to being provided for, they experience significant cognitive changes that lead them to express feelings of altruism toward their children that are correlated with asking for less help than might be preferable based on self-interest alone (see figure 6.5). Along with a focus on how life stage influences caregiving preferences, Wong (chapter 2) notes the importance of considering caregiving transitions, with a focus on how people move in and out of these roles over time. Her research indicates that most parents and children are engaged in some form of reciprocal care and caregiving and thus take on the roles of both donor and recipient throughout adulthood.

Like caregiving, emotional ties between parents and children can change over the life course, depending on developmental stages and life transitions. For example, Belsky et al. (2003) found that as children became young adults, they experienced less conflict and greater warmth with parents. In their work, life course events in young adulthood such as delaying childbirth, being married or in a committed relationship, and being engaged in work or other productive activities were also linked to more positive parent–child relationships. Unlike caregiving, which has a fairly consistent trend favoring downstream transfers until old age, researchers have recognized that the affective component of parent–child relationships is characterized by change and reciprocity over the life course.

Where Do Caregivers Live?

Care and caregiving are not necessarily bound by geography, although research indicates that certain types of transfers are more likely to occur as proximity between parent and child increases, with coresidence being a particularly strong correlate of caregiving. For example, Bianchi et al. point out that sharing a home creates a resource-rich environment for caregiving in terms of economies of scale and efficiency in personal care and emotional support. Furthering this point, Billari and Liefbroer (chapter 3) note that "coresidence not only *facilitates* other types of support but is itself an *indicator* of support and perhaps of the prevalence of specific norms" (emphasis added, 57). In addition to influencing the parent–child care and caregiving relationship, coresidence influences how families distribute obligations to provide assistance. For example, Pezzin, Pollak, and Schone draw on game theory to explore how siblings use distance to bargain with one another in deciding which adult child will take care of their aging mother. In this two-stage game, if the mother lives with one of the children, that child has less bargaining power in future caregiving decisions and more responsibility to provide for the mother than the other sibling. The noncoresident sibling is likely to reduce contributions to the mother, knowing that the coresident sibling will have to make up the difference.

Moving beyond this binary measure to a general assessment of proximity between parent and child can also be useful in explicating research findings in situations where coresidence is not a factor (Billari and Liefbroer). In fact, although coresidence is not a necessary condition for many types of daily support, a certain level of proximity is. For example, parents are less likely to name a son or daughter as a potential caregiver if that person lives far away; conversely, parents are more likely to provide certain kinds of resources (e.g., help during an illness or grandchild care) to an adult child who lives nearby (Pillemer and Suitor). However, even though proximity offers important clues about the type or frequency of transfers given, this indicator does not determine the occurrence of all such transfers. As Billari and Liefbroer have documented, financial transfers between immigrants to the United States and family members still in their country of origin are distributed across borders without regard to geopolitical boundaries or parent–child proximity.

How Are Transfer Decisions Made?

People make decisions to provide resources based on information available regarding recipient need, perceptions of others' responsibilities, and their own personal sense of obligation. Nock, Kingston, and Holian used a vignette study to measure when a person is more likely to provide financial resources. Their findings indicate that a person feels a greater obligation to help when the recipient has close biological or familial ties, has a high income, is either very young or elderly, or appears not to be responsible for the problem. Some people make transfer decisions on the basis of their perception of governmental or familial alternatives to assistance, and family obligation may be less salient when help is readily obtained elsewhere (chapter 5, Cox; chapter 14, Jackson et al.). Although this "crowding out" phenomenon may not accurately describe responses to government aid in Western countries (chapter 8, Zarit), there is some indication that it occurs within families. For example, Pezzin, Pollak, and Schone found that children determine the amount of resources they will provide their elderly mothers after evaluating their siblings' potential offers. However, this decision is not just up to the person providing care; the person in need of assistance can actively participate in constructing alternatives for care by preemptively refusing undesirable offers.

Furthermore, Pillemer and Suitor suggest that a number of factors influence parents when they must make transfer choices among multiple children—including the number of adult children to choose from, the quality of each parent–child relationship, and the personal characteristics of the individuals involved. Taken as a whole, these studies indicate that transfer decisions are based on a wide range of factors including the characteristics of the parent and child and their affective ties (Pillemer and Suitor), the perception of sibling responsibility (Pezzin, Pollak, and Schone), the number of other nonfamily agents obligated to help (Nock et al.), and the possibility of individual or government intervention (Cox; Jackson et al.).

Why Do People Engage in Care and Caregiving?

Although this volume's authors use many theoretical approaches to explain why people engage in care and caregiving, the primary theoretical approach they used was either exchange/reciprocity (e.g., Bianchi et al.; chapter 11, McHale and Crouter; Pillemer and Suitor; Seltzer et al.) or altruism/caring (e.g., Bianchi et al.; Nock et al.; chapter 16, Willis). A core distinction between these approaches is an assumption about what motivates relationship cohesion among family members. Specifically, scholars have argued about whether the family is a cohesive group held together by the emotional ties of its members or an economic unit brought together by financial or economic exigency. The altruistic/caring approach to intergenerational relationships suggests that the loving, nurturing ties between parents and children bind families and dyads together and that this affection motivates resource transfers. Conversely, the exchange/reciprocity approach argues that economic necessity and exchange are what keep family units intact.

If economic bonds are largely responsible for keeping family units intact, then exchange theory may best explain caregiving behavior. Exchange theory predicts resource transfers on the basis of the need to reciprocate past help or buy future obligations. If families are organized and maintained around emotive relationships, transfer behavior may follow an altruistic model, where caregiving transfers occur out of love and require no direct reciprocation. Although these two models conceptualize family cohesion differently, they are not mutually exclusive. Any attempt to pit altruism and exchange against one another oversimplifies the real-world processes that underlie motivations for caregiving, especially because altruism and exchange likely work in tandem across social settings to produce variations in intergenerational ties and transfers.

Contextualizing Future Research

The context surrounding family life is critical for understanding caregiving behavior. Proximal forces such as individual and family-level processes should be considered when modeling intergenerational care, and more distal trends should be incorporated into future research designs and modeling. To this end, we examine a number of demographic patterns that will influence intergenerational ties over the next half century: the aging population; fertility declines; increased age at first marriage; the large-scale entrance of women into the workforce; changes in family forms (i.e., increased single parenthood, divorce, remarriage, and cohabitation); changes in the racial and ethnic composition of the United States; increased immigration; and changes in social class.

The Graying of America

One of the most important population trends to affect intergenerational ties is the "graying of America." The U.S. Census Bureau projects that the proportion of the U.S. population older than 65 years will nearly double, from 12.4 percent in 2000 to 20.7 percent in 2050. Large increases are also expected in the group 85 years and older, which will expand from 1.5 percent of the total population in 2000 to roughly 5 percent by 2050 (Marks 2006). Increases in life expectancies mean that more parents will survive into old age and will therefore live long enough to require care from their adult children. The need for upstream resources, however, is tempered by increases in the "health life expectancy" of parents; as the number of years of life increase, so do the number of years before parents might need caregiving assistance (Riche 2006). Therefore, the potential burden of care is not increasing for *individuals* per se, although more individuals will face caregiving decisions (Riche 2006). As a result, more adults than before will find themselves part of the "sandwich generation," those people sandwiched between responsibilities to provide care for elderly parents and dependent children.

Future research should consider how members of the sandwich generation view their multiple caregiver roles and how concepts such as role conflict, role strain, role overload, and role quality may affect decisions to provide care as well as the positive and negative outcomes associated with caregiving. Further, public policy will need to better address this increased strain during midlife and provide alternatives for allocating individual- and family-level supports that expand caregiving options and address well-being concerns for those lacking access to needed family transfers.

Shrinking Family Size

The decline in fertility rates for American women over the past 30 years is also critical to the study of family life and intergenerational care. In 1976, women ended their childbearing years (40 to 44 years old) with an average of 3.1 children. By 2002, that number had dropped to a record low of 1.9 children for the same age group (Marks 2006). Furthermore, the number of American women who were childless at the end of their fertile years nearly doubled over this period (10 percent in 1976 vs. 18 percent in 2002) (Riche 2006).

As a result of the dramatic changes to family size over the past quarter century, intergenerational relationships and caregiving are also likely to change in several important ways: (1) fewer children may influence transfer behavior by creating less competition for parent-to-child assistance, while simultaneously increasing the concentration of responsibility for child-to-parent help; (2) shrinking family size may lead to an earlier identification of adult child caregivers (especially in families with one child), which may radically alter the amount of preparation and thought given to upstream transfers before they are required; and (3) an increasing number of childless individuals and couples will not be able to rely on offspring to provide upstream transfers when they are elderly and will likely have to create bonds with extended family, nonfamily members, or privatized care providers to ensure adequate care and caregiving. The increase in childlessness has a direct impact on public policy related to elder care and suggests that a stronger safety net of publicly available care may be needed for more elderly parents now than in previous generations. Further research should consider how self-identification as a caregiver at earlier stages of the life course might influence actual caregiving behavior later on, and whether crowding out is more or less likely to occur in single-child families, childless families, or multiple-child families.

Increases in Age at First Marriage

People are currently getting married at older ages than at any other time in the past century. Over the past 30 years, for example, the age at first marriage increased from 21 in 1970 to nearly 25 in 2000 (Marks 2006). Women who are postponing marriage appear to use these extra years to get more education and work experience; over this period the number of women graduating from college has nearly doubled and the number of women entering the labor force has shown a 40 percent increase (Marks 2006). The extra unmarried years impact women and men in other important ways, as delays in marriage are associated with declines in ever-married rates, lower overall fertility, and delayed childbearing. Taken together, these changes may affect intergenerational caregiving in three significant ways: (1) delays in marriage and childbirth may alter caregiving over the life course as people enter and exit roles of donor and recipient at different points than before; (2) more middle-aged adults are likely to be "sand-wiched" by responsibilities for children in the home while also caring for older parents; and (3) the increased exposure to education and paid work may enhance a woman's ability to adequately provide resources for herself and her family throughout adulthood. Future research should explore changes in the timing of these life course transitions and how they play a role in intergenerational transfers, family well-being, and the work–family dynamic.

Women in the Workforce

Arguably, one of the most important population trends to affect the family over the past century was the entrance of women into the U.S. labor market. In 1940, about 28 percent of women were working (Parcel and Menaghan 1994); by 1978 the number had increased to 66 percent, and by 1998, fully 79 percent of women were active in the labor force (Bianchi and Casper 2000). This large-scale entrance of women into work was particularly influential for families because it led to an increase in the use of day care for babies and preschoolers (Parcel and Menaghan 1994). Women's entrance into the labor force has important implications for contextualizing intergenerational ties because it may influence women's abilities to provide particular types of resources to either parents or children and has important policy implications for family members throughout the life course.

Maternal work is important for defining the context for intergenerational care because of mothers' increased ability to provide economic resources. Indeed, working women tend to provide more monetary resources to their elderly parents than nonworking women (Gerstel and Sarkisian 2006), although less is known about how work affects the nonmonetary transfers made available to elderly parents. For downstream transfers, the amount of time spent with children has not suffered due to the increase of women in the workforce, but rather, the changes in women's work can be counterbalanced to a certain extent by other interfamilial processes to counter negative outcomes for children (see Bianchi 2000). Future work on intergenerational ties should explore whether a similar continuity between upstream transfers and increases in women's workforce participation exists. Research assessing the context of women's work as a predictor of caregiving would be invaluable; for example, work hours, job characteristics, the constellation of family and civic responsibilities, and the preferences of working women are important factors in determining how work will influence caregiving and exchange.

Though not a completely new issue, the prevalence of women in the workforce continues to signal the need for a new set of policies and programs to deal with the limited time and resources of working families. Public programs for elderly parents were formed under the assumption that women were available to care for the elderly; however, the baby boom generation that is now responsible for elderly care was also the first to see large numbers of women enter the workforce (Riche 2006). There is now a discrepancy between the adequacy of public provision of care and the reality of working women being responsible for their elderly parents and relatives. This conflict may lead women with low-paying jobs to leave work to provide care. For economically better-off women, there is an option to outsource responsibilities to another service provider for duties such as child care or housecleaning. Future policies will need to create support structures for families at both ends of the economic spectrum, as well as introduce measures that are more reflective of the convergence of men's and women's work and home lives.

Changing Family Forms: Divorce, Remarriage, Cohabitation, and Nonmarital Childbearing

The evolving nature of U.S. families offers another set of population trends relevant to intergenerational care and caregiving. Over the past century, American family life has faced dramatic transformations, including increasing divorce, decreasing rates of marriage and remarriage, and a rise in cohabitation and nonmarital childbearing. According to Amato (2000), one of the most far-reaching and dramatic changes to the family has been the rise in divorce rates from about 5 percent in the mid-19th century to about 50 percent in 2000. This increase in marital instability has been linked to "increasing economic independence of women, declining earnings among men without college degrees, rising expectations for personal fulfillment from marriage, and greater social acceptance of divorce" (Amato 2000, 1269).

Divorce and remarriage provide important contexts for intergenerational care, but it is important to consider the increasingly diverse context of post-divorce family life, which has been altered as much by marital dissolution as it has by new forms of union formation. Whereas divorce in America was once a transitional phase between marriage and remarriage, the majority of children who experience a parental divorce now will remain in mother-only families for the remainder of their childhood, with about half of young children in the United States spending some time in a single-parent family (Bumpass 1990). Further, the nature of growing up in single-parent families is also being altered by the interjection of single parenthood with relatively short-term, serial cohabiting unions. Currently, about 40 percent of all children spend some time living with their mother and a cohabiting partner, about 40 percent of unmarried births occur in two-parent cohabiting families, and nearly half of all stepfamilies are formed by cohabitation (Bumpass and Hsein-Hen 2000). One of the most important effects of cohabitation on the family context is that it changes the nature of what single-parent time actually is, largely because about one-third of the time children spend with a single parent is actually spent in a two-parent cohabiting family (Bumpass and Hsein-Hen 2000). In addition to cohabitation, the rising rates of nonmarital childbearing are linked to single parenthood as a chosen family form, often because of the greater number of years spent unmarried, decreases in the propensity to marry upon becoming pregnant, and increased childbearing rates among the unmarried (Bumpass and Hsein-Hen 2000).

These new family forms are likely to have profound impacts on intergenerational caregiving over the next half century and, when taken together, they suggest the potential for new approaches to the study of intergenerational transfers. First, the increases in family diversity may challenge, contradict, or obscure current norms of obligation and reciprocity. For example, Coleman, Ganong, and Rothraff (2006) found that norms based on nuclear families do not necessarily apply to stepfamilies unless the stepparents are viewed as kin, and individuals tend to feel a diminished obligation to provide transfers to nonnuclear family members (Nock et al.). Future research should consider how norms of obligation are created and reinforced between children and their parent figures (e.g., stepparents, cohabiters, nonresident parents, and custodial grandparents). Second, future research needs to consider the influence of cohabitation on caregiving relationships. On the one hand, cohabitation is characterized by instability, so children may experience more family disruptions than previously thought given the stabilized divorce rate. These disruptions may lead to less secure ties between the generations and more ambiguous obligations between parents and children. On the other hand, focusing on increases in divorce and nonmarital births may underestimate children's time with their fathers, as children born to so-called single-parent families often do have a mother and father present in the home. This phenomenon suggests that children may have more access to fathers' downward investments of time, involvement, and money than previously thought. When a mother is cohabiting with either the biological father or a father figure, it increases the financial security for her children, because adults tend to spend money on the people in their households, even if they are not related. Future research should consider whether the downward transfers provided by cohabiting partners influence later upward transfers to that individual, or if these transfers influence the child's feelings of obligation to provide care for the mother who maintained these relationships. Third, future work needs to consider the long-term impacts of increased time in single-parent families. Research has demonstrated that individuals from divorced families tend to score lower than those from two-parent families on a variety of indicators of well-being (Amato 2000). Furthermore, the children of single parents are more likely to experience a variety of negative outcomes, including increased poverty, poor school performance, earlier sexual activity, premarital births, and a higher likelihood to cohabit, marry early, and divorce more frequently than other children (Amato 2000). Future research is needed on how the nature of children's early family life influences subsequent feelings of obligation, and whether exposure to negative outcomes influences the long-term viability of children and their parents to provide resources for one another throughout the life course.

Race and Ethnicity

The changing racial and ethnic composition of the U.S. population will likely alter how intergenerational caregiving is studied and practiced in the future. U.S. Census Bureau population projections suggest that the Hispanic proportion of the population will nearly double between 2000 and 2050, from 12.6 percent to 24.4 percent of the total population. Likewise, the Asian proportion of the population is expected to increase from 3.8 percent to 8 percent, while the black non-Hispanic population is projected to increase only slightly, from 12.7 percent to 14.6 percent of the total population. Non-Hispanic whites are the only racial/ethnic group projected to decline over this period, falling from 69.4 percent of the total population in 2000 to about 50.1 percent by 2050 (Marks 2006). Empirical research has documented differences in the caregiving behaviors and attitudes of non-Hispanic whites, African Americans, Asians, and Hispanics (Nock et al.; Jackson et al.; Seltzer et al.). In one study of the norms of obligation, white European Americans reported lower expectations for adult children to provide assistance to their elderly parents than all other racial/ethnic groups in the sample (Coleman et al. 2006). Minority groups have also been found to place more value on extended families compared with whites; specifically, African Americans, Latinos, and Asians tend to coreside, live closer to, and have more contact with extended kin (Gerstel and Sarkisian 2006). This distinction across groups may be due to variations in such cultural values as collectivism, familism, and filial obligation. According to Coleman, Ganong, and Rothraff (2006, 585), "Past experiences of slavery and past and current experiences of racial discrimination have made African Americans less willing to embrace an individualistic ideology. As a result, African Americans may have a tradition of relying on family and fictive kin help more than White European Americans, and therefore, are more likely to believe that older persons should be helped." Like African Americans, Asians are more collectivistic and centered on filial piety than white Europeans (Coleman et al. 2006).

The omission of race from much of the current research on intergenerational caregiving skews the bulk of what is known toward a white European American perspective, which is increasingly problematic as the U.S. population reflects more diverse racial and ethnic groupings and, subsequently, diverse caregiving patterns. Although several authors in this volume considered race in their work (e.g., Billari and Liefbroer; McHale and Crouter; Nock et al.; Wong), only Jackson and colleagues fully articulated the multiple ways race might influence intergenerational caregiving. Over-looking race and ethnicity has serious consequences when trying to understand how norms and feelings of obligation influence intergenerational assistance. Because people of diverse racial and ethnic backgrounds are differentially exposed to a range of family processes such as divorce, remarriage, and cohabitation, there may be racial distinctions in feelings of obligation for caregiving and in exposure to norms on intergenerational ties. For example, African Americans are much more likely to cohabit and much less likely to marry than non-Hispanic whites. As a result of participation in these "incomplete" institutions, family obligation may be more ambiguous for African Americans, leading to more varied and less normative intergenerational caregiving behavior.

Immigration

Associated with, yet distinct from, changes in the racial/ethnic composition of the American population are important changes in immigration patterns and the economic viability of these immigrant families. Currently, the United States has the highest immigrant population of any industrialized country in the world, with the lion's share of immigrants hailing from Mexico (Billari and Liefbroer; Wong). The current wave of immigrants tends to be economically vulnerable, frequently working in low-paying jobs, facing poverty, and often transferring this disadvantage to their children (Marks 2006).

Poverty, country of origin, and cultural values make immigration-focused research a prime area for future studies of intergenerational ties. Although most types of transfers in the United States go downstream from parents to children, this pattern is reversed for Mexican immigrants, who are more likely to transfer resources upstream from children to parents (see Wong).When Mexican immigrants follow cultural norms to provide resources to their parents, these caregiving obligations may make them particularly vulnerable to resource depletion. A promising area of future research is to consider how Mexican immigrants deal with the conflicting demands of simultaneous upstream and downstream transfer norms, and how parents choose between providing resources for their aging parents or their economically disadvantaged children. Future work might also benefit from assessing whether the creation of ethnic communities and proxy families ("ethnic enclaves" and "fictive kin," respectively) are used to offset the resource depletion caused by upstream transfers.

Finally, it is important to note that although immigration patterns may influence the type and direction of caregiving among immigrants, these behaviors may also influence the caregiving patterns of the larger society. Billari and Liefbroer suggest that inflows of migrants bring with them new ideas about intergenerational ties that may be diffused in the population. Thus, current U.S. immigration may indirectly drive the context of future intergenerational transfers.

Class

Perhaps the most overlooked context for care in this volume is social class. Lower-income offspring are more likely to provide care personally rather than give monetary aid to parents in need (Bianchi et al.) and are less likely to report willingness to help others financially (Nock et al.). These references to one component of social class (i.e., income) suggest that the norms and realities of caregiving may vary across families depending on socioeconomic status.

Future research should consider how class interacts with other social groupings to influence caregiving behavior. As previously noted, minorities place more value on extended families and have a stronger sense of filial obligation than whites do. However, the confounding of race and socioeconomic standing add complexity to such findings. As Gerstel and Sarkisian (2006, 255) point out, scholars recognize that "minorities are more often poor and therefore more in need of extended family support networks than Whites." Other future work could test the concurrent influences of race and class on feelings of obligation and preferences for care and care work. Incorporating race and class into future models will help unpack the processes that lead some groups to develop closer, more obligatory ties with one another and distinguish whether cultural explanations are linked to poverty or particular racial/ethnic experiences.

Although family members often belong to the same class, this is not always the case. In fact, there may be considerable heterogeneity in social class within and between generations that may affect the type and quality of resources transferred. Revealingly, family members might not share the same socioeconomic standing even when they live together. For instance, mothers and fathers who are both employed may have substantially different types of jobs and keep their money separate, such that one does not share the class identification of the other (Gerstel and Sarkisian 2006).

Just as husbands and wives may experience different class realities, elderly parents, adult children, and grandchildren may also identify with different social classes. Future work could address how both between- and within-family class differences affect the type, quality, and amount of transfers and care family members exchange. Specifically, how do within-family differences in income affect parents' preferences for care or the type of care children provide? Other research might develop between-family comparisons that consider how families of different classes deal with caregiving. This research may be particularly important in answering a key public policy question: how does the availability of public support for the elderly change the nature of caregiving and exchanges among families who have few resources?

Methodological Directions for Future Research

The wealth of information contained in this volume reminds us of the great complexity involved when studying intergenerational relationships. Although there are many approaches to addressing the intricacies of intergenerational research, three key methodological issues emerge from this volume as promising avenues for future research: reexamining the unit of analysis, viewing caregiving in a longitudinal framework, and using innovative data collection techniques.

Unit of Analysis

Intergenerational caregiving researchers would benefit from assessing the family as a unit of analysis rather than examining concepts from a single individual's perspective. By altering the focus to include the entire family, researchers would be better able to understand the ways in which familial relationships influence the link between the receiver and donor. Within-family designs also can account for variability across family members that "target child" studies omit, such as having a child with a disability (Seltzer et al.). Further, when the family is the unit of analysis, both within-family and between-family differences can be studied. For example, McHale and Crouter suggest that studies with between-family designs tend to conclude that parents do not treat children differently on the basis of gender, whereas within-family comparisons of sisters and brothers find the opposite. Likewise, within-family designs can control for between-family differences such as socioeconomic status that may be confounds in studies that rely on between-family designs (Pillemer and Suitor).

The motivation for incorporating the entire family into a research design is that care and exchanges made between elderly parents and their adult children cannot be fully described by either the personal character-istics of those involved or the nature of their affective ties to one another. Rather, the adult child's spouse's feelings about the parents and the exchange must be considered, as must the siblings' preferences for care, and the public and private options for purchasing care for the elderly par-ent. The study of sibling relationships by McHale and Crouter recognized the important role other family members play in an individual's devel-opment. Pillemer and Suitor also considered the importance of the fam-ily system when they studied each parent–child dyad as an independent unit, distinct from other pairings yet embedded in the context of other family relationships. Economists such as Pezzin and colleagues furthered this idea when they included multiple informants in their model of care-giving decisions through the use of game theory.

Future work that incorporates the family as the unit of analysis might encourage research on sibling relationships, in-laws, and disrupted mar-riages. For example, does the gender makeup of sibling groups influence caregiving preferences? How do interpersonal sibling ties affect parental preferences for care? Is the quality of the daughter-in-law–mother-in-law relationship a predictor of caregiving and exchanges later in life? Does closeness between a stepparent and stepchild early in the life course influ-ence children's feelings of obligation to provide care for their biological parent in middle age?

Longitudinal Design

Although cross-sectional designs predominate in survey research on intergenerational caregiving, this approach only "makes sense if the social phenomena under investigation are reasonably stable. One of the defining features of contemporary family life, however, is its fluidity" (Eggebeen 2002, 205). For researchers to adequately capture the nature of contemporary intergenerational relationships and caregiving, they must incorporate data that are contextually sensitive and acknowledge the important changes in roles, responsibilities, and relationships in indi-viduals' lives over time that affect family care and caregiving (Higgins, Duxbury, and Lee 1994). Research designs that attempt to capture how life events unfold over time are often informed by the life course perspective, which several of this volume's authors incorporated into their work (Bianchi et al.; McHale and Crouter; Pillemer and Suitor; Seltzer et al.).

In addition to implicitly promoting a longitudinal study design, a life course perspective allows for a fully developed theoretical explanation for caregiving behavior over time; this approach stresses that decisions made early in one's life can profoundly shape life outcomes and that the principals of *linked lives* of family members, *developmental change* across the lifespan, *timing of life transitions,* the *role of individual agency,* and *time and place* offer important considerations when undertaking research on family relationships (see Elder 1997). When examining intergenerational care and exchange, life course transitions such as entrance and exits in the labor market, age at first marriage, number of children, timing of births, and the relationships among these transitions aid in understanding the context of caring and exchange in middle and late adulthood. For example, when women leave the labor market to raise children, it may economically disadvantage them and their families as compared to women who stay in the labor market, especially if the former leave well-paid jobs. Loss of pay, work experience, and job security may limit the total possible financial contributions women provide to their children over their lifespan. Further, this decision to leave work and raise children early in the life course might lead to a greater need for upstream transfers from children to mothers later in life due to lost earning potential, smaller retirement and saving funds, and lower Social Security support. This lost earning potential may further decrease the ability of mothers to provide upstream transfers to their elderly parents when the need arises.

Future investigations should consider how early life choices such as leaving (or staying in) the workforce after a child is born influence later caregiving behavior. In fact, numerous hypotheses regarding intergenerational caregiving could be fleshed out with longitudinal data and a life course approach. For example, researchers could study how preferences about caregiving may differ at various ages and life stages; shed light on early precursors of caregiving decisions later in life; or demonstrate that exchanges do not happen simultaneously—there may be lag time in reciprocal transfers within the family. Further, longitudinal designs would allow researchers to study whether transfers even out over time for parents' spending on children and children's caregiving toward parents, and they would also provide more information on the range of currencies used to reciprocate caregiving behaviors throughout life (Bianchi et al.).

Innovative Techniques for Data Collection

The authors in this volume exhibited several innovative data collection methods, including vignette studies, directly asking respondents questions about caregiving preferences, mimicking experimental designs, and incorporating a biological approach into research designs (see Nock et al.; Pillemer and Suitor; Silverstein; and Cox, respectively). These approaches to data collection illustrate new methodological directions for the field as a whole.

Nock, Kingston, and Holian used vignette studies to better understand the norms of obligations people use in making decisions to help others. They used computer-assisted scenarios with a hypothetical decisionmaking framework to provide information about why people choose to engage in caregiving and how people perceive their obligations to provide assistance relative to the obligations of others. Hypothetical vignettes such as these are useful to capture variability in a wide range of situations that may not be as accessible through surveys of family members' current behaviors.

Pillemer and Suitor improved current data collection strategies by directly querying respondents about caregiving preferences over a variety of domains. They found that by and large, parents can articulate preferences for children on a number of dimensions. Asking parents directly about their domain-specific preferences offers a new and important avenue for data collection because it increases variability, which may allow for greater accuracy when predicting family-related phenomena such as caregiving decisions, and may decrease pressures to respond in socially desirable ways.

Third, although many family processes cannot be manipulated experimentally, variants of experimental design can still be useful. For instance, Silverstein suggests seeking out cultural niches that may prove useful for exploring bioevolutionary hypotheses. Further, both Billari and Liefbroer and Wong noted empirical ways to answer the counterfactual dilemma, what if some people received transfers while others did not? Would the people who received transfers be better off? Do countries that provide resources for the elderly do better or worse economically? While researchers cannot use random assignment to test what would happen if some transfers were made while others were withheld, there are methods for approaching this experimental design, such as using other countries as the counterfactual (Billari and Liefbroer) or employing propensity score analyses.

Cox uses the fourth innovative technique, introducing an evolutionary perspective to the study of caregiving that can be used to address some of the most intriguing questions posed in this volume. For example, Nock, Kingston, and Holian found that one's sense of obligation to provide care is stronger where there are biological ties, and that the more closely related a person is to another the more responsibility he or she feels to provide resources. Does this connection between biology and caregiving occur because individuals are socially conditioned to value biological ties, or do people have biologically based impulses to provide for closely related kin? The latter idea has intrigued researchers across disciplines and is the foundation of a number of living systems theories that incorporate biological data collection techniques, study designs, and theoretical principals to unravel the multiplicative effect of biology, physiology, and cognitive processes on family relationships. Several chapters in this book consider evolutionary theory and behavioral genetics, and other areas of study might also prove worthwhile in answering this question, including anthropological approaches to biology, hormone/endocrinology work, and genetic research and twin studies.

Substantive Directions for Future Research

One of the key findings of this book is that while intergenerational care and exchange may occur between a parent and a child, neither the behavior nor the affective bond can be fully understood without considering the parent and child relative to other family members and relationships. This section provides substantive directions for future research that build upon this notion of interconnectedness by addressing several important but neglected family ties, such as fathers, grandparents, in-laws, and siblings. Further, we advocate greater attention to values, the health and well-being of family members, and connections between research and policy.

Including Family Ties in Family Research

Family members are uniquely positioned to provide help with unexpected problems, such as unemployment, sickness, death, child care needs, major repairs around the house, or other financial, emotional, or physical difficulties. The "insurance value of kin" is a leading theory explaining why intergenerational transfers occur in times of difficulty (Wong) and has been used to describe how siblings, grandparents, parents, and in-laws may provide help for a family member rather than requiring those in need to arrange alternate sources of support. The motivation for providing these resources may be tied to feelings of obligations for family members (Nock et al.), information asymmetries between family members involved in the transfer and between public and private care providers, enforceability of transfer arrangements, efficiency, and ease of quality assessment related to care options. Because a variety of inter- and intragenerational relationships are targeted for "insurance" help, these ties are important to include in a substantive discussion of intergenerational care, and as such we will consider them more fully here.

Fathers

One of the groups targeted to provide support in times of need is fathers, although a number of societal changes (i.e., increases in divorce, cohabitation, and nonmarital childbirth) have transformed their role over the past century:

> A father may or may not be biologically related to his child, may or may not be married to his child's mother, may or may not have a relationship with his child's mother, may or may not reside with his child, may or may not have legal ties to his child, may or may not have custody of his child, may or may not support his child (either emotionally or economically), and may or may not establish paternity. Who then are fathers? (Tamis-LeMonda and Cabrera 2002, 600)

As a result of changes in family formation and dissolution, fathers often do not reside with their children, and the ties between children and nonresidential fathers tend to weaken over the life course as mothers and fathers form new unions and increase their physical distance from one another. Paradoxically, current norms of family life lead coresident fathers to be more involved in childrearing than in centuries past, which may increase care and caregiving behavior between fathers and children, while fathers as a whole are less available to their children than ever before,[1] a phenomenon that diminishes the opportunities for developing strong, caring relationships and providing an environment for intergenerational transfers to thrive.

Future research should examine how the increasing diversity in fathering roles influences upstream transfers in late adulthood. Specifically, who will provide for nonresident fathers in the future? Similarly, who will provide for residential, nonbiological fathers? Will norms of obligation connect fathers and children regardless of residential status in childhood? And is biological fathering more important than social fathering in predicting later caregiving behavior? Future work linking research to policy should consider whether laws that require provisions of care from parent to child influence feelings of obligations that go from child to parent in later life. For example, do fathers who consistently provide child support receive more caregiving transfers when these children reach adulthood than fathers who do not? Finally, public programs need to devise ways to create a larger safety net for fathers who have not maintained strong parent–child relationships and therefore may not receive needed transfers from their children.

Siblings

Siblings are central to intergenerational research because they influence both within- and between-generation transfers and represent the longest lasting personal relationships experienced in life (McHale and Crouter). Among adult children, sibling relationships can predict the amount of resources provided to elderly parents, with children each giving less when they think their siblings will provide more (Pezzin et al.). Further, the emotional bonds between siblings and between parents and siblings influence parental caregiving preferences in late adulthood (Pillemer and Suitor). Future research might consider how differential treatment and sibling preference across the lifespan affects caregiving strategies (see McHale and Crouter; Pillemer and Suitor). For example, do sibling rivalries influence the amount, quality, or type of care provided to parents? And conversely, does within-generation sibling support and caregiving affect the distribution of obligations for parental care? That is, does sibling support buy out the need to provide parental caregiving, or does such support reinforce one's role as a family caregiver?

In addition to the adult sibling relationship, our understanding of intergenerational transfers would benefit from including longitudinal research designs that consider the sibling relationship over the life course. From an early age, siblings provide care for one another, but whether this care is translated to adult transfers is unknown. In a review of the "understudied and unacknowledged" sibling caregiving literature, Dodson and Dickert (2004, 320) found that in single-parent homes, older siblings were often channeled into caregiving roles during childhood to cover for parents who were absent from home because of work. Specifically, siblings were involved in after-school care, feeding and washing children, babysitting, helping with school work, missing school to care for sick siblings, cooking, cleaning, doing laundry, performing household maintenance, and often acting as a confidant or emotional supporter to the single parent. Future scholarship should focus on whether sibling caregiving during adolescence influences elderly parents' preferences for who should provide care later on; when parents choose among their children; and whether and how these preferences change over time. Further, researchers should determine whether early adolescent caregiving solidifies sibling roles and feelings of obligation from an early age, such that younger siblings feel less responsible to provide care in adulthood, while older siblings feel more responsible to continue in their role of family provider throughout their life.

Grandparents

Grandparents provide a host of important resources for their children and grandchildren, including custody, coresidence, child care, and other forms of emotional and financial assistance. One of the most important ways grandparents provide for their children and grandchildren is by assuming parenting responsibilities when their adult child cannot fulfill them, often because of serious problems such as drug abuse, child abuse, child neglect, incarceration, HIV/AIDS, mental illness, or death (Dolbin-MacNab 2006). Over the past 30 years, the number of grandparents who have taken on the role of primary caregiver has more than doubled to 4.5 million, which represents primary caregiving for 6.3 percent of all U.S. children (Dolbin-MacNab 2006). In addition to becoming full-time caregivers, grandparents may also provide important assistance through coresidence. In 2002, 13 percent of children raised by single parents had at least one grandparent living in the household, which may offer important advantages for children, such as increased school achievement (Marks 2006). Less intensive grandparent involvement has also influenced the well-being of grandchildren, as seen in maternal grandmothers' ability to deflect the negative consequences of maternal depression away from grandchildren (Silverstein 2006).

Grandparents' roles are central to the study of intergenerational ties because they influence the parent–child relationship as well as the parent–grandchild relationship. When grandparents provide intensive help raising a child or providing housing, is this intergenerational assistance viewed as an exchange with the child or the grandchild? Does providing grandchild care change the likelihood, type, or quality of upward transfers later on? Further, how does grandparent involvement affect the parent–child relationship and the creation of norms of obligation between the two younger generations?

In-Laws

In-laws provide a unique component to the study of intergenerational ties. In-laws are usually biologically related to some members of the family but not to others. Although studies of ambivalence, ambiguous norm socialization, and kin-keeping all inform studies on in-laws, little work has been done in this area. Future studies might consider who provides care for whom and whether a matrilineal preference for care extends to a preference for matrilineal caregiving and exchanges at the exclusion of caregiving for patrilineal family members. In a related vein, knowing the conditions under which parents and in-laws receive different types or amounts of care and exchanges during late adulthood or equitable treatment by adult children over time would be valuable. More research needs to consider how daughter-in-law–mother-in-law relationships influence the type, quality, or availability of care, given the roles of both women as kinkeepers in their own families (see Turner et al. 2006). Finally, research needs to elucidate how siblings-in-law influence the type and amount of care provided to parents. That is, do children assess their responsibilities for care on the likely input of their siblings' spouses?

Incorporating Values

A main thrust of this volume has been to explore possible motivations for caregiving. The inclusion of values in future research is an innovative approach to this issue. At their core, caregiving behaviors presuppose an orientation toward helping others, and this belief is central to the value of benevolence, or more broadly, collectivism. Collectivism is in part measured by support for family and family bonds (Bengston, Biblarz, and Roberts 2002), and this value thus represents a core motivation for caregiving today. Incorporating values more explicitly into care and caregiving work may (1) aid in explaining cross-cultural differences within and across nations and (2) lead to gains in cross-disciplinary understandings.

Nock, Kingston, and Holian set up the need for the inclusion of values in their concluding remarks, citing that it is difficult to "specify where culture resides (other than in the mind)" (315). A values approach can address this problem, as value orientations are subject to cultural background and teachings as well as the influence of media, religion, and other socializing forces. In effect, couching cultural variation within a values perspective can serve as a way to frame cultural differences in feelings of obligation and caregiving behaviors. The chapters in this volume point to both cross-cultural differences in caregiving norms and behaviors (Billari and Liefbroer; Davey; Jackson et al.) and cultural variability within nations (Jackson et al.; McHale and Crouter). A values approach would offer a parsimonious explanation for cultural differences in caregiving behaviors.

Although the inclusion of values into care and caregiving models would *not* likely revolutionize what we know about the caregiving process, it would add precision in defining preferences and motivations for action that are studied across many areas of social science. A values approach would open doors to a large literature that examines the degree of similarity in values between parents and their children and the implications of this similarity (Bengston et al. 2002; Pillemer and Suitor). Future work on intergenerational caregiving may also benefit from intentionally integrating the topic of value similarity into explanatory models. Value similarity could directly influence caregiving decisions or indirectly lead to caregiving decisions via its impact on family relationships. Moreover, examining within-family variation in values of family obligation, altruism, and reciprocity speaks to the influence of the family environment versus larger social change in caregiving choices across time and generations.

Incorporating Assessments of Health and Well-Being

Several authors acknowledged the link between caregiving decisions and the health and well-being of the parent and child (e.g., Jackson et al.; McHale and Crouter; Pillemer and Suitor; Seltzer et al.). In line with their thinking, a large body of literature already speaks to the importance of parent–child relationships for well-being in childhood, adolescence, and into adulthood (Jackson et al.; Pillemer and Suitor; McHale and Crouter), although the connection has not been made as thoroughly at the later end of the lifespan. Exploring these relationships longitudinally is needed. McHale and Crouter offer future research questions on this subject that are quite useful here: Does differential treatment in the care given to adult siblings affect the well-being of these adult offspring? Does this treatment affect sibling relationships? If the answer to both of these questions is no, it would be of less consequence to know whom the mother plans to choose for support later in life. If the answers are yes, however, future research should address how differential treatment affects adult well-being on a variety of domains, which can be broadly construed as an individual-level or family-level variable.

Future work on caregiving should be explicit in its definition of *health* and *well-being* and endeavor to find consensus measurements of both physical and social constructs. Furthermore, the relationship between well-being and caregiving could go both ways. For example, conflictual relationships may have important consequences for caregiving situations, as shown by Jackson and colleagues' and Seltzer and colleagues' work. Notably, Seltzer and colleagues found that children with disabilities can have positive effects on the family despite needing more care, and this positive effect is more likely when the child's behavior is less conflictual. Other researchers have already begun examining the impacts of individual and family well-being in the face of such changes in family structure as divorce, remarriage, and the introduction of stepchildren. Jackson and colleagues pointed out that the well-being of certain adults may be compromised as they accept more of the burden for caring for their aging parents along with the more elongated time of supporting their children. It is plausible that one's psychological reactions (and subjective well-being) in response to these transitions may have long-term implications for the caregiving behaviors of children in these situations. Thus, the bidirectional and longitudinal relationships between well-being and caregiving decisions are open areas for future research. Overall, it is important to assess health and well-being because they bring to life the key question: "Do intergenerational transfers matter for people?" Future research on the physical and social outcomes of caregiving will allow us to answer such questions, determining the impact of transfers and whether intergenerational caregiving is a beneficial behavior for families and their members.

Policy Implications

In light of the aging population and the need for elderly care, U.S. policymakers have increasingly turned their attention to issues relevant to older

Americans. Parts of this volume offered intriguing avenues for public policy regarding caregiving at inter- and intragenerational levels. Although there is a substantial interest in intergenerational care, Jackson and colleagues found that the United States provides less assistance and lower quality care than the other developed countries surveyed. They also concluded that a country's policies are reflected in their citizens' beliefs about providing for elderly, and this connection points to the potential formative role of government policies in shaping the perceived personal obligations of individuals in that country. In this way, policymakers are leaders in influencing how citizens will treat the elderly and the disadvantaged among them.

The vignette work of Nock, Kingston, and Holian implied that individuals perceive the U.S. government as having a smaller caregiving role than it actually does. As a result, individuals may favor private or semiprivate solutions to health care, housing, or education rather than the sweeping public reforms that require increased government intervention. For example, Nock, Kingston, and Holian mention the possibility of compensating individuals through existing policies (e.g., Medicare) for providing care for relatives at home. Family-oriented policies such as kinship care provisions of the current welfare laws give preference to keeping families together, and these relatives receive subsidies akin to those given to foster parents (Nock et al.). Creating similar policies for elder care may be a direction that would both interest and meet the needs of many American citizens.

Finally, several authors point to the need for policy to address the needs of individuals who are disadvantaged or who do not have family support. Davey raises the potential problem of diffusion of responsibility—where some individuals will inevitably fall through the cracks as more institutions and people offer help—and he provides an example of Scandinavian countries that provide a safety net to individuals when families are unable to provide the necessary resources. A group that may fall through the cracks is fathers who are divorced, unpartnered, or otherwise unconnected to their families and who thus may have no one to care for them later in life (Bianchi et al.; Pezzin et al.). Pezzin, Pollak, and Schone also point to the lack of symmetry that often exists between siblings in providing care, such that one typically bears the brunt of the time and financial costs. These authors give plausible policy suggestions for this dilemma, such as taxing the noncoresident child more than coresident children or subsidizing the caregiving expenses of the coresident child.

Finally, Seltzer et al. argue that more government intervention is needed for parents who provide care for adult children with disabilities because they are "an exceptional example of the sandwich generation" (240) who are expected to provide downstream and upstream transfers with little hope of future support from their neediest child.

Conclusions

The expansions we have suggested for future intergenerational care and caregiving research involve a more intentional consideration of within-family processes along with a greater recognition of the various demographic changes that contextualize intergenerational interactions. These new directions can best be approached by drawing upon cross-disciplinary knowledge. This volume has already demonstrated that research on intergenerational ties can be greatly enhanced by incorporating the insights, methodologies, and theories of various disciplines. As Tamis-LeMonda and Cabrera (2002, 599) note, "Exposure to the perspectives of distinct traditions in the social sciences challenges researchers to confront their own epistemological assumptions and to grapple with the discipline-specific, theoretical, and methodological discourse of others. This approach inevitably leads to a different type of scientific inquiry, one that not only stimulates a different set of research questions, but also presents a more integrative, complex, but perhaps less-tidy picture of the phenomenon under study." Researchers' efforts to grapple with the complexities of caregiving by incorporating a cross-disciplinary approach will produce scholarly agendas that better reflect the interrelated nature of families' lives and policy prescriptions that address intricacies of the real world.

NOTE

1. As stated by Tamis-LeMonda and Cabrera (2002, 616), "Fewer fathers may be participating in their children's lives today than in any period since the United States began keeping reliable statistics."

REFERENCES

Amato, Paul R. 2000. "The Consequences of Divorce for Adults and Children." *Journal of Marriage and Family* 62:1269–87.

Belsky, Jay, Sara R. Jaffee, Avshalom Caspi, and Terrie Moffitt. 2003. "Intergenerational Relationships in Young Adulthood and Their Life Course, Mental Health, and Personality Correlates." *Journal of Family Psychology* 17:460–71.

Bengston, Vern L., Timothy J. Biblarz, and Robert E. L. Roberts. 2002. *How Families Still Matter.* Cambridge: Cambridge University Press.

Bianchi, Suzanne M. 2000. "Maternal Employment and Time with Children: Dramatic Change or Surprising Continuity?" *Demography* 37(4): 404–14.

Bianchi, Suzanne M., and Lynn M. Casper. 2000. "American Families." *Population Bulletin* 55(4): 1–42.

Bumpass, Larry. 1990. "What's Happening to the Family? Interactions between Demographic and Institutional Change." *Demography* 27:483–98.

Bumpass, Larry, and Lu Hsein-Hen. 2000. "Trends in Cohabitation and Implications for Children's Family Contexts in the United States." *Population Studies* 54(1): 29–41.

Coleman, Marilyn, Larry H. Ganong, and Tanja C. Rothrauff. 2006. "Racial and Ethnic Similarities and Differences in Beliefs about Intergenerational Assistance to Older Adults after Divorce and Remarriage." *Family Relations* 55:576–87.

Dodson, Lisa, and Jillian Dickert. 2004. "Girls' Family Labor in Low-Income Households: A Decade of Qualitative Research." *Journal of Marriage and Family* 66(2): 318–32.

Dolbin-MacNab, Megan. 2006. "Just Like Raising Your Own? Grandmothers' Perceptions of Parenting a Second Time Around." *Family Relations* 55:564–75.

Eggebeen, David J. 2002. "Sociological Perspectives on Fatherhood: What Do We Know about Fathers from Social Surveys?" In *Handbook of Father Involvement: Multidisciplinary Perspectives,* edited by C. S. Tamis-LeMonda and N. Cabrera (189–209). Mahwah, NJ: Lawrence Erlbaum Associates.

Elder, Glenn H. 1997. "Life Course and Human Development." In *Handbook of Child Psychology, Volume I: Theoretical Models of Human Development,* 5th ed., edited by R. M. Lerner and W. Damon (939–91).

Gerstel, Naomi, and Natalia Sarkisian. 2006. "Sociological Perspectives on Families and Work: The Import of Gender, Class and Race." In *The Work and Family Handbook: Multidisciplinary Perspectives, Methods, and Approaches,* edited by M. Pitt-Catsouphes, E. Kossek, and S. Sweet (237–65). Mahwah, NJ: Lawrence Erlbaum Associates.

Higgins, Christopher, Linda Duxbury, and Catherine Lee. 1994. "Impact of Life-Cycle Stage and Gender on the Ability to Balance Work and Family Responsibilities." *Family Relations* 43(2): 144–50.

Marks, Steven R. 2006. "Understanding Diversity of Families in the 21st Century and Its Impact on the Work-Family Area of Study." In *The Work and Family Handbook: Multidisciplinary Perspectives, Methods, and Approaches,* edited by M. Pitt-Catsouphes, E. Kossek, and S. Sweet (1–65). Mahwah, NJ: Lawrence Erlbaum Associates.

Parcel, Toby L., and Elizabeth G. Menaghan. 1994. "Parents' Jobs and Children's Lives." New York: Aldine de Gruyter.

Peters, Cheryl, Karen Hooker, and Anisa Zvonkovic. 2006. "Older Parents' Perceptions of Ambivalence in Relationships with Their Children." *Family Relations* 55:539–51.

Riche, Martha F. 2006. "Demographic Implications for Work-Family Research." In *The Work and Family Handbook: Multidisciplinary Perspectives, Methods, and Approaches,* edited by M. Pitt-Catsouphes, E. Kossek, and S. Sweet (125–40). Mahwah, NJ: Lawrence Erlbaum Associates.

Silverstein, Merril. 2006. "Breaking the Chain: How Grandparents Moderate the Transmission of Maternal Depression to Their Grandchildren." *Family Relations* 55(5): 601–12.

Tamis-LeMonda, Catherine S., and Natasha Cabrera. 2002. "Cross-Disciplinary Challenges to the Study of Father Involvement." In *Handbook of Father Involvement: Multidisciplinary Perspectives,* edited by C. S. Tamis-LeMonda and N. Cabrera (599–620). Mahwah, NJ: Lawrence Erlbaum Associates.

Turner, M. Jean, Carolyn R. Young, and Kelly I. Black. 2006. "Daughters-in-Law and Mothers-in-Law Seeking Their Place Within the Family: A Qualitative Study of Differing Viewpoints." *Family Relations* 55:588–600.

About the Editors

Alan Booth is distinguished professor of sociology, human development, and demography at Penn State. He has been a senior scientist in Penn State's Population Research Institute since 1991. Dr. Booth has co-organized the University's National Symposium on Family Issues since its inception in 1993. His research has focused on marital and parent–child relationship quality, nonresidential fathers and their children, adolescent transition to adulthood, as well as hormones and family relationships. He is the author of more than 100 scholarly articles, four books, and editor of 16 volumes.

Ann C. Crouter is the Raymond E. and Erin Stuart Schultz Dean of the College of Health and Human Development and professor of human development at Penn State. Her research, funded by the National Institute for Child Health and Human Development and the Alfred P. Sloan Foundation, focuses on the interconnections between work circumstances and family processes in a variety of populations.

Suzanne M. Bianchi is professor and chair of sociology at the University of Maryland. She is a past president of the Population Association of America and a former director of the Maryland Population Research Center. Dr. Bianchi's research focuses on the American family, time use, and gender equality. Her most recent book (coauthored with John P.

Robinson and Melissa Milkie), *Changing Rhythms of American Family Life*, is winner of the 2008 William Goode Book Award of the American Sociological Association. She was awarded the District of Columbia Sociological Society's 2008 Stuart A. Rice Award for Career Achievement.

Judith A. Seltzer is professor of sociology at the University of California, Los Angeles. She is chair-elect of the family section of the American Sociological Association and a member of the National Academy of Sciences Panel on the Design of the 2010 Census Program of Evaluations and Experiments. Seltzer studies kinship institutions that are in flux and instances in which family membership and coresidence do not coincide. Her research examines marriage, cohabitation, divorce, and nonmarital families in the United States. She has a long-standing interest in custody, child support, and visiting patterns in separated families and in the quality of data used to study families.

About the Contributors

Toni C. Antonucci is the Elizabeth M. Douvan Collegiate Professor of Psychology and program director in the Life Course Development Program of the Institute for Social Research at the University of Michigan. Her research focuses on social relations and health across the life span, including multigenerational studies of the family and comparative studies of social relations in the United States, Europe, and Japan.

Francesco C. Billari is a professor of demography at the Department of Decision Sciences and director of the Carlo F. Dondena Centre for Research on Social Dynamics at Università Bocconi, Milan, Italy, and secretary-general of the European Association for Population Studies. His research focuses on methods for life course analysis, comparative family and fertility behavior, and the transition to adulthood.

Edna E. Brown is an assistant professor at the University of Connecticut, Department of Human Development and Family Studies. Dr. Brown's research focuses on life transitions in adulthood (marital relations, divorce, and health) in the context of race and gender. She also studies the influence of culture, social relations, spirituality, and religiosity on health and well-being.

Donald Cox is a professor of economics at Boston College and has served as a consultant to the World Bank. His primary research interest concerns intergenerational transfer behavior in developing and developed countries. Dr. Cox has recently published on the connection between reproductive and evolutionary biology and the economics of family behavior. Dr. Cox takes an interdisciplinary approach to teaching and research, drawing from biology, psychology, and anthropology to improve economic models.

Svein Olav Daatland is a social psychologist and a leading Norwegian expert in aging research. He has served two periods as a research director of the Norwegian Social Research (NOVA), and is now a research professor at NOVA. He has been coordinating a number of Scandinavian studies and has been partner on several European projects, among them the OASIS project. He is also the founding editor of the *Norwegian Journal on Ageing and the Life-Course.*

Adam Davey is an associate professor in the College of Health Professions, Temple University. Dr. Davey is a developmental psychologist whose research addresses issues of marital and intergenerational relationships, family caregiving, and comparative analysis of the interface between formal and informal care networks, particularly in the United States, Great Britain, and Sweden. He is investigating longitudinal changes in care networks within families and couples' navigation of the retirement process.

Cassandra Rasmussen Dorius is a doctoral candidate in sociology and demography at Penn State. Cass's dissertation focuses on the trends and prevalence of women's multipartner fertility and the consequences of this family pattern on children's lives. Other research interests include family formation patterns, father involvement, and the intersection of biosociology and family life.

Jeremy Freese is a professor of sociology and fellow of the Institute for Policy Research at Northwestern University. His research interests are in articulating relationships among biological, psychological, and social processes, especially in the contexts of technological or social policy innovation. He was formerly a Robert Wood Johnson scholar in health policy research at Harvard University.

Jan S. Greenberg is a professor in the School of Social Work, University of Wisconsin–Madison. His research focuses on the challenges faced by aging families caring for adult children with major mental illnesses, in particular schizophrenia. In collaboration with Dr. Marsha Mailick Seltzer, Dr. Greenberg has conducted a series of NIH-funded studies comparing different groups of aging parental caregivers to understand how the effects of caregiving are determined by the unique characteristics of the adult child's disability (e.g., an adult child with schizophrenia versus an adult child with developmental disabilities).

Melissa Hardy is a distinguished professor and director of the Gerontology Center at Penn State. Dr. Hardy's research has focused on work and retirement, including family decisionmaking; public policy, including Social Security, pensions, and the Age Discrimination and Employment Act; political attitudes; and older workers, including training and displacement. She serves on the editorial board for *Sociological Methodology, Research on Aging,* and *Journal of Gerontology: Social Sciences.*

Laura M. Holian is a research analyst at CNA Education in Alexandria, Virginia. Her work focuses on accountability systems, school transitions, and at-risk populations.

V. Joseph Hotz is the arts and sciences professor of economics at Duke University and is a research associate of the National Bureau of Economic Research and the Institute for Research on Poverty. In his research, Dr. Hotz has analyzed such issues as the costs and consequences of teenage childbearing in the United States, the effects of regulations on the availability and quality of child care services, how parents interact with and influence their adolescent children's risk-taking behaviors, and how adult children care for their aging parents.

James S. Jackson is the Daniel Katz Distinguished University Professor of Psychology, professor of health behavior and health education, and director of the Institute for Social Research at the University of Michigan. His research focuses on adult development and aging, attitudes and attitude change, immigration, race and ethnic relations, and cultural influences on mental health. He is currently directing the most extensive social, political behavior, and health surveys on the American and Caribbean black populations ever conducted.

Paul W. Kingston is a professor of sociology at the University of Virginia and is currently serving as associate dean for arts, humanities and social sciences. His research has focused on social stratification, especially in its connections to education.

Aart C. Liefbroer is the head of the Department of Social Demography at the Netherlands Interdisciplinary Demographic Institute in The Hague and professor of demography of young adulthood and intergenerational transmission at the VU University in Amsterdam. His research focuses on trends, determinants, and consequences of demographic transitions in young adulthood, like leaving home, union formation, and entry into parenthood.

Laura Wray-Lake is a doctoral candidate in human development and family studies at Penn State. Laura's research interests center on the life-span development of personal values and social responsibility. Her dissertation explores the processes of value socialization for parents and their adolescent offspring.

Kathleen McGarry is the Joel Z. and Susan Hyatt 1972 Professor in Economics at Dartmouth College and a research associate at the National Bureau of Economic Research. She was previously a senior economist at the Council of Economic Advisers. Dr. McGarry's research focuses on the economics of aging, primarily on the roles of public and private transfers in affecting the well-being of the elderly. She has examined the long-term care and medigap insurance markets, and the effect of expansions in the Social Security program on living arrangements of the elderly.

Susan M. McHale is the director of the Social Science Research Institute; director of the Children, Youth, and Family Consortium; and professor of human development at Penn State. Dr. McHale's research focuses on children's and adolescents' family relationships, roles, and everyday activities. Highlighted in her work are sibling relationships and the family experiences, including gender dynamics in the family, that foster similarities and differences in the development of sisters and brothers.

Steven L. Nock was professor of sociology and psychology at the University of Virginia. Dr. Nock's research focused broadly on the causes and consequences of change in the American family, concentrating on the intersection of social science and public policy. He studied issues of privacy, unmarried fatherhood, cohabitation, divorce, and marriage. He also studied covenant marriage and fault-based divorce laws in Marriage Matters, a project supported by the National Science Foundation. Dr. Nock passed away suddenly in January 2008.

Gael I. Orsmond is an associate professor in the Department of Occupational Therapy at Boston University. She is a developmental psychologist whose research focuses on developmental and family issues for individuals with developmental disabilities, specifically autism, across the life span.

Liliana E. Pezzin is a professor of economics and health policy in the Department of Medicine at the Medical College of Wisconsin. Her research focuses primarily on issues related to long-term care, aging, and disability, with special emphasis on the interplay between public policy and family behavior.

Karl Pillemer is a professor of human development at Cornell University, professor of gerontology in medicine at the Weill Cornell Medical College, and director of the Cornell Institute for Translational Research on Aging. Dr. Pillemer's research focuses on intergenerational relations in later life, with a particular interest in the determinants and consequences of the quality of adult child–parent relationships. He also studies family members who provide care to disabled relatives and the relationship between families and community institutions that serve older persons.

Robert A. Pollak is the Hernreich Distinguished Professor of Economics at Washington University, St. Louis. His research interests include the economics of the family and demography; labor economics; consumer demand analysis; and environmental policy. Dr. Pollak is the author of more than 70 articles and three books, including *From Parent to Child: Intrahousehold Allocations and Intergenerational Relations in the United States*, with Jere R. Behrman and Paul Taubman.

Barbara S. Schone is a senior economist at the Agency for Healthcare Research and Quality and a visiting professor at Georgetown University Public Policy Institute. She conducts research related to long term care and caregiving decisions within families and also on employment-based health insurance.

Besangie Sellars is a Kellogg postdoctoral health scholar at the University of Pittsburgh Center for Minority Health. Her research focuses on the role of social relations in the healthy development of African Americans and how social relations influence the multiple pathways to longevity.

Marsha Mailick Seltzer is a Vaughan Bascom Professor and director of the Waisman Center, University of Wisconsin–Madison. Authoring over 130 publications, the focus of her research is on the life course impacts of disability on the family and how lifelong caregiving affects the well-being of parents and siblings of individuals with disabilities such as autism, Down syndrome, and schizophrenia.

Merril Silverstein is professor of gerontology and sociology at the University of Southern California. Dr. Silverstein's research focuses on aging within the context of family life, including intergenerational transfers and support, grandparenting, migration in later life, public policy toward caregiving families, and international perspectives on aging families in China, Sweden, and Israel. He is currently a principal investigator of the Longitudinal Study of Generations.

Matthew James Smith is a postdoctoral research fellow in the Department of Psychiatry and Behavioral Sciences at Feinberg School of Medicine, Northwestern University. His research focuses on the pathogenesis of schizophrenia and the impact of schizophrenia on the psychosocial development of siblings across the life span.

J. Jill Suitor is a professor of sociology and a member of the Center on Aging and the Life Course at Purdue University. Dr. Suitor's research focuses on the effects of status transitions on interpersonal relations, particularly between parents and their adult children. She is currently conducting a longitudinal study of the causes and consequences of parental favoritism in later-life families.

Julie Lounds Taylor is an assistant professor of pediatrics and special education and investigator at the Vanderbilt Kennedy Center, Vanderbilt University. Her research focuses on how individual, family, and society characteristics interact to promote healthy development among families of individuals with intellectual and developmental disabilities.

Robert J. Willis is a professor of economics at University of Michigan, where he is also a research professor in the Survey Research Center and the Population Studies Center. Dr. Willis is past director of the Health and Retirement Study and past president of the Society of Labor Economists. His research interests include economic development, the economics of aging, economic demography, and labor economics. He is currently pursuing a new interest in cognitive economics as a principal investigator of a National Institute on Aging program project.

Rebeca Wong is a professor of sociomedical sciences at the University of Texas Medical Branch and director of its World Health Organization/Panamerican Health Organization Collaborating Center on Aging and Health. Dr. Wong's research focuses on the social and economic consequences of population aging in Mexico and among Hispanic immigrants in the United States. She has recently completed research on poverty, health behaviors, and utilization of health services among the elderly, international migration and old-age well-being, and served as coinvestigator of the Mexican Health and Aging Study, sponsored by the National Institute on Aging.

Steven H. Zarit is the department head and professor of human development and family studies at Penn State and adjunct professor, Institute of Gerontology, Jönköping University, Sweden. Dr. Zarit has conducted pioneering work on the problems faced by families of people with Alzheimer's disease and related memory disorders, and on interventions such as adult day services to relieve the stresses of family caregiving.

Index

distinction between altruism and
exchange, 25
as family transfer, 354
game theory perspective on, 262, 268
Generations and Gender Programme
and, 64–65
immigrants and, 356
income levels and, 23, 24, 25–26, 86
intergenerational ties and, 18, 22–23,
56, 60
marriage and, 217
measurement of, 282, 284, 317, 356
from men, 353
in Mexican Family Life Survey, 27
proximity of parent/child, 57–58
time assistance vs., 339
from women, 361
Financial transfers. *See* Financial assistance
Firstborn. *See* Birth order
Fishbein, Morris, 335
Fisher, R. A., 87
Fitness. *See* Extended fitness
Folbre, Nancy, 267–68
Foster care, 315
Fragile Families data set, 111
France, grandparental care in, 130
Free rider problems, 347–48
Freese, Jeremy, 96–97, 145
Freudian theory, 182, 185

Gale, William G., 22
Gambia, child mortality in, 119*n*13
Game theory, 258, 259–60, 262–71,
355–56, 368
Ganong, Lawrence, 99, 363
Gaugler, Joseph E., 190
Gender. *See also* Men; Sex and sex ratios;
Sons and daughters; Women
allocation of assistance and, 214, 217
bioevolutionary selection and, 129, 134
children with disabilities and, 235, 236,
238
choice of caregiver and, 219, 220–21,
234, 353
chores and, 72–73, 250

closeness to grandparents and, 132
differential treatment of children and,
248–50, 252, 367
elder care and, 325, 326
emotional support and, 214
grief upon loss of child and, 152
nursing home care and, 322
obligations and, 284, 293, 302, 310–11,
314
occupational choice and, 163
General Social Survey (GSS), 64
Generations and Gender Programme
(GGP), 33, 62, 64–65
Generosity. *See* Philanthropy and
generosity
Genes and genetics
differential treatment and, 247–48,
253
evolutionary biology and, 128, 183–85,
190, 371
family ties and, 16
fertility rates and, 171
helping genes, 89–91, 119*n*12, 119*n*13
importance to social life, 147
nonshared family environments and,
250
Genotypes, 183
Germany, elder care in, 325, 326–27
Gerotranscendence theory, 129
Gerstel, Naomi, 37*n*10, 366
GGP. *See* Generations and Gender
Programme
Ghana, elder care in, 138
Glaeser, Edward L., 116
"Golden rule hypothesis," 312
Goldscheider, Calvin, 34
Goldscheider, Frances K., 20, 34
Government, responsibility of. *See also*
Public policies
beliefs about, 279–81, 282, 286, 290–92
diffusion of responsibilities, 336, 337
for education, 314
for elder care, 299, 326–27
entitlement and, 311, 312
magnitude of assistance, 294, 341, 378
for strangers, 309, 312–13, 315